BOREDOM

BOREDOM

The Literary History of a State of Mind

PATRICIA MEYER SPACKS

THE UNIVERSITY OF CHICAGO PRESS
Chicago and London

PATRICIA MEYER SPACKS is Edgar F. Shannon
Professor of English and chair of the Department of English
at the University of Virginia. Her books include *Gossip* and
*Desire and Truth: Functions of Plot in Eighteenth-Century English
Novels*, both published by the University of Chicago Press.

The University of Chicago Press, Chicago 60637
The University of Chicago Press, Ltd., London
©1995 by The University of Chicago
All rights reserved. Published 1995
Printed in the United States of America

04 03 02 01 00 99 98 97 96 95 1 2 3 4 5

ISBN: 0-226-76853-8 (cloth)

Library of Congress Cataloging-in-Publication Data

Spacks, Patricia Meyer
  Boredom: the literary history of a state of mind / Patricia Meyer
Spacks.
    p. cm.
  Includes bibliographical references and index.
    1. English literature—History and criticism. 2. Boredom in
literature. 3. Boredom—History. I. Title.
PR408.B67s67 1995
820.9'353—dc20   94-17109
                                                      CIP

⊗ The paper used in this publication meets the minimum
requirements of the American National Standard for Information Sciences—Permanence of Paper for Printed Library
Materials, ANSI Z39.48-1984.

For Nan Heinbaugh,
who knows about boredom but is never boring

CONTENTS

PREFACE

The title of this book straightforwardly announces its subject but hardly suggests that subject's complexity. A literary history of boredom necessarily involves cultural history as well. Neither kind of history can focus, in this instance, simply on textual allusions to boredom as a state of mind (or soul, or society), since the importance of the state may reveal itself by the very absence of allusion. The expanding definition of boredom in our own time means that by now one might argue that virtually every word currently written speaks of the condition in one way or another. Conversely, in the eighteenth century almost no one spoke directly of boredom, and indirections sound more ambiguous: the concept was new; the word smacked of fashionable jargon; and the person who claimed to endure the condition thereby revealed moral insufficiency.

The story that emerges here illuminates issues even larger than the pervasive psychic situation it purports to describe. It speaks, for example, of changing notions of responsibility: an eighteenth-century belief in personal theological obligation giving way to nineteenth-century sociological fatalism and twentieth-century location of responsibility outside the self. It explores the ways of subjectivity and the operations of social theory. The story begins in eighteenth-century England because the concept of boredom begins there. And the narrative comes to a stop if not an end in the present moment, when comic strips and advertisements as well as novels and sociological or psychological treatises (not to mention the speech of children and adolescents) attribute to boredom enormous and essentially unalterable power.

As my allusions will already have suggested, the texts that concern me here are not all "literary" in any orthodox sense. They include familiar letters by often obscure writers, conduct books, magazine and newspaper articles, psychoanalytic arguments, sociological investigations, and the occasional comic strip and advertisement, as well as many novels both canonical and neglected. The increasing body of academic work labeled "cultural studies," in other words, has influenced and inflected my procedures. Yet this book also pursues a literary agenda, seeking to reveal the energy and power of the written word and to investigate the operations of language by examining ways that writers employ well-worn cultural constructs as starting points for subtle interrogations of verities.

Boredom's status as cultural construct becomes increasingly apparent as its verbal records multiply. It was born in the same era as the ideas of "leisure" and the pursuit of happiness, and its social and literary functions have charted the development of civilization's discontents. As a category of interpretation it shapes perceptions, but in different ways at different times. Persistently it has associated itself with ideas of victimization and entrapment, summing up for James Boswell the dreariness of being confined in a castle paying court to a man he despises, epitomizing for Anita Brookner, two centuries later, an aspect of the female condition. Often it condenses gender distinctions. In the eighteenth century women attributed it to men; in the nineteenth, men attributed it to women. It can imply passivity—as moral sin for Samuel Johnson, as female luxury for Charlotte Brontë—or aggression: the steady repudiations of George Eliot's Grandcourt in *Daniel Deronda*. Sometimes, especially for women, it conveys selfishness as opposed to the benevolence that engages one in meaningful action. Almost always it suggests disruptions of desire: the inability to desire or to have desire fulfilled.

Such random examples indicate that boredom, examined, characteristically appears to mean something beyond itself. Emotions like love and fear carry their own sufficient signification. We may inquire why someone fears dogs or water, we may even construct an elaborate etiology of emotion, but we do not anticipate—unless we are psychoanalysts—that fear, although it may coexist with other emotions, will itself disguise some quite different psychic state. But boredom in its verbal renditions usually masks another condition. Hence, perhaps, its literary usefulness as a measure of psychological entanglements.

Although the spread of boredom has coincided with and reflected an increasing stress on subjectivity and individualism, the state of mind carries social as well as personal meanings. From the eighteenth century on, one can note a tendency to attribute boredom to members of groups other than the writer's own. Middle-class journalists in the eighteenth century believe the nouveaux riches to be bored. In the nineteenth century (encouraged by Lord Byron) the middle class assigns the condition to the aristocracy. The old think the young are bored. The young think the same of the old. Given the residuum of moral opprobrium some circles attach to being bored, many people vigorously deny boredom in themselves while seeing it in others, in those of another "kind." Moreover, with increasing emphasis various forms of public discourse attribute the causes of boredom to a set of social and political conditions, from the repetitiveness inflicted on assembly-line workers to the deadness of television comedy, seeing it as social inevitability rather than personal plight. Boredom is a capitalist plot, by one interpretation. By another, it is a necessary by-product of technological advances.

Such analysis insists on the externality of boredom's causes. It marks a far-reaching change from the eighteenth-century insistence on boredom as individual ethical failure, its causes always internal. The change—one of the many interpretive shifts I propose to examine—epitomizes the malleability of a concept that many employ as though its meaning were self-evident and stable.

Boredom has figured in literary and cultural history as a moral state, a psychic condition, a social ailment, a form of passive aggression, and a cause for active aggression (teenagers go out and shoot people, newspapers tell us, because they're bored). Although unlike its more dignified cousin ennui it is often considered a trivial emotion, boredom has at various moments provided a mode of speech and even a way of life for its practitioners. Repudiated, embraced, attributed, claimed, it turns up everywhere, changing shape with the times. It offers an overwhelmingly rich subject for investigation.

It also supplies a way to think about the dynamic of writing and reading. Dr. Johnson, characterizing his own writing of the periodical called *The Idler*, pointed out that the act of writing alleviates the boredom of the writer and the product of that act combats readers' potential boredom. Roland Barthes, much later, offered essentially the same observation. The writer by implicit contract with readers promises to interest them; they in turn tacitly agree to allow themselves to be interested. But their power inheres in their capacity to declare themselves bored, thereby repudiating the object of their temporary attention. This book will investigate the histories of a few works that exemplify the possibility of dramatic shifts in the assignment of interest. At their first publication, they apparently interested thousands of readers. Within half a century, widespread sentiment dismissed them as boring. Perhaps such books as *Coelebs in Search of a Wife* threatened the assumptions of their later readers. Perhaps they no longer performed acceptable ideological work. Possibly their versions of romance ceased to answer their readers' fantasies. Their publishing careers provide ample material for speculation about boredom's origins, meanings, and importance as a register of response.

The critical act derives from a commitment to pay attention to a text. Boredom in all its manifestations implies failure of full attention, as cause or effect of the feeling. Critics perform their verbal operations in order to interest themselves and to claim the interest (for others and for themselves) of their own intellectual processes. If they bore their readers they have failed—as has the novelist, given a comparable result, or the letter writer with an audience of one. This book thus embodies as well as examines complex exchanges, processes, compacts. It both exemplifies and narrates ways of escaping boredom as it explores through varied examples the protean history of a forever indeterminate state of mind.

ACKNOWLEDGMENTS

Many people have helped me during the long process of thinking and writing about boredom. Those who have offered provocative suggestions—ideas about what to read, where to look, how to think about a problem—include Martin Battestin, Ruthe Battestin, Sara Blair, Liz Clark, Christy Dennis, Ann Diamond, Denis Donoghue, Jaroslav Folda, Marcia Folsom, Carol Gilligan, James Gilligan, Clement Hawes, Nan Heinbaugh, Claudia L. Johnson, Robert Kunkel, Milton Miller, Adrienne Munich, Catherine Parke, Mary Lee Settle, Mark Taylor, and Herbert Tucker.

Others have read parts of the manuscript, providing abundant insight, criticism, encouragement, and stimulation. They include Jessica Feldman, Paul Hunter, Myra Jehlen, Clare Kinney, Steven Marcus, Jerome McGann, Mary Price, Joseph Reed, Margery Sabin, Joan Stewart, Sara Suleri, Aubrey Williams, and Bryan Wolf. With yet greater endurance, Liliane Greene and Deborah Kaplan read and commented on the entire book.

To all these people I feel intensely grateful: for the delight of their conversation and the profit as well as pleasure of their criticism. I am grateful also to the staff of the National Humanities Center, where I spent a semester in 1989 working on this project.

Some material on boredom that has been incorporated into this book in different form appeared in essays in the *Yale Journal of Criticism* and the *Virginia Quarterly Review*.

ONE

Reading, Writing, and Boredom

As action and as product, writing resists boredom, constituting itself by that resistance. In this sense all writing—at least since 1800 or so—is "about" boredom, as all physical construction is "about" entropy. The act of writing implicitly claims interest (boredom's antithesis) for the assertions or questions or exclamations it generates. At the very least, any autonomous process of writing protects the writer for a time against the vacuity we call boredom. Often, words written down will interest someone else as well: the letter's recipient, the report's reader, the detective story's consumer. As Henry James knew, the obligation to be interesting focuses the publishing writer's enterprise.

For reading too, in another sense, resists boredom. Voluntarily picking up a book, we expect—indeed *demand*—to have our interest engaged. Removing the reader from immediate actuality, reading liberates us from routine and tedium as well as the pain life more actively inflicts. Even the kind of verbal production read only for information or ideas involves us in alternative worlds of conceptualization and imagination. If a text fails to interest me, I can set it aside, or skim through it, or substitute some other work I will value for its wisdom, knowledge, or imagination—but first for its interest.

The ideal dynamic between writing and reading depends in part on boredom as displaced, unmentioned, and unmentionable possibility. The need to refute boredom's deadening power impels the writer's productivity and the reader's engagement. In the best of all possible arrangements, an author's energy and a reader's reciprocate, establishing a "dialectics of desire" (Barthes 4). The act of writing both draws on and generates imaginative vitality. So does the act of reading. The mutual dependence of writer and reader declares their human likeness in shared defiance of psychic entropy.

But the implicit contract between creator and responder—the promise "I will interest you" corresponding to the demand "you must interest me"—remains, like other contracts, subject to default. The writer may fail to engage the reader's interest, the reader may refuse to be interested. The writer, Roland Barthes observes, may "prattle," failing to consider the reader as a real presence. In such a case, "this text bores me" (Barthes 4). Boredom, acknowledged, mocks meaningful literary experience as well as every other kind. The writer writes, the reader reads, with submerged awareness of the possibility they avert by their action. The tension of that possibility informs both creativity and response: readers' capacity to declare themselves uninvolved threatens the writer's project as it menaces their own pleasure. All literary endeavor occurs in a context of conceivable rejection, the embracing refusal of engagement figured by Pope's Goddess of Dulness. Indeed, it is possible to construct a literary history founded on the notion that successive waves of readers' boredom generate literary innovation. John Sisk has sketched a partial version of just such a history: Wordsworth declared the boredom of traditional poetry and offered the excitement of *Lyrical Ballads*; realists and naturalists revealed that by their time "romanticism had also become a bore" (Sisk 26), and so on.

As a matter of fact, all endeavor of every kind takes place in the context of boredom impending or boredom repudiated and can be understood as impelled by the effort to withstand boredom's threat. I am not the first to say so. Nietzsche, for example, toward the end of the nineteenth century, suggested that men of rare sensibility value boredom as an impetus to achievement:

> They do not fear boredom as much as work without pleasure; they actually require a lot of boredom if *their* work is to succeed. For thinkers and all sensitive spirits, boredom is that disagreeable "windless calm" of the soul that precedes a happy voyage and cheerful winds. They have to bear it and must wait for its effect on them. Precisely this is what lesser natures cannot achieve by any means. (108)

Bertrand Russell observed, "Boredom as a factor in human behavior has received, in my opinion, far less attention than it deserves. It has been, I believe, one of the great motive powers throughout the historical epoch, and is so at the present day [1930] more than ever" (56). The anthropologist Ralph Linton hypothesized that "the human capacity for being bored, rather than man's social or natural needs, lies at the root of man's cultural advance" (qtd. in Sisk 25). As an explanatory hypothesis, boredom serves many purposes: such hypotheses accord enormous power to a commonplace and ostensibly trivial psychic state.

The position hinted by Nietzsche, Russell, and Linton suggests that the dynamic of promise and threat between writing and reading typifies the tension of all production and consumption. Every producer evades boredom, as does every consumer. Like the reader seeking entertainment and enlightenment, the housewife yearning for a vacuum cleaner to relieve her drudgery wants something to make the world new. The designer of vacuum cleaners, like the purveyor of poetry, generates novelty. All "cultural advance" derives from the need to withstand boredom; literature is a single instance among many. Boredom, in this theory, explains everything: a new version of the doom assigned to humankind in the original fall from grace. That it recurs insistently as literary subject only reiterates an embracing truth.

One may feel appropriately suspicious of so inclusive a hypothesis, but much twentieth-century commentary confirms the centrality of boredom in our culture, though only rarely its status as creative impetus. The condition figures more typically as malady than as inspiration. "Boredom has become the disease of our time." The *Reader's Digest* said it (in 1976), so it must be a truism (qtd. in Healy 36). A French survey reports "that twenty-three per cent of Frenchmen and thirty-one per cent of Frenchwomen now acknowledge being bored when they make love—a condition described as `l'atrophie du désir'" (Brubach 77). Steadily increasing in the twentieth century, according to Sean Desmond Healy, boredom's omnipresence reveals cultural decline and loss of authenticity. Healy argues that boredom and anxiety constitute allotropes of one another (69); Haskell Bernstein contrasts the two states, maintaining that since World War II "our former Age of Anxiety has given way to an Age of Boredom" (536). Orrin Klapp documents an enormous increase in the use of the word *boredom* between 1931 and 1961 (23–24), calls attention to "the large vocabulary of English words connoting boredom," and hypothesizes that this lexicon "not only registers the prevalence of boredom but helps create it" (32). Other statistical evidence, focusing on effects rather than putative causes, supports the view that boredom increasingly manifests itself as a social problem. A 1981 West German study, for instance, shows that between 1952 and 1978 the percentage of the population who found boredom "a great problem" in filling leisure time changed from 26 percent to 38 percent, almost a 50 percent increase (Iso-Ahola and Weissinger 357).

Although boredom as universal infirmity has received more documentation—in the twentieth century and earlier—than boredom as universal stimulus to achievement, both interpretations allegedly account for widely disparate phenomena. The notion of boredom as an all-embracing explanation for psychic distress has startlingly wide currency. High-school teachers report that students' complaints of boredom constitute a growing pedagogical problem; mothers moan that their young children constantly demand relief from boredom. A comic strip (Bill Griffith, "Zippy," 3 June 1988) suggests boredom's perverse glamour. "There are so many boring things to be bored with . . . cross-indexing, school board meetings, computer literacy, Gary Hart. . . . It's exciting to be so bored!! Is that boring? Am I bored yet? . . . Boredom . . . th' next big thing!!" I note in a bibliography a remarkable title: "Excitement and Boredom as Determinants of Vocalization in Infants." I hear of parents who worried lest their three-month-old infant suffer boredom. When he cried inexplicably, they declared boredom his malady. Reacting to such data, commentators—sociologists, psychologists, philosophers, psychoanalysts—investigate symptomatology, etiology, and remedies for the condition. They offer, according to their disciplines, social, psychological, or metaphysical exegeses of something they often fail to define fully.

The exegeses lend dignity to an embarrassingly commonplace state. When Sean Healy describes the root of increasing boredom as "the growing metaphysical void at the center of Western civilization, not such more obvious conditions as wealth, leisure, personal pathology, or human nature" (87), he perhaps provides comfort for readers who find their social lives tedious. But even the "more obvious conditions" offered as explanations relieve the putative sufferer of personal responsibility. Otto Fenichel's classic 1934 essay "The Psychology of Boredom," for one case in point, defines boredom usefully if self-evidently as "an unpleasurable experience of a lack of impulse" (292). Fenichel calls attention to the apparent paradox that one might expect "lack of impulse" to be a pleasurable condition. Boredom, however, includes as a component the "need for intense mental activity," a need that in the bored person cannot find gratification by generating its own impulse but seeks "incitements" from the outside world as a means of decreasing tension. Fenichel concludes,

> Boredom must be a state of instinctual tension in which the instinctual aims are repressed but in which the tension as such is felt; and therefore one turns to the external world for help in the struggle against repression. The person who is bored can be compared to someone who has forgotten a name and inquires about it from others. (292)

As the psychoanalyst's speculations about the state continue, it becomes increasingly clear that he finds it puzzling. Boredom connects itself, he points out, with depression, with loneliness, with restlessness. He tries to distinguish between "pathological" and "normal" boredom, achieving some clarity about the difference in causality but remaining bewildered about why particular causes produce this particular effect. The common property of "pathological" and "innocent" boredom, he suggests, is that in both situations *"something expected does not occur."*

> In pathological boredom it fails to occur because the subject represses his instinctual action out of anxiety; in normal boredom it fails to occur because the nature of the real situation does not permit of the expected de-tension. . . . It is difficult to predict, however, when a frustrating external world will mobilize aggressiveness in the subject, when it will be tolerated by him, and when it will be experienced as "boring." One should not forget that we have *the right to expect* some "aid to discharge" from the external world. If this is not forthcoming, we are, so to speak, justifiably bored. (301)

The distinction between the pathological and the innocent or normal depends on how justifiable boredom appears. The cause of pathological boredom lies within; normal boredom derives from inadequacies of "the external world."

Fenichel's notion that "we have *the right to expect*" (his italics) helpful stimulation from our environment finds an echo in many subsequent utterances. It articulates a widespread twentieth-century assumption that helps to generate what it purports to explain. To posit the right of being stimulated virtually guarantees that one will from time to time be "justifiably bored" as the external world proves less than satisfactory. (Adam Phillips, discussing boredom as a possible "developmental achievement" for children, observes that "it is one of the most oppressive demands of adults that the child should be interested. . . . Boredom is integral to the process of taking one's time" [69].) Even the kind of boredom Fenichel declares pathological, the kind that depends on anxiety and repression and links itself to depression and loneliness, sounds inevitable in his formulation. Given that one has little control over the experience of anxiety or the mechanisms of repression, the sufferer from pathological boredom simply exemplifies a particular form of civilization's discontent.

Like the other commentators—like most of us—Fenichel hypostatizes boredom. His analysis usefully suggests the complexity and perplexity of the psychic experience while assuming its inevitability. He, and we, his successors, take the condition as a fact of social and personal life. The problem of boredom then becomes to understand it, or to remediate it, or to deny it.

But what if we instead understand boredom as a social construction, and a fairly recent construction at that, dating from the mid-eighteenth century? In the context of such understanding, the twentieth-century proliferation of the malaise—boredom at work, boredom in leisure, boredom while making love—signals not only an experiential but a conceptual problem. Boredom appears to have become a remarkably useful, remarkably inclusive explanatory notion—and a historically explicable one.

Everything I have said so far, as well as everything I have quoted, issues from a set of uniquely twentieth-century assumptions. The notion that the dynamic of reading and writing can be described as implicating boredom, the idea that all activity responds to boredom's threat—such hypotheses depend on belief in boredom as a universal, like fear and desire. Like fear and desire, it possesses interpretive force. Like them, despite its association with inertia, it can generate discourse. Yet its comparatively brief linguistic history suggests that it is by no means universal.

This book's project is to investigate boredom's imaginative functions during the past two and a half centuries, mainly in England, where speakers first labeled the condition early in the second half of the eighteenth century. Such investigation will reveal the shifting cultural purposes served by the construction of boredom. My cases in point will come from published writing—fiction, poetry, conduct books, sociological and historical description, personal letters—by members of the white middle class. Middle-class boredom, often associated with idleness, and middle-class attributions of boredom to members of other groups reveal with peculiar distinctness certain forms of boredom's social utility, forms that have changed over the course of two centuries.

I do not, of course, mean by my narrow focus to suggest that the working classes fail to suffer psychic malaise comparable to that of those higher on the social scale. Plausible reasons for boredom abound in the occupational and living conditions of assembly-line workers, computer operators, telephone salespersons, domestic servants. Middle-class commentators often report how bored such workers feel, on and off the job. The workers themselves, until recently, offered such reports less frequently. John Burnett's two compilations of autobiographical material by "working people," for instance, evince a striking absence of boredom as a complaint. Men and women alike report arduous, repetitive work with little opportunity for recreation and limited chances of entertainment. They grumble about many aspects of their lives, but the closest thing to a mention of boredom is Winifred Griffiths's observation that filling sugar bags was a "rather monotonous task" (Burnett, *Useful Toil* 118). (This task lasts, however, only "a few days.") Sunday school may seem boring (Burnett, *Destiny* 93, 118, 119), but leisure time is not. "The evenings of my childhood stand out," writes Stella Entwistle, a vicar's daughter, "as happy and peaceful times, without any of the frustration and boredom felt nowadays when the television breaks down!" (*Destiny* 111). The miner's son Fred Boughton summarizes: "They were happy in those days because they made their own pleasure" (*Destiny* 297).

In any case, the putative boredom of the working class differs from the amply documented dullness of middle-class experience, and its forms of social usefulness presumably differ as well. Like the endemic boredom postulated in nineteenth-century European literary production, like the complicated forms of boredom expressed in early American writing, working-class boredom deserves its historian. Afflicted by an excess of data, I have limited my own agenda. My record here is not complete, nor can my analysis presume to comprehensiveness, given the subject's vastness. The instances offered in this book will serve, however, as examples to help elucidate shifting cultural patterns and shifting literary strategies. And they will illustrate Adam Phillips's provocative observation that "we should speak not of boredom, but of the boredoms, because the notion itself includes a multiplicity of moods and feelings that resist analysis; and this, we can say, is integral to the function of boredom as a kind of blank condensation of psychic life" (78).

When I lecture about boredom, suggesting its status as an early modern invention, someone in the audience often objects that boredom existed in classical times, citing as evidence Horace's satire called "The Bore." That satire offers an instructive exemplum. Satire 1.9 originally appeared with no title, only a number. It tells of a morning stroll interrupted by the unwelcome companionship of a man whom the speaker had previously known only by name. The stroller tries to get rid of his unwanted escort, but the other man, aware of being unwanted, announces (in the Loeb translation), "It's no use, I'll stick to you; I'll stay with you to your journey's end" (lines 15–16). He claims the rights of friendship, praising his own talents; he asks for an introduction to Maecenas; he insists on detailing his plans. The poem's protagonist tries to enlist a friend's help in shaking himself loose, but the friend only laughs, "pretending not to understand" (66). "To think so black a sun as this has shone for me!" the victim exclaims (72–73), just before an unexpected intervention rescues him.

By the seventeenth century, Horace's satire had become in England a favorite subject for translation and adaptation. John Donne's energetic, disgusted "Satire IV" elaborates Horace's hints with an extensive account of an irritating, tedious courtier: "A thing more strange, then on Niles slime, the Sunne / E'r bred" (18–19). Herbert Grierson, in his 1912 edition of Donne, observes that "Donne, like Horace, describes a bore" (Donne 2: 117), and throughout his commentary he refers to the figure as "the bore." Donne himself does nothing of the sort. When Alexander Pope, in 1733, published (anonymously) his own version of Donne's satire, he assigned it a title: *The Impertinent: Or, A Visit to the Court.* He associates the courtier with "Dulness":

> I whisper, gracious God!
> What Sin of mine cou'd merit such a Rod?
> That all the Shot of Dulness now must be
> From this thy Blunderbuss discharg'd on me!
> (62–65)

He does not, however, call him a bore: the word did not yet exist.

Eighteenth-century translations typically connected Horace's interloper with the idea of impertinence: indeed, S. Dunster's early eighteenth-century version uses as a title "The Description of an Impertinent." Not until two centuries later does the uncomfortable companion get called a bore and does a new translation receive the title "Bored to Distraction" (Horace, ed. Bovie). As the reiterated question from lecture audiences indicates, Satire 1.9 is now thought of as "The Bore."

This capsule history of nomenclature records a sequence of cultural change. To call the pest Horace describes "an impertinent fellow" or "a forward coxcomb" characterizes his social sin as a violation of decorum and restraint. It assigns to an observer's judgment defining force. To call the nuisance a bore, on the other hand, makes the observer's emotional response to his companion definitive. Instead of commenting on the interloper's failure to conform to objective standards, such a designation notes his effect on another. Twentieth-century reliance on the concept of boredom accompanies other evidence—evidence so familiar as to constitute cliché—of increasing emphasis on subjective experience. When we invoke boredom to explain or condemn increasingly diverse circumstances, we declare our participation in a "culture of narcissism."

We speak of an effect, not of its causes. We care about the effect—the emotion we experience in the presence of someone who refuses to let us alone—more than about its meaning.

To conceive boredom as an invention, an idea that became both useful and necessary only at a relatively recent historical moment, demands further explanation. (The word *boredom* dates from the nineteenth century; the verb *to bore* as a psychological term comes from the mid-eighteenth century.) What social and psychological conditions would require the construction of boredom as a concept? Conversely, what social and psychological circumstances would allow the world to get along without it? Available historical data do not altogether resolve the issues. For the moment I will allow myself the luxury of speculation.

In the hypothetical world that lacks a concept of boredom, people would tend to accept their condition in life as *given*—like the dogs whose experience of the world Elizabeth Marshall Thomas attempted to share, imagining it as utterly free of boredom. My hypothetical world has its utopian aspects, in the putative psychic stability that acceptance generates. But for a citizen of postmodern culture—even a citizen who sometimes feels herself marooned in postmodernism—this stable environment must prove difficult to imagine in detail, as difficult as the life of dogs. How would it *feel?* To its inhabitants, that question would seem beside the point—beside any conceivably relevant point. The world without defined boredom would not appear from the point of view of a twentieth-century observer less boring than our own. Perhaps, indeed, it would provide more abundant pretexts or causes for boredom than do the frenetic environments of modernism and postmodernism. But the hypothetical inhabitants of a world without the notion of boredom—they're *not* dogs, after all—invoke categories other than those of feeling to assess their experience. Perhaps they judge what happens around and to them in terms of *meaning:* meaning in relation to a theological order of things or to a system of family and local responsibilities. Or do they not judge at all, only take their lives for granted, thinking about one happening in relation to another but aware of no need to assess events? Their condition depends on assumptions so different from our own that it is hard to avoid either romanticizing it or denying its possibility. (As we shall see, social historians trying to describe premodern culture far less impressionistically than I am doing face the same difficulty.) Its most essential aspects, from my immediate perspective, derive from the shared conviction that merely personal feelings, however powerful, do not necessarily illuminate circumstances external to the observer. Here too vocabulary supports the hypothesis: premodern England lacked a detailed nomenclature now excessively familiar. If life was never *boring* in premodern times, neither was it *interesting, thrilling,* or *exciting,* in the modern sense of these words. And one has to assume that people without such terminology didn't need it— not necessarily because they weren't by our standards bored or interested or whatever, but because other categories of interpretation satisfied their understanding of their own situations.

The impossibility of describing an event as thrilling or boring, of thus readily emphasizing its emotional effects, might imply the need to offer more precise description of what the event *is*, as well as what it means. The development of *boring* as an all-purpose term of disapproval among the young emphasizes the word's capacity to blur distinctions. Its apparently increasing usefulness in our culture may derive partly from just that capacity to blur. As an all-purpose designation of pain, the idea of boredom, while declaring the world inadequate, also subtly acknowledges our own insufficiency. As Richard Wilbur puts the point,

> Not that the world is tiresome in itself:
> We know what boredom is: it is a dull
> Impatience or a fierce velleity,
> A champing wish, stalled with our lassitude,
> To make or do.
>
> (12–16)

The tension of lassitude with the wish to accomplish, of active impatience with stultifying dullness, infects our perceptions and thus makes a vivid world tiresome.

Did the world never seem tiresome in premodern times? Wilbur, implicitly linking boredom with narcissism, hints that both maladies entered human experience when Satan first set foot in Eden,

> dragging down
> And darkening with moody self-absorption
> What, when he left it, lifted.
>
> (43–45)

But that interpretation, like the rest of Wilbur's poem, betrays twentieth-century dread of the colorless, the abruptly meaningless. Hippolyta, in *A Midsummer Night's Dream,* complains of the actor playing Moonshine, "I am aweary of this moon. Would he would change" (5.1.256). The performance has gone on too long; she's tired of it. To impose the category of boredom on Hippolyta's reaction would transform it into a weightier judgment, of herself and of the actor, registering her inability to take interest, his incapacity to interest her. Boredom, unlike weariness, carries intimations of despair.

Conversely, the category of boredom implies a set of expectations of the external world that apparently did not afflict our remote predecessors. The details of life in the distant past may sound boring to us; indeed, some have imagined Eden itself as boring. Adam and Eve, before the Fall, found little occupation and no excitement. A medieval peasant endured an existence of grinding routine. Even a medieval lord, except in time of war, led a relatively "uninteresting" life—though he probably did not think so.

Medieval monks, we know, on occasion experienced something quite recognizable to the modern student of boredom. John Cassian describes in detail the monastic who

> looks about anxiously this way and that, and sighs that none of the brethren come to see him, and often goes in and out of his cell, and frequently gazes up at the sun, as if it was too slow in setting, and so a kind of unreasonable confusion of mind takes possession of him like some foul darkness, and makes him idle and useless for every spiritual work, so that he imagines that no cure for so terrible an attack can be found in anything except visiting some one of the brethren, or in the solace of sleep alone. (267)

But Cassian's categories of interpretation derive from assumptions far different from ours. His tone indicates disapproval approaching contempt. The "unreasonable confusion of mind" the monk suffers makes him "imagine" himself afflicted with an incurable condition. In fact he need only focus on appropriate spiritual concerns to alleviate a personal situation that constitutes, in Cassian's view, a form of self-indulgence. This monk does not endure boredom, he commits acedia: a sin. Acedia makes people "idle and useless for every spiritual work." A combination of what we call boredom and what we call sloth, it was understood as a dangerous form of spiritual alienation, a misery of the soul that could, like other sins, be avoided by effort or by grace.

The world that did not know boredom as boredom would necessarily have been one whose inhabitants believed in, lived by, a notion of personal responsibility. That notion survived with full force into eighteenth-century England, in which the most relevant locus of responsibility remained theological. Even in the period when the bore emerged as a concept, Christian faith still implied individual accountability. Emotional apathy, given a Christian context, reflected reprehensible spiritual apathy. The medieval characterization of acedia locates the danger: "For in truth the soul which is wounded by the shaft of this passion does sleep, as regards all contemplation of the virtues and insight of the spiritual senses" (Cassian 268). When midway through the eighteenth century the bore entered the language, moralists, unwilling to locate boredom explicitly as a sin, nonetheless continued to believe that focused spiritual endeavor might effectively combat psychic malaise. Not your stars or your employment or your friends but your self was at fault if apathy and discontent submerged you.

Boredom was not (*is* not) the same as ennui, more closely related to acedia. Ennui implies a judgment of the universe; boredom, a response to the immediate. Ennui belongs to those with a sense of sublime potential, those who feel themselves superior to their environment. Robert Lowell adapts Baudelaire's description of the condition, using the figure of a king:

> nothing cheers him, darts, tennis, falconry,
> his people dying by the balcony;
> the bawdry of the pet hermaphrodite
> no longer gets him through a single night;
> his bed of fleur-de-lys becomes a tomb;
> even the ladies of the court, for whom
> all kings are beautiful, cannot put on
> shameful enough dresses for this skeleton;
> the scholar who makes his gold cannot invent
> washes to cleanse the poisoned element
> ("Spleen" lines 5–14; Lowell 50)

These lines come from an elaborate simile, comprising the entire poem, that characterizes the poem's speaker ("I'm like . . ."). The defining element of his situation is its irremediability: nothing can cleanse the poisoned element. No sensation, no stimulation, no activity arouses the victim of ennui, who proudly? despairingly? attests the permanence of his cheerlessness. In another poem also called "Spleen," Baudelaire observes, more economically, "L'ennui, fruit de la morne incuriosité, / Prend les proportions de l'immortalité" (Baudelaire 312). (In Anthony Hecht's translation, "Indifference expanding to Ennui / Takes on the feel of Immortality" [Baudelaire 91].) The lines convey the totalizing force of ennui and hint the curious pride that sometimes marks its victims.

If only because it seems more dignified, many people would rather suffer ennui than boredom, despite its presumably greater misery. Given that ennui and boredom exist by virtue of interpretation (if we labeled our experience differently, we would *feel* it differently), a person's self-construction as bored or *ennuyé* carries crucial meaning. When Lowell's speaker uses figures of death (tomb, skeleton, poison) to elucidate his situation, when he moves from one extremity to another, he makes a claim significantly different from that of, say, James Harthouse in *Hard Times*, who says of himself, "The result of the varieties of boredom I have undergone, is a conviction (unless conviction is too industrious a word for the lazy sentiment I entertain on the subject), that any set of ideas will do just as much good as any other set, and just as much harm as any other set" (Dickens, *Hard Times* 162). Unable to separate the pose from the reality of boredom, Harthouse characteristically defines himself in inconsequential terms. He would not claim analogical kinship with a king. One might argue that his willful reductionism and Lowell's series of comparatively grandiose instances amount finally to the same thing—but the difference in terminology makes exactly the kind of difference this book will attend to.

Boredom presents itself as a trivial emotion that can trivialize the world. As an interpretive category, it implies an embracing sense of irritation and unease. It reflects a state of affairs in which the individual is assigned ever more importance and ever less power. Surely a society that got along without it felt better than our own.

When one arrives at the point of reflecting about the preferability of the past to the present, it's time to change direction. A shift from speculation to evidence seems in order. I shall offer a cursory historical overview of developing attitudes toward boredom, less manifestly value laden than my past few sentences, then sketch more fully my plans for this book and their theoretical justification.

The *Oxford English Dictionary* asserts that the verb *to bore*, as a psychological description, arose "after 1750" (it does not appear in Johnson's *Dictionary* of 1755). The word can claim no clear etymology, although the dictionary notes and dismisses efforts to connect it with the reiterative action of the bore as drill and with the French *bourre*, meaning padding. The first occurrence cited comes from a private letter of 1768, Earl Carlisle announcing his pity for "Newmarket friends, who are to be bored by these Frenchmen." *Bore*, meaning "a thing which bores," comes along in 1778; the bore as tiresome person is assigned to 1812 (although in fact the word in this sense appears several times in the eighteenth century); the first citation of the noun *boredom* belongs to 1864.

The English-speaking world, in other words, long managed to sustain itself without recourse to the concept of boredom. French *ennui* (which came into English usage in the late seventeenth century) greatly predates it. Derived from *inodiare,* associated with hatred of life itself, the French term in all its metaphysical dignity belongs to the twelfth century. The more commonplace response to commonplace inflictions did not demand expression until much later. If people felt bored before the late eighteenth century, they didn't know it. "Recent work in social history," Neil McKendrick writes, "has reminded us forcibly that there are fewer constants in the human condition than we have usually imagined, or has often been assumed" (35). Boredom, that intimate, familiar malaise, does not necessarily inhere in being human.

My favorite impressionistic definition is "psychic anorexia" (Healy 60). Equivalent to denial of hunger is the denial of desire implicit in boredom as condition. (In Adam Phillips's astute formulation, boredom presents "two impossible options: there is something I desire, and there is nothing I desire" [76].) The anorectic cannot allow herself to be nourished, nor can boredom's victim. Outside observers of the sufferer from anorexia frequently feel that she willfully refuses food; those doomed to the company of sufferers from boredom may believe that such persons could interest themselves in something if only they really *tried.* But the malady, which often descends without warning, feels to its victim incurable by personal effort. If only the lecture would draw to a close, if the school day miraculously ended, if a magic carpet could transport us to the South Pacific, away from interminable meetings or demanding toddlers. . . . The causes of boredom, to someone afflicted, appear to inhere in external circumstances.

The expanding usefulness of boredom as a late twentieth-century concept compounds the problem of definition. To express intense distaste, teenagers may chant, "Bor-*ring.*" Nominally more mature companies of intellectuals indulge in a euphemism of comparable meaning: "He's just not *interesting.*" "Fly around the world in the Concorde," an advertisement urges. "Everything else is boring." Everything else! And sometimes, yet more categorically, *everything.*

No single definition can compass the meanings of so culture-bound a term, a word that in less than two and a half centuries has accrued multifarious ideological associations and complicated emotional import. Its history has intimate involvements with that of leisure, a new concept in the eighteenth century, an increasingly troubling one in the nineteenth.

In the third decade of that century, Charles Dickens published (anonymously) a tiny work called *Sunday under Three Heads,* an attack on proposed legislation to restrict recreational activity on the Sabbath. Central to his argument was his imagining of working-class boredom, although he does not use the word. Addressing members of Parliament and speaking of the workingman, Dickens writes,

> You offer no relief from listlessness, you provide nothing to amuse his mind, you afford him no means of exercising his body. Unwashed and unshaven, he saunters moodily about, weary and dejected. In lieu of the wholesome stimulus he might derive from nature, you drive him to the pernicious excitement to be gained from art. He flies to the gin-shop as his only resource. (18)

Other Victorian commentators located the malady elsewhere. A foreign visitor to London in the 1830s sees it among the aristocracy: "On the one hand there is the busy population of the city whose only motive is desire for profit, on the other there is the haughty, disdainful aristocracy who comes to London each year to escape from boredom" (Tristan 5). A feminist perceives it as a problem particularly for women: "As soon as a woman rises out of the class in which the smallest earnings and savings are valuable, the irresistible force of public opinion deprives her of all but paltry sources of interest and activity" (Taylor 111). A social observer who offers a generally idyllic account of life at all social levels and of English political institutions nonetheless remarks that "there is amongst us an immense number of persons of both sexes who are not merely ready but anxious to make, by their patronage and favour, the fortune of any one who will be good enough to invent for them a new mode of agreeably, and more or less athletically, beguiling the passing hours" (Escott 1: 179). He apparently alludes to the middle classes, those sufficiently prosperous to have "patronage and favour" at their disposal, but not to aristocrats. "Existence for the fashionable and the wealthy," Escott believes, "is . . . one unending whirl of excitement" (2: 9).

To attribute boredom to other people, other classes (or conversely, to believe their lives "one unending whirl of excitement") suggests the importance that had accrued, by the beginning of the Victorian period, to the notion of the interesting, and the anxiety by then associated with the problem of "beguiling the passing hours." Logan Pearsall Smith has called attention to "a curious class of verbs and adjectives which describe not so much the objective qualities and activities of things as the effects they produce on us, our own feelings and sensations" (246). All these words, he notes, belong to the modern period. *Interesting*, in its current sense, comes from the late eighteenth century, its first use occurring in Laurence Sterne's *A Sentimental Journey* (1768) (Smith 247).

Such linguistic change of course signals a shift of sensibility. The social commentators quoted above concern themselves not directly with their own feelings and sensations, not with the "interest" inherent in their own experience, but with their imaginings of feelings and sensations experienced by other people, whose emotional lives by implication prove inferior to that of the observer. (The aristocrats with their whirl of excitement, it turns out, admit "small opportunity for the cultivation of the domestic affections" [Escott 2: 9–10].) The increasing concentration on self suggested by the proliferation of such terms as *boring*, *interesting*, *exciting* reveals itself indirectly in a new cognizance of others: what they do, how they feel. It does not self-evidently belong to the province of the moralist and the social observer to remark on the emotional lives of their subjects. Before the middle of the nineteenth century, though, such remarking—often on posited rather than observed emotional experience—had become commonplace.

The concerns implicit in the new vocabulary did not altogether depend on that vocabulary for expression. If words like *boring* signal a cultural shift, the shift conveys itself in other ways as well. Preoccupation with the problems of "leisure," the kind of perception and anxiety signaled by Dickens's commentary, registers one dimension of change. Like boredom (not coincidentally), leisure, as a wealth of recent scholarship has demonstrated, is a modern construct. "In pre-industrial society work was part and parcel of everyday life and leisure was not a separate section of the day" (Parker 24). Peter Bailey provides a particularly cogent summary of the shift that began in the eighteenth century from a unified conception of ordinary experience toward a more differentiated one. By the mid-nineteenth century, he writes,

> Work and leisure were no longer intertwined in the continuum of shared activities that characterised the daily and yearly round within the closed world of the small and homogeneous traditional community. In the populous and extensive industrial city, leisure was time clearly marked off from work, to be pursued elsewhere than in the workplace and its environs, and undertaken in company no longer in the nature of things comprised predominantly of workmates. Moreover, the activities of this leisure time were no longer regulated as a whole by the tight mores and collective obligations of traditional social life. (4)

In the perception of those reflecting on this new space of leisure, the fact of empty time had ominous implications.

> In the bourgeois ideology of the reformers, leisure was less the bountiful territory in which to site Utopia, than some dangerous frontier zone beyond the law and order of respectable society. Traditionally it dispensed its own

licence, and it was its abuse which had imprinted itself most deeply in middle-class consciousness; in a work-oriented culture it represented an invitation to idleness and dissolution—the weakness of an ill-disciplined working class, the badge of an unduly privileged aristocracy. (P. Bailey 170)

The temptation to idealize the past afflicts even social historians. Bailey's account of an idyllically harmonious "traditional" arrangement of life may not be accurate; J. M. Golby and A. W. Purdue, for instance, term "mythical" the "notion of a fall from a society that was `traditional,' customary, organic and pre-capitalist to one that was modern, individualistic, commercial and capitalist" (11). Yet considerable evidence suggests an increasing separation of work and leisure in English life during the eighteenth and nineteenth centuries, a separation that came to imply ever higher valuation of work as activity, and that thus plays its part in the development of capitalist society.

The split between work and leisure implicates the problem of boredom. Sebastian de Grazia reports the results of a Roper poll inquiring about the perceived desirability of a four-day or three-day workweek: 20 percent of those answering agreed that "people would simply get bored having too little to do" (140). Such an attitude, de Grazia demonstrates, develops from deep historical roots.

> The Reformation had seen to making [Sunday] a dismal bore, and enterprising businessmen thought that the move was in the right direction. . . . With all the joy gone out of the Lord's day, it might as well not have existed. To take all joy out, one must say, seems too often to have been precisely the purpose. The thought seems to have been that if there were nothing but work for a man to do, he would no longer see any point to stopping work once he had earned the exact number of pennies he needed. (202–3)

The familiar notion of a "right to work," established only after 1848, implied—still implies—that "only through work, a new fundamental right, can men (all adult males and some females) pursue happiness. The original idea was the reverse: only through not having to work can men pursue happiness" (de Grazia 283).

The "original idea" de Grazia refers to has nothing to do with a concept of leisure as a space for recreation. It bears rather on the notion of the contemplative life as the noblest human occupation. According to Hannah Arendt, before the modern age (which she locates as beginning in the seventeenth century) "all activities of the *vita activa* had been judged and justified to the extent that they made the *vita contemplativa* possible" (291–92). To declare work the antidote to boredom degrades the psychic function of productive activity. Such understanding of work also sensitizes workers to the potential for boredom inherent in that activity itself, a potential barely acknowledged before the twentieth century. And of course the idea that work offers more satisfaction than alternative pursuits can supply intensifies the problem of leisure. As early as 1780, an essayist in the *Mirror* notes the difficulty inadequately educated men find in filling up time. As long as such men work, they face no difficulty:

> I believe it may be true, that neither learning, nor a taste for the elegant arts, is requisite to enable a person engaged in the ordinary business of life, to succeed in his profession; and, while so engaged, the occupations of that profession will prevent his feeling any vacuity. (*Mirror* 279; no. 106, 13 May 1780)

In retirement, however, poorly educated men encounter unpleasantness: "Instead of pleasure, they find satiety, weariness, and disgust; time becomes a heavy burden upon them, and in what way they may kill the tedious hours, grows, at length, their only object" (279). The rich man's posited inability to enjoy himself ("He either becomes a prey to chagrin and *ennui*, or he gives himself up to the coarsest intemperance" [280]) reveals his lack of adequately developed inner resources. Had his mind been properly cultivated, the writer concludes, he might have enjoyed his fortune.

Early discourse about methods of occupying time suggests that the problem of leisure not only provides alternative ways of talking about boredom, it constitutes one of the causes for the new concern with boredom as itself a problem. By the nineteenth century, however, the notion that satiety, weariness, disgust, chagrin, ennui—inability to enjoy leisure—reflect internal inadequacy appears to yield largely to belief that such unpleasant states will dissolve given adequate external stimulation. Both contemporary and later commentators testify to the rapid proliferation of new forms of entertainment in the late eighteenth and nineteenth centuries. "Appetite for the new and the different, for fresh experience and novel excitements," as well as "for the getting and spending of money . . . lies," J. H. Plumb maintains, "at the heart of successful bourgeois society" ("Acceptance" 316). Eighteenth-century England generated comic opera, equestrian circuses (including "wild-animal trainers, conjurers, jugglers and trapeze artists"), increasing numbers of horse races (Plumb, "Commercialization" 276, 282). "Exhibitions of curiosities; museums; zoos; puppet shows; circuses; lectures on science; panoramas of European cities; automata; horseless car-

READING, WRITING, AND BOREDOM / 19

riages; even human and animal monstrosities were available in provin-
cial cities as well as in London" (Plumb, "New World" 307). In the country, crowds resorted to such affairs as grinning competitions to entertain themselves (Burton 281). By 1807 Robert Southey, offering a
pseudonymous account of life in England, tells of tulip raisers, pigeon
fanciers, and butterfly breeders. "Even as any thing may become the
object of superstition," he writes, "an onion or a crocodile, an ape or an
ape's tooth, so also any thing does for a pursuit" (Espriella 1: 233). In
an 1823 work titled *A Compendious History of the Cotton Manufacture*, someone named R. Guest complained about the "effeminate cast" of members of the laboring class who "are now Pigeon-fanciers, Canary-breed-
ers, and Tulip-growers" (qtd. in Cunningham 60). A quarter century
later, H. Shimmin observes that "the craving for amusement is common
to all. The people, in their eagerness to obtain some, are ever ready to
accept any, and, in the absence of anything better, take what they can
get with least inconvenience to themselves" (122).

Anton Zijderveld, writing provocatively about boredom "as a typically modern characteristic of the experience of subjective time" (77),
suggests that

> it can be observed that speech becomes gross and hyperbolic, music loud
> and nervous, ideas giddy and fantastic, emotions limitless and shameless,
> actions bizarre and foolish, whenever boredom reigns. A bored individual
> needs these irritants of body, psyche and mind because he is not behav-
> iourally stimulated in any other way. (84)

He evokes in this summary recognizable aspects of late twentieth-century culture. Accounts of eighteenth- and nineteenth-century "craving
for amusement," however, call attention to the fact that our ancestors
too sought "irritants of body, psyche and mind" as ways to deal with a
new relation to time. The notion of leisure implies a principle of dif-
ferentiating time. But once kinds of time—"leisure time," "work time"—
become sharply distinguished, it seems, further differentiation proves
necessary. "When we are bored," a modern commentator argues, "our
attitude toward time is altered, as it is in some dreamlike states. Time
seems endless, there is no distinction between past, present, and future.
There seems to be only an endless present" (M. Waugh 541). Equestrian circuses and canary breeding mark temporal divisions, helping
spectators or participants to separate spaces of time.

The eighteenth- and nineteenth-century commentators I have
quoted do not use the word *boredom* or its cognates, although one mentions ennui (and Tristan's "boredom" in the original French would have

been *ennui*). Nor do the twentieth-century historians and sociologists who discuss leisure as a problem of the past comment on boredom as implicated in concern over the use of free time. (Recent social scientists writing about the present, on the other hand, have announced that "leisure should be optimally arousing for it to be psychologically rewarding" [Iso-Ahola and Weissinger 357].) Yet the "craving for amusement" allegedly "common to all" implies fearful awareness of boredom as an alternative possibility. And the eagerness of observers to attribute desperation for new pursuits to groups other than themselves suggests displaced anxiety over being afflicted by the dreariness of nonengagement. To perceive leisure as a "problem" entails awareness of emotional danger in idleness. The devil finds work for idle hands to do because of the nature of idle minds. Recurrent words like *weary, dejected, anxious,* and *satiety* call attention to observers' consciousness of and concern about the infirmity of the soul that people were learning to call *boredom.*

Not only twentieth-century scholars but eighteenth- and nineteenth-century moralists, it seems, consider this malaise a property of groups—workingmen, aristocrats, nouveaux riches, the middle class—rather than of individuals, although in fact boredom, if sometimes infectious, remains an intensely personal experience. Even the few examples of commentary cited, however, suggest historical distinctions in ways of thinking about it, distinctions whose nature I have already suggested, bearing on the problem of the personal. Although the eighteenth-century essayist considers the entire category of poorly educated businessmen, his little fable about imaginary rich men without the mental training to use their leisure constructs their plight as an issue of individual responsibility. His nineteenth-century successors find causes beyond the self, external difficulties afflicting large classes, for the experienced inability to find "interesting" occupation.

The writer in the *Mirror* expresses an attenuated sense of boredom as a kind of vice. Medieval theologians had readily proclaimed acedia the root of many evils. It seems sometimes identical to boredom, sometimes a vice caused by boredom, sometimes itself boredom's cause. Siegfried Wenzel documents in detail its shifting meanings, but all suggest the moral and theological danger of insufficient engagement with life's obligations and possibilities.

The *Mirror* essayist, inheriting the view that individuals bear public responsibility, converts the terms of that view from Christian to social. He sees victims of boredom as suffering from "diseased imagination" (283), but he condemns them finally in a moralistic vocabulary:

Had their minds been cultivated in their youth, had they then acquired the
first principles of elegance and taste, they would have been enabled, after
attaining a fortune, to have enjoyed it with propriety and dignity: while they
were reaping the fruits of their honest industry and success, they might have
been useful to others and proved ornaments to their country. (287)

The inability to enjoy becomes equivalent to a failure of usefulness.
Bored rich men are more to be censured than pitied.

The nineteenth-century moralists I have quoted, on the other hand,
pity rather than condemn members of the working class or upper-class
women deprived of occupation. T. H. Escott adopts a neutral tone for
his comments on middle-class folk who want something new to do.
One may discern faint overtones of amusement in his account, but no
blame. The change from a moralistic to a sociological view of boredom
marks a significant moment of cultural development.

If the emergence of leisure as condition and as problem suggests one
reason for boredom's arrival in the eighteenth century, a hypothetical
reason connecting boredom closely with the rise of capitalism, the
decline of orthodox Christianity suggests another. As a twentieth-century theologian has pointed out, boredom can usefully be understood
as faith's opposite. "Where faith, for good or bad, is a tremendous drive
toward relationship and contains all the energies that we associate with
the life of wishing and longing, boredom moves in just the opposite
way" (Lynch 99). Moreover, Christian faith provides constant occupation: lack of interest in what the world offers can encourage focus on a
life beyond. And faith supplies clear standards for action and for
thought. The history of commentary on boredom and associated states,
and on the problem of leisure, shows a steady decline in faith: medieval
writers, with their assured vocabulary of sin and virtue, give way to
moralists apparently certain of their standards but vague about what
systems or sanctions support them. By Dickens's time social morality
has made serious inroads on the realm of personal morality.

A third possible cause for boredom as an eighteenth-century concept involves the newly elaborated notion of individual rights. A brief
excursion into the twentieth century will show an important line of
development. We might consider two instances of recent attitudes.
One is recorded in a 1986 book titled *Overload and Boredom: Essays on the
Quality of Life in the Information Society.* At the outset, the author comments
on the "major paradox that growing leisure and affluence and mounting
information and stimulation we call progress lead to boredom—a
deficit in the quality of life" (Klapp 1). Shortly thereafter, he makes
explicit his intent to criticize the current notion of progress. "What can

progress be," he inquires, "if it does not banish boredom?" (4). The implicit conviction, apparently felt to need no examination, is that people have a right not to be bored, that society's obligations include preventing their boredom, preserving not only the physical but the psychic "quality of [their] life." This conviction marks a postmodern moment.

Equally vivid in implication is an observation from a 1990 *New Yorker* article on problems of Rembrandt attribution and deattribution. One controversial pair of portraits, of a middle-aged man and his wife, display sections of careless painting that cause certain critics to consider it impossible that Rembrandt executed them. The painting of the woman, with an "awkwardly foreshortened" arm, seems especially dubious (A. Bailey 65). A contrary view, articulated by John Brealey, head of conservation at the Metropolitan Museum of Art, explains the master's sloppiness by the personality of the woman he painted. "She was a dreadfully boring woman, and you can see it looking at her face," he maintains. "It was one of those commissions that portrait painters have to do to earn money" (A. Bailey 66). Such a judgment rests on the assumption that certain human beings possess inherently boring characters. Others, inevitably bored by them, therefore have the right to ignore or reject them.

From an eighteenth-century, even a nineteenth-century, point of view, the attitudes conveyed by both Brealey's comments and Klapp's would seem astonishing. The notion that boredom inheres in the consciousness of its experiencer appears to have vanished. Now to call something boring describes an object rather than a subject. Progress should banish boredom by making life objectively interesting. A boring woman simply *is* boring—you can see it in her face; anyone can see it. The new point of view inhabits the same continuum as eighteenth-century moralizing and nineteenth-century sociologizing, extending the development away from a tendency to condemn the person who suffers boredom, toward attributing the misery to external causes. But something qualitatively different has also taken place. A new form of moralizing directs opprobrium toward the cause rather than the victim of boredom. The hypothetical "dreadfully boring woman," the deadening cultural environment: these become, implicitly or explicitly, objects of condemnation.

And it all started in the eighteenth century, with such notions as, for instance, a *right* to "the pursuit of happiness." A right to pursue happiness at least hints the possibility of achieving it. Dr. Johnson, maintaining the ethos of older, sterner forms of Christianity than those that flourished around him, thought human life a state in which much was to be endured, little to be enjoyed. People were coming to believe in enjoyment, though: in the desirability of seeking it and the yet greater desirability of finding it. By the nineteenth century, the Utilitarians could speak of a "calculus of pleasure." The calculation and calibration of pleasure imply comparably refined awareness of "unpleasure." To consider human existence an arena for seeking happiness virtually guarantees heightened consciousness of how little happiness daily routine necessarily provides. Hannah Arendt observes that "the universal demand for happiness and the widespread unhappiness in our society . . . are but two sides of the same coin" (134). Given constant assessment of degrees of pleasure, boredom becomes an essential category of experience. Human beings perceived as causing boredom, and cultural situations understood to promote it, ultimately focus the primitive anger of unfulfilled entitlement.

The rise of individualism, a development long associated with the seventeenth and eighteenth centuries—my fourth posited cause for boredom's invention—implies a concomitant increase in personal sense of entitlement. The story of eighteenth-century individualism has often been told: the proliferation of new forms of Protestantism, the increase in affectively motivated marriage, the intensifying stress on personal accomplishment and achievement, the interest in individual psychology that had originated with Locke. Paradoxically, the new stress on the dignity of individuals may have implied increasing trivialization of experience. As individual life is accorded more importance, focus on daily happenings intensifies. Keeping an eye on small particularities has positive consequences but, inviting constant evaluation, also calls attention to the lack of emotional satisfaction in much ordinary experience. The inner life comes to be seen as consequential; therefore its inadequacies invite attention. The concept of boredom serves as an all-purpose register of inadequacy.

Exploring the connection between attention to individual interior experience and words like *boring* and *interesting*, Logan Pearsall Smith construes the shift in vocabulary as symptomatic of the modern era of self-consciousness inaugurated by Descartes (Smith 249). Edward Peters, also reflecting on the link between self-awareness and boredom, makes a broader claim:

> The virtually limitless increase in the range of conversational and literary taste, convention, and vocabulary across a broadened social bond, a new, commonplace interest in medical subjects and in scientific projects, the systematic ordering of ideas and (initially audacious, occasionally outrageous)

topics in dictionaries and encyclopedias, outside the universities and schools, and even the consequences of the rise of anthropological discourse in the sixteenth and seventeenth centuries, all these contributed to a widening and transformation of public consciousness, not only of the world of things but of the vaster interior world of the self and the personality. (504)

To delineate the history of introspection obviously exceeds the scope of my inquiry. But Peters's association of more detailed forms of self-knowledge with increasingly elaborated knowledge of the external world provides a useful perspective on the deliquescence of subject and object that we have noted in developing attitudes toward boredom. The "world of things" and that of the self, alike objects of study, impinge forcefully on one another. If knowledge comes from both, so do feelings. Boredom derives perhaps from who one is, perhaps from what surrounds one. Eighteenth-century confidence in the culpability of the person experiencing boredom rapidly gave way to more ambivalent nineteenth-century judgments. The need to make such judgments at all registers the growing tendency to take feeling seriously.

I have sketched four hypotheses to explain the new importance of boredom in the eighteenth century: the development of leisure as differentiated psychic space; the decline of Christianity; the intensification of concern with individual rights; and the increasing interest in inner experience. None of these developments can be taken as a definitive cause for *boredom* the word or boredom the experience, nor do all together suffice as total explanation. All are historically associated circumstances that help define more fully the psychological and social circumstances in which the concept of boredom developed. To contemplate them even briefly begins to suggest the intricacies of boredom itself as a bearer of cultural meaning.

Paradox inheres in the apparent fascination with boredom felt by many makers of fiction. Antithetical to energy and desire, to all forces of action, boredom by its nature stands in opposition to the activity of literary invention, as to all other activity. An emblem of stasis, it, like Pope's Dulness, brings every mind to one dead level. The banality of evil is arguable, the banality of boredom manifest. Why then its attraction for novelists, for whom dullness must be the worst of sins?

Why, for that matter, its attraction for me as a critic? The *so what?* question, that question critics should constantly ask themselves, presents itself loudly at this point. Which brings me to the rationale for this book.

We have learned by now both the possibility and the urgency of investigating the taken for granted. Recent cultural history has made it seem more conceivable to examine the culturally invisible, to see what we previously have not seen at all, often because we have thought it not worth looking at. Boredom feels like an inevitable and, well, *boring* concomitant of civilized existence. All the more reason to scrutinize the discourse surrounding it.

It was the word and its history that first aroused my interest in the subject. That the word has not always existed, has not even existed for long, suggests not necessarily that the experience is new but at least that the concept has not always been necessary. If we can answer the question why such a notion demanded formulation, we will have achieved some insight into the necessity of boredom, both cultural construct and social myth. Like other myths, it helps explain us (and our social world) to ourselves. William Barrett has speculated that the idea of boredom focuses a universal and ultimately metaphysical fear, that of running out of things to do. "Our craving for the open [i.e., infinitely various] universe . . . comes down to this: we want to be left something to do, something to create. Above all, we do not want to be bored" (554). Understanding the universe as rich in unsolved problems, we take comfort from that understanding. "In the end, it is our own creativity that we want to be reassured about" (555). But why should it be so terrible to run out of things to do? The fear and resentment of boredom even as a possibility, the desperation with which, as glossy advertisements testify, twentieth-century Westerners struggle to avert it— such emotions demand social as well as metaphysical exegesis, particularly because they appear not to be historical constants.

So the examination of articulations and representations of boredom must take place in a historical context. The French historian Lucien Febvre, cofounder of *Annales*, more than half a century ago called for a history of *sensibilité*, "the emotional life of man and all its manifestations" ("Sensibility" 13), as essential to any adequate social history. He speaks of the danger

> of wanting to switch directly . . . from feelings and ideas belonging to ourselves to feelings and ideas that similar words or the self-same words seem to describe perhaps several centuries back in time; such words can cause the worst sorts of confusion by persuading us that they have the same meanings as the ones we know. ("History" 6)

The difficulty of recovering past emotional conditions is, of course, enormous: "The task is, for a given period, to establish a detailed inventory of the mental equipment for the men [sic] of the time, then by dint of great learning, but also of imagination, to reconstitute the whole physical, intellectual and moral universe of each preceding generation" ("History" 9). A tall order, not likely to be filled by any single social or cultural historian.

Lacking the resources to provide the kind of inventory Febvre calls for, one can yet accumulate evidence of shifting associations and meanings for at least a single term of heavy emotional weight. Edward Peters, inspired by Febvre, began the effort, in relation to boredom, in 1975. His sketchy but provocative account, however, fails to specify why boredom should offer a particularly significant case in point. One answer might call attention to the especially clear status of boredom as both social and psychological happening. All emotions bear social meanings. As Febvre points out, "They imply relations between one man and another—group relations" ("Sensibility" 14). Even self-loathing and, for that matter, self-glorification depend implicitly on comparison between the self and others. But boredom, unlike love, hate, and self-loathing, has been increasingly understood as itself a product of social conditions. To investigate it over the course of two centuries involves interrogating institutions as well as individuals.

Febvre, with the perspective of a historian, recommends the study of "sensibility" as a way to contextualize past events and to comprehend more fully the meaning of actions and responses from periods before our own. As a literary scholar, I pursue a somewhat different agenda. I am interested in (i.e., I resist boredom by investigating . . .) developing verbal responses to an evolving concept. Those responses—representations and repudiations of boredom, polemics and instructions about confronting it, narratives of avoidance—record a cultural process. They also constitute, often, works whose imaginative and emotional persuasiveness rewards exploration. Examining them under the rubric of boredom reveals surprising connections among them and uncovers unpredictable animating energies. My purposes here are "literary," resting on the assumption that verbal constructs contain ascertainable meanings that speak their writers' conscious and unconscious intentions, respond to their readers' assumptions, and suggest processes both of cultural work and of individual effort. But my project also participates in the undertaking Febvre envisioned, inasmuch as the sequence of generically diverse texts of boredom indeed helps to specify the "mental equipment" (meaning psychological as well as intellectual orientation) of men and women in different historical periods. Unlike Febvre, I, as a twentieth-century feminist, find myself wondering how far gender determines modes of confronting boredom. This book offers tentative answers to that question too.

Boredom is worth exploring partly because it is so hard to look at, so much taken for granted as an aspect of life. "Big" emotions—love, hate, jealousy—generate the kinds of conflict that readily engage most people, in their direct experience and on the page. Trivial emotions connect themselves less readily to dramatic happening (although violent crime, these days, quite frequently gets accounted for as a product of boredom) and appear implausible as literary subjects (although many a novel and play develops out of and concentrates on protagonists' boredom). Yet the trivial weaves the texture of lives. Boredom, as a historically locatable manifestation of trivialization, provides a paradigm of the ordinary and, examined, helps elucidate the gradual construction of ordinariness.

With a generally historical perspective, I hope to examine boredom as an explanatory myth of our culture, looking at what the trivial and the profound have in common. Most psychological and sociological commentators on boredom distinguish two varieties: "One is a responsive feeling and the other is a malaise" (Bernstein 513; see also, e.g., Healy 46). What Healy calls "simple boredom" (Bernstein's "responsive feeling") appears to derive from specific circumstances—the prolonged meeting, the repetitive job—and to be remediable. The "malaise" corresponds more precisely to the French *ennui*, a state of the soul defying remedy, an existential perception of life's futility. As I have already suggested, it possesses more dignity than does its commonplace sibling, and it has attracted more attention in print. The only full-length study of boredom as a literary subject (Kuhn) focuses on ennui and rejects as beneath consideration the emotion of the bored housewife.

But the bored housewife and her sisters and brothers interest me. And it is not always easy to distinguish between dignified and trivial forms of boredom. Someone's general psychic and "metaphysical" situation—ennui—may predispose him or her to find external stimuli troublesome, but the stimuli themselves, at least on occasion, help to generate specific, immediate feeling (boredom). Boredom, as many imaginative writers know, provides a handy catchall for emotion. To categorize it rigidly risks limiting it excessively.

Inasmuch as I can separate kinds of boredom, however, I shall concentrate in the main on the kind that appears to be caused by not having enough to do, or not liking the things one has to do, or existing with other people or in a setting one finds distasteful—with the caveat that the definition of "not having enough to do," like that of the other states listed, depends on perception. Thus the "remediability" of "simple boredom" may depend, like the irremediability of ennui, on psychic rather than external conditions.

The data of boredom exist, for my purposes, in written records: testimony, imagining, commentary. Like other cultural constructs, boredom thrives also as a literary construct. References to it multiply astonishingly from the eighteenth to the twentieth century. I confine myself in this book almost entirely to England (with a small excursus into twentieth-century America, which provides revealing and usefully explicit accounts of boredom's functions), mainly because the subject becomes patently unmanageable if one considers France and Germany and Russia and Scandinavia, where boredom, its trivial and metaphysical meanings intertwining, supplies an enormous mass of literary material, particularly in the nineteenth century. But England alone provides such abundance as to make exhaustiveness a ludicrous fantasy. I offer, therefore, a series of essays that examine certain representations of and responses to boredom from various points of view in order to adumbrate the development of its social, psychological, and narrative functions and to argue the importance of these functions in defining and maintaining modernity (and postmodernity).

It is by no means essential to my argument to maintain that boredom came into existence only when it was first named. One can never prove that a new feeling has entered the world. The emotion Shakespeare's Hippolyta experiences may in fact have precisely corresponded to what we understand as boredom, but the language assigned to her emotion differs from the twentieth-century vocabulary of boredom, and I maintain the importance of the difference. If new feelings arguably never manifest themselves, new concepts unequivocally do. Boredom was in the eighteenth century a new concept, if not necessarily a new event. The emergence of a new concept marks a significant cultural happening because it allows articulation of fresh ways to understand the world.

This book will develop its argument—its thesis about how boredom has enabled us to understand the world, about the psychic, social, and literary purposes it has served—in two directions. One thrust concerns the implication of boredom (and its antithesis, interest) in the processes and the consequences of writing and reading. I have already sketched the broad outline of my contention that writers write and readers read in order to keep life interesting. Specific implications of this contention reveal themselves in, for instance, reception history, as works almost universally considered "interesting" at the moment of publication come to seem self-evidently "boring" some years later. Society at large has a stake in what its members will recognize as interesting. The experientially personal act of reading a book inflects itself differently according to the reader's historical moment and social circumstances. To survey the shifting reputation of even a few works can suggest kinds of cultural meaning inherent in individual acts of judgment.

The other line of argument draws on ways boredom has figured as overt or covert subject as well as stimulus of literary investigation. Men and women write (and have written) not only to avert boredom but to deny it, to represent it, to investigate it, to embrace it, to deplore it. They speak of boredom sometimes without mentioning its name; they tell its story even when they narrate excitement. Tacitly and explicitly, they reveal the steadily expanding range of social and personal purposes the concept has served since its eighteenth-century articulation. As point of reference or focus of opposition, as means of characterization, repudiation, or definition, as social indictment or as personal grievance, the idea of boredom as articulated in language condenses a spectrum of crucial meanings and attitudes. I propose to delineate that spectrum.

To investigate various forms and moments of written expression under the rubric of boredom calls attention to literary content. But this is not a thematic study—not an examination of boredom in literature— and it moves among various approaches. The next chapter investigates eighteenth-century male attitudes toward boredom, focusing mainly on that exemplary eighteenth-century male Samuel Johnson. Neither Johnson nor the other men briefly discussed will rely on the new word, but all register their awareness of the stance toward being that the word *boredom* would soon commonly designate. The concept of boredom has come to express a complex system of sensibility, the beginnings of which predate reliance on the word. Johnson, in his violent repudiation of the experience of tedium, expresses a prescient horror of boredom's potential.

In the subsequent two chapters, dealing with eighteenth-century women, various forms of the word *bore* occasionally appear as part of the texts considered, but the *absence* of boredom as an acknowledged part of female experience constitutes the main subject. In women's novels of the eighteenth century (chapter 3), boredom characteristically belongs mainly to men, sometimes as a cultivated stance. Misery— exaggerated, complicated misery—replaces boredom as a female experience in these fictions. Eighteenth-century conduct books for women make it clear that females who admit to boredom thereby violate an important standard. Women's private letters (chapter 4), like their novels, consequently deny the experience even while relating uneventful lives. Sometimes, scornfully, women's letters too explicitly identify boredom as a problem troublesome only to men, more self-indulgent and less disciplined than their female counterparts. The two chapters argue that systematic verbal construction of alternatives to boredom marks women's writing in this period.

An interlude on the "interesting" precedes chapter 5, which returns to the subject of readers as arbiters of boredom by examining the reception of three novels (Hannah More's *Coelebs in Search of a Wife*, Samuel Richardson's *Sir Charles Grandison*, and Mrs. Humphry Ward's *Robert Elsmere*). The eleventh edition of the *Encyclopaedia Britannica* describes Ward's novel as "the talk of the civilized world" when it first appeared, to run through five editions in its first seven months. The other books in this assortment likewise created enormous popular interest at their initial publication, only to be universally dismissed as "boring" by the twentieth century. Investigation of the perceptual shift involved focuses on the relation between the didactic and the boring.

Chapter 6 concerns the nineteenth-century shift, in novels centered on women, to emphasis on boredom as a peculiarly female experience. In chapter 7 I take up the nineteenth-century pose (in contrast with the nineteenth-century female experience) of boredom as represented mainly in novels by Dickens and Trollope. The succeeding two chapters touch on connections between boredom and the assumptions of modernism and postmodernism.

TWO

Vacuity, Satiety, and
the Active Life
Eighteenth-Century Men

On the island of Skye, during his tour of the Hebrides (7 Sept. 1773), James Boswell found existence temporarily burdensome. He reports his emotions in the *Life of Johnson* as well as in the journal of his travels:

> I was happy when tea came. Such, I take it, is the state of those who live in the country. Meals are wished for from the cravings of vacuity of mind, as well as from the desire of eating. I was hurt to find even such a temporary feebleness, and that I was so far from being that robust wise man who is sufficient for his own happiness. (5: 159)

A twentieth-century reader has no trouble understanding Boswell's condition. He was, we might say, *bored,* lacking adequate occupation. We might even sympathize, since his narrative evokes the severely circumscribed possibilities for entertainment supplied by the barren islands he has been traversing.

Strangely, though, considering his general propensity for self-pity, Boswell hardly seems to sympathize with himself. He understands his sense of tedium as an index of moral weakness ("feebleness"), a sign of his inability to duplicate the energy of a companion whom—at least sometimes—he considers a "robust wise man." He believes that his craving for event marks his insufficiency, his emptiness of mind. Although he apparently imagines that all who live in the country share his moral malady, he yet preserves his dream that one can be "sufficient to his own happiness." Both his vocabulary and his self-castigation may well derive from Johnson, whose propensity to discover or to fear

31

"vacuity of mind" matches his readiness to worry about "satiety," an equal but opposite sign of spiritual inadequacy.

Both Johnson and Boswell meditate about the moral and psychological problems implicit in intermittent experiences of life's apparent vacuity, although they do not employ the word *boredom* to focus their concerns. The specific label would give heightened reality to something still vague and disturbing. An essayist in the *Observer* (a periodical published as individual essays in *Town and Country Magazine* from 1773 to 1790) who congratulates the English on the absence of such a word from their vocabulary implicitly worries lest the term create the experience. Describing the face of a dissipated man, he concludes that in it, "all is languor, *nonchalance* or *ennui*." "(I help out my description with French)," the writer adds, "(for, thank Heaven! we have yet no words in our language to express it)" (*Observer* 32: 203; no. 28). He was wrong, of course: the English had already found a word of their own to designate a condition not unique to depraved dwellers on the Continent and not necessarily associated with dissipation, one that had started to trouble English people. The essayist, however, did not know that word; possibly neither did Johnson.

The entrance of the word *bore* into the English language as a psychological description coincides chronologically with an increase in the number and urgency of discussions reflecting on boredom as a circumstance. Whether or not the discussants label the condition in a single word, they call attention to their concern with the experience, its causes and consequences. In the previous chapter I argued that the intensifying conceptual usefulness of boredom coincided with heightening stress on subjectivity. Eighteenth-century England supplies clear evidence of how the problematic aspects of subjectivity reveal themselves in the concept of boredom. Boredom implies a dwelling on the self, specifically a sense of victimization. Commentary on it explored what it means to allow oneself to be a victim, to define oneself as victim. Imaginative reconstructions of boredom often suggest the emotional tug of victimization—an appeal all too familiar in the late twentieth century—even as they deplore its moral implications.

Jonathan Swift had dramatized in *A Tale of a Tub* ways that a focus on the self, its needs and demands, opposed communal and historical stability. Johnson's implicit and explicit denunciations of boredom's self-indulgence show his awareness of threats to ethical order in the very idea of boredom, which depends on the belief in the importance of individual feelings that Swift had challenged. Subjectivity in its nature evades established systems of control: the self proclaims its own laws.

The complaint of boredom, subjectivity's product, violates the Christian ethical imperatives of faith and good works, which together fruitfully occupy mind and body and improve the hope of salvation. The bored man, insisting that nothing can interest him, denies the discipline of faith and the obligation of occupation.

Indeed, all secular concentration on the self implies such denial in its acknowledgment of emotion's power and of the possibility that moods and feelings may fluctuate unpredictably. The unexamined assumptions of the late twentieth century often associate psychological introspection with freedom: to follow one's feelings expresses one's liberty. From the point of view of an eighteenth-century conservative, just the opposite would be the case. Feelings can enslave their possessor. Feelings indulged become tyrannical. To discriminate emotions with increasing specificity implies a dangerous move toward solipsism. To allow feelings power may make the moral self powerless: such, at least, was a prevailing fear.

Such generalizations appeared plausible only to those committed to moral orthodoxy. Eighteenth-century England also contained men and women more firmly oriented toward new ways of thinking: more concerned, for instance, with psychological particularities than with moral generalization. Nonetheless, the characteristic imaginative uses of boredom in the eighteenth century (whether or not the psychic state received its new label) emphasize its moral valence. Its sufferers might consider it a psychological malady, but their way of conceiving it usually suggested its moral dangers. Such commentators as Johnson stressed the need to combat it. Boredom, in typical eighteenth-century representations, provided an emblem of helplessness. It menaced ethical energy. To write about it opened a way to discuss or to deplore the threat of undesired passivity. Boredom's meanings coalesced through a dynamic of communal responsibility versus individual susceptibility.

Living at a historical moment when boredom seems a universal malady, we may find it hard to recapture the sensibility that finds it a mark of moral deficiency, a sickness curable only with great effort. Our mothers perhaps proclaimed that if you're bored, you're boring. I can remember telling my own daughter that boredom wasn't allowed at our house. From time to time, even now, in other words, we acknowledge ethical issues implicit in the concept of boredom, but for the most part we have lost a sense of their urgency. I shall try to recapture that feeling of urgency by looking closely at Johnson's comments on boredom the actuality, as opposed to *boredom* the word—comments contained mainly in his periodical essays and in *Rasselas*. Johnson's dense commentary uncovers the apparent psychological necessity even while it exposes the ethical insufficiency of boredom as a human response to experience. A more cursory look at three other eighteenth-century writers, less morally rigorous, who themselves confessed to experiencing boredom will help focus the meaning of Johnson's position. Boswell, Gray, and Burney appear more inclined than Johnson to give themselves the benefit of the doubt. Yet finally they have much in common with him, for they too understand boredom as a state epitomizing the painful and increasingly troubling experience of feeling oneself acted upon rather than active.

A student passed on to me a photocopy of a cartoon showing Johnson pontificating in a tavern: "So I say, `You *have* Lord Kames. Keep him; ha, ha, ha!'" Around him sit a group of men manifestly in terminal stages of boredom. The caption reads, "Dr. Johnson gets off a good one."

Eighteenth-century buffs may prickle at such a representation, but it is true enough that Johnson's insistent high seriousness in public utterance encourages twentieth-century association of the sage with boredom, given the common current connection of boredom to lack of sufficient entertainment. Eighteenth-century assumptions suggest quite different connections. Johnson's seriousness, his contemporaries would have thought, marked his active engagement with life. Such engagement, those contemporaries believed, resists boredom for its possessor and, inasmuch as it is communicated, for others.

To be sure, Johnson did not much concern himself with his effect on his company. (Boswell, according to the Boswellian version of events, needed to tell him when he was rude.) His contemporary Samuel Richardson used a letter-writing manual to warn young men against social sins, including being bores. They should avoid "silly digressions" (Richardson, *Letters* 16), keep from making their wife and children "the constant Subject of . . . Praise and Conversation" (87), convey a sense of self-esteem that would prevent "many of the *yawning* hours spent in companies composed of men not incapable of behaving agreeably" (15). Such matters did not interest Johnson, who worried not about the aggression implicit in being boring but about the dangerous passivity of being bored.

To make others yawn is only a social sin. Understood as a psychological state, though, boredom in the eighteenth century, like other forms of unease, signaled moral misstep. John Mason, in his popular treatise *Self-Knowledge,* warned against allowing *"fretful* and *discontented* Thoughts, which do but chafe and wound the Mind to no purpose. To harbour these, is to do yourself more Injury, than it is in the Power of your greatest Enemy to do you. It is equally a Christian's Interest and Duty to *learn, in whatever State he is, therewith to be content,* Phil. iv. ii" (Mason 114). Emphasizing the point, he adds that "it is of as great Importance for a Man to take heed what Thoughts he entertains, as what Company he keeps; for they have the same Effect upon the Mind" (126). To permit oneself the experience of "vacuity" and "satiety," for instance, as Johnson would more sharply specify the problem, implied a potentially fatal fall into inattention. Christian responsibility mandated steady attention to the inner life. Mason's language makes it clear that he understands *"fretful* and *discontented* Thoughts" as potential *invaders* of the mind. The good man repels them by active mental resistance, rejecting the passivity that would permit their incursions.

Johnson and others found diverse ways to emphasize that only active involvement in moral struggle protected against boredom and other forms of discontent. James Harris, for instance, in 1744 published as one of his *Three Treatises* a discourse "On Happiness." The search for happiness, he argues, typically focuses on two areas, business and leisure. Business can be divided into the political and the lucrative, leisure into the contemplative and the pleasurable (124–25). These classifications speak eloquently of Harris's historical moment, not only in the separation of "business" from "leisure" but in the subdivisions that pair classical categories (the political, the contemplative) with their up-to-date counterparts, involving attention to money and to pleasure. Neither divisions nor subdivisions, however, finally matter much to Harris. He claims that in every sphere of activity human beings find all enjoyment "cancelled by *Satiety,"* pleasure passing hastily "away into the tedious Intervals of *Indifference"* (130). The opposite of business, implicitly, is the tedious state of not caring. Neither business nor leisure itself generates happiness, in the writer's view. Only the life of virtue, Harris's logic leads him to conclude, the life governed by moral duties, can produce happiness. Such a life involves constant effort, sustained moral action. Happiness, this treatise insists, consists in action rather than in its results (196–200).

Other moralists concurred, although Harris was unusual in directing his investigation specifically toward the attainment of happiness. With an altogether different emphasis—on education—David Fordyce, writing in dialogue form, imagines each of his characters as concerned with the need for action. When Phylax suggests that action constitutes the highest virtue, no one dissents. Eugenio deplores the idea of the solitary life as a locus of goodness, since "it approaches too near the Life of a *Vegetable*, and has nothing to stir the Passions, or keep them awake" (Fordyce 1: 169). Even Cleora, who would rather "calm than agitate" her mind (1: 169), redefines rather than repudiates action. Observing that her sex is confined to "a small Circle of Pleasures" (1: 172), she advocates contemplation of nature and rational conversation as appropriate forms of action for women (1: 171). These conversationalists do not discuss vacuity or satiety or any other equivalent for boredom. Instead, all concur in celebrating learning as lifelong action and declaring the inherent interest of the natural and the cultural world. Such stress on the importance of active involvement suggests the impermissibility of boredom.

The kind of action appropriate to human beings includes other people. The dialogue form dramatizes this circumstance, and many moralists commented on it. Thus Henry Mackenzie (probably) in the *Lounger*:

> Men were born to live in society; and from society only can happiness be derived. The station of life requires activity and effort. For these was mankind formed; and those who do not contribute to the happiness of themselves and others by strenuous exertions of virtue, are unworthy of a place in the great theatre of the universe. (Johnson, *Lounger* 30: 73; no. 9, 2 Apr. 1785)

The essay explicitly repudiates pleasure seeking as a viable way of life. Mackenzie tells a first-person story about a man who retires to the country for the sake of self-indulgence. Its denouement merits full quotation, for it epitomizes in every detail the standard eighteenth-century attitude toward boredom as an index of moral failure.

> I now found my *ferme ornée* gave me little amusement; the charm of novelty was worn off, and I grew tired of having always under my eye the same objects, however beautiful; there was not a tree the shape of which I was not acquainted with, nor a walk which I had not a thousand times measured with my steps. My books, too, had lost their charms. . . . The enjoyment which I received was of a kind which rested in itself, and led to no further pursuit; so that I became more and more languid, weakened, and inactive. This I have experienced to be the case with all pleasure arising from inanimate beauties, and from every thing that may be termed an object merely of taste; they all terminate in themselves, and lead to weariness and satiety, unlike the exercise of the social affections, where every enjoyment multiplies itself, and leads to still fuller and more endearing sources of delight. . . . When the morning came, I have been unwilling to get out of bed, because I knew not what to do when I should get up; and at night I have been afraid to lie down,

because I knew that, when the night was spent, it would only lead to the nothingness of the next day. (*Lounger* 30: 70–71; no. 9, 2 Apr. 1785)

This paragraph implicitly specifies the complex relation between internal and external facts in the bored man's situation. The victim's account makes clear how fundamentally boredom derives from passivity. Someone who expects satisfaction to arise from objects outside himself becomes increasingly "languid," increasingly dependent on external stimulation. He can eliminate his boredom by the same general means Harris and Fordyce recommend: activity. Mackenzie, however, emphasizes the connection between the life of action and that of community. The social affections demand exercise and consequently supply delight. Fear of nothingness as an aspect of experience speaks not of insufficiency or futility in the organization of things but of personal inadequacy: failure to maintain social responsibilities.

Johnson's moral thought rests on the same assumptions that govern Fordyce, Mackenzie, and Harris. He differs vividly from them and most of their contemporaries, however, in his sense of how problematic the life of virtue might be for any individual. Granting the excitement of learning and of the external world, acknowledging the connection between the struggle for virtue and the achievement of what small happiness human beings can hope for, believing in social as well as theological responsibility, Johnson believed also that the possibilities of moral failure, for any given individual, exceeded those of success, even as the likelihood of misery in any human experience exceeded the chance of happiness. Like other forms of moral failure, boredom must be sternly resisted, especially because it implied the sufferer's acceptance of the distressing view that helpless man, in ignorance sedate, must roll darkling down the current of his fate. Boredom might nonetheless entrap any man or woman—even, on rare occasion, Johnson himself.

In a letter to Boswell written two years after Boswell mused on the importance of tea in the Hebrides (27 Aug. 1775), Johnson writes of his own visit to the Midlands.

I was glad to go abroad, and, perhaps, glad to come home; which is, in other words, I was, I am afraid, weary of being at home, and weary of being abroad. Is not this the state of life? But, if we confess this weariness, let us not lament it; for all the wise and all the good say, that we may cure it. (Boswell, *Life* 2: 382)

The odd qualifiers ("perhaps," "I am afraid") convey the hesitancy with which Johnson confesses his moral inadequacy before summoning up the rhetorical resources to withstand it. Boswell imagines the "robust wise man" who does not suffer Boswellian problems; Johnson, for comparable reasons, invokes the ghosts of "all the wise and all the good." His question, "Is not this the state of life?" betrays the anxiety at the foundation of all his discussions of tedium. *This* has vague grammatical reference, but the question's point is clear: weariness with what one has generates desire for what one has not. ("Life is a progress from want to want, not from enjoyment to enjoyment," Johnson observed a year later [*Life* 3: 53].) The alternation between satiety and vacuity, weariness and want, according to this view, keeps us in motion. Yet humankind can avoid the futile, reciprocal pattern: a cure exists for weariness (which I take as here roughly equivalent to boredom). Johnson investigates boredom in order to specify the cure.

In the periodical essays, he on occasion adopts the persona of a chronic victim of boredom. Thus he writes in the voice of a figure made familiar by Restoration comedy and by Pope: the young woman of fashion forced into rural retirement.

> I go out and return; I pluck a flower, and throw it away; I catch an insect, and when I have examined its colours, set it at liberty; I fling a pebble into the water, and see one circle spread after another. When it chances to rain, I walk in the great hall, and watch the minute-hand upon the dial, or play with a litter of kittens, which the cat happens to have brought in a lucky time. (Johnson, *Rambler* 3: 230; no. 42, 11 Aug. 1750)

Euphelia finds no solution to her difficulties, but she dimly knows that others in the same situation might not suffer them. "I have heard, Mr. Rambler, of those who never thought themselves so much at ease as in solitude, and cannot but suspect it to be some way or other my own fault, that, without great pain, either of mind or body, I am thus weary of myself" (231). The movement from blaming circumstances—the lack of entertainment in the country—to blaming herself points to a moral advance. Like Johnson and Boswell in the passages previously quoted, however, she remains vague about the precise nature of her failing. Begging Mr. Rambler to teach her "the art of living alone," she promises that "a thousand and a thousand and a thousand ladies" (231) who share her dilemma would feel grateful for help.

But women are of course not the only sufferers. Johnson suggests in the *Rambler* (no. 5, 3 Apr. 1750) that "when a man cannot bear his own company there is something wrong." Such a man flies from himself, either to avoid painful ideas or "because he feels a tediousness in life from the equipoise of an empty mind, which, having no tendency to one motion more than another but as it is impelled by some external power, must always have recourse to foreign objects" (3: 27). Again, passivity is the problem. The matter of "foreign objects" creates one of the great difficulties about comprehending boredom. To what extent is boredom an externally caused problem, to what extent internal? In a characteristically vigorous evocation of boredom, Boswell, in the guise of Hypochondriack, declares the intolerability of country living. "Even plantations, the rearing of which is by much the highest rural enjoyment, advance so imperceptibly; that a Hypochondriac proprietor is sick and sick again and again with *ennui,* and is tempted with wild wishes to hang himself on one of his own trees long before they are able to bear his weight" (*Hypochondriack* 2: 26; no. 37, Oct. 1780). Like Euphelia, this hypochondriac blames his spiritual state on lack of occupation. Unlike Euphelia, he does not contemplate the possibility that he bears responsibility for his own condition. Nor do most of Johnson's imaginary sufferers. Melanthia and Philotryphus, one of many unhappy couples who inhabit the pages of the *Rambler,* marry for bad reasons, Melanthia governed by her "insatiable desire of pleasure" (*Rambler* 3: 214; no. 39, 31 July 1750), Philotryphus seeking only money. Since neither is "vitious," "they live together with no other unhappiness, than vacuity of mind, and that tastelessness of life, which proceeds from a satiety of juvenile pleasures, and an utter inability to fill their place by nobler employments" (215). Suffering vacuity and satiety at once, these two are in a bad way, victims of their desires and of their excessive valuation of desire. The sentence evoking their plight not only emphasizes their internal inadequacies but also suggests that "nobler employments" would alleviate their difficulty. But what, exactly, does that phrase mean? Euphelia and Boswell's hypochondriac foretell the future in their suggestions that environments providing little in the way of satisfying occupation necessarily generate boredom. In effect they embrace passivity. What form of nobler employment could sufferers from the environment devise?

In the *Rambler* (no. 6, 7 Apr. 1750), Johnson considers the Stoic maxim that "man should never suffer his happiness to depend upon external circumstances" (3: 30) and declares it a doctrine repeatedly overthrown by experience. If human beings cannot hope for such "absolute independence" (31), however, they can at least aspire to rise beyond being "wholly at the mercy of accident" (31). As a case in point, the essayist contemplates the state of the idle rich, deprived of regular occupation and "having nothing within that can entertain or employ them" (31). He compares their situation to that of "a trader on the edge of bankruptcy": rich in literal monetary terms, they yet do not possess what they need. Their abject dependence on external stimuli appears reprehensible, but once more Mr. Rambler fails to explain how his imagined family can avoid it. Passivity constitutes moral danger, but alternative forms of action prove hard to locate.

Writing in another voice, however, in the persona of William Payne, author of *An Introduction to the Game of Draughts* (London, 1756), Johnson suggests a mental condition that might help boredom's victims. In a dedication to William Henry, earl of Rochford, Johnson writes,

> Triflers may find or make any Thing a Trifle; but since it is the great Char-
> acteristic of a wise Man to see Events in their Causes, to obviate Conse-
> quences, and ascertain Contingencies, your Lordship will think nothing a
> Trifle by which the Mind is inured to Caution, Foresight, and Circumspec-
> tion. (Hazen 150)

Even a game of checkers, rightly understood, supplies enlightenment. One might consider it a trifle, might even be bored by it. On the other hand, it is possible to take seriously the qualities of mind necessary to success in the game—and thus to take the game itself seriously as more than a distraction. Nothing is too little for so little a creature as man. People must form the "habit of turning every new object to [their] entertainment" (*Rambler* 3: 28; no. 5, 3 Apr. 1750). Thus "foreign objects" can indeed help sufferers from tedium—but only if they know how to use them properly, if they treat elements of their environment as opportunities for action.

Yet to say this does not do justice to the complex way Johnson grasps the problem of the external. He recognizes the genuine diffi-culty that Euphelia and the hypochondriac face.

> So few of the hours of life are filled up with objects adequate to the mind of
> man, and so frequently are we in want of present pleasure or employment,
> that we are forced to have recourse every moment to the past and future for
> supplemental satisfactions, and relieve the vacuities of our being, by recol-
> lection of former passages, or anticipation of events to come. (*Rambler* 3: 221;
> no. 41, 7 Aug. 1750)

The world does not supply sufficient "foreign objects" to gratify the mind, to fill "the vacuities of our being"; hence our dangerous reliance on memory, hope, imagination. Fundamentally the problem of bore-dom, as Johnson imagines it, involves the focusing of desire. The fable of Almamoulin exemplifies the dilemma. Child of a wealthy merchant, Almamoulin inherits vast amounts of money, which, his father tells him on his deathbed, "it must be thy business to enjoy with wisdom" (*Rambler* 4: 277; no. 120, 11 May 1751). Failing in his first enterprises, the heir finally contracts "his desires to more private and domestick pleasures" (278), happily building and landscaping. Languor and weariness soon "invade" him, however. "Change of place at first relieved his satiety, but all the novelties of situation were soon exhausted; he found his heart vacant, and his desires, for want of external objects, ravaging himself" (278). When he finally goes to a philosopher for help, the wise man tells him that riches are not much use to anyone except as they contribute to the acts of benevolence that "will afford the only happiness ordained for our present state, the confidence of divine favour, and the hope of future rewards" (280).

This pessimistic view, corresponding to that dramatized in Johnson's *The Vanity of Human Wishes*, glosses the phrase "nobler employments" in his earlier sketch of unsatisfying marriage. Nobler employments alleviate the misery of others. Although the wealthy have fuller scope for benevolence than do those in restricted financial circumstances, everyone, by redirecting desire, can do something for other people. Only thus may one fill the vacancies of the heart and avoid the ravages of desire, making boredom irrelevant.

This is a theoretical solution, however, and Johnson knows it. Experientially, boredom remains perplexing. Johnson's most vivid evocation of boredom as plight and as dilemma occurs in one of his contributions to the *Adventurer*. Number 102, like other eighteenth-century periodical essays we have encountered, tells the first-person story of a businessman ("Mercator") who finds retirement an agony of tedium. An allusion to Satan suggests the seriousness of his condition: "I now seldom see the rising sun, but `to tell him,' with the fallen angel, `how I hate his beams'" (Johnson, *Idler* 438; 27 Oct. 1753). Although he himself makes the Satanic connection, Mercator sees his condition not as sin but as misery, a psychic situation he has not deserved and cannot remedy. He hates the sun not from enmity to light but from inability to occupy himself in the daylight hours. Like Boswell in the Hebrides, he looks forward to meals to alleviate his sense of tedium. "If I could dine all my life, I should be happy: I eat not because I am hungry, but because I am idle" (438).

Mercator has made a series of concerted efforts to remedy his misery. He has tried hunting, reading, and hospitality, but he does not enjoy killing defenseless animals, he does not know how to read to any purpose, he finds his rural peers mindless in their talk and disgusting in their "turbulent and obstreperous" drinking (440). Summarizing at the end of his letter, he looks back nostalgically to a time when "I toiled year after year with chearfulness, in expectation of the happy hour in which I might be idle" (440). Idleness, however, brings no happiness.

The retired man in the *Lounger* essay cited earlier in this chapter makes the mistake of seeking stimulation in external objects rather than in "social affections." For Mercator, social possibilities prove no more satisfactory than aesthetic ones—and one can hardly blame him for disliking the company of boisterous squires. The educated reader may deplore his inability to find pleasure in books, but such condescension would miss the point. Without ever making the case directly, Johnson's essay emphasizes the truth that eighteenth-century moralists frequently insist on: only a life of focused action brings satisfaction. Mercator's years of "toil" involved just such action. His years of leisure offer less apparent possibility. Although concentration on the afterlife and dedication to active benevolence are theoretically as possible for him as for anyone else, the psychological authenticity of his narrative makes his experience so vivid that it becomes hard to imagine for him some totally different psychic condition. Mercator sees himself as victim. The reader, vicariously enduring the merchant's victimization, encounters his terror of psychic helplessness—as well as his luxurious dwelling on the details of his own experience. Although his suffering sounds authentic, one also catches overtones of a claim to specialness in the range and intensity of that suffering. A Christian perspective would provide rescue by emphasizing the insignificance of all pleasure and pain here below, but nothing in the essay suggests it as a possibility. Mercator inhabits a vacuity created by his self-concentration as well as by his lack of preparation for a life of leisure.

Johnson's *Adventurer* essays frequently emphasize the immanent possibility of tedium in human experience. Number 111 (27 Nov. 1753) considers the nature and the conceivable location of "felicity." Those who inherit fortunes, Johnson points out, rarely possess the ease and pleasure that money is sometimes thought to supply: "Their time seems not to pass with much applause from others, or satisfaction to themselves" (Johnson, *Idler* 453). Some indulge in debauchery. Others

> lie down to sleep and rise up to trifle, are employed every morning in finding expedients to rid themselves of the day, chase pleasure through all the places of public resort, fly from London to Bath and from Bath to London, without any other reason for changing place, but that they go in quest of company as idle and as vagrant as themselves, always endeavouring to raise

some new desire that they may have something to persue, to rekindle some
hope which they know will be disappointed, changing one amusement for
another which a few months will make equally insipid, or sinking into languor and disease, for want of something to actuate their bodies or exhilarate
their minds. (454)

This kind of boredom derives from and exemplifies the fallen state of
humanity. The pattern of seeking new desires and rekindling futile
hopes, ever pursuing something to "actuate" the body and exhilarate
the mind—that pattern belongs, as *The Vanity of Human Wishes* makes
clear, not only to morally inadequate potential heirs to wealth but to
morally inadequate humankind as a whole. Johnson would not have
said that fear of boredom motivates all accomplishment. Yet the paradigm of constant striving for distraction insistently evoked in Johnson's
writing records a comparable perception.

Johnson of course differs from later thinkers who restated the same
insight in his insistence that the pattern, however universal, must yet
be resisted. Acknowledging that men like Mercator—those absorbed
in gaining or enlarging fortunes—avoid "the insipidity of indifference,
and the tediousness of inactivity" (454), he imagines the possibility of
similar activities with other ends. "To strive with difficulties, and to conquer them, is," he concludes, "the highest human felicity; the next, is to
strive, and deserve to conquer" (455). Such action, the action of resistance and of moral combat, withstands boredom by drawing on and
creating mental energy. Without such energy, without the psychic
resources created by a life of action, men doom themselves to futile
time filling or empty inactivity.

But what can retirement confer upon him, who having done nothing can
receive no support from his own importance, who having known nothing
can find no entertainment in reviewing the past, and who intending nothing
can form no hopes from prospects of the future: he can, surely, take no wiser
course, than that of losing himself again in the croud, and filling the vacuities
of his mind with the news of the day. (*Idler* 473; no. 126, 19 Jan. 1754)

Lasting happiness evades human beings. Nonetheless, the option of
striving for worthy ends, even while knowing the unlikelihood of their
achievement, opens a way to avoid vacuity and satiety alike.

Although men who confront their condition create the greatest
probability of evading tedium, those of limited imaginations can also
escape ennui. Tim Ranger, an imaginary figure in the *Idler*, reports his
own difficulties in filling his time but also evokes the happier state of

the rich uncle from whom he inherited his money. "Having his mind completely busied between his warehouse and the 'Change, he felt no tediousness of life" (*Idler* 194; no. 62, 23 June 1759). The practical man demonstrates the saving virtue of concentration on a single object. Activity, for him as for others who evade boredom, provides salvation, but only his lack of ability to conceive alternatives makes possible his single-minded focus of energy. No explicit reservations about this uncle emerge in the text. He stands as an exemplar of happiness, the only such figure in Johnson's essay.

From one point of view, the character of the uncle exemplifies Johnson's notorious suspicion of the imagination. A man who does not let his mind wander from his business will not suffer life's tedium. Imagination creates boredom as it creates the other ills of human consciousness. On the other hand, the uncle's moral ambiguity qualifies the point. Unaware of spiritual or even social responsibility, he trudges through life with repellent complacency. Imagination, which might bring him misery, might also generate his salvation.

Imagination enlarges desire. Periodical essays serve the same purpose for their readers.

> When I consider the innumerable multitudes that, having no motive of desire, or determination of will, lie freezing in perpetual inactivity, till some external impulse puts them in motion; who awake in the morning, vacant of thought, with minds gaping for the intellectual food, which some kind essayist has been accustomed to supply; I am moved by the commiseration with which all human beings ought to behold the distresses of each other, to try some expedients for their relief, and to inquire by what methods the listless may be actuated, and the empty be replenished. (*Idler* 11; no. 3, 29 Apr. 1758)

The writer of such essays fulfills his social obligation by producing "intellectual food" to fill the mental vacuity of those who lack desire and will.

The adjective *intellectual* denies the possibility that activation—the "external impulse" that puts the inert in motion—and replenishment depend only on imagination. But the essayist's meditations on the distress of others, his perception that his publication might energize a jaded consciousness, his ingenious transformation of his own act of writing into one of the "nobler employments" through which human beings fulfill their obligations to one another—such textual strategies appear to modern eyes as imaginative achievements. Johnson in his persona as Idler assimilates himself to the "artists" who entertain the idle rich. "The idle and luxurious find life stagnate," he writes, "for want of some desire to keep it in motion. This species of distress furnishes a new set of occupations, and multitudes are busied, from day to day, in finding the rich and the fortunate something to do" (*Idler* 93; no. 30, 11 Nov. 1758). Implicitly, the task of manufacturing desire for the idle and luxurious solves the problem of boredom for those who do the manufacturing. Just so with the Idler: his self-designation itself makes the point. Keeping his own imagination vigorous by exercising it in the service of others, he evokes a Barthesian dialectic between writer and reader. Some people condemn those who serve the rich, he grants. "But this censure will be mitigated, when it is seriously considered, that money and time are the heaviest burthens of life, and that the unhappiest of all mortals are those who have more of either than they know how to use" (93). Helping others spend their money and fill their time constitutes a worthy activity: a "nobler employment," a way to contribute to human welfare.

This manifestation of Johnson's characteristic melancholy realism makes boredom—lassitude, lack of desire, inability to engage wholeheartedly in internal or external action—a central problem of civilized existence. People find diverse expedients for escaping it. Johnson's periodical essays almost always sound a note of sympathy when they consider the plight of those seeking such expedients. The man who gives up business to seek pleasure and then finds pleasure impossible to attain emerges as the pathetic type of mortals yearning for something to desire. "It would be undoubtedly best," Johnson writes in his most sententious voice, "if we could see and hear every thing as it is, that nothing might be too anxiously dreaded, or too ardently pursued" (*Idler* 158; no. 50, 31 Mar. 1759). But the conditional mode in which he articulates this classical ideal suggests his severe doubt about whether mortals can hope to achieve it. When he speaks of life as it is, rather than as it might be, he acknowledges the psychic value of ardent pursuits, even after trifles. Whatever fills time and spends money innocently is to be welcomed.

"It would seem impossible to a solitary speculatist," Johnson writes, "that a human being can want employment." Precisely this impossibility, daily realized, repeatedly occupies his attention. The reason the "speculatist" would consider unfulfilled need for employment impossible involves his awareness of humankind's intellectual gifts. "To be born in ignorance with a capacity of knowledge, and to be placed in the midst of a world filled with variety, perpetually pressing upon the senses and irritating curiosity, is surely a sufficient security against the languishment of inattention." Not only does the world we inhabit provide infinite stimulation for the mind, the world beyond should also press on the attention, recalling us from boredom's shadow. "That mind will never be vacant, which is frequently recalled by stated duties to meditations on eternal interests; nor can any hour be long, which is spent in obtaining some new qualification for celestial happiness" (*Rambler* 4: 299; no. 124, 25 May 1751).

The emotional tension of the three sentences I have just quoted epitomizes the central paradox of Johnson's attitude toward boredom. He believes in and experiences the wonder of the physical world and of his own mind. Yet his tentativeness emerges in such phrases as "it would *seem* impossible" and "*surely* a sufficient security"—the intensifier suggesting an effort to shore up fragments against the ruins. Once more his prose conveys the gap between ideal and actuality. This world and the next provide abundant occupation for mind and soul; human beings need not languish. And yet, perversely, they do. Minds feel vacant, hours seem long. Despite abundant potential occupation, people find themselves wanting—both lacking and desiring—employment they cannot find. As his prayers and meditations testify, Johnson suffered from reiterated discrepancies between his sense of how he should behave and his actual behavior. In his allusions to the vacuity of minds and of lives and to the satiety that makes experience flavorless, he generalizes the awareness of discrepancy. Desire—as *The Vanity of Human Wishes* tells us—makes human beings miserable. So does the absence of desire that we call boredom. Christian doctrine tells us that we should direct our wishes toward heaven. Human experience tells us that we can fruitfully focus our yearnings on the search for knowledge, or indeed on activity of almost any kind. But no moral or pedagogic imperative, internal or external, suffices to make us do or be what we should.

Johnson's fullest investigation of the problem of boredom, confirming and amplifying what I have suggested, occurs in *Rasselas*. The young prince's situation in the Happy Valley (which, according to Imlac, duplicates the plight of many other inhabitants) dramatizes boredom's ravages and the kinds of solution those not "vitious" seek. After the travelers escape the valley and dedicate themselves to making a "choice of life," they inadvertently explore further reaches of boredom. By the time *Rasselas* reaches its conclusion, it has clarified the insoluble paradox integral to the idea of boredom as Johnson understands it.

Everyone in the Happy Valley is "required to propose whatever might contribute to make seclusion pleasant, to fill up the vacancies of attention, and lessen the tediousness of time." The next sentence suggests the necessary futility of such enterprise: "Every desire was immediately granted" (10). The concept of the Happy Valley makes vacancy and tediousness inevitable, since the granting of all desires, as Rasselas will soon demonstrate, devitalizes experience. Johnson provides in his character a detailed etiology of boredom. Rasselas compares himself with a beast, noting that "I am, like him, pained with want, but am not, like him, satisfied with fulness" (14). Like Boswell and Mercator, he sees food as entertainment. "The intermediate hours are tedious and gloomy; I long again to be hungry that I may again quicken my attention" (14–15). "Man has surely," he concludes, "some latent sense for which this place affords no gratification, or he has some desires distinct from sense which must be satisfied before he can be happy" (15).

The unfulfilled desire that creates boredom is the desire for desire. As Rasselas tells an old man at the end of chapter 3:

> That I want nothing, or that I know not what I want, is the cause of my complaint; if I had any known want, I should have a certain wish; that wish would excite endeavour, and I should not then repine to see the sun move so slowly towards the western mountain, or lament when the day breaks and sleep will no longer hide me from myself. (18)

"Surprized at this new species of affliction" (18–19), the old man tells the prince that he would appreciate his lot if he compared it with the miseries of the world. Rasselas, temporarily comforted, asserts that now he has something to desire: encounter with the world's miseries. In the next few months he discovers that simply *imagining* the world suffices for a time. But a need for actuality supervenes: the prince must leave his valley.

In an early interview with Rasselas, Imlac generalizes the point about the need for desire into a thematic statement linking the tale's subsequent events: "Some desire is necessary to keep life in motion; and he, whose real wants are supplied, must admit those of fancy" (39). He then reports his own exemplary experience. Fulfilling a youthful longing to go to sea, he imagined that he "could gaze round forever without satiety." Soon, however, he found himself bored with the ocean's "barren uniformity" and troubled lest all his experience prove equally disappointing. "I may hope to find variety in life," he concluded, "though I should miss it in nature" (42). This comment acquires increasingly ironic resonance as the narrative continues.

Readily accepting Imlac as moral guide, Rasselas seeks wisdom from him. Of Imlac's various pronouncements, the most important recapitulates Johnson's notion of the significance of knowledge. Imlac posits in every human mind a "natural desire" to increase its ideas. Ignorance, he says, "is mere privation, by which nothing can be produced: it is a vacuity in which the soul sits motionless and torpid for want of attraction" (56). Ignorance as vacuity corresponds to boredom's torpidity. The mind's desire to increase its ideas justifies Rasselas's hope to travel through the world.

The four travelers find, predictably, repeated insufficiency and futility. Apparent happiness masks discontent, superficiality, or illusion. Neither private nor public life supplies true gratification. When Imlac suggests that they direct their attention to history, they visit the Pyramids for a lesson in the power of imagination. The pyramid they have examined, Imlac explains, "seems to have been erected only in compliance with that hunger of imagination which preys incessantly upon life, and must be always appeased by some employment. Those who have already all that they can enjoy, must enlarge their desires" (145). The king who erected the pyramids, in other words, duplicated Rasselas's initial situation. He was "compelled to solace, by the erection of a pyramid, the satiety of dominion and tastelessness of pleasures, and to amuse the tediousness of declining life, by seeing thousands labouring without end, and one stone, for no purpose, laid upon another" (145).

This account elucidates the opposition between imagination and boredom. If one can, like the rich uncle adequately fulfilled by his business, escape boredom by limiting imagination/desire, one also—more typically—avoids boredom by generating ever more grandiose desire. The hunger of imagination, a wild beast, *preys* on human beings. But satiety, tastelessness, and tediousness feel equally destructive. To subdue tedium, people indulge imagination. In effect, Imlac says, they welcome madness, since "all power of fancy over reason is a degree of insanity" (190).

That well-known Johnsonian pronouncement comes from the story of the mad astronomer, which Imlac presents as an exemplum of far-reaching application:

> When we are alone we are not always busy; . . . the ardour of enquiry will sometimes give way to idleness or satiety. He who has nothing external that can divert him, must find pleasure in his own thoughts, and must conceive himself what he is not; for who is pleased with what he is? He then expatiates in boundless futurity, and culls from all imaginable conditions that which for the present moment he should most desire, amuses his desires with impossible enjoyments, and confers upon his pride unattainable dominion. (190–91)

The explanation suggests one reason why the world's abundant sources of knowledge and the mind's aptitude for grasping them do not adequately protect us from boredom. We can't work all the time—or for that matter pray all the time. Satiated with rigorous mental activity, we welcome laxities of imagination, which can create both desire and its gratifications, combating satiety and vacuity alike.

Reading *Rasselas*, one sees the process again and again as the characters generate fantasies briefly adequate to satisfy them, are disillusioned, and construct further fantasies. In the tale's conclusion, recapitulating their experiences, they reveal their individual "schemes of happiness" (219): full-blown products of the imagination. Pekuah, Nekayah, and Rasselas have all elaborated dreams of dominion, in convent, college, or kingdom. "Of these wishes that they had formed they well knew that none could be obtained" (221). They return to Abyssinia.

In a reading of Johnson's tale that takes as thematic Imlac's assertion that "some desire is necessary to keep life in motion; and he whose real wants are supplied, must admit those of fancy," this might seem to constitute a happy ending. *Rasselas* opens with an announced problem: a young prince, given nothing to desire, suffers from life's tedium. The narrative resolves the problem. By the end, Rasselas and his companions have defined clear desires that they know cannot be satisfied. No matter where they go, they can no longer experience the kind of tedium that sent them on their travels.

But the value of desire itself has been compromised by the protagonists' discovery of universal futility. Their apparent satisfaction with their schemes of happiness, despite their knowledge that they will never obtain them, tells us again that contentment depends more on internal than on external arrangements. To balance between the states of boredom—the claim of insufficiency in the environment—and imaginative indulgence—a commitment to excess that makes no demands on the environment—requires superhuman dexterity. In practice, human beings manage no more than alternation. The travelers' realization that fulfillment never matches hope constitutes the wisdom of their experience, the wisdom implicitly recommended to readers. They have learned the usefulness of activity for providing distraction, the importance of maintaining an illusion of control over one's own life. No longer feeling helpless, at the mercy of arrangements made by others, they can acknowledge that happiness remains unlikely and settle for contentment. Like Johnson himself, they try to move beyond futile self-concentration. Like Johnson, they succeed only intermittently.

Johnson's account of tedium as threat, of the constant likelihood of suffering from depletion ("vacuity") or surfeit ("satiety"), of the need to struggle against insufficiency as well as excess, reveals to us once more the figure Boswell made familiar: the hero engaged in endless conflict. The man who on his deathbed announced his determination to be conquered rather than capitulate to illness refused also to capitulate to boredom. In discussing boredom's threat, he elevates it to symbolic status. The tendency to be bored despite the abundant stimulation the world provides, despite the need to labor for a reward in heaven, becomes a manifestation of fundamental human perversity. To defy that tendency in oneself, to preach the need for others to defy it, displays Johnson's typical determination to make himself and his disciples master the moral possibilities open to humanity—despite his awareness that moral achievement will always prove insufficient.

But Johnson's heroic struggles often derive from his way of constructing experience. When he confesses to Boswell that he talks for victory, he reminds us how consistently he forces conversation into the pattern of combat. His interpretation of the problem of boredom, often acute, implicitly insists on the possibility of triumphing over tedium in any given instance, although not invariably. Perhaps a specific human being will not choose "nobler employment" that might fully engage his or her powers, but the choice, Johnson implies, is always available. Even while he describes the endemic pattern of moral failure in human life, he insists that decisions remain for us to make and that the right decision may imply victory. While reminding us of the painful experience of feeling our helplessness, he preserves a vision of control.

The desperation behind that vision emerges most clearly when Johnson confronts boredom not as public moralist but as private person. His discussions of melancholy with Boswell suggest his attitude toward combating psychic ailments of all sorts. When Boswell, seeking his mentor's approval, reports that he sometimes tries to *"think down"* distressing thoughts, Johnson declares him "wrong" (Boswell, *Ominous Years* 276). Recurring to the subject three days later, he terms himself "shocked" by the very idea. Boswell claims his own "spirit and resolution"; Johnson calls it "the spirit and resolution of a madman." Then he suggests a preferable technique:

> While we were in the chaise driving to Birmingham to breakfast, he said, "When you have a place in the country, lay out twenty pounds a year upon a laboratory. It will be an amusement to you." I said I had last summer taken a course of chemistry. "Sir," said he, "take a course of chemistry, or a course of rope-dancing, or a course of anything to which you are inclined at the

time. Contrive to have as many retreats for your mind as you can, as many things to which it can fly from itself." (Boswell, *Ominous Years* 287)

(Boswell, characteristically, thinks to himself that "a course of concubinage" might be fun.)

The mind needs to "fly from itself" for many reasons. Johnson is thinking at the moment about depression, his recurrent nemesis, not about boredom. But the two states, as modern psychoanalysts have noted, are closely related. Both involve the horror of experienced helplessness. Johnson's outrage at the idea that one might attempt direct combat against misery, mobilizing thought against thought, presumably stems from his conviction that consciousness remains always the realm of danger. Trying to think down thoughts locks the victim of depression into his own mind when he needs above all to locate himself in the world outside himself. Johnson recommends evasive action as the primary resource in the struggle against internal disorder. One can resort to the outside world to remedy interior difficulty: quite a different thing from attributing such difficulty to external causes. Only thus can one regain the vital sense of control. Johnson's recurrent considerations of boredom, despite their firm moral orientation, often sound surprisingly sympathetic to boredom's sufferers. They consistently stress the danger of allowing control to be lost by supinely accepting the role of victim.

Boswell, equally ready to declare himself a victim or to proclaim his power and dominance, did not invariably remember the distinction between using and blaming the outside world. Worried not only about the "hypochondria" or "melancholy" that recurrently plagued him but about the possibility of tedium, he often blamed his boredom on external circumstance even while he demonstrated how imaginative activity combats it. Thus the prospect of confinement to his apartments during treatment for venereal disease worries him because of the likelihood of dullness. Visitors help: "I found a little intercourse with the living world was necessary to keep my spirits from sinking into lethargic dulness or being soured to peevish discontent" (Boswell, *London* 183). Even taking medicine entertains him: "I have a sort of genius for physic" (184). He fears "a dreary vacancy" in his journal as in his life (186) but discovers that his verbal gifts ("words come skipping to me like lambs upon Moffat Hill" [187]) withstand the threat. The action of writing combats or evades the stasis of boredom.

Not always, though. If young Boswell in London proved the kind of "robust wise man who is sufficient for his own happiness," Boswell as an older man often considered himself the victim of circumstance. Indulging hypochondria,

> I called up into my fancy ideas of being confined all winter to an old house in the north of Scotland, and being burthened with tedium and gnawed with fretfulness. It is humiliating for me to consider that my mind is such that I can at any time be made thus wretched, merely by being placed in such a situation. But let me comfort myself that I can keep out of it. My body would be tormented were it put into a fire, as my mind would be tormented in such a situation. But as the one thought gives me no uneasiness, neither should the other. As I would not wish to have my body of stone, so I would not wish to have my mind insensible. (Boswell, *Ominous Years* 54)

The ideal of the robust wise man seems to have vanished, replaced by celebration of psychic sensitivity. Security depends on keeping out of tedious situations, not on surmounting tedium by action. Having dinner alone with three members of one family in London, Boswell complains that "it was rather dull compared with what society I can have in London. There was not enough" (97). At church in Edinburgh, "The tediousness of the service . . . was really tiresome" (179). Listening to a dull story, he manages patience "for I suppose eight or ten minutes, but the story was so uninteresting, and Hunter spoke so tediously and so insipidly, that my mind was in such uneasiness as the lungs are when in want of air, when they are just teased with as much as keeps them in a wretched feeble motion. I could endure it no longer, and made my escape" (270). The metaphor of boredom as suffocation provides an intense image of danger—and a rather precise evocation of the *kind* of danger boredom represents.

Escape rather than struggle direct or indirect (indirect struggle being Johnson's kind of evasion) has become Boswell's dominant strategy for dealing with boredom, now associated distinctly with particular locales (typically Scottish) and particular people. Is not London, Boswell inquires rhetorically of himself, "so extensive a place, such a world, that a man may always find novelty and vivid relish in it?" (218). Vivid relish proved harder to discover in Edinburgh, which could, to someone preoccupied with his own social and professional status and his own psychic condition, seem a trap.

He experienced boredom's entrapment intensely in his association with Lord Lonsdale, whom Lord Eglinton definitively characterizes: "I think Lord Lonsdale a great bore" (Boswell, *English Experiment* 87). To profit from Lonsdale's patronage, Boswell had to endure his company. Contradicting all Boswell's fantasies of nobility, the patron provided inadequate food and wine, an unendurably cold castle, and a series of tedious evenings marked by his interminable talking about himself and mostly unrelieved by card playing. About one of these evenings, Boswell comments, "While LONSDALE was drowsy after dinner, we sat in stupid silence, and I groaned inwardly. . . . the dreary waste of the cold house, with nobody but Saul, a sycophantish fool, to talk to made me almost desperate. I fancy my mind was in a state very similar to that of those wretched mortals who kill themselves" (167). The desperation of boredom could drive a man to suicide.

Boswell blames Lonsdale for the misery he suffers in the nobleman's presence. He occasionally blames himself for experiences of domestic boredom: "I am ashamed to say that dining at home seemed dull to me" (98). The moral responsibility adumbrated by that verbal gesture of shame, however, did not suffice to keep him home. Instead, he rationalized a life of constant dissipation, even while his wife lay dying. (If he stayed home, he writes, he would only be peevish; better to store up funds of delightful memory.) Out of Johnson's presence, and especially after Johnson's death, he retained little understanding of the view that a man must assume the moral burden of his own boredom. Most of the time, for Boswell, boredom inheres in circumstance. Johnson's diagnosis of the condition, his understanding of it as epitomizing the inadequacy of fulfillment to hope, would apply precisely to Boswell, for whom the Lonsdale episode might represent the pathos of his entire legal career. Boswell, however, rarely sustains a Johnsonian vision. Often he assimilates boredom to his chronic melancholia. Johnson, of course, condemned this state too as self-indulgence; Boswell typically thinks of it in a more modern light, as disease.

The difference in the two men's characteristic stances toward boredom echoes the contrast in their rhetoric. Johnson relies heavily on the deployment of weighty abstractions; Boswell dwells in concrete particularities. Johnson moves from an individual experience to "the state of life." Boswell may generalize about the nature of noblemen or about life in London or Edinburgh, but his interest focuses on his own experience. For him boredom, a private state of suffering, constitutes something to be lived through (complainingly) or avoided. His specificity about its manifestations reflects his unfailing interest in the day-to-day texture of event. Johnson's eagerness to move from an individual state to the nature and condition of humankind urges him toward the kind of moral reflection that always seems to him the most fruitful way of understanding humanity.

Indeed, the difference between Johnson's and Boswell's ways of constructing and confronting the problem of boredom calls attention to many of the two men's crucial divergences. Johnson, as the story of Mercator indicates, acknowledges the category of "leisure," but it has far less importance than that of "empty time." The distinction between activity (pleasurable) and inactivity (destructive and dangerous) matters more than that between business and freedom from business. Given sufficient imagination, properly controlled by reason, Mercator could find new forms of action less narrow than that of pursuing business. Business is better than nothing, but only because it provides a type of action. Conversation, composing dictionaries, cleaning pieces of orange peel: all occupy the mind and protect it from debilitating depression. Boredom invades in the absence of activity. Boswell, on the other hand, a more "modern" man, finds the separation of business and recreation significant. His frequent recourse to womanizing and to hard drinking suggests the predicament that "leisure" created for him. The "business" of law rarely delighted him. It did not protect him from boredom: its action did not fully engage him. His pleasure in his profession came from moments when it made him feel important and from infrequent emotional engagement with clients. From leisure, on the other hand, he expected consistent gratification. His sense of grievance over the experience of boredom typically connects itself with the nonbusiness time he considered an appropriate space for recreation. When the companions he expected to entertain and be entertained by prove unsatisfactory, he falls readily into boredom. Although his penchant for close observation often rescues him, his lapses into emotional inertness illustrate the futility of expecting consistent pleasure from leisure.

For Boswell the social connections that Mackenzie explicitly and Johnson implicitly thought a source of salvation from boredom could instead become boredom's cause. And Boswell does not, as Mackenzie and Johnson both enjoined, combat boredom with "strenuous exertions of virtue." Despite the moralistic implications of his comment on his own boredom in the Hebrides, he apparently came to think of the state not as something to be resisted by moral effort but as something to be endured and lamented—even something that might make one jokingly think of suicide. The passivity that Johnson and Mackenzie considered an avoidable cause of boredom to Boswell seemed inevitable. He imagines himself "placed in such a situation" as to be doomed to boredom. The possibility of active choice—choice both of situation and of what to do in it—recedes for him. His brooding about determinism eventuates in a sense of helplessness that makes him in effect embrace passivity.

Some of these contrasts may derive from the fact that Boswell wrote personally, about himself and his experience, whereas Mackenzie and Johnson chose mainly public forms of discourse. But the relatively scanty evidence of Johnson's surviving prayers and meditations suggests that Boswell's mentor judged himself at least as severely as he judged others, and by the same standards. Boswell's imagination operates in a different mode.

Many of the differences I have sketched will sound familiar from historicized accounts of the shift in sensibility from the eighteenth century to the nineteenth. Indeed, some of them appeared in more generalized form in the first chapter, with its overview of how attitudes toward boredom shifted between the eighteenth and the twentieth centuries. In general it can be said that Johnson looks backward, preserving and articulating the beliefs associated with Christian humanism. Boswell, despite his efforts to imitate his moral guide, typically speaks for a newer acceptance of subjectivity. He resembles many of his successors.

Like most historical generalizations, though, those of the first chapter cannot account for individual differences. Boswell did not deviate from Johnson in his attitudes toward boredom simply because he was thirty-one years younger. One finds a yet more "modern" view of boredom in writing by Thomas Gray (1716–71), born only seven years after Johnson and twenty-four years before Boswell. Gray's letters, as S. H. Clark has recently pointed out, contain a series of "meditations on the psychology of boredom, and its concomitants of repetition, futility, and isolation" (277). Begging Walpole to give him "the minutest Circumstances of your Diversions & your Indiversions," at the age of nineteen Gray explains that he has no comparable material to offer, since in Cambridge "there is nothing so troublesome, as that one has nothing to trouble one. every thing is so tediously regular, so samish, that I expire for want of a little variety" (Gray 1: 16; To Walpole, 12 Jan. [1735]). "Every thing" is to blame that the victim "expire[s]." Elsewhere, to be sure, Gray claims that his normal state of mind predisposes him to boredom regardless of circumstance. Describing to West his "white Melancholy, or rather Leucocholy," he comments, "The only fault of it is insipidity; which is apt now and then to give a sort of Ennui" (27 May 1742; 1: 209). Like Boswell, Gray reports with interest his psychic states, despite frequent apologies in his letters for his tendency to write about himself (e.g., 1: 84, 1: 231). He takes little responsibility for those states.

The specific malady of boredom seems to him to belong more to men than to women. Johnson's periodical essays acknowledge that

women too may be afflicted, on occasion implying that the triviality of
their concerns more or less guarantees boredom. Boswell, preoccupied
with his own condition, never considers the possibility of female boredom. Gray, on the other hand, explicitly (and rather patronizingly)
blames his malaise partly on his gender.

> To find oneself business (I am persuaded) is the great art of life. . . . some
> spirit, something of Genius (more than common) is required to teach a Man
> how to employ himself. I say *a Man*, for Women commonly speaking never
> feel this distemper: they have always something to do; time hangs not on
> their hands (unless they be fine Ladies) a variety of small inventions & occu-
> pations fill up the void, & their eyes are never open in vain. (2: 666; To Whar-
> ton, 22 Apr. 1760)

The vision of occupation as inherent in gender belongs to a self-construction as passive. Things *happen to* Gray, as to Boswell. Even the finding of business, in his interpretation, inheres not in a unified self but in
some "spirit" or "Genius" that appears external to the self.

Clark's acute analysis of Gray's self-presentation points out how the
writer avoids "privileging . . . subjectivity." "The first person pronoun
can easily be transposed into another case without loss: even when
dealing with obsessive states of mind, it remains singularly colorless"
(277). Clark attributes the curious sense of distance in Gray's personal
writing to the poet's acceptance of Lockean psychology, which makes
the mind a passive inlet for impressions, and his commitment to Lockean analysis, in which the self becomes a representative object of study.

Although I perceive more urgent self-concern than Clark acknowledges in the letters, it is quite true that Gray's introspection carries an
odd atmosphere of neutrality. His comments about his own boredom,
as about male difficulties in self-employment, strike a different note
than do Johnson's passionate injunctions and Boswell's self-referential
intensities. All three men, however, despite their tonal divergencies,
share the association of boredom with helplessness and passivity. They
differ in their beliefs about possibilities of remediation. Johnson's faith
in arduous self-improvement (accompanying his conviction that no
amount of effort will remedy humankind's flawed nature) corresponds
to Boswell's hope that both circumstances and he himself will somehow
change. Gray, on the other hand, embraces his own passivity, expecting no alteration of his condition from within or without. Johnson,
Boswell, and Gray alike recognize boredom as signifying forces that
make meaningful action difficult or impossible, a trap it may or may not
prove possible to elude.

Inasmuch as the "trap" belongs to temperament, as Gray often suggests, it presumably is inescapable. Traps of circumstance, in contrast, for him as for Boswell and Johnson, can be evaded. It is not so clear that women, despite Gray's assertions about them, have the same evasive resources. Frances Burney's early diaries, written from 1768 to 1778 when the author was aged sixteen to twenty-six, provide suggestive grounds for comparison.

"Alas, alas! my poor Journal! how dull, unentertaining, uninteresting thou art! —oh what would I give for some Adventure worth reciting— for something which would surprise—astonish you!" (Burney, *Early Diary* 1: 16). So Burney writes in 1768, sounding like the heroine of many an epistolary novel, conscious of the lack of public interest in female lives. In this passage she turns tedium into a joke. A few pages later, she sounds more despairing:

> So it is, and so it seems likely to be; that I am to pass my days in the dullest of dull things, insipid, calm, uninterrupted quiet. This life is by many desired—so be it—But it surely was design'd to give happiness after (and not one ounce before) twenty *full* years are past, but till then—no matter what happens—the spirits—the health—the never dying *hope* are too strong to be *much* affected by whatever comes to pass—Supper bell, as I live! — (1: 28)

Like virtually all the figures Johnson evokes, the diarist lives by hope. Her hope, however, focuses not on any specific fantasy, only on the possibility that *something*, almost anything, will happen.

On 16 November 1768 Burney has "the first real conversation I ever had in my life, except with Mr. Crisp" (the much older man who serves as her surrogate father) (1: 33). Mr. Seaton, apparently a Scot, comments on the habits of English young women. "The truth is, the young women here are so mortally silly and insipid, that I cannot bear them. —Upon my word, except you and your sister, I have scarce met with one worthy being spoke to. Their chat is all on caps—balls—cards— dress—nonsense" (1: 35). Flattered, Fanny hardly defends her sex. And indeed, as we soon learn, her sense of the dullness of life comes mainly from the demands of social experience, the tedious young women (and others) she has to associate with.

> Miss Crawford called here lately—she is very earnest for us to visit her— but *we* are not very earnest about the matter: however, the code of custom make [sic] our spending one evening with her necessary. O! how I hate this vile custom which obliges us to make slaves of ourselves! —to sell the most precious property we boast, our time; —and to sacrifice it to every prattling impertinent who chooses to demand it! —Yet those who shall pretend to

> defy this irksome confinement of our happiness, must stand accused of inci-
> vility, —breach of manners—love of originality, —and . . . what not. (1: 54;
> ellipsis in the text)

Five years later: "We have returned the Ellerkers' visit, though they did
not return their Entertainment! No music! . . . —everything stupid and
heavy" (1: 219; my ellipsis). Four years after that, to her sister: "We
walk, talk, write, read, eat, drink, thrum, and sleep" (2: 150). She
explains each activity, emphasizing their monotony and suggesting that
her own imagining of *Evelina*, then in progress, keeps her entertained.
One final instance, also from 1777:

> Well! to return to Sir Herbert and my fair self, —why, perhaps you will be
> glad to hear our conversation; for we had a tete a tete of full two hours long;
> and in that time much might be said. I have known many a good thing hit
> upon in a quarter of the time. I can't pretend to give you all the *particulars*;
> but the *heads* of the discourse, they were as follow, viz.; —the Weather, —
> the Hay, —and Dr. Dodd. (2: 200)

These examples should suffice to suggest how Burney constructs the
problem of boredom: as a function of social existence. Only by violat-
ing decorum might a young woman avoid tedium. She can *hope* that
something will happen; she lacks the power—or the sense of power—
to *make* anything happen. With great psychic and literary energy, she
yet remains by virtue of her age and gender at the mercy of other people. She effectively defines herself as victim, less in self-pity than in a
bemused and faintly melancholy acceptance of things as they are.
Unlike Johnson, she cannot manage even a brief fantasy of control.
Unlike Boswell, she cannot imagine that some other place (after all, she
lives in London) would hold automatic excitement. Unlike Gray, she
does not attribute her condition to temperament, and only in clandes-
tine fashion (her stepmother disapproved) could she escape from it by
writing. The situation of women in relation to boredom, her case indicates, was less straightforward than Gray believed.

For all the rigorous moral exhortation that appears to differentiate
Johnson from this chapter's other subjects, he in fact defines his century's understanding of boredom as enemy of action, product of inaction. In its subtlety and range, his moral and psychological analysis of
the condition describes Gray's situation and Burney's and Boswell's by
evoking the plight of Rasselas and Mercator and the rest. Specific
causes and manifestations of the variously labeled disability we call
boredom change through the century, but Johnson's evocation of the
state as implicated with helplessness, a condition of being acted upon

rather than acting, establishes the emphasis that would seem most cogent to his immediate successors as well as to his contemporaries.

Johnson and the others vivify the notion that writing, as action and as product, exists to resist boredom. Johnson speaks directly for this view in explaining the function of periodicals: as product, his writing provides the idle with mental occupation. As he elaborates his treatment of boredom through its various avatars, he gives the reader cause to suspect that writing rescues him as well as his audience. Boswell, taking pride in words that skip like lambs, suggests the same thing. Gray and Burney, acknowledging in more detail their sense of entrapment, do not directly allude to writing as escape, except in Burney's comment about her pleasure in working on *Evelina*. Yet what other form of meaningful action—boredom's remedy—might they find?

Only Johnson, of the figures considered in this chapter, apparently considers boredom something it is possible to defy openly—by benevolent action or by playing draughts or by constructing useful forms of unsatisfiable desire. We shall see in chapter 4 that eighteenth-century women—including Burney—also found plausible ways to resist. Increasingly, though, the usefulness of boredom as a trope would inhere in its intractability. It would gradually come to represent an uneasiness of the spirit that left its victim powerless to resist. For the eighteenth century, the sense of powerlessness was characteristically temporary and usually thought to be resistible.

THREE

The Consciousness of the Dull

Eighteenth-Century Women,
Boredom, and Narrative

The invention of boredom as concept and of the novel as genre coincided in time and implicated one another. In the mid-eighteenth
century, a steady proliferation of novels helped provide the mass entertainment demanded by a developing culture of leisure. J. Paul Hunter
associates reading, like freak shows, with "the desire to wonder in a
world increasingly explored, understood, and (it seemed) conquered"
(34). Some people went to grinning competitions, others patronized
circulating libraries—according to their taste. Novels and horse races
alike could occupy leisure and forestall boredom.

Respectable women, nonfrequenters of circuses and races, might
stay home and read novels without manifest impropriety, but perhaps
not without moral danger. Eighteenth-century commentators generally
believed that women and young people, both groups imagined as
morally vulnerable, composed the bulk of novel readers and the
patrons of circulating libraries. (As Hunter points out, the precise
nature of novels' actual readership remains incalculable [61–81].) In
response to a posited female audience, female novelists proliferated.
They wrote, by and large, about women. Inasmuch as they attempted
to provide recognizable social detail and circumstance, they faced a
fundamental problem. The "small inventions & occupations" that
according to Gray supply the "void" in female life do not suggest obvious narrative possibilities. One cannot readily construct a novel on the
subject of needlework. Such a novel would seem, even to an audience
of women, . . . *boring.*

"It is of great consequence," Hester Chapone wrote, "to have the
power of filling up agreeably those intervals of time which too often

hang heavily on the hands of a woman, if her lot be cast in a retired situation" (137). Appropriate time fillers for women included such pursuits as drawing, singing (of course only as amateurs), and reading aloud. Where is the plot potential in that kind of thing? Where is the excitement? Jane Austen could make novels of lives without conspicuous happening, but earlier novelists could not, and one understands why. Boredom defies narration. A storyteller whose matter does not engage the reader's attention has failed. In a society that understands conventional female occupations as ways of filling dead time, the conventional female will hold little interest. Stories in which a lot happens (*Moll Flanders, Tom Jones, Roderick Random*), stories about men or about unconventional women, possess a manifest advantage in attracting readers.

All writing provides a space of freedom for its creator—a space for fantasy, invention, openness. The writing of fiction implies especially great freedom and possibility. But if we try to imagine the psychological situation of the respectable woman setting out to write a novel in the middle or late eighteenth century, we may quickly realize the limitation of her imaginative freedom. If the novelist we call to mind is Charlotte Lennox, she knows Richardson and Johnson and is awed by them and their literary and moral standards. If she is Frances Burney, she has long since learned that a young woman must postpone her writing (even in a journal) until she has done her needlework and performed her social visits for the day. Burney's well-known early repudiation of the novel is worth quoting for the eroticized intensity of its writer's implicit attraction to writing fiction as well as of her explicit rejection:

> So early was I impressed myself with ideas that fastened degradation to this class of composition, that at the age of adolescence, I struggled against the propensity which, even in childhood, even from the moment I could hold a pen, had impelled me into its toils; and on my fifteenth birth-day, I made so resolute a conquest over an inclination at which I blushed, and that I had always kept secret, that I committed to the flames whatever, up to that moment, I had committed to paper. And so enormous was the pile, that I thought it prudent to consume it in the garden. (Burney, *Wanderer* 8; "To Dr. Burney")

Lennox and Burney and their sisters wished to preserve propriety while interesting and instructing their readers. They would not risk Defoe's recourse to writing about women outside the realm of social decorum, nor could they write about the female adventures of the respectable: as the countess in Charlotte Lennox's *The Female Quixote* points out, good women don't have adventures. Yet female novelists, like male ones, needed to forestall their readers' imaginable boredom. In this sense, projected boredom provided their narrative impetus.

A complex relation links boredom as assumed or posited female experience with fictional narratives of female lives. I shall argue for a way of reading such narratives that suggests an imagination of boredom as their precondition. In many female novels—novels by and about women—the represented lives of young women oscillate between boredom and far more dramatic forms of anguish. To constitute fiercely imposed misery as boredom's only alternative and then build stories around these alternatives implies devious but intelligible social protest. The taken-for-granted probability of boredom in a woman's life provides the starting point for narrative—and perhaps for female anger.

It is not a twentieth-century imposition to say that for most eighteenth-century Englishwomen of the middle and upper classes, a life of what observers might perceive as tedium seemed a foregone conclusion. Commentators of the period tacitly or explicitly assume the high probability of repetitiveness, triviality, and tedium in female experience. John Gregory's notorious advice to his daughters—they should learn "needle-work, knitting, and such like" not because of the "intrinsic value" of anything they can do ("which is trifling"), but "to enable you to fill up, in a tolerably agreeable way, some of the many solitary hours you must necessarily pass at home" (39)—emphasizes that unmarried women, at any rate, can do nothing really useful and can expect at most "tolerably agreeable" ways of passing the time. Maria Edgeworth and Richard Lovell Edgeworth articulate a similar point: "Accomplishments have . . . a value [for young women] as resources against ennui, as they afford continual amusement and innocent occupation" (2: 522). The pervasive eighteenth-century anxiety over novel reading reflects a comparable view of female experience. Young women's lives in particular lacked occupation and obvious interest: hence presumable female susceptibility to the temptations of the printed word and, perhaps partly as a consequence, to more sinister temptations. As Thomas Brown put the problem at the very beginning of the century, eventually young women's "continual Idleness grows tedious; yet being unwilling to shake it quite off, and in the room of it take some *profitable* Employment unknown to them, they indulge themselves in irregular Desires, and this leads them to base and dangerous Attempts" (149).

Both the anxiety over the possibility of "irregular Desires" generated by boredom and the implicit recommendation of a solution in *"profitable Employment"* persisted through the century. Brown acknowledges that women may not know the nature of the employment they should find, although he implies their responsibility to discover it. Others consider proper female occupation self-evident. To cite one final example from almost the beginning of the nineteenth century, here is Thomas Gisborne in 1797:

> How are well-bred women to support themselves in the single state through the dismal vacuity that seems to await them? This question it may be sufficient to answer by another. If young and well-bred women are not accustomed, in their single state, regularly to assign a large proportion of their hours to serious and instructive occupations; what prospect, what hope is there that, when married, they will assume habits to which they have ever been strangers, and exchange idleness and volatility for steadiness and exertion? (212)

But the problem of female boredom, before and after marriage, did not, by the time Gisborne wrote, lend itself to such ready solutions. The small range of socially acceptable "serious and instructive occupations" would not suit every sensibility. Anna Howe's account of how Clarissa arranged her time adumbrates the feminine ideal. The paragon allotted only six hours for rest. She spent the first three hours of the day "in her study, and in her closet duties" (Richardson, *Clarissa* 4: 506): that is, praying, meditating, and reading improving and pious books. "Domestic management" occupied two hours; "needle, drawings, music, etc." (4: 507) took five hours; an hour passed in "visits to the neighbouring poor" (4: 507). The rest of the time went in conversation, reading aloud, and paying and receiving social visits.

Only three hours of Clarissa's eighteen-hour day—the time spent in domestic management and in visits to the poor—involve her in activity of manifest social value. Recent social historians have conclusively demonstrated, differing in their assignment of dates for changes brought by industrialization but agreeing about the fundamental facts, that England's "modernization" in the eighteenth century entirely deprived many middle-class women of meaningful occupation. With industrialization, Ann Oakley explains, "the idle dependence of the married woman became a practicable ideal for the rising middle classes" (49). Earlier, women had shared with their men the work of the household and of moneymaking, both integrally connected with their family lives. Given such a social system, "all adults work, and status in the community, for adults of both sexes, derives as much from identification with a family as from identification with a particular kind of work" (10). As status became connected with leisure, middle-class women separated themselves from work both domestic and public. Trying to emulate the aristocracy and to distinguish themselves from lower classes, such women sought servants to perform the tasks of the household. But in giving up both responsibility and occupation, many leisured women found their lives empty.

> Had [their] labour been replaced by other interests, and an expansion of the educational and cultural horizons of such women, it could have represented an advance. But all too often, their newly won leisure was barren of interest. Their withdrawal came to mean not merely a retreat from active labour but a social contempt for labour, particularly manual labour, of any sort. Hence the desperate desire to separate themselves from those they saw as their social inferiors—those who needed to work in order to live. (Hill 52)

For such women, "accomplishments" like needlework and drawing might fill time but obviously had no genuine utility. One can understand why excessively leisured women, married or single, might yield to irregular desires: that is, at the very least, indulge erotic fantasy.

Both Clarissa and her admirers consider her daily occupations worthy and satisfying. She keeps herself busy, and erotic fantasies do not appear to inhabit her imagination. One may fancy, though, that a woman less dedicated than Clarissa to propriety ("*Propriety*, another word for nature, was . . . her law, as it is the foundation of all true judgment" [4: 501])—a woman even as minimally rebellious as the young Frances Burney—could feel a need for more excitement. She might, for instance, wish to read a novel. Reading novels, many commentators suggested, encouraged forbidden fantasies. In a period of deliquescent generic distinction (the difference between "novel" and "romance" remained elusive; the line between "fact" and "fiction" frequently blurred [see Hunter, McKeon]), the influence of novels over readers who were often uncertain what relation pertained between text and world would arguably possess special intensity. Middle-class female readers, perhaps lacking what they themselves could perceive as meaningful occupation, might turn to fiction for kinds of interest their lives could not supply. They might also seek in fiction representations of female experience relevant to their own.

But how could female lives posited as either empty or simply dutiful generate compelling narrative? I return to the question I implied at the outset. The monotonous story of women's experience conveyed by the proliferating conduct books of the eighteenth century acquires only limited drama from the female struggle against natural depravity, the arduous effort toward goodness, because women had such limited possibilities for choice and action. James Fordyce's popular *Sermons to Young Women* (1765) typifies the implicit narratives of tedium that characterize advice to the female. Fordyce defines woman's role in terms of her responsibilities, primarily to men. Women, he writes,

> were manifestly [How, then, could one disagree?] intended to be the mothers and formers of a rational and immortal offspring; to be a kind of softer companions, who, by nameless delightful sympathies and endearments, might improve our pleasures and soothe our pains; to lighten the load of domestic cares, and thereby leave us more at leisure for rougher labours, or severer studies; and finally, to spread a certain grace and embellishment over human life. (1: 208)

He warns emphatically against any revelation of female wit (1: 188–92) and elaborately urges his readers toward domestic activity and learning domestic skills. "By men the knowledge of the world is commonly gathered in it," he explains (2: 15). Women, however, must not risk direct experience of "the world." They rely, rather, on reading—which can prove dangerous. But the more fundamental danger, to which Fordyce devotes insistent rhetoric, is women's perception of the tedium their mentor himself conveys as a fact of their premarital experience. The sermonizer deploys heavy moral artillery in forbidding such perception.

> Nor would I have you despise any one of [the domestic skills] as trivial or dull. If they should seem either, you must give me leave to say the fault is in you. If on any pretence whatever you should affect to call them so, I should deem it a mark of— But I forbear. (1: 233)

Perception of boredom is bad enough, but *acknowledgment* of boredom implies literally unspeakable sin.

The point recurs again and again.

> There is not, methinks, any thing more contemptible, or more to be pitied, than that turn of mind, which finding no entertainment in itself, none at home, none in books, none in rational conversation, nor in the intercourses of real friendship, nor in ingenious works of any kind, is continually seeking to stifle reflection in a tumult of pleasures, and to divert weariness in a crowd. (1: 246)

The alternatives suggested here—Clarissa's routine of virtue or "a tumult of pleasures"—emphasize the limitation of female opportunity. Although, as we shall see, the letters of eighteenth-century women suggest that "real friendship" indeed provides genuine pleasure and that for a talented worker "ingenious works" also gratify, many women, by virtue of their circumstances, found little genuine friendship and little rational conversation. If they lacked artistic gifts or intellectual power and will, they had few resources.

Again, Fordyce complains about the sinister probabilities facing women who seek pleasure. If they wish to escape boredom, they risk the fate of prostitution:

> What numbers of miserable beings are now lost . . . , whose first deviations were occasioned by nothing more than a desire of escaping from inactivity or dulness to something that might divert or employ! (2: 7)

Or, claiming sympathetic understanding of the female plight, he nonetheless threatens that efforts to escape that plight will produce dire consequences:

> Dulness and insipidity, moroseness and rigour, are dead weights on every kind of social intercourse; nor will I conceal it from you that I wish, as much as any of you can do, to make my escape from them on all occasions. But tell me, my lively friends; when the heart overflows with gaiety, is there no danger of its bursting the proper bounds? Is not extreme vivacity a near borderer on folly? (1: 173)

Men, like women, wish to escape boredom. But men have a larger number of legitimate resources for doing so. The dullness frequently implied as inherent in the well-bred young female's condition derives partly from the prohibition of most possibilities for action outside the home. Women risk the miserable state of being "lost" if they try to avoid the miserable state of being bored.

Other conduct books, including those by women, tell with varying degrees of cheerfulness the same story about the female difficulty, particularly for the young, of filling time. Catharine Macaulay, presumably not without irony, recommends needlework as a remedy: "Let us not give up one of the great privileges of female life, which is the consent of the world, that we may amuse ourselves with trifles" (65). Mary Wollstonecraft, predictably, argues directly (as Macaulay does elsewhere) that women need the opportunity to engage with serious issues. The emptiness of their minds and of their lives, she maintains, derives from the insufficiency of their educations. "For the little knowledge that they are led to acquire, during the important years of youth, is merely relative to accomplishments; and accomplishments without a bottom, for unless the understanding be cultivated, superficial and monotonous is every grace" (253). Women, in other words, are not only bored but, partly as a consequence, boring. They may rest in the satisfaction of their trivial accomplishments or they may, as many moralists recommend, concentrate on higher things ("It is a much kinder and a much shorter way to make us [women] happy, to teach us to be satisfied with external circumstances, and to look for an atonement for their deficiencies in a higher region" [Hawkins 1: 125]). Neither course necessarily lends immediate interest to their day-to-day experience.

The message of the conduct books constructs a neat double bind. On the one hand, these books convey the sense that youthful female life should contain little of interest: a woman must constantly strive to fill her empty time. Young women's lives, in short, are mostly boring. But—the other half of the bind—women must under no circumstances allow themselves to be bored. They should learn to satisfy themselves with limited possibilities.

Although they speak of tedium and emptiness, none of the eighteenth-century commentators describes women's lives as specifically *boring*. The mid-eighteenth-century coinage had not yet achieved currency except as upper-class slang. Hester Thrale, writing in December 1777, calls attention to the term *bore*, with a typically false etymology, but she never mentions it again:

> It has been the mode of late to call every thing that's tiresome or disagreeable—a *Bore*, taking the Allusion from an ill bitted Horse, who pulls without meaning, & is heavy in your hand. Among the many People who *bore* their Friends as it is called with tedious & futile Talk, Mr Holford the Master in Chancery is most eminent; so that he is known now by the Name of *Bore Holford*. —Coll: Bodens was to meet him somewhere at Dinner—but I wish says George that he might be served up with an Apple in his Mouth like any other *Boar*, & so be kept silent. (221)

The brutal joke suggests the profound social sin implicit in the notion of a *bore*. Thrale makes no connection to the situation of women, but links are easy to find. If women led lives that often appeared, even to them, "tedious & futile," they must keep silent of their own accord or risk some equivalent of the apple in the mouth. And men at least on occasion betrayed their own conviction that domestic occupations are necessarily boring. Dr. Johnson, for instance, made it clear to Mrs. Thrale that she could expect her husband to feel nothing but boredom in her presence:

> One Day that I mentioned Mr. Thrale's cold Carriage to me, tho' with no Resentment, for it occasioned in me no Dislike; He said in Reply—Why how for Heaven's Sake Dearest Madam should any Man delight in a Wife that is

to him neither Use nor Ornament? He cannot talk to you about his Business, which you do not understand; nor about his Pleasures which you do not partake; if you have Wit or Beauty you shew them nowhere, so he has none of the Reputation; if you have Economy or Understanding you employ neither in Attention to his Property. You divide your Time between your Mamma & your Babies, & wonder you do not by that means become agreable [sic] to your Husband. (309)

Men, Dr. Johnson suggests, perceive domestic women—women deprived of opportunity for public functioning—as dull. (He neglects to explain why he chooses to spend so much time in Mrs. Thrale's company.) Women, of course, would get Johnson's message, reiterated implicitly and explicitly by many men in many contexts.

Hester Thrale, imagining future readers who might acknowledge her fascination, evaded boredom for herself and asserted her right to notice by writing copiously about her own life. The best female alternative to silence was to convert the "tiresome or disagreeable" into the entertaining. Women's consciousness of fundamental and unavoidable painful facts of their experience—the lack of publicly interesting material in their lives and the possibility that such lack makes women boring—informs many of the narratives they construct, in indirect and frequently ambivalent ways.

As novelist and as journal writer, Frances Burney devises stories that more or less covertly convey the intimate pain and suffering of boredom, the fear of being thought a bore. In her adolescence, as we have already seen, she became sharply aware of tedium. Many of her comments on it focus on limitations inherent in a woman's highly codified social existence. Over and over she makes the same point.

We have nothing but visiting here, and this perpetual round of constrained civilities, to persons quite indifferent to us, is the most provoking and tiresome thing in the world; but it is unavoidable in a country town, where everybody is known, as here. [She is visiting at Lynn Regis.] It's a most unworthy way of spending our precious and irrecoverable time, to devote it to those who know not it's [sic] value—why are we not permitted to *decline* as well as *accept* visits and acquaintance? It is not that we are ignorant of means to better employ ourselves, but that we dare not pursue them. (*Early Diary* 1: 62)

One wonders what means of better employment the young woman dares not pursue.

Burney wrote her complaint at the age of seventeen. Four years later (9 Sept. 1773), matters had not improved: "We had the Hurrels with us in the evening. That stupid couple, to whom Mr. Rishton has taken a most unaccountable liking, *ennui* both his wife and me to death. Her good nature is so tiresome and officious that I would prefer even a bad temper, with a little portion of understanding" (1: 260). In 1774—twenty-two years old now—she encourages the fantasy that she is writing a book about politeness.

"It will contain all the *newest fashioned* regulations. In the first place, you are never again to cough."

"Not to *cough*?" exclaimed every one at once; "but how are you to help it?"

"As to *that*," answered I, "I am not very clear about it myself, as I own I am guilty sometimes of doing it; but it is as much a mark of ill breeding, as it is to *laugh*; which is a thing that Lord Chesterfield has stigmatized." . . .

"And pray," said Mr. Crisp, making a fine affected face, "may you *simper*?"

"You may *smile* Sir," answered I; "but to *laugh* is quite abominable; though not quite so bad as *sneezing*, or *blowing the nose*." . . .

"But pray, is it permitted," said Mr. Crisp, very drily, "to *breathe*?"

"*That* is not yet, I believe, quite exploded," answered I; "but I shall be more exact about it in my book of which I shall send *you* six copies. I shall only tell you in general, that whatever is natural, plain, or easy, is entirely banished from polite circles." (1: 325–26)

Early in Burney's first novel, *Evelina* (published four years after this conversation occurred), the heroine writes to her guardian, "But, really, I think there ought to be a book of the laws and customs *à-la-mode*, presented to all young people upon their first introduction into public company" (72). Evelina's creator had already imagined the conceivable shape of such a book: a manual of repression. The "natural, plain, or easy" interdicted by social custom includes expression of feeling as well as freedom of behavior. Forced to endure a "perpetual round of constrained civilities," a young woman can in her private writing declare the routine "provoking and tiresome" (cf. Thrale's definition of the bore as "tiresome or disagreeable"), but she "dare not" alter her socially mandated behavior. The energy of her distaste animates her prose. Her account does not replicate the tedium it reports. By the time she jokingly presents herself as an arbiter of decorum, she has learned to convert anger into comedy, to shape an actual social encounter to allow indirect self-expression, and to preserve comic dialogue for the benefit of an epistolary audience.

Boredom as subject, risking the fallacy of imitative form, seems to mark the boundary of narrative possibility. Recollected in tranquillity, however, it becomes—in Burney's treatment—intelligible as a metonym for many forms of social discomfort and a stimulus for wit.

The writer tells the story, *makes* the story, of her boredom. By telling the story, she triumphs over the condition.

Told directly, however, even with comic distancing, the story of female boredom provides limited narrative resources. As the romance tradition began to yield to or merge with the fiction of mimetic plausibility, female novelists attempting to write versions of female lives confronted the paucity of obvious external interest in respectable female existence. (Indeed, male novelists presenting female characters faced a version of the same difficulty.) The notion of narratability has a certain inconclusiveness: no fixed quotient of story inheres in any given life. Stories must be perceived in order to be told. (Who but Jane Austen would recognize a Harriet Smith or a Miss Bates as containing potential for narrative?) Although eighteenth-century familiar letters by women demonstrate their perception of great interest in the details of their own lives, that kind of interest could not readily be communicated to any imaginable "public." Ordinary day-to-day experience, for either gender, did not supply the stuff of fiction. Male characters could evade the commonplace by *doing* something—seeking their fortunes, combating obstacles, struggling with enemies, going on protracted travels. Novelists—especially female novelists—customarily resolved the problem of eventlessness for female characters by making something (usually something disastrous) happen to them.

Yet boredom haunts the margins of much women's fiction. As we have seen, boredom never constitutes an objective fact but is always a category of interpretation, a way (a *dangerous* way, from orthodox eighteenth-century points of view) to understand experience. Male and female moralists who worry lest young women find their lives tedious in effect posit the relevance of the interpretation even as they inveigh against it. The period's gender distinctions demanded that a virtuous young woman's life contain little event, and Burney, for instance, as a girl indicates clearly that on occasion she found much conventional female existence annoying, in effect boring. But her irritated outbursts occupy a minute proportion of her early journals. Far more characteristic is her record of feeling entertained and gratified by the details of her ordinary life. Her irritation typically derives from her sense of being controlled by the will of others, specific or generalized and internalized. In finding much of her conventional occupation enjoyable, she resembles those of her female contemporaries who have left records of themselves. All women, however, faced the problem of resisting others' constructions of the tedium inherent in the good young woman's life. One response, possibly not uninflected with irony, emerged in the fictional narratives of female experience.

Burney herself, of course, created such fictions. *Cecilia,* her second novel (1782), 919 pages long in the Virago Classics edition, provides an intricate plot centered on immediate contemporary issues about money and its uses, reveals subtle awareness of idiomatic possibility, and contains a wealth of social detail. Despite these "realistic" elements, it does not convey a sense of female experience obviously corresponding to that evoked by the conduct books, partly because its protagonist leads much of her life outside the domestic setting. Yet it comments on boredom as interpretive trope and on the alternatives to boredom imaginable for a woman.

Cecilia, an intelligent, beautiful, orphaned heiress approaching her twenty-first birthday at the beginning of the action, appears to have plenty to do. First she involves herself in London social life; later she performs acts of benevolence. She confronts and resolves constantly changing personal problems. Typically surrounded by people, she never needs to resort to needlework. Her life abounds in interest, for herself and for others.

Nonetheless, boredom exists in the text, troubles Cecilia herself, and contributes to the making of the narrative. The novel's most conspicuous exemplar of the state, a man, employs it as a socially powerful stance. Mr. Meadows, refusing all concern for others, insists on his own malaise: "I am tired to death! tired of every thing! I would give the universe for a disposition less difficult to please. Yet, after all, what is there to give pleasure? When one has seen one thing, one has seen every thing. O, 'tis heavy work!" (268). Taking pride in his difficult disposition, claiming his superiority by his refusal to take pleasure, he indeed, according to the testimony of others, achieves social distinction as a result. His avowed boredom records not the emptiness of his experience but the assertiveness of his ego. With all the occupations open to every male available to him, with, specifically, the possibility of active benevolence before him, he rejects engagement and willfully rests in his psychic fatigue. Both Cecilia and the narrator manifestly scorn him.

Entirely lacking in significant plot function, Mr. Meadows acquires narrative importance solely by exemplifying boredom, which figures in Burney's fiction not only as pose but as threat. Men can indulge in it; women suffer it. Mrs. Harrel, the wife of one of Cecilia's three guardians, widowed by her husband's suicide after a course of heedless extravagance, wishing only to gratify herself by returning to comparable extravagance, endures a version of boredom that demonstrates her moral inadequacy but also expresses her pain. Deprived of husband and of habitual occupation, she finds herself "a prey to all the misery of unoccupied solitude: torn from whatever had, to her, made existence seem valuable, her mind was as listless as her person was inactive, and she was at a loss how to employ even a moment of the day" (525). Although she terms her condition "sorrow," the narrator severely characterizes it as the "helplessness of insipidity" (525), calling attention to the power of interpretive terminology. One might equally well describe her state as boredom: listlessness of mind, inability to employ oneself, generalized insipidity. The orthodox eighteenth-century view, Johnson's view, of such psychological reactions explains them as derived from lack of personal resources or from unwillingness to use properly the resources one has. Given this explicit perspective, the reader would hardly expect to find the paragon Cecilia suffering a comparable malady. Yet for a time Cecilia too endures a version of the "helplessness of insipidity," helplessness precisely the source of her misery, her boredom not her fault but her fate.

In the social world Cecilia unwillingly inhabits, where Mr. Meadows practices determined boredom and Mrs. Harrel has developed no habits to protect her from inertia, only one person—Albany, who preaches the necessity for active benevolence—gets called a bore. An idle captain terms Albany "the greatest bore in nature" (282). "He has so frequently inconvenienced me by his impertinences," the captain adds, "that he really bores me to a degree" (283). Injunctions to virtue, irrelevant to the fashionable, of course bore them. The captain belongs to the group of society people whose moral inertia entails rejecting involvement. Cecilia, eager for virtue, breathes the same air as they and suffers, for different reasons, a comparable malady. Living with the Harrels, whose sole occupation is pleasure, she can find no meaningful friendship or meaningful action. What interests her associates bores her; what bores them interests her. Her situation as unmarried, unparented, wealthy young female prohibits useful activity. As she explains to her old friend, Mr. Monckton,

> Where the mind is wholly without interest, everything is languid and insipid; . . . how ever can I reconcile myself to a state of careless indifference, to making acquaintance without any concern either for preserving or esteeming them, and to going on from day to day in an eager search of amusement, with no . . . view beyond that of passing the present moment in apparent gaiety and thoughtlessness? (158)

The life she describes, one that other women of her acquaintance appear to enjoy, provides no interest for her mind and makes both the external and internal realms languid and insipid. Cecilia has not chosen it, and she cannot escape. Although she makes plans for virtuous action, she lacks the freedom—despite money, beauty, and intelligence—to engage in it. She can only refuse to participate in meaningless social life and stay home in solitude. If the others by their boredom testify to their moral insufficiency, Cecilia's boredom measures her ethical impulse. But she too feels powerless within a constricting environment.

What rescues her from boredom is yet more complicated and emphatic forms of misery. Two-thirds through the novel, this telling meditation occurs:

> "What continual disturbance," cried she, when left alone, "keeps me thus forever from rest! no sooner is one wound closed, but another is opened; mortification constantly succeeds distress, and when my heart is spared my pride is attacked, that not a moment of tranquillity may ever be allowed me!" (678)

This statement may belong among cries we doubt ever got cried, but it accurately characterizes the bulk of the novel's events. Continual disturbance indeed keeps Cecilia from what she here characterizes as "rest": likewise from passivity, inaction, and boredom—other labels for nondisturbance. Deprived of tranquillity, she only thus escapes insipidity. A series of wounds, mortifications, attacks descend on her; withstanding them supplies painful interest to her life. She resembles in this respect many—indeed, most—other heroines of eighteenth-century novels by women.

An unorthodox eighteenth-century conduct book sheds light on the remarkable narrative emphasis female novels give to female suffering. The guides to behavior I have cited so far differ in details but resemble one another in focus. *Letters from a Peeress of England to Her Eldest Son* (1784), however, unique as far as I know in being addressed by a woman to an audience defined as male, provides a new perspective on the female situation. The project of these letters originated, the text explains, in a conversation between two women who agree that "it is indeed impossible for one human being to be more in the power of another, than an English wife is in that of her husband" (3). The mother therefore decides to advise her son about how to be a good husband. In the process she reveals her angry perception of the female condition.

Two sentences in particular illuminate the relation between boredom and other forms of unhappiness for upper-class women. One invites the reader to

> view the chance for happiness a woman has in small domestic concerns in England, where the sports of the field, the houses of parliament, and, above all, the clubs, forbid a woman to hope for comfort in the society of her husband, brothers, or friends; for their conversation, engrossed by these three grand objects, is more insupportable to women than solitude. (123–24)

The other comments on the difficulty of female action:

> All those who have given [women] rules to follow, have not considered that our state of dependence makes it impossible for us to act for ourselves: the men we belong to are the first causes of every action, good or bad, that we commit. (10)

Aristocratic women, in other words, cannot count on men to alleviate with their companionship the tedium of uneventful lives. On the contrary, it appears that men's conversation only intensifies female boredom. And since men "are the first causes of every action" women commit, they must also bear responsibity for their forced inaction, presumably the root of women's boredom.

Novels besides Burney's frequently document the relation between women's good behavior and their subordination to men. (Not without occasional unexpected and provocative commentary: "Be assured of this, my good friend, that it is our submission which enables men to become tyrants—we have ourselves only to blame—and yet you gentle ones are not entitled to the merits you affect to have, as you yield more from indolence than resignation, and never comply without repining" [Griffith 2: 31].) Over and over they demonstrate that the other forms of suffering composing the sole alternative to boredom derive specifically from the agency of those to whom women submit: men. As Eliza Haywood's Betsy Thoughtless puts it, reflecting on her brothers' good advice to her, "They know their sex, and the dangers to which ours are exposed, by the artifices of base designing men" (3: 28). The stories women tell in their fiction imagine diverse ways base designing men afflict good women and bad alike. *Memoirs of Miss Sidney Bidulph*, Frances Sheridan's spectacularly successful novel, with its relentless exposition of female distress, provides the most extreme case in point, but even more cheerful female fictions rely heavily on narratives of women's suffering.

Edward Said speaks of "the desire to create an alternative world, to modify or augment the real world through the act of writing" as "one

motive underlying the novelistic tradition in the West" (81). How curious that the alternative world evoked by eighteenth-century woman
novelists consistently differs from the world reported, for instance, in
female letters—what we customarily call the "real world"—by its
relentless punishment of one sex at the hands of the other. Women in
actuality may have bored men and been bored by them; they were presumably often neglected, usually restricted, and sometimes abused. But
they did not customarily suffer as Cecilia suffers, or Sidney Bidulph, or
even Betsy Thoughtless. Instead of fantasizing escape or triumph or
successful independence, women novelists imagined heightened versions of oppression. Sometimes they conceived anguish as the penalty
of deviance: Haywood's History of Miss Betsy Thoughtless educates its protagonist through suffering presumably warranted by her light-minded-
ness. She likes to flirt, to play off one lover against another, to experience her sexual power. As a result, predictably, she loses the good man
who truly loves her, enters a marriage of convenience that threatens
lasting boredom, alleviated only by the constant seeking of individual
pleasure, and after almost four volumes' worth of affliction finds happiness in the true lover's return. But Cecilia's distress and Sidney's do not
by any moral system seem deserved.

Misguided Betsy believes in the possibility of lasting enjoyment
found elsewhere than in marriage. She wonders to herself, "What can
make the generality of Women so fond of marrying? . . . Just as if it
were not a greater pleasure to be courted, complimented, admired, and
addressed by a number, than be confined to one, who from a slave
becomes a master, and, perhaps, uses his authority in a manner disagreeable enough" (4: 23–24). The point recurs in many novels by
women, a corollary to their stress on man-caused calamity. A particularly striking example enlivens one of the century's most popular works,
The History of Lady Julia Mandeville, in which sprightly Lady Anne con-
verses with an older woman:

> "But, my dear Lady Anne, an unconnected life—"
> "Is the pleasantest life in the world. Have not I three thousand pounds a
> year? am I not a widow? mistress of my own actions? with youth, health, a
> tolerable understanding, an air of the world, and a person not very dis-
> agreeable?"
> "All this I own. . . . But what is all this to the purpose, my dear?"
> "Now I protest I think it is vastly to the purpose. And all this you advise
> me to give up, to become a tame, domestic, inanimate—Really, my dear
> madam, I did not think it was in your nature to be so unreasonable." (Brooke
> 111)

More explicitly than Betsy, Lady Anne specifies the pleasure of free-dom—the freedom available to her as a prosperous young widow—and the tedium of its alternative ("tame, domestic, inanimate"). But of course she must marry in the end: the only alternative resolution for female existence, eighteenth-century fiction suggests, is death.

Betsy Thoughtless suffers more dramatically for having questioned the notion of female subordination and betrayed her pleasure in a female form of power. First of all, she has bad dreams. "Sometimes she imagined herself standing on the brink of muddy, troubled waters; — at others, that she was wandering through deserts, overgrown with thorns and briars; or seeking to find a passage through some ruin'd building, whose tottering roof seemed ready to fall upon her head, and crush her to pieces" (4: 24). Her effort as a woman to find a viable path through deserts and ruins cannot succeed. She goes about it the wrong way, failing to understand marriage as the only acceptable fate. Her life itself reads like a bad dream. Only full acknowledgment of her errors, full submission, can rescue her. The happy ending of this cautionary fable—and a fair number, though by no means all, of the female narra-tives of torment work their way to happy endings—does not obviate the preceding emphasis on the suffering that, after all, creates most of the story.

As for Burney's Cecilia, unlike Betsy she does nothing very wrong. She makes mistakes about her money, she misjudges an old friend, she inadvertently misleads her new husband, but she usually acts with intel-ligence as well as integrity, and shows a remarkable willingness to take responsibility for her own actions. Although men cause her distress, she does not relax into blaming them. Her errors derive from inexperience, and she readily takes advantage of the experience available to her. She struggles to avoid even self-pity. On the whole, she seems more active and more resourceful, as well as more upright, than her lover.

But if Betsy's moral flaws guarantee her tribulation, Cecilia's abun-dant virtues do not enable her to avoid the calamities, culminating in madness and near death, that provide her only apparent alternative to stasis ("rest") and the boredom that often accompanies inaction. Despite her willingness to judge and act for herself, men, in her case as in Lady Anne's, supply the "first cause" for most of her actions. At men's behest she spends much of her fortune, changes residence, and bestows benevolence. The psychic and physical torment Cecilia undergoes derives from the fact that she can keep her considerable inheritance, once married, only if her husband takes her name. And given aristo-cratic primogeniture, for a man to change his name at marriage—as women routinely do—is perceived as a horrifying impossibility. Cecilia must finally give up her money and her name, the signs of her independence, for the sake of a "happy ending" in marriage.

The shadow of boredom hovers strangely about this ambiguously happy ending. In the final scene, flighty Lady Honoria Pemberton, a minor character "who was accidentally in town" (909), shows up for little apparent reason other than to remind Cecilia, and the reader, of the tedium associated with Delvile Castle, where Cecilia will live hereafter. "If you are tempted to an unseasonable laugh," Lady Honoria advises, "think of Delvile Castle; 'tis an expedient I commonly make use of myself when I am afraid of being too frisky: and it always succeeds, for the very recollection of it gives me the head-ache in a moment" (911). Later she adds that she hates dignity—the most conspicuous characteristic of the Delvile family—"for it's the dullest thing in the world" (913). One need not take Lady Honoria's word for anything. Still, she has raised a disturbing possibility: the end of Cecilia's afflictions, her return to "rest," may bring the recurrence of tedium. The putative boredom of her marriage will have new causes, inasmuch as in marriage she will comply with standards different from those of the Harrels and their society. But in marriage as in girlhood, Cecilia may find that the need to conform to restrictive rules entails a closing off of possibility.

Not that she necessarily will consciously experience boredom as a result. Lady Honoria would no doubt feel bored married to Delvile; Cecilia almost certainly will not. She did not, like the captain, find herself bored with hearing about good works; she would not, like Mr. Meadows, cultivate boredom; she could not, like Mrs. Harrel, respond to the abrupt cessation of a course of extravagance by suffering boredom. For these characters, the stance of boredom provides certain rewards; for Cecilia it does not. Burney's novel reminds its readers repeatedly of boredom as idiosyncrasy, a personal response to external stimuli. Cecilia has experienced it only when cut off in all directions from meaningful choice. Marriage, as the conduct books promised all well-bred young women, will enlarge her sphere of action. This cheerful view, however, does not respond quite adequately to Lady Honoria's intercession.

At one moment of extreme distress, Cecilia comes close to reproaching (though only in thought) Lady Delvile, her lover's mother. The narrator takes pains to comment that "her grief was unmixed with anger, and her tears streamed not from resentment, but affliction" (686). Cecilia's status as female paragon depends partly on her denial of rage. The narrator likewise expresses no resentment. And the plot insists that the outcome of marriage to the man she loves fills Cecilia's needs and guarantees her happiness, obviating the weight of all her previous suffering.

But Lady Honoria, one of the verbally indiscreet women who appear in each of Burney's novels, by her intrusion announces alternative possibilities. Giving a name to dullness, a young woman exercises her freedom to speak the unspeakable. Dullness, boredom, tedium pop up rather awkwardly from time to time as incidental issues in *Cecilia*, quickly disappearing again from the text. The marginalized possibility of boredom, however, remains the largely unspoken threat to female happiness. Burney's novel, as recent commentators have noted, deals with the difficult necessities implicit in a young woman's socialization into marriage. Denying the very possibility of boredom may be one of these necessities.

As the conduct books insist, young women must not allow themselves to think their experience boring because they have so little opportunity to enlarge it. Far better eliminate the category of boredom from their interpretive repertoire. To consider *Cecilia* under the rubric of boredom reminds the reader of Burney's deftness at suggesting the existence and the power of what good girls never speak about. Cecilia can permit herself boredom at a life of social emptiness and can disapprove of those who indulge in boredom for reasons of self-aggrandizement or moral insufficiency. She cannot acknowledge boredom's possibility at Delvile Castle: only the improper female can do that.

Attention to this marginalized subject in *Cecilia* may also alert readers to its equally peripheral (but also equally suggestive) appearances in other eighteenth-century novels by women. Often tedium attends compliant virtue. As one fictional young woman writes to a friend, in another novel, "I am seriously considering, whether or not I can find any thing to amuse you, which I have not repeated to you five hundred times" (J. Marshall 1: 115). She can report her gratitude to the relatives who are helping to support her, or tell of local theatricals, or summarize social routines she has summarized often before. But since nothing happens in the normal life of a well-bred woman, the fictional letter writer, like her real-life counterpart, may find it difficult to discover communicable interest in the doings that fill her daily experience. At the edge of female awareness, many novels indicate, lies always the consciousness of the dull.

If the imagined persecutions of men in a more or less realistic mode provided one novelistic alternative to dullness, the Gothic novel supplied almost limitless possibilities for painful infliction—infliction frequently intensified by the imaginations of its victims. "The taste for the horrible, is the consciousness of the dull" (91), wrote someone named Charles Bathurst in 1850, providing no elucidation. The remark raises the possibility that the efflorescence of female Gothic in the late eighteenth century may bear on women's awareness of tedium in female lives. Most Gothic novels never state the alternatives of commonplace boredom or uncommon anguish, on the contrary figuring a vaguely imagined domesticity as bliss. A novel that remains on the fringes of Gothic, Eliza Fenwick's *Secresy: Or, The Ruin on the Rock* (1795), on the other hand, renders explicitly the opposed possibilities of boredom or nightmare in female experience. (I quote from the badly printed Pandora edition, full of typographical errors though it is, because of its comparative accessibility.) *Secresy* tells the story of Sibella Valmont, a virtual parable of male oppression. Confined to a remote castle at the will of her uncle, Sibella lives in utter subjection to a man who speaks "mysteriously of his systems, and his plans, of his authority, his wisdom, and your [Sibella's] dependence, of his right of chusing for you, and your positive duty of obeying him without reserve or discussion" (17). Mr. Valmont complains that he has spent hours pondering her welfare, "yet you are not the docile and grateful creature I expected to find you" (6). His plans depend on keeping Sibella from human contact. Aside from her aunt and uncle, whom she sees rarely, she encounters only servants with defects of speech or hearing and one boy her own age, Clement, allegedly her uncle's adopted son, with whom she inevitably falls in love and from whom she is arbitrarily separated.

The details of the tragic denouement hardly matter to my present argument. Sibella, too innocent to understand the social meaning of her action, insists on sexual union with Clement, to her mind equivalent to the marriage her uncle appears to interdict. She becomes pregnant as a result. Eventually she dies, as does the virtuous man who has loved her with no return. Self-seeking Clement, having made a dreadful prudential marriage, survives in unhappiness and remorse. The explicit moral of these events, according to the normative figure Caroline Ashburn, is that "however plausible and even necessary in appearance, yet artifice and secrecy are dangerous vicious tools" (278). The uncle has concealed his devious plans for them from Sibella and Clement alike, has concealed his true fatherhood of Clement, has concealed the existence of Sibella's fortune, insisting always on her "dependence." Murden, the unrewarded lover, has operated in secrecy to see and know Sibella.

Even Caroline has used secret methods to try to remedy the devastation caused by previous secrets. Disaster results from the elaborate structures of concealment.

The original secrets, the source of all the trouble, depend on the uncle's sense of his absolute right to absolute power. Caroline herself comes to see this, inveighing against George Valmont's stress on "obedience."

> The perpetual hue and cry after obedience . . . has almost driven virtue out
> of the world, for be it unlimited unexamined obedience to a sovereign, to a
> parent, or husband, the mind, yielding itself to implicit unexamined obedi-
> ence, loses its individual dignity, and you can expect no more of a man than
> of a brute. (290)

As Caroline's language indicates, men as well as women fall victim to the exercise of power. But the differences between Clement's and Sibella's fates distinguish the operations of power on females and on males. Caroline predicts of Clement, "His sorrow will abate; he will be again reconciled to himself, and live abounding in all things but esteem" (291). Sibella will stay dead.

The plot of *Secresy*, as my summary must suggest, owes more to romance tradition than to any obvious notion of "realism." Yet its deviations from the plausible only emphasize its approximation of psychic and social actuality for women. As the peeress writing letters to her son observed, Englishwomen literally live in the absolute power of their husbands. Before marriage, they function at the will of their fathers, or father substitutes. Fenwick's novel broods over the implications of such facts. Clement escapes George Valmont to enter a larger world. His lack of moral preparation for that world testifies to his father's errors, but his ability to choose his environment emblematizes a possibility of self-sufficiency not available to Sibella, who cannot leave until "rescued" by a man. The young woman's life and death exemplify female victimization, apparently women's necessary condition. For even Caroline, with far more apparent freedom of choice than Sibella (like Cecilia, she is rich, clever, and beautiful), becomes a victim. She cannot choose a man for herself: the man she wants, wants another. Nor can she escape the social environment that oppresses her. For women, the novel suggests, no freedom obtains.

All of which has little obvious connection to boredom. But boredom is never far away in *Secresy*. Sibella suffers it in and because of her seclusion; Caroline endures it in and because of her social activity. These opposed possibilities indeed delineate the common determinants of

boredom for women, both deriving, like the causes of Cecilia's temporary boredom, from the imposition of other wills on that of the female
victim. Sibella, of course, has not the slightest opportunity for self-
determination. Her first letter to Caroline claims that her correspondent has "bestowed upon me the only charm of existence that I have
known for many and many a tedious day" (5). Despite her courage and
hardihood (she spends much time outdoors, undeterred by rumors of
ghosts in the local ruin), she suggests that she feels bored even with the
progression of seasons because of her confinement at her uncle's behest.
"Imprisoned, during so many years, within the narrow boundary of this
castle and its parks, the same objects eternally before me, I look with
disgust from their perpetual round of succession. Nature herself, spring,
summer, autumn, degenerate into sameness" (33). Like the bored characters in *Cecilia*, she reveals boredom as a construction of consciousness.
Turning from an external world that has become to her the emblem of
her helplessness, she decides to rely on "the resources of [her] own
heart" (35). Hence her disaster: female emotions undisciplined by
knowledge offer no dependable guide.

As for Caroline, she undergoes constant experiences of social
tedium. Although the ways of passing time she reports sound altogether
attractive, they epitomize the tiresome (for her and implicitly for the
others who engage in them) because they represent no real choice but
instead evoke the impossibility of choice. In one instance she describes
a lavish entertainment, complete with music, fishing, and delicate food.
"Notwithstanding all this costly care," she concludes, "it is very possible we shall pass a listless morning, return without any increase of
appetite, or animal spirits, and be mighty ready to bestow loud com-
mendations on the pleasures of a morning, from which we derive no
other secret satisfaction than the certainty of its being at an end"
(40–41). Aristocratic idlers, associating with one another for no reason
other than passing the time, do not satisfy one another's needs, but Caroline cannot choose her company and consequently cannot enjoy the
entertainment provided her. The impossibility of female autonomy
dooms her as much as Sibella to "many and many a tedious day."

Acknowledging boredom as an aspect of female victimization, Fenwick, like Burney, constitutes her narrative on tribulation as its alternative. Sibella experiences calamity directly, Caroline only vicariously.
The use of personal letters to transmit the stories of human suffering
underlines the assumption that affliction makes interest, that both private and public audiences will be engaged by accounts of disaster.

Sibella and Caroline, of course, no more choose their painful fates than they chose the imposed conditions of their early lives. Yet their anguish and Sibella's death result from their efforts to assert personal choice. Sibella determines on an act of sexual freedom, Caroline dares to desire a man who has shown no interest in her. Disaster ensues. Fenwick's novel thus overtly teaches compliance even though it allows one of its characters to inveigh against "obedience." Yet its construction of female possibility as bounded on every side by misery also implies dimly articulated protest. Women, such fiction suggests, can rest in obedience, denying active desire, and suffer the flaccid unhappiness of boredom, or they can deviate from conformity at the cost of more dramatic suffering that frustrates desire's fulfillment. No other choice opens for them.

Freud, Said reminds us, defined the objective of "the reconstructive techniques, whether history, philosophy, or personal narrative" as "both to create alternatives to a confusing reality and to minimize the pain of experience" (94). Novels imitate such techniques. Women's novels of the eighteenth century, however, resentfully *maximize* the pain of experience in their rendition of it. They thus convey the subjective meaning of desire constantly deflected in the service of propriety and of men as the agents of social power.

The fantasies of popular romance—the Harlequins that abound in every supermarket—it has been argued, encourage female conformity by providing vicarious satisfactions to obviate the necessity for direct gratification. These eighteenth-century fantasies of extravagant oppression, perhaps issuing from imaginations less fully resigned to social actuality, supply different forms of comfort. By exaggerating the indignities women endure, they offer female readers the pleasure of being understood: someone comprehends how they suffer. The books may thus encourage self-pity or, conversely, assure their readers that matters could, after all, be worse: women should perhaps be willing to settle for only moderate misery. More furtively, the novels of female misery encourage indignation. The boredom to which women are destined, according to conduct books by men and women alike as well as women's novels, is not a condition of the soul, like that professed by Burney's Mr. Meadows. It does not reveal consciousness cut off from the possibility of will or desire. The boredom of women, as it emerges in these texts, constitutes an imposition of intricate social pressure: pressure to conform to the rules that forbid free choice or action, and pressure to deny their conceivable understanding of their relatively inactive lives as tedious. Narratives of female misery, however fantastic, reveal resentment of such imposition.

FOUR

"Self Is a Tiresome Subject"
Personal Records of Eighteenth-Century Women

If male moralists in the eighteenth century consistently recommended action as the antidote to boredom, women living private lives understood that not action alone but interpretation as well provides boredom's remedy. Even Dr. Johnson, for all his wisdom, failed to see that the condition he called "weariness" might not constitute, even temporarily, a necessary fact. All the wise and all the good tell him of the state's curability. They do not tell him that his weariness derives from his way of understanding, or feeling, his own experience.

Many women knew what Johnson did not. Themselves victims of others' interpretation (for instance, the typical understanding of most female occupations as trivial), they apparently grasped that people impose meaning on their own and others' experience. Not that they say so directly: the women considered in this chapter rarely venture large generalizations. But their ways of describing their own lives, of invoking the category of boredom only to reject it, of contemplating the possibility that they may bore others—these and other aspects of their personal writing implicitly claim and openly manifest the power of interpretation. Boredom is not, from these women's point of view, a necessary condition. It does not inhere in leisure, it does not signify passivity. The citations in the previous chapter from Burney's early journal, as well as from contemporaneous moralists, remind us of the severe restrictions on eighteenth-century women's ways of spending time. Nonetheless, the period's female letter writers rarely complain of boredom. They demonstrate specific and powerful ways in which writing, even private writing, resists any such condition.

Lives, like novels, depend on narratability. Only by telling stories of ourselves to ourselves and others do we make sense of what we think, what has happened to us, what we have caused to happen. Alasdair MacIntyre insists that the possibility of a meaningful notion of virtue depends on belief in "the narrative unity of human life" (212).

> To be the subject of a narrative that runs from one's birth to one's death is ... to be accountable for the actions and experiences which compose a narratable life. . . . [P]ersonal identity is just that identity presupposed by the unity of the character which the unity of a narrative requires. Without such unity there would not be subjects of whom stories could be told. (202–3)

By this argument, everyone has a vital stake in life's narratability, which defines both the self and other people and makes possible the concept of responsibility.

Potential narratives of circularity, oscillation, and repetition, however, abound in even the most privileged lives. "All great books contain boring portions, and all great lives have contained uninteresting stretches" (Russell 62). Often the pattern of a day, a month, a lifetime requires severe excision and dramatic intensification to feel interesting in retrospect, even to the experiencer. Eighteenth-century women living the lives recommended by conduct books—not "great lives" but "good" ones—would find it difficult to narrate their literal experience in compelling terms. The blandness of identity and the relative blankness of personal history implicit in conventional notions of female virtue do not, as novelists made clear in their practice, possess obvious interest.

Perhaps partly for this reason, autobiographies of eighteenth-century British women do not abound. Women like Laetitia Pilkington and Charlotte Charke published putative accounts of their lives so highly colored that subsequent critics have considered them largely fiction. Members of the aristocracy occasionally related their experience, assuming public interest in the lives of the privileged and, in particular, interest in the important people they had encountered in their social functioning. Working-class women rarely left detailed written records. Respectable females of the middle and upper classes wrote letters. On occasion (I am thinking of Elizabeth Montagu, Hannah More, Lady Mary Wortley Montagu, Elizabeth Carter) they also produced a treatise on Shakespeare, a translation of Epictetus, a guide to behavior, a group of poems, or other forms of published material, but their direct claims for the narratability of their own lives exist mainly in their correspondences.

Elizabeth Montagu, More, and Mary Delany lived into their eighties. Although nineteenth-century editors have expurgated and tidied their surviving letters, multivolume collections remain. Along with the authoritatively edited correspondences of Lady Mary and Frances Burney and with less voluminous assortments of letters by other women, they provide a basis for speculation about what kind of narrative unity and interest respectable women discovered and constructed in their lives: how they interpreted their lives for purposes of verbal rendition. Like Alasdair MacIntyre, although with more limited objectives, these women concerned themselves with "virtue" and understood it as implying responsibility, and therefore choice—autonomy. Only occasionally did any of them perceive herself as oppressed or even severely restricted by men. They make of their lives extended stories, thus denying boredom by verbal action. The construction of interest in their epistolary accounts of themselves delineates the shape of their freedom.

Such generalizations suggest once more the possibility that the subject of boredom, in relation to eighteenth-century women, becomes most significant in its denial and avoidance. Because of propriety, and perhaps for deeper reasons, women whose correspondence has survived typically rejected, both implicitly and explicitly, interpretation of their own experience as boring. Such refusal, like Johnson's and Mackenzie's analyses, implies ethical rejection of boredom as a form of self-indulgence. It may also on occasion imply a covert sense of female superiority. Like Gray, but in a very different tone of voice, many women of the period apparently believed that only men allowed themselves the reprehensible luxury of boredom. Women were made of sterner stuff.

Although the young Frances Burney frequently deplored the boredom of social compliance, she also on occasion denied personal experience of tedium, her denial expressing attitudes familiar in other female writers of her century.

> I seldom quit home considering my age and opportunities. But why should I when I am so happy in it? following my own vagaries, which my papa never controls I never can want employment, nor sigh for amusement. We have a library which is an everlasting resource when attack'd by the spleen—I have always a sufficiency of work to spend, if I pleased, my whole time at it— musick is a feast which can never grow insipid—and, in short, I have all the reason that ever mortal had to be contented with my lot—and I *am* contented, I *am* grateful for it! (*Early Diary* 1: 46)

The diarist records her contentment at age seventeen, in 1769, the year for which the journal also preserves her complaint of the tedium of compulsory visiting. Her italics and exclamation point hint the excess of her protestations, suggesting effortful self-conviction. Various forms of effort—self-reminders that needlework always awaits her, that books and music should alleviate any conceivable discontent, that her father permits her to do what she wants (within, of course, the severe restrictions of propriety)—comfort her.

Insistence on individual triumph over boredom recurs in her own and other women's personal writing. "I have nobody but little Sally for a companion. But I have no dread of *ennui*, nor fear of idleness or listlessness. I am going (as soon as I have finished this letter) to study *Italian*, which I can do alone at least as easily as I did French" (2: 142; 27 July 1776). Hester Thrale, much older, sounds precisely the same note:

> It is a backward melancholy Spring—I'll study Hebrew to divert Ennui & pass the Summer Months away: —Shameful! if not criminal Resolution! to endeavour to rid myself of *Time*, who is so near ridding the World of *me*—yet one cannot all Day be praying for Grace to do well, nor in Spinning for the poor, wch after all is the only *Good Thing* one *can do*: and learning Hebrew is no harm. (2: 1065; 20 May 1805)

And Lady Mary Wortley Montagu:

> I know by Experience it is in the power of Study not only to make solitude tolerable but agreable. I have now liv'd almost seven years in a stricter Retirement than yours in the Isle of Bute, and can assure you I have never had halfe an hour heavy on my Hands for want of something to do.
> Whoever will cultivate their own mind will find full employment. (3: 35; To Lady Bute [her daughter], 6 Mar. [1753])

These women who explain that study or needlework or music alleviates ennui—by which they appear to mean something more like what we call boredom—believe that they can and should control their reactions to circumstance. As twenty-two-year-old Lady Mary wrote to her friend Anne Justice, "I endeavour to make my Solitude as agreable as I can. Most things of that kind are in the power of the mind; we may make our selves easy if we cannot perfectly happy" (1: 107; [c. 4 Aug. 1711]). But ethical imperatives do not always govern immediate response. Lady Mary sounds more authentic, if less high-minded, in a letter to the same friend a year earlier: "Yes, yes, my dear, Here is Woods and Shades and Groves in abundance; you are in the right on't. Tis not the place, but the solitude of the place that is intollerable. Tis a horrid thing to see nothing but trees in a wood, and to walk by a purling stream to ogle the Gudgeons in it" (1: 42; [c. 5 July 1710]).

This tone of irritation disappears from her letters after her move to the Continent—a move thought to derive from her finding England, and her husband, boring. As a malicious 1740 letter from Elizabeth Montagu to an unspecified recipient explains,

> Lady Shadwell saw Lady Mary Wortley at Venice where she now resides, and asked her what made her leave England; she told them the reason was people had grown so stupid she could not endure their company; all England was infected with dullness; by the bye what she means by insupportable dullness is her husband, for it seems she never intends to come back while he lives. (*Mrs. Montagu* 1: 25)

Although Lady Mary indeed returned to England only after her husband's death, her letters suggest that the dullness of England, for her as for the young Frances Burney, derives from social restrictions. While still in England she wrote to her sister, "Here, what between the Things one can't do and the Things one must not do, the Time but dully lingers on, tho I make as good a shift as any of my Neighbours" (2: 30; [Oct. 1723]). By summarizing her complicated motives for self-exile as a perception of dullness, she implies her superiority to the merely conventional—which, in her view, guarantees tedium.

Life in Italy provided little stimulation or excitement. "I play at Whist every night with some old Priests that I have taught it to, and are my only Companions. To say truth, the decay of my sight will no longer suffer me to read by Candle light, and the evenings are now long and dark, that I am forc'd to stay at home" (2: 391; To Lady Bute, 17 Dec. [1747]). But Lady Mary had *chosen* this life, had indeed created it, in a sense quite different from any of her previous choices, in a sense available to few women of her era. She could not therefore find it boring.

Instead, she worries about the possibility that she and her letters might be tiresome. As we shall see, she was by no means alone in this anxiety, which issues from awareness of possible discrepancies between one's own perceptions and those of others. Perhaps her daughter will find dull what she considers urgent: "I should excuse the Length of this Letter (duly considering the dullness of it) but I hope you can forgive it, as it comes from your most affectionate Mother" (2: 422; To Lady Bute, 6 Mar. [1749]). "I slide, insensibly, into talking of my selfe, tho I allwaies resolve against it. I will releive you from so dull a subject by concluding my Letter" (3: 49; To Lady Bute, 1 Mar. [1754]). "This Letter is as Long and as Dull as any of Richardson's. I am asham'd of it, notwithstanding my Maternal Privelege of being tiresome" (3: 89; 22 Sept. [1755]).

The boring, in epistolary contexts, from Lady Mary's apparent point of view consists in the personal. She makes no apologies for letters composed almost entirely of conventional protestations of affection and concern ("I beg of you with the utmost earnestness, that you would be carefull of your selfe; I can receive no proofe of your Freindship so obliging to me, tho I am yours by every Tye that can engage a gratefull Heart" [2: 342; To Lady Oxford, 14 Sept. 1744]), or for paragraphs of scandal about members of the aristocracy, or certainly for detailed accounts of what she has seen on her travels. She assumes, in other words, that the world outside herself holds interest for her correspondents, but that she imposes the burden of dullness on them by speaking of herself.

Hannah More states with some precision the narrative problem inherent in the notion of the self, and of ordinary female life, as dull:

> *"Heureux le peuple dont l'histoire ennuie,"* says somebody. The best times to live in are often the worst to write about. In a novel or a comedy, the moment the lovers are settled and happy they become so insipid that another page of the one, or an additional scene of the other, would be quite surfeiting. If any body were to write a play about good sort of quiet, reasonable, orderly, prosperous people, the audience would not be able to sit out the first act; they would long for the relief of a little distress, and languish for the refreshment of a little misery [precisely the "relief" and "refreshment" supplied by the novels considered in my previous chapter]. . . All this verbiage means to say that I have during the whole summer, kept the "even tenour of my way," with such sober and quiet uniformity, that the history of my adventures would make as dull a novel as could be had at a circulating library, and that is saying a great deal. I do not however *complain;* I have lived much to my own taste. (Roberts 2: 130–31; To William Pepys, Sept. 1788)

She has no story to tell, in other words. Indeed, in the four volumes mainly comprising her letters (she lived to the age of eighty-eight) she tells little of herself beyond her ailments, her good works, her travels, and the people she visits. She allows herself description of social occasions—what others wear, what others say—and sometimes full accounts of her reading. She comments on the political situation in England and in France, mainly in religious terms. (God's vengeance seems likely.) She reports deathbed scenes in excruciating detail.

In a late-century epistolary novel, the heroine writes the story of her life for a friend. She introduces her account in these words: "To any one but my Lucy, the enclosed narrative would afford little entertainment: it is not a series of events, but a continued conflict of the mind, and is a history of passions, not of persons" (Griffith 2: 160). Our own post-

Freudian sensibilities may lead us to believe that everyone could, if she or he would, leave a record of "continued conflict of the mind," and that a "history of passions" would almost necessarily prove interesting. An obvious solution to the putative narrative boredom of women's lives lies here. But More does not fully avail herself of this possibility, nor does Lady Mary, or Burney, or Mary Delany. More, her memoirist reports, had an unhappy romantic engagement in her youth and at least one subsequent proposal. The letters say nothing of all this. Delany in her first widowhood expected a proposal from a man who had given her every reason to think him committed to her. He made a pretext for quarreling and disappeared from her life. Only in the most guarded terms does she report these matters to her sister.

Delany's letters and More's are available to us now only in hagiographic nineteenth-century editions. Perhaps they wrote of their passions, but we cannot read what they wrote. For Burney and Lady Mary, on the other hand, we have excellent twentieth-century collections of correspondence. Burney endured a false courtship comparable to Delany's. Although she tells the story to her sister, she records virtually nothing of the "passion" that must have attended it. Lady Mary in her middle age fell desperately in love with a younger Italian man, bisexual, himself perhaps romantically involved with Lord Hervey. Her surviving letters to Algarotti unmistakably reveal the intensity of her feeling for him. Her letters to others, even her intimates, barely allude to the relationship.

From most women's novels of the eighteenth century, one might conclude that the vicissitudes of love generate the only tellable story of female experience. Yet literal female correspondences often suppress precisely this aspect of the writers' lives. The fear of "egotism" must partly account for the suppression. When More lapses into a revelation of how intensely she fears "an unkind look, a severe word, or a cool letter" from someone she cares for, she instantly apologizes: "Can your lordship forgive all this egotism? I have been betrayed into it by my subject, and I am afraid it is so pleasant to talk of oneself that one had almost rather talk of one's faults, than not talk of oneself at all." Immediately she goes on to speak of her concern for someone else (Roberts 2: 375). In the female orthodoxy, preoccupation with self constitutes betrayal. As one young woman writes to another in 1795, "I could fill volumes with telling you all my *thoughts*, but that w^d be only tiresome" (*Jerningham Letters* 1: 83; Fanny Dillon to Lady Jerningham, 17 June). Or in Betsy Sheridan's summation, "Always self is a tiresome subject" (LeFanu 120; To her sister, 1 Oct. 1788). We can expect to find few epistolary narratives of personal feeling or purely personal reflection. On the other hand, women, largely confined to private settings, could provide little news of public interest. When Gray, for instance, lacks material apart from himself for letters, he simply refrains from writing: "I well remember how little you love Letters, where all the Materials are drawn out of oneself; yet such mine must have been from a Place, where nothing ever happens but Trifles, that it would be mere impertinence to think of entertaining You with" (Gray 1: 231; To Walpole, 7 July [1746]). Women who waited for something beyond trifles to happen in their lives might wait a long time. What were they to do in the meantime? What could rescue their letters from the charge of being boring? What could give them narrative intelligibility and interest?

The intelligibility they claim does not, for the twentieth-century reader, always coincide with that they provide. Nor do women's frequent apologies for the tedium of their letters necessarily locate stretches of uninteresting material. Lady Mary's letters to her daughter, full of reflection on the situation of women, seem especially compelling now, implicitly telling a new story, offering a new interpretation, of her personal history. No letter in the three-volume collection alludes explicitly to her unhappiness with her husband. If she complains (as, in the early years, she does) directly to Wortley, she couches her grievances in the language of love: she wishes he would write more often because she cares so much for him. She continues to send him letters—and to refrain from seeing him, even when he visits the Continent—until he dies, always professing her immense concern for his health and welfare. In advising Lady Bute about the education of her daughters, on the other hand, Lady Mary reveals her own sense of female constriction. In effect she generalizes her condition. She also reveals it. The narrative her letters supply exposes a character unified by her will to achieve self-determination despite all forces forbidding it. The correspondence tells the story of a woman's gradual self-discovery and self-assertion.

Here is Hannah More, writing to Horace Walpole in 1793:

I have been much pestered to read the "Rights of Women," but am invincibly resolved not to do it. Of all jargon, I hate metaphysical jargon; besides there is something fantastic and absurd in the very title. How many ways there are of being ridiculous! I am sure I have as much liberty as I can make a good use of, now I am an old maid, and when I was a young one, I had, I dare say, more than was good for me. If I were still young, perhaps I should not make this confession; but so many women are fond of government, I suppose, because they are not fit for it. To be unstable and capricious, I really think, is but too characteristic of our sex; and there is perhaps no animal so much indebted to subordination for its good behaviour, as woman. (Roberts 2: 371)

Like Lady Mary writing to Lady Bute, More makes limited narrative claims. The story she purports to tell mainly concerns a set of opinions—of rejections. She will not read a certain book, she does not like a certain kind of language, she thinks she has had too much liberty, she considers women unfit for government. The excess of negation demands interpretation. A woman whom surely no one ever called "unstable and capricious" declares instability and capriciousness the qualities of her sex. A woman who has made herself an arbiter of public morals announces her own unfitness for government. A year earlier, she had reported that in London a woman who "gave a very great children's ball" had set on a platform at the end of the room a figure representing Hannah More, "with a large rod in my hand prepared to punish such naughty doings" (Roberts 2: 322; To Wilberforce, 1792). For others, in short, More herself constituted an image of stern government. But she denies her authority, implicitly denies the very possibility of her own interest in "government." And she attributes to "subordination" the good behavior of her sex.

More resembles other literary women in claiming interest for her letters based on not their narrative but their intellectual qualities, the putatively "masculine" capacity for abstraction and generalization revealed in them. If readers find narrative a more compelling basis for interest, they can readily construct the story implicit in the set of generalizations about women quoted above. It is "not a series of events, but a continued conflict of the mind": between the writer's desire for female propriety and her will to effective force in the world. One can perceive comparable conflicts in the private writings of Burney, Lady Mary, and Thrale. Their letters seldom bore an attentive modern reader—not, as the writers anticipate, because they avoid excessive personal revelation, not only because of the weight of their ideas, but because of the narratives they imply, narratives that restore a sense of possibility to experience declared by the writers to fit readily into the established mold of female conformity. The most compelling stories, in other words, exist in the gaps of female correspondences.

A phrase like "most compelling" raises the question, Compelling to *whom?* The stories implied in letters that dwell largely on trivia may interest twentieth-century feminist readers, but they also clearly interested the letters' original recipients. The richest communications

between women depend on mutually understood subtle transforma-
tions of male orthodoxies. Their letters embody as well as narrate the
escape from boredom.

A n eighteenth-century commonplace had it that women excelled in
  writing letters. As Jane Austen's Henry Tilney ironically puts it,
"Every body allows that the talent of writing agreeable letters is peculiarly female" (Austen, *Northanger Abbey* 27). The presumed epistolary
excellence of females depended partly on their posited gift for the personal. Thomas Gisborne worried that young women, lacking the public concerns of their male counterparts, might concentrate too heavily
in their letters on the effectiveness of their composition, forgetting the
authentic—and for women appropriate—force of directly expressed
emotion. "They are exposed to peculiar danger," he writes, of women,

> a danger aggravated by the nature of some of the fashionable topics which
> will proceed from engrossing conversation to employ the pen, of learning to
> clothe their thoughts in studied phrases; and even of losing simplicity both
> of thought and expression in florid, refined, and sentimental parade. Fre-
> quently, too, the desire of shining intermingles itself, and involves them in
> additional temptations. They are ambitious to be distinguished for writing,
> as the phrase is, *good* letters. Not that a lady ought not to write a good let-
> ter. But a lady, who makes it her study to write a good letter, commonly pro-
> duces a composition to which a very different epithet ought to be applied.
> Those letters only are good, which contain the natural effusions of the heart,
> expressed in unaffected language. (111–12)

In other words, the *really* good woman letter writer does not strive for
epistolary excellence, does not allow herself "studied" display ("parade")
of her thoughts and feelings, but spills out simple "natural effusions"
unmarked by art or artifice. Her unpremeditated utterance reveals a
heart needing no disguise, open to investigation. On the page as in person, a woman must show her innocence. Her feminine concern with
feeling, uncontaminated by excessive thought, should be part of that
innocence, the nature of her feelings irreproachable.

To twentieth-century readers who understand collected letters as
psychic autobiography, the female predilection for the personal as
recorded in letters may seem less gift than accomplishment. The correspondences that remain engaging conform to the stringency of Gisborne's implicit and explicit requirements, not only for correspondence
but for daily life, yet manage to convey unexpected emotional complexities, especially through their ways of avoiding the tedium the writ-

ers fear. Early modern commentators on letters as a literary genre frequently remark on the capacity for *interest* that characterizes the successful letter writers. J. C. Bailey, writing of Lady Mary Wortley Montagu, comments on her possession of "the good health and multiplicity of interests which together defeat the monster *ennui*" (69) and adds, about her life in Italy, "The most striking thing about it is the abundance of resources, and the astonishing activity of interests, which she must have possessed in herself to enable her to continue it so long" (98). George Saintsbury notes "that extraordinary power of making anything interesting—of entirely transcending the subject—which belongs to the letter-writer in probably a greater measure than to any man-of-letters [sic] in the other sense, except the poet" (43). Elizabeth Drew observes that the most famous letter writers "have always been highly intelligent, interested in and curious about the world around them and the variety of people they meet or hear of in it" (15).

Commenting on a letter writer's capacity for interest in the world means, I suspect, that the writer has succeeded in interesting the commentator. Perhaps the three critical statements above can all be translated, "The good letter writer does not bore us." In the context of eighteenth-century injunctions for female conduct on and off the page, the very possibility of entertaining female correspondences seems remarkable. If woman novelists made melodramatic misery the alternative to the mundane and predictable misery of boredom, woman letter writers, the ones who still seem worth reading for their own sakes, insist on the interest of their routine experience. Believing that to be bored or boring registers moral failure, they reject both temptations. In order to construct "interesting" narratives of their lives, they must construct interest within those lives. They face not only the literary problem of the reader's response—the reaction of that first reader, the letter's original recipient—but the immediate personal problem of experiencing their own existence, however conventionally circumscribed, as narratable: possessing shape, immediate meaning, *interest*.

Collected letters have a special value as autobiography because they record not the distillation but the dynamic of experience. Formal autobiography presents itself as the product of a life reflected upon. The sort of informal autobiography amassed in a published accumulation of letters represents the processes of life (and especially of relationship) rather than a product. Unlike diaries, letters are composed with consciousness of specific and shifting audiences. Their communications focus on more than self-revelation. Yet this very fact guarantees foci of self-exposure more various than those of a diary, more inadvertent than those of formal autobiography. Sheer bulk has special advantages for the kinds of representation a published correspondence provides: the mass of Mary Delany's letters, first primarily to her sister, then to that sister's daughter, then to the daughter's daughter, itself dramatizes the shifting sequence of accommodation by which she both came to terms with her life and made that life the stuff of story.

Born Mary Granville, the protagonist of this correspondence (1700–1788) married young, at her uncle's will, an apparently monstrous (physically ugly, morally repellent, pathologically jealous) much older man named Alexander Pendarves. Before she was twenty-three, she had been widowed. For the next twenty years she lived in apparently contented celibacy. At forty-three she married, for love, the Irish clergyman Patrick Delany, Swift's friend. She outlived him, her beloved sister, her parents, and her closest friends. Endlessly active, she created artifacts ranging from chandeliers made of shells to exquisite paper mosaics of flowers (recently exhibited at the Morgan Library). Although virtually blind, she continued to write letters almost until her death.

The uniqueness of personality that familiar letters convey defines much of their appeal. Mary Delany, with a particular life and particular ways of living it, cannot tell us how her contemporaries lived or interpreted their experience. Her ways of creating interest, however, in her life and on her pages, exemplify strategies of self-definition and self-assertion that correspond to those employed by many other female correspondents who asserted their own lack of specialness and declared the interest of the commonplace. Suppressing direct statement of intense feeling, she nonetheless conveys it.

Writing to her sister, Anne Dewes, in 1754, Delany offers a rare and revealing bit of self-analysis: "I was not born to be a philosopher: nature has not thrown in enough of indifference in my composition, nor has art attained it; in short, I *like*, and *love*, and *dislike* with *all my might*, and the pain it sometimes costs me is recompensed by the pleasure" (First Series 3: 294; 30 Oct.). This self-delineation provides a clue to the special intensity of Delany's letters. Emphasizing pleasure more than pain, she characteristically conveys the vitality with which she experiences even the everyday. Her refusal of (or inaptitude for) indifference forces her to respond to the natural world and the social world alike with the energy of a mind determined to make the happiness she does not find.

She goes to the prince's birthday celebration and writes of it to her sister:

I was a *good foil* for those that were there. I never saw so much finery without any mixture of trumpery in my life. Lady Huntingdon's, as the most extraordinary, I must describe first: —her petticoat was black velvet embroidered with chenille, the pattern a *large stone vase* filled with *ramping flowers* that spread almost over a breadth of the petticoat from the bottom to the top; between each vase of flowers was a pattern of gold shells, and foliage embossed and most heavily rich; the gown was white satin embroidered also with chenille mixt with gold ornaments, *no vases* on the *sleeve*, but *two or three on the tail*; it was a most laboured piece of finery, the pattern much properer for a stucco staircase than the apparel of a lady, —a mere shadow that tottered under every step she took under the load. (Second Series 2: 28; 23 Jan. 1738–39)

A year later, at another social event, she makes another characteristic comment on clothes: "My Lord Baltimore was in light brown and silver, his coat lined *quite throughout* with ermine. His lady looked like a *frightened owl*, her locks strutted out and most furiously greased, or rather gummed and powdered" (Second Series 2: 72; 22 Jan. 1739–40).

Even the most high-minded eighteenth-century female correspondences—the letters of the Bluestockings, for instance—display a preoccupation with what other people wear. Clothing constituted an appropriate female concern. Not all letter writers, however, used their reports on costume as Delany does, to convey social and psychological judgment. Lord Baltimore, he of the ermine-lined coat, had courted Mary Delany when she was the widowed Mary Pendarves. Appearing about to come to the point of proposing, he instead found a pretext for anger, departed, and promptly married a richer woman: the frightened owl. Delany devises decorous expressions for her continuing anger, emphasizing Lord Baltimore's use of riches, his wife's tastelessness and unattractiveness. The vigor with which she describes Lady Huntingdon's stone vases, on the other hand, owes nothing to premeditated malice—although perhaps something to a sense of her own superior propriety in modest dress ("a *good foil* for those that were there"). The detailed description conveys the writer's delight in observation as well as pleasure in "the most extraordinary." Her sheer attentiveness embodies the incapacity for indifference she would later claim.

Many of Delany's letters include extended sequences about what people wear. As a subject for correspondence, women's dresses might appear unpromising. To contemplate Delany's epistolary achievement, however, reminds the reader that "subject" hardly determines literary effect. The quality of consciousness the writer brings to routine social and domestic life redeems the potentially boring, makes boredom a meaningless literary category.

Not, however, a necessarily meaningless category for experience. A woman's life, as Mary Granville, Mary Pendarves, and Mary Delany lived it, does not lack occupation, but its structure of external demands need not prove immediately entertaining.

> If it is possible for me to write next post I will; but I will give you a sketch of what I am to do, and then you may be judge how much time will lie upon my hands. We dine to-morrow with Sir John at Somerset House: at four o' the clock in the afternoon comes my lawyer and my taylor, two necessary animals. Next morning I send for Mrs. Woodfelds to alter my white tabby and my new clothes, and to take my black velvet to make; then comes Mrs. Boreau to clip my locks, then I dress to visit Lady Carteret, then I come home to dinner, then I drink coffee after dinner, then I go to see my niece Basset and Mrs. Livingstone, then *they reproach me*, then I give them as good as they bring, then we are *good friends again*, then I come back, then if it is a possible thing, I will write to mama, then sup and go to bed. (First Series 1: 123–24; To Anne Granville, 8 Nov. 1726)

The tone of impatience that marks this summary narrative suggests that its creator does not expect to enjoy the events she reports, although she knows they are unavoidable. As in her accounts of clothes, though, she transforms what she narrates by the energy of her language.

Later letters make it clear that Delany accepts the obligation to prevent her correspondence from sounding boring, whatever the nature of her experience. Writing to the Viscountess Andover (21 Jan. 1771), Delany, in her seventies, comments on the activities of women she sees in the social world.

> Pleasure, or rather vanity and folly, *run high*. Ladies lose *vast sums!* it answers their purpose by killing that which will kill them (*time*), little thinking of that bar where they must inevitably appear and be arraigned for *that murder!* It mortifies my sex's pride to see women *expose themselves* so much to the contempt of the men, over whom I think from nature and education, if they were just to their own dignity, they have so *many advantages!* and then men plead excuses women have nothing to do with, that they are necessarily from their situations and employments in life exposed to temptations. My dear Lady Andover, how I run on! But it is your own fault; why won't you come to town? Writing to a friend is so like conversation that one forgets that what will pass off tolerably well in talk, is dull and tedious on paper. Forgive my tediousness, I entreat. (Second Series 1: 326–27)

One may speculate that Delany's uneasiness derives as much from her subject matter as from her indulgence in a kind of stream of consciousness. She may wish to apologize not so much for tediousness as for presumption in claiming women's essential superiority to men. Still, her acknowledgment of the difference between conversation and writing implies her recognition of the need for artifice in correspondence. The point is important. Bruce Redford's study of eighteenth-century letter writers insists on the need to investigate the artificial components of the most "natural" seeming letters. Letters, Redford points out, create as well as reflect context. When the writer does both,

> the resulting artifact straddles the barrier between "fictive" and "natural" discourse, between "verbal artwork" and "event in nature." At its most successful, in fact, epistolary discourse accomplishes something even more inventive: it fashions a distinctive world at once internally consistent, vital, and self-supporting. (9)

What Redford calls "the complex interplay between the natural and the fictive" (13) may develop (so Delany's remark hints) out of the letter writer's desire to avoid the tedious. The writer must at the very least edit her material, convert the possible tedium of her life or her thoughts into a form that will engage her correspondent. Those effusions of the heart that Gisborne admired do not in uncensored form necessarily prove engaging.

As Delany aged, she became increasingly concerned that her letters might bore their recipients—even when what they relate does not even come close to boring her. In one amusing instance, she apologizes to her brother for a "tedious description" of a flower and in the same breath elaborates that description: "I wish my tedious description has not tired you, but I was so pleased with the flower, &c., I could not help communicating it: one extraordinary beauty I forgot, which is that the flower as it hangs down is *transparent*" (Second Series 1: 385; 17 Dec. 1771). She has learned how to prevent boredom in her own passing of time, but she fears others may not share her view of her experience.

> Now I know you smile, and say what can take up so much of A.D.'s [Aunt Delany's] time? No children to teach or play with; no house matters to torment her; no books to publish; no politicks to work her brains? All this is true, but *idleness never grew in my soil*, tho' I can't boast of any very useful employments, only such as keep me from being a burthen to my friends, and *banish the spleen*; and therefore, are *as important* for the present use as matters of a higher nature. (Second Series 2: 327; To her niece Mary Port, 20 Oct. 1777)

The dejection, gloom, and melancholy associated with "the spleen" are close neighbors to boredom. Delany's claim of constant activity, even at age seventy-seven, records an achievement of will. Her refusal of inertia, moral or physical, focuses the story she can tell of herself. The assertion that *"idleness never grew in my soil"* constitutes her fundamental claim of unified identity, the identity that makes and is made by the possibility of narrative. Many eighteenth-century female correspondences allow comparable interpretations. In the face of the encroaching boredom that even moral commentators considered a feminine danger, women committed to "virtue," unable and presumably unwilling to live out the fantasies novelists manufactured as alternatives to female tedium, finding conventional social life tiresome, intellectual conversation rarely available (and not necessarily pleasurable), and the display of "accomplishments" inadequate occupation, systematically created for themselves ways of escape. One source of interest in their letters derives from their records of escape.

Cause and effect intertwine in a reader's perception of these letters. Delany and others manifestly accept the obligation of keeping their own letters from tedium. Did they verbally construct their lives as interesting in order to make their letters so, or did the construction take place in action and perception, preceding the verbal record? In other words, did the process of creating narrative from experience manufacture the interest of that experience, or did the sense of value inhere in lived events, making it possible to devise story even from routine? The letters themselves do not unambiguously answer such questions. Reading the vast collection Delany produced, however, reveals her assertion—on the page, perhaps also in her day-to-day life—of three strategies for averting boredom.

The most insistent, reflected in the letter quoted above, is the valuing of activity. Everyone who has written about Delany has noted the furious pace of her productivity. Germaine Greer summarizes her astonishing range: "She worked at the making and sticking of pincushions, Japan-work, pastel portraits, copies of great masters, designs in shell-work, lustres, candelabra; cornices and friezes in cut-paper on wood, chenille work, cornices made of shells painted over like fine carving, upholstery, quilt-making, embroidery, cross-stitch carpets, miniature playing-card painting, chimney boards . . ." (291). Such endeavors obviously gave their maker pleasure in the doing and won her praise she enjoyed, in particular from her devoted second husband. The letters reveal that she also understood them quite consciously as a psychic resource, a bulwark against tedium. Writing to Mrs. Dewes (10 Nov. 1752) she reports: "I painted Wednesday, Thursday, and Friday, and part of Saturday, for Mr. Steward (to whom the Transfiguration belongs) is in great haste to have it home. They say I am going on very well with it, it amuses my thoughts, and gives me pleasant and comfortable ideas" (First Series 3: 175). To amuse one's thoughts and provide pleasant and comfortable ideas justifies activity.

Nothing in the tone of Delany's utterance suggests that she shares with Dr. Johnson the desperate need to have as many things as possible to which the mind can fly from itself. Her notion of action as protection against boredom, however, echoes Johnsonian injunctions. As Gray observed, it is easy for women to find things to do. Delany shows that females' finding of occupation may derive from accepting the responsibility—as Gray himself did not—to fill life with action. Her narratives of her own pursuits reveal her awareness that action matters because it helps the performer to construct her life as not only meaningful but "interesting." The quality of her activity's product is irrelevant. Delany claims no intrinsic value for the results of her labors, only for the process. Sometimes she worries about doing things primarily for her own psychic welfare. Thus, describing to her sister her procedures in fitting up a storeroom (6 Oct. 1750), she feels troubled about her ways of spending time:

> But trifling and insignificant is my *store-room* to what yours is! Mine fits only an idle mind that wants amusement; yours serves either to supply your hospitable table, or gives cordial and healing medicines to the poor and the sick. Your mind is ever turned to help, relieve, and bless your neighbours and acquaintance; whilst mine, I fear (however I may sometimes flatter myself that I have a contrary disposition), is *too much filled* with amusements of no real estimation; and when people commend any of my performances I feel a consciousness that my time might have been better employed. (First Series 2: 601)

Although Delany herself does good works on occasion ("after supper I make shirts and shifts for the poor naked wretches in the neighbourhood" [First Series 2: 362; To Mrs. Dewes, 11 June 1745]), she worries that "virtue" does not always occupy her.

Less troubling is her second major expedient for forestalling boredom: her reliance on friendship as psychological resource and moral bulwark.

> Three days together spent abroad is being a downright rake, but the sobriety of my own dwelling is much pleasanter to me than all the flirtations of the world; though the society of it I will always keep up to the *best of my power*, as it is a duty incumbent on us to live sociably, and it is necessary to keep up good humour and benevolence in ourselves, or the qualities of the heart contract and grow useless, as our limbs would do without any proper exercise. (First Series 2: 418; To Mrs. Dewes, 1 Feb. 1745–46)

To define as *duty* the exercise of friendship converts social life into moral necessity. But association with other people also provides a satisfaction that makes experience meaningful, as Mackenzie and Johnson knew. "The seal of all my pleasures," Delany writes her sister on 8 March 1750–51, "is communicating them to you" (First Series 3: 23). The energy and determination of her voluminous correspondence testify to the high value she places on intimate connection. To Mrs. Dewes she writes (13 Feb. 1745–46):

> The Dean has subscribed to some philosophical lectures, and they are to be three times a week for six weeks, which with my other employments will fill up my time pretty well; but no occupation shall interfere with my devoirs to my absent friends. I dedicate a certain portion of my time to them, and make my other engagements as much as possible subservient to that. (First Series 2: 422)

Eighteenth-century idiom made *friend* a synonym for *relative*. Delany, in her devotion to sister, niece, and great-niece, justifies the equivalence. But her correspondences with other women such as the duchess of Portland and Viscountess Andover also reveal how the act of communication to an intimate could add worth to every mundane occupation and feeling. Both the emotions of friendship and the conversion of experience to language that friendship demands or allows helped to generate the lasting interest of Delany's life (and, their correspondences suggest, of the lives of many female contemporaries). "The world is a *sort of julep*," Delany observes, "which sometimes may relieve, though not *cure* any complaint, as the true cordial drop in it is love and friendship" (First Series 3: 163; To Mrs. Dewes, 14 Oct. 1752). She drank heavily of the cordial.

Friendship made possible the deployment of a third resource against tedium, the articulation of ideas arrived at by personal reflection. Many eighteenth-records survive of women's anxiety that they might be known to indulge in intellectual pursuits. Burney, for instance, worried obsessively lest "the world" become aware of Dr. Johnson's project for teaching her Latin. Delany herself, at age thirty-eight, "had two or three lectures of cosmography in the library." When an unexpected visitor intruded, "I blushed and looked excessively silly to be caught in the fact, but the affair, which I have endeavoured to keep secret, is discovered, and I must bear the reflection of those who think me very presuming in *attempting to be wise*" (First Series 2: 19; To her sister, 22 Dec. 1738). To presume to male knowledge marked a woman as arrogant, noncompliant: well might she blush. Yet if women should not claim to *know*, they could not be prevented from *thinking*. Delany's letters reveal her pleasure in using her mind: not to display knowledge, but to indulge in sharp observation and speculation—often about men. For instance:

> Shall I devote my life, my heart, to a man, that after all my painful services will be glad of an opportunity to quarrel with me? What security have I, more than my neighbours, to defend me from this fate? I am frail, my temper is apt to be provoked, and *liberty of speech* all womankind has thought their privilege, and hard it is to be denied what has so long been allowed our prerogative; the greatest chance for avoiding the above-mentioned misfortune, will be choosing a man of sense and judgment. But there's the difficulty; *moneyed men* are most of them covetous, disagreeable wretches; *fine men* with titles and estates, are *coxcombs:* those of *real merit are seldom to be found.* (First Series 1: 204–5; To her sister, 1 Apr. 1729)

> [Of *Sir Charles Grandison*, a book she greatly admired:] I think [his having his daughters bred papists] . . . the only blot in Sir Charles's character. Had a woman written the story, she would have thought the *daughters of as much consequence as the sons* . . . ; but on the whole it is a most excellent book, calculated to please and improve all ages. (First Series 3: 257; To her sister, 21 Dec. 1753)

> You say true many are the rules given for women's behaviour in the married state, and *much* might be *addressed to the men;* but you can't expect they will do it by one another, and they would exert their lordliness, should we presume to prescribe to them. (First Series 3: 218; To Mrs. Dewes, 30 Mar. [1753])

She has a clear sense of assigned gender responsibilities, believing women by their nature suited for domestic tasks. This belief fosters a conviction of female superiority:

> I think of my journey cheerfully, and set about preparing for it *manfully! That* expression does *not suit the occasion*, for if *the men* were to go through all domestic bustle as we are obliged to do when we acquit ourselves properly, they would think themselves *somewhat obliged* by the trouble we *save them!* (First Series 2: 552; To Mrs. Dewes, 8 June 1750)

Respect for herself as a woman marks many of Delany's utterances. Although she sounds deferential toward her brother when she writes to him, her communications with others of her gender reveal a strong awareness of female solidarity, a high valuing of women's capacity, and even a tendency to deprecate men.

Delany recognized that her life might hold little interest for the spectator. Writing to her brother Bernard, she apologizes for its uneventfulness: "I can tell you no news; we are at a dead calm after our

stormy winter; a little rolling of the waters to a bystander is more amusing than gliding on so smoothly" (Second Series 1: 64; 3 July 1766).
Like her contemporaries among the novelists, she understood that the
ordinary course of female life ran too smooth to make compelling narrative. Yet she felt apparent contempt for those lacking the resource-
fulness to find interest in the pleasures of nature and in female occupations. To her niece, Mary Ann Port, she observes scornfully, "As to the
other guests they were in another strain: cards and china their idols;
and would you believe it, they could not find entertainment enough at
Bulstrode [the estate of the duchess of Portland] for *one evening* without
a pack of cards; and to prevent their ennui the Duchess and I were
obliged to make up a cribbidge party" (Second Series 1: 554; 1 Oct.
1773). Delany's letters show that she, like Johnson, believed everyone
was responsible for preventing her own ennui.

If occupation, friendship, and intellectual play made such prevention
possible for her, writing letters provided all three. The bulk of her correspondence attests to the time it must have taken. The content of that
correspondence affirms and reaffirms her close relationships and
demonstrates the freedom they provided for observation and speculation. Verbal freedom supplied the space that conventional restrictions
on conduct appeared to eliminate. The plot of Mary Delany's life, as
developed in her letters, lacks the excitement of Gothic or even sentimental novels. If her first marriage, with the jealous husband in effect
confining her to his bedside, provided potential material for sensation-
alism, her restrained accounts of it, even after the fact, emphasize her
determination to remain virtuous (not merely chaste, but "good") rather
than the luridness of her suffering. The happy widowhood, the happy
second marriage, as she narrates them, acquire value by proving devoid
of turmoil. The interest of the letters depends not on any overt "conflict of the mind," not on the rolling of the waters, but on the subtle
possibilities of what might seem to the observer "dead calm."

Yet to discover such possibilities raises far-reaching critical questions. If Delany manufactured the interest of her life by imposing on
her experience a personal and communal system of values that revealed
both its worth and its hidden variety, the twentieth-century reader who
asserts such interest performs her own constructions. Formal autobiography manifestly requires the excision and shaping that I spoke of at
the outset of this chapter as necessary to the effective narration of even
the most drama-filled life. Letters of course depend on their own exci-
sions: not even the intimate, continuous narratives that many eighteenth-century women provided for those closest to them constitute

total records of daily existence. On the other hand, like diaries, they often set down the trivial, and they often repeat themselves. Although letters to different recipients sometimes hold interest in the varying ways they tell a single story, often their accounts virtually duplicate one another. If a description of other women's clothes can on occasion convey complicated attitudes and assumptions, on other occasions such descriptions may register as relatively meaningless assemblages of detail. Seeing how linguistic, psychological, and social convictions, responses, and habits change or persist over long stretches of time holds considerable fascination—but to trace such transitions, the reader must plod through much language that does not immediately pronounce itself meaningful.

A collection of letters by its nature tells no determinate story. The story a critic discovers in it, she must also construct. No single recipient of the letters could have known that story, nor would it have belonged to the consciousness of a writer concerned in each letter with an individual relationship, a particular set of conditions. To see in Delany's letters the narrative of her refusal of boredom, her unearthing of interest in her own experience, to declare those letters paradigmatic of eighteenth-century female culture, exemplary in their mode of transforming the commonplace—to find such meanings calls attention to how the critic duplicates the letter writer's strategy. We too, in the acts of reading and of writing about reading, insist on unearthing interest. We too find the boring intolerable. And like Delany commenting about her fellow guests at Bulstrode, we condescend to those so blind as to believe that what interests us—in this instance, the six volumes of letters—has no power to engage. The critical act in its essence constitutes the refusal of boredom.

In a posthumous letter to her literary executor, Anna Seward announces that she is leaving him the exclusive copyright to twelve volumes. "They contain copies of letters, or of parts of letters, that, after I had written them, appeared to me worth the attention of the public" (Seward 1: vi). The letters, as one might expect, emphasize political, moral, and religious subjects and virtually ignore personal experience. Eighteenth-century readers apparently shared Seward's assumption that "deep" topics must be preferable to trivial ones. In the preface to a collection of Elizabeth Carter's letters to Elizabeth Montagu, the editor quotes an unnamed "literary friend," who observes of this correspondence,

> The latter Letters are, as might be expected, less interesting than the early
> ones. Old age, I presume, brought on a certain degree of languor; and
> induced the writer to fill up her pages more with common chit-chat, and to
> avoid the attempt to develope deep and interesting topics. What I consider
> most worthy of selection are opinions on books, life, and morals. (*Letters*, ed.
> Pennington xvi–xvii)

The justifications nineteenth-century editors found for printing collections of letters typically centered on the alleged value of the writer's
opinions and ideas. "Common chit-chat," however, now often appears
more revealing—as well as more entertaining—particularly when its
recorders reflect, directly or indirectly, on the value of what they
record.

"I shall be the heroine of my own story," Elizabeth Montagu writes
to the duchess of Portland, in a letter assigned no date but by its tone
and its placement in her collected letters apparently belonging to her
youth. "I have generally observed that the writers of memoirs remember nothing but themselves; thus, being very important to myself, and
insignificant to the rest of the world, I will proceed to write my own
history, and talk of myself rather than not be spoken of" (*Letters* 2: 98).
Despite her self-protective irony, the writer in a sense means exactly
what she says. She too will produce a voluminous assortment of letters,
through which she in effect writes her own history.

It is partly a history of her anxiety about boring others. Unlike
Delany, especially in her youth Montagu worries that her letters might
seem dull and suffers from the tedium of a life not fully chosen. At the
age of eighteen, she writes to the duchess,

> The surprising and entertaining incidents so frequent at Bulstrode, are so
> scarce at Mount Morris [her family home], that it is hardly possible to amass
> a parcel of circumstances together. Here we sleep with our forefathers, and
> all the acts that we do, which are to eat, drink, sleep, and die, are they not
> written in the book of the Chronicles! (*Letters* 1: 40; 17 Dec. 1738)

Two years later, to the same recipient, from Bath: "The waters employ
the morning, visits the afternoon, and we saunter away the evening in
great stupidity. I think no place can be less agreeable; How d'ye do? is
all one hears in the morning, and What is trumps? in the afternoon"
(*Letters* 1: 73; 27 Dec. 1740). The two kinds of complaint exemplified
by this passage, about the tedium of the country and of social life ("It
is a most unreasonable thing to give up all one's time to people one does
not like, merely because their footman brings one a card, and they light
ten candles instead of two" [*Letters* 2: 34; To Mrs. Donnellan, 2 Dec.

(year unspecified)]), recur in many letters until after her marriage. Montagu demonstrates that her life's monotony does not infect her consciousness. Declaring the freedom of her pen, she converts experienced tedium into verbal comedy—a short-term expedient also pursued by many of her contemporaries.

"Variety and change (except in a garden)," she writes to Gilbert West, "make the happiness of our lives" (*Letters* 3: 201; 26 Nov. 1752). She sees around her sufferers from ennui, although like Delany she seems to designate by that word a state readily alleviated by activity, which she believes is closely associated with virtue. On 1 January 1742, to Mrs. Donnellan, she observes,

> Every day ought to be considered as a period apart: some virtue should be exercised, some knowledge improved, and the value of happiness well understood; some pleasure comprehended in it; some duty to ourselves or others must be infringed if any of these things are neglected. Many look upon the present day as only the day before to-morrow, and wear it out with a weary impatience of its length. (*Letters* 2: 90)

Like Delany, and like many of her contemporaries, she considered existence an arena for moral exercise.

Necessary moral exercise included resisting boredom. "The polite world has no way of driving away l'ennui but by pleasure," she writes to Mrs. Donnellan (30 Dec. 1750); "we country gentlefolks know it may be banished by occupation" (*Letters* 3: 13). She finds it hard to understand why "any one will prefer a stupid companion to the converse of their own imagination," yet notes that some court the society of the insipid "rather than live in solitude." "For my own part," she concludes, "I am so happily partial to myself, that if I find I am tired of myself, I think it so strong a symptom of dulness, that I am for a time discouraged from producing myself to others" (*Letters* 2: 168–69; To Sarah Robinson, n.d.). For a time, happy in pregnancy, she believes that having a child will provide an unfailing source of interest. "Without the dearest concerns, life has no interesting scenes for us" (*Letters* 2: 239; To the duchess of Portland, 5 Dec. 1742). But the son she bears, and adores, soon dies, and she never has another. She resolves to find continuous interest in her life, fearing the ennui she sees about her at Tunbridge Wells ("the mental disease of idleness and inoccupation" [*Letters* 3: 121; To her husband, 1749]). Her increasing commitment to literary endeavor, culminating in her 1769 publication of *An Essay on the Writings and Genius of Shakespear*, provided the source of interest she sought.

Women, trained to please others, display constant anxiety about "entertaining" the recipients of their letters. Sarah Byng Osborn, whose letters reiterate the theme, appears to believe that only "news"—information about events of public interest—can make her letters worth reading. "I can send you no news from this place but what is in the public prints," she apologizes to her brother Robert (2 June 1722), "for I have no men belong to me, so of course can have no news that is authentic" (Osborn 8). Mary Lepel, Lady Hervey, writing to the Reverend Edmund Morris at the age of fifty-eight, apologizes, "As I am grown too old and too dull to afford you any amusement by my letters, but from the matters of fact I can transmit to you, I have hardly now any justifiable reason for writing to you" (Hervey 237–38). A woman had the obligation to make herself interesting. The contempt the notorious duchess of Marlborough expresses for Queen Anne focuses on the monarch's alleged inability to sustain entertaining conversation:

> Her conversation, which otherwise might have been enlivened by so great a memory, was only made the more empty and trifling by its chiefly turning upon *fashions* and rules of precedence, or observations upon the weather, or some such poor topics, without any variety or entertainment. Upon which account it was a sort of unhappiness to her that she naturally loved to have a great crowd come to her; for when they were come to Court, she never cared to have them come in to her, nor to go out herself to them, having little to say to them, but that it was either hot or cold; and little to enquire of them, but how long they had been in town, or the like weighty matters. (Marlborough 2: 119–20)

Even if she had to make something out of nothing ("I am so secluded from the world and all amusing subjects that, like the spider, I must spin out of my own bowels, and that is but a flimsy Manufacture at the best" [Anson and Anson 291; Hannah More to Mary Dickenson, 30 July 1788]), a woman should help keep the world interesting for others. As Dickenson confides to her diary, "I esteem'd it a mark of their affection to wish to have my company in preference to any other person; I endeavoured to amuse them & succeeded pretty well" (Anson and Anson 175).

Men, in the female view of things, allow themselves the indulgence of boring and being bored. Their narcissism incapacitates them from fulfilling the kind of responsibility that women assume for themselves:

> Every Man of high character for wit comes into company with an idea that he has that character to support, and therefore, if he does not feel himself unusually brilliant, is apt to become unusually dull, from sinking into a sort of ill humoured and hopeless silence. Whereas people of less name [including, presumably, virtually all women], not being burthened with any reputa-

tion to keep up, try to be as cheerful and as entertaining as they can, and often bring in a larger contribution to the general stock of pleasure, than persons whose name gives you a right to make larger demands on them. (Anson and Anson 117; Hannah More to Mary Dickenson, 18 June 1782)

Men, unlike women, feel themselves objects of public contemplation. Women, understanding the male need for external stimulation, tolerate men's tendency to lapse into boredom. Thus Lady Sarah Napier writes to her friend Lady Susan O'Brien about a dinner attended by Lady Susan's husband, who wishes to engage in some unspecified enterprise that his wife disapproves. Lady Sarah believes he should be encouraged: "It is rather a laudable than a wild scheeme for him to occupy his mind in some pursuit from which he secures the absence of *ennui*, a chance for fortune, & a certainty that if he *does* obtain any it will be in a pleasant way." She continues, to draw a contrast between male and female responses, "I don't say that I am of his opinion, for *I myself me*, should think myself perfectly content to be in his situation, viz, with a reasonable income & no children to provide for" (Lennox 2: 39; 10 Nov. 1783). Again, in an undated letter to the same recipient, she tells of a social evening in which her own husband played cribbage with his hostess,

& they seemed pleased to find a person ready to be usefull to them all; for, as young Mrs. Crewe says, there are so many men in these days who are *ennuyé* to death if they are not exactly in their own set, & at their own amusements, that a man who likes anything is quite a treasure in the country. (Lennox 2: 51).

For men, these observations suggest, boredom presents fewer or less intense moral risks than it offers women. The numerous passages I have cited from women's letters more often describe than name the state. One may speculate that the word *bore* and its cognates rarely appear not only because they had just recently entered the language but because the women writing feared, for moral reasons, to designate their condition in such terms. The case of Betsy Sheridan (described in the title of the modern edition of her letters to her sister as "Sheridan's sister": everyone knows who Sheridan is, but who knows Betsy?) is instructive. The published letters belong to four years. During most of this time Betsy, as the unmarried sister, took care of her ailing and apparently tyrannical father. She complains only indirectly, but she consistently relates details of a life characterized by deadly boredom:

Still the same old life—Airing—home and cards, not very enchanting but to say the truth I am not in spirits to enjoy any other. (LeFanu 45; 25 Apr.–3 May 1785)

> Apropos to Women our present set are as tiresome, as exacting, as prating, as observing, and as illnatured as one could wish. (74; 1–6 Oct. 1785)

> What you say respecting the fuel required by the mind no one feels more strongly than I do: mine is not only starved, but to use your own figure, overwhelm'd with Slack and choack'd with smoke (80; 21–23 Jan. 1786

> Mrs Paterson has been sending me cards and invitations, but when I have dullness without trouble I always give it the preference. (99; 11–16 Sept. 1786)

Meanwhile, she refers to the fact that other people bore her by trying to get her to influence her father (54), or describes a scene in which the duke of York and the prince of Wales "bore" her brother, the playwright Richard Brinsley Sheridan (138). She does not, however, directly assert that the routine of her dutiful life causes boredom or that anyone bores her except for the sake of her father.

On 4 July 1789, at the age of thirty-one, Betsy Sheridan married her brother-in-law, Henry LeFanu. Shortly thereafter, she received a visit from her "sentimental Cousin William Chamberlain." "He bored me so much on the subject of marriage and children, that recollecting that he acts as Surgeon and Accoucheur I was sure that his visit was intended in the fair way of trade and was heartily glad when he took his leave" (183; 20 Aug. 1789). A new assertiveness registers in her willingness to openly claim her boredom. The conduct-book writers accurately intuited the hidden aggression—every mother knows it—in proclamations of boredom. If women permitted themselves to find their mandated daily experience boring, they would by that recognition take one tiny step toward rebelling against the ordained. Sheridan's self-repression during the years of caring for her father derives partly from her sense of her own lack of social importance, almost of social identity. "I cannot make my Father feel the difference the world makes between a man of talents and the women of his Family unless these are at least independent [meaning, of course, financially independent]" (44; 8–14 Mar. 1785). Once married she acquired, in her own eyes and in the view of "the world," more social standing. She could let herself not only know but say that someone else bored her.

It would be wrong to say, on the evidence of surviving letters, that eighteenth-century women struggled with boredom. They would have articulated their struggle in other terms, as an effort to lead "good" lives. By that they would mean, of course, lives that conformed to their society's notions of female virtue. But they also evidently wished, perhaps less consciously, to retain their capacity to take pleasure in their own experience, and to judge that experience. Sometimes "goodness" and judgment might appear incompatible. Silence could seem to reconcile the two: a good woman kept her judgments to herself or confided them to her sister or her intimate friend. Thus Mary Dickenson comments to her diary on her success in entertaining a Mr. Pepys: "People that love to talk themselves require nothing more from one than a look of attention, the words `Yes' & `No,' a well timed smile, a grave face." Obviously troubled by the implications of her reflection, she manages to convert it to an injunction about ethical responsibility: "I detest *Art* of every kind, but it is a duty we owe Society to appear perfectly attentive to every one" (Anson and Anson 216; 10 July 1784).

Read from the perspective of two centuries later, however, much female musing over ethical responsibility turns in one way or another on questions of tedium. The moralists' anxiety that they would claim lack of occupation seems irrelevant to the women glimpsed in their letters. Most keep very busy indeed. But the nature of their activity, when it centers on social life, raises questions in their minds, and several of them appear conscious that they manufacture occupation to avoid tedium. If concentrating on the self is by definition boring, as these women believe; if social duties are a woman's central responsibility ("Remember we are creatures formed for Society & that we must not so wholly converse with old Authors, as to neglect the cheerful conversation of our acquaintance; too severe an application to study naturally gives the mind too serious a turn, & indisposes it for the Social duties of Life" [Anson and Anson 11; Mrs. Dickenson to her daughter Mary, age fifteen, 12 Nov. 1772]), one risks opprobrium from the self and from others by judging another boring. Yet one risks losing herself by refusing to assess experience.

Personal letters, in their assumed confidentiality, helped resolve the dilemma. To a trusted confidante, a woman might reveal uneasiness with the texture of her life, might hint negative judgments of others, might even reflect, if only indirectly, on herself. In such letters, women often appear to tell authentic stories of themselves. "To be the subject of a narrative that runs from one's birth to one's death is . . . to be accountable for the actions and experiences which compose a narratable life" (MacIntyre 202). Letters in their nature can neither begin with the birth nor end with the death of their creator. Yet they declare the existence of narratable life, and they demonstrate the accountability of their maker. The letters of eighteenth-century women, more specifically, show a set of devious ways to wrest meaning from the asserted boredom of their existence.

INTERLUDE

The Problem of the Interesting

Stating his objectives for *Lyrical Ballads* in the 1802 preface, William Wordsworth declares his intent to make the incidents and situations of common life "interesting by tracing in them, truly though not ostentatiously, the primary laws of our nature" (Wordsworth and Coleridge 238–39). His claim for "interest" in his work, however, appears to stimulate him to increasing defensiveness. Elaborating his purpose, he insists on "the general importance of the subject":

> The subject is indeed important! For the human mind is capable of being excited without the application of gross and violent stimulants; and he must have a very faint perception of its beauty and dignity who does not know this, and who does not further know, that one being is elevated above another, in proportion as he possesses this capability. . . . [A] multitude of causes, unknown to former times, are now acting with a combined force to blunt the discriminating powers of the mind, and unfitting it for all voluntary exertion to reduce it to a state of almost savage torpor. The most effective of these causes are the great national events which are daily taking place, and the encreasing accumulation of men in cities, where the uniformity of their occupations produces a craving for extraordinary incident, which the rapid communication of intelligence hourly gratifies. To this tendency of life and manners the literature and theatrical exhibitions of the country have conformed themselves. (242–43)

(Charles Bathurst, quoted in chapter 3, said it more economically: the taste for the horrible is the consciousness of the dull.)

Wordsworth's evident anxiety focuses on his perception that his contemporaries, failing to discriminate properly, find meretricious stimuli "interesting." Will they, then, agree with his judgment that the emotions of an idiot's mother warrant interest? Without assigning a term to interest's antithesis, the poet describes a dynamic of interest and boredom. Men restricted to tedious occupations seek excitement outside them. Publishers and producers try to gratify their desires. The writer who wishes to concern himself with "important" matters and to prove that the mind needs no "gross and violent stimulants" to maintain its concern with the operations of human nature risks boring his readers even as he insists on his capacity to interest them. And that risk matters to Wordsworth not only for reasons of vanity. In the *Lyrical Bal-*

lads preface, he tacitly and explicitly attempts to reclaim the social momentousness of the interesting, to make it a matter not of individual taste but of communal commitment.

The first two sentences of the Wordsworth passage suggest a provocative logic. The "for" beginning the second sentence declares a relation of causality between excitement and importance. What proves the importance of the subject, these sentences allege, is that it can excite people. In other words, excitement—but only certain kinds of excitement: those not dependent on "gross and violent stimulants"— implies importance. What is important is, or should be, interesting, Wordsworth implicitly argues, and conversely, what is interesting should be important. In effect he glosses the problematic status of the interesting as the eighteenth century turned into the nineteenth, and he struggles to preserve an old meaning of the word. According to the *Oxford English Dictionary, interest* derives from a Latin verb form meaning "it makes a difference, matters, is of importance." The original sense of *interesting,* now obsolete, centers on the idea of importance: "That concerns, touches, affects, or is of importance; important." More familiar to us now is the later meaning: "Adapted to excite interest; having the qualities which rouse curiosity, engage attention, or appeal to the emotions; of interest."

The first cited instance of the modern meaning dates from 1768; the last occurrence of the obsolete sense belongs to 1813. In the first decade of the nineteenth century, the word *interesting* would have reverberated with two significantly opposed meanings. The modern definition—"adapted to excite interest; having the qualities which . . . appeal to the emotions," and so on—designates a set of responses by the observer: interest, curiosity, attention, emotion. The older meaning implies more objectivity. Although importance, the crucial concept in the obsolete definition of *interesting,* may be subjectively designated, relatively impersonal criteria can be invoked for assessing it. An assumption of communal standards operates in the old definition: everyone is presumed to agree about the location of the important. The new meaning suggests individualism, centered on the uniqueness of every personal set of emotions. On the other hand, as Raymond Williams points out, the distinction is not always clear. "The problem is that the sense of objective concern and involvement . . . is not always easy to distinguish from . . . later more subjective and voluntary senses" (143). Moreover, in the old definition the idea of importance mingles with less dispassionate alternatives: "that concerns, touches, affects." And the relation among the concepts evoked remains problematic. Is something conceived as important *because* it concerns, touches, or affects? Is whatever touches and affects necessarily important? Or are the notions of the touching and of the important independent of one another? The newer definition of *interesting* avoids the difficulty by eliminating the notion of importance.

In the first years of the nineteenth century, a writer might invoke either sense of *interesting*. Wordsworth, for all the originality of his poetic project, finds it urgent to preserve the old meaning. As his indictment of modern taste reveals, he prefers old rural ways (around which a faint aura of mythologizing already clings) to new urban ones. Implicitly he attaches a moral imperative to the notion of interest. One *should* be interested in what he offers rather than in "frantic novels" or "idle and extravagant stories in verse" (243). Failure to respond to his text may imply human failure to respond to the needs and natures of others perceived as unlike the self. The idea of importance inherent in the old meaning of *interesting*, as I have already suggested, involves reliance on communal values—and Wordsworth proposes to reestablish ancient community.

—All of which implies the importance to the writer of *interesting* the readers of *Lyrical Ballads*. Why, then, does Wordsworth make certain poems so ostentatiously and insistently "uninteresting": linguistically flat, repetitive, commonplace? "The Idiot Boy," for instance, challenges the reader with its slow narrative and pedestrian language.

> He quite forgot his holly whip,
> And all his skill in horsemanship,
> Oh! happy, happy, happy John.
> (Wordsworth and Coleridge 88; lines 94–96)

> And Susan's growing worse and worse,
> And Betty's in a sad quandary;
> And then there's nobody to say
> If she must go or she must stay:
> —She's in a sad quandary.
> (91; lines 177–81)

Language, rhythm, subject all seem trivial. The poetic presentation supplies no obvious thrill. An arrogant writer flaunts his power over the reader and dares that reader to reject his offering. It would seem perverse to declare such verse *interesting*. One must wonder about the relation between the claims of the preface (written, of course, after the poetry) and the fact of the poem.

The interesting (in its modern version) and the boring imply one another. Without the concept of engagement, disengagement has no meaning. Interesting means not boring; the boring is the not interesting. The preface and the poems of *Lyrical Ballads* call attention to that reciprocal relationship and emphasize what is at stake in it. Other works of the same period do the same thing. Before discussing "The Idiot Boy" more fully, I shall take a long detour through *Sense and Sensibility*.

The first description of Marianne in Austen's novel includes this sentence: "She was generous, amiable, interesting: she was every thing but prudent" (Austen, *Sense* 6). In a list of qualities accorded or denied to the character, *interesting* has a curious ring. Unlike *generous, amiable,* or *prudent,* it sounds remarkably vague. Indeed, it hardly designates a property of personality. Rather, it calls attention to a way others respond. It sounds like one of Marianne's words, not an item in the vocabulary of Jane Austen's precise narrator.

Willoughby, it turns out, is also "interesting." In the two pages that introduce him after Marianne sprains her ankle and he rescues her, the adjective occurs twice and the noun *interest* once. This time the context provides clues about the concept's meaning. Willoughby's "interest" bears some relation to his age and appearance: "Had he been even old, ugly, and vulgar, the gratitude and kindness of Mrs. Dashwood would have been secured by any act of attention to her child; but the influence of youth, beauty, and elegance, gave an interest to the action which came home to her feelings" (42). The romantic rescuer becomes "still more interesting" because he departs "in the midst of a heavy rain" (42). As Marianne reflects about him and his actions, she concludes that "every circumstance belonging to him was interesting" (43). The specific circumstances mentioned include his name, his residence, and his shooting jacket. Clearly, the assignment of "interest" to Willoughby tells more about the assigners than about the object of their judgment. Indeed, "interesting" appears to mean something very like "answering to self-interest"—given a fairly subtle definition of self-interest.

The best that can be said for Edward Ferrars, Elinor's lover, as far as interest is concerned is that he "was no longer uninteresting when [Mrs. Dashwood] knew his heart to be warm and his temper affectionate" (17). Elinor beholds in Colonel Brandon "an object of interest" (50), but Marianne, denying him "genius, taste, [and] spirit" and adding that "his understanding has no brilliancy, his feelings no ardour, and his voice no expression" (51), does not concur. As for Elinor herself, the category seems not to apply: no one in the novel explicitly perceives her as either interesting or uninteresting.

The references to interest as attached to Willoughby, Brandon, and Edward emphasize the notion's subjectivity. Willoughby appears interesting to observers predisposed to value youth, beauty, elegance, unconventionality. Edward becomes not uninteresting when Mrs. Dashwood finds reason to interest herself in him. Brandon interests some and not others. Marianne, on the other hand, simply *is* interesting. And Elinor's degree of interest for others apparently does not merit comment.

New and old meanings of *interesting* jostle in *Sense and Sensibility*, on which Austen began work in 1797. (The novel appeared in 1811.) Marianne, representative of new ways of valuing feeling, believes herself sufficient standard of interest. Whatever interests her therefore becomes "interesting." For the narrator, on the other hand, as for Wordsworth, the idea of importance remains alive in the word. The novel raises the question of what constitutes importance, hence interest. In its wider exploration of the costs of subjectivity, *Sense and Sensibility* may make its readers realize the kind of loss involved in translating "interesting" only as "personally appealing."

The possibility of fusing the idea of the important, traditionally associated with the public realm, and that of the touching, a matter conventionally of private concern, calls to mind other sets of opposed assumptions—old versus new—that demanded reconciliation in the early nineteenth century. Public and private, reason and imagination, thought and feeling . . . sense and sensibility. The word *interesting* in effect miniaturizes a central issue of Austen's novel. Marianne, one might speculate, would want to appear "interesting," at least to people she values. *Pride and Prejudice* provides a retrospective gloss on her character in a critical comment Darcy makes about Bingley: "You are really proud of your defects in writing, because you consider them as proceeding from a rapidity of thought and carelessness of execution, which if not estimable, you think at least highly interesting" (48–49). Like Bingley, Marianne separates the "estimable" from the "interesting" and takes pride in being assigned the latter characteristic. Elinor, who wishes for herself moral significance, might prefer to be appreciated for such qualities as those Marianne acknowledges in Edward, without considering them "important": "I have the highest opinion in the world of his goodness and sense. I think him every thing that is worthy and amiable" (20). One can reformulate the obvious dynamic of the novel, the one readers have always seen, by saying that the book's pedagogy requires that Marianne make herself "interesting" in the old rather than the new sense of the word, intensifying qualities of moral "importance," and that Elinor should manage to embody more obviously, along with her uprightness, the "touching" or "affecting" aspects of the interesting.

Other dynamics implicit in *interest* as a word ("There is much that is obscure in the history of this word," the *OED* observes) also operate in Austen's novel. I have already mentioned the overtones of self-interest that cling around the initial uses of "interesting" in *Sense and Sensibility*. If the earliest sense of *interest* involved "the relation of being objectively concerned in something" (first cited from 1450), by the sixteenth century another meaning included "the relation of being concerned or affected in respect of advantage or detriment": in other words, self-interest. And the notion of advantage quickly focused on "esp. a pecuniary share or stake in or claim upon anything," the first cited instance of this meaning dating from 1674. In other words, money is at stake in certain assignments of "interest," quite apart from the word's most familiar economic meaning ("money paid for the use of money"). Although Austen rarely says so directly, she allows at least metaphoric hints of financial concern in characters' readiness to discriminate between the "interesting" and its alternatives. I have spoken of "value," of "costs," and of "loss" in relation to the issues Austen raises. Such language develops almost inevitably from the ambience of appraisal established by emphasis on the interesting.

Many readers find Elinor the reverse of interesting. In *Sense and Sensibility*, as later in *Mansfield Park*, Austen works to involve readers' feelings with a woman who might be called priggish. The novelist creates for herself a difficult challenge, confronting the reader with immediately engaging presences in Mary Crawford and Marianne, then severely chastising these figures and demanding her audience's assent to a higher valuation of their upright foils, Fanny Price and Elinor. The problem of the interesting, as it exists in *Sense and Sensibility* and *Mansfield Park*, centers on the issue of the appealing: How much worth should be assigned to it, how much value accrues as a result of it? Both novels constitute arguments that the appealing, never sufficient, must not be separated from the morally significant: the "important." The important manifests itself in small details of domestic life. Rightly understood, it may often also embody the appealing, but its emotional urgency does not always reveal itself plainly. The argument implicit in Austen's plots demands that readers interest themselves in Elinor as much as in Marianne, in Fanny more than in Mary, but the novels must draw on resources beyond rational argument to enforce the quality of interest. A kind of coercion comparable to that involved in bringing Marianne to accept Brandon works on the reader.

To formulate the patterning of sense and sensibility as a problem of the interesting calls attention to the fact that the matter, as a narrative issue, involves effects as well as causes, within and beyond the text. Since novelistic characters exist only as words on a page, absorbed into the consciousness of readers, the modification of Elinor's sense and of Marianne's sensibility takes place by virtue of a manipulated change in readers' perceptions. To call Marianne and Willoughby interesting at the outset and Edward "not uninteresting," to avoid the category altogether in relation to Elinor—this verbal arrangement corresponds to the initial impressions of most readers. The reader must learn to understand Elinor and Edward as interesting in a direct emotional sense (it's pretty hard with Edward!), Marianne as not only appealing but morally significant, Willoughby as neither "affecting" nor "important," and to concur with Elinor rather than Marianne (the unchastened Marianne) in judging Brandon. The narrator's maneuvers to this end constitute the novel.

Such a description of the novelistic enterprise calls to mind the novelist's primary obligation to interest readers. As Henry James perceived, the necessity to be interesting takes precedence over all other considerations in writing fiction. Readers' commitment to the text persists only while that text engages their interest. In demanding that we assess Elinor as interesting, the narrator risks her own status. At stake is the narrator's notion of the important and the affecting as well as ours. She demands that we move beyond a confined sense of self-interest, of response to what immediately engages our emotions. The vocabulary of interest in *Sense and Sensibility* urges readers toward a specific pattern of response. That response of "interest" involves both judgment and feeling, sense and sensibility: the fusion indicated by the early definition of *interesting*.

Although the novel typically uses *interesting* with overt or subtle emphasis on its subjectivity, it nonetheless often preserves the traditional overtones of "importance" as part of its meaning. When the narrator offers the judgment that compared with the repulsiveness of Lady Middleton's "cold insipidity . . . the gravity of Colonel Brandon, and even the boisterous mirth of Sir John and his mother-in-law was interesting" (34), the comment implies primarily the comparative attractiveness, for the Dashwood family and for the narrator, of both dignity and boisterousness over the insipidity that implicitly rejects human

contact. (Indeed, this insipidity finally is implicitly defined as the incapacity to take an interest in others. Elinor, in time of stress, takes comfort in her ability "to be sure of exciting no interest in *one* person at least
among their circle of friends" [215]: Lady Middleton's nature precludes
interest.) But the account of Elinor's self-control in not betraying to her
family her knowledge of Edward's engagement to another, and of what
that self-control conceals, emphasizes a different aspect of the term:
"Her thoughts could not be chained elsewhere; and the past and the
future, on a subject so interesting, must be before her, must force her
attention, and engross her memory, her reflection, and her fancy" (105).
The power to engross memory, reflection, and fancy belongs inherently
to the interesting, understood as the exciting, to return to
Wordsworth's perception, rather than merely the attractive—as that
which "must" preoccupy. In Lucy Steele's early youth, "simplicity . . .
might . . . have given an interesting character to her beauty" (140). That
is to say, her beauty might have seemed more significant because it
could be imagined as an emanation of character rather than partly a
product of artifice. Elinor introduces to Lucy the "interesting subject"
of her relation to Edward (145): the subject of primary emotional
importance to them both. The newspaper notice of the birth of a son
and heir to the Palmers constitutes "a very interesting and satisfactory
paragraph, at least to all those intimate connections who knew it
before" (246): the paragraph's importance depends on personal involvement. Mrs. Dashwood, in Elinor's view, "must always be carried away
by her imagination on any interesting subject" (336). Such is the nature
of the interesting: it stimulates the imagination as well as—or dangerously, instead of—the intellect.

The reader's education in the proper location of the interesting
derives partly from such varied uses of the word. If predisposition helps
to determine interest, accidental conjunctions shape it, and imagination intensifies it, then to direct its location from outside, as the novelistic narrator must try to do, involves many pitfalls. Yet these textual
instances of how the interesting is constituted contain implicit warn-
ings, moral directives to the reader. To contemplate Mrs. Dashwood's
far-fetched conclusions, to note the narrator's gentle irony at the
expense of those who consider the births and marriages of friends or
relatives the most interesting of all news, even perhaps to note the
intensity of Elinor's preoccupation with a depressed and self-absorbed
young man—such moments of consciousness may help keep us wary of
our own self-centered assignments of interest. The emphatic irony at
the expense of Marianne, who throws aside a book in order to engage

in "the more interesting employment of walking backwards and for-
wards across the room" (166), calls sharp attention to possibly ridiculous aspects of subjective definitions of the interesting.

During my freshman year in college, I learned from a revered English teacher that *interesting* is not a critical adjective, because it comments
on the reader's reaction rather than on any quality of the text under
consideration. For years I passed the dictum on to my own students,
circling the word in their essays. Only recently has it occurred to me
that perhaps *interesting* in fact *is*, or can be, a critical adjective: an adjective conveying a cultural as well as a personal situation. Relatively
rarely, in fact, does an individual's location of the interesting prove altogether idiosyncratic. When teenage mutant ninja turtles interest one
preadolescent, they turn out to interest many others. Marianne's tendency to allow herself idiosyncratic responses reveals what in her
requires rebuke.

The didactic effort of *Sense and Sensibility* involves trying to move its
readers toward communal, therefore weighty, definitions. Inasmuch as
the effort works successfully on late twentieth-century readers, it must
work against the insistent trivialization of the interesting. A student
passed on to me a newspaper clipping reporting the words of Rabbi A.
James Rudin: "'Interesting' is arguably the most damning word in the
English language. . . . Its use by a member of the congregation conceals
the real opinion: two thumbs down. . . . When applied to a sermon,
'interesting' often means, 'I had trouble staying awake'" ("Watch Sermon"). The word now in many contexts seems virtually noncommittal.
Austen claims commitment for it.

If the notion of the interesting, even in its older sense, never approx-
imates objectivity, it yet avoids solipsism by a discipline of sharing. The
vocabulary of that sentence—*discipline, sharing*—belongs to the kind of
moral lexicon that Elinor employs. Marianne accuses her of believing
that one should "be guided wholly by the opinion of other people," that
"our judgments were given us merely to be subservient to those of our
neighbours" (94). Elinor denies the charge, claiming that she has tried
to influence her sister's conduct, not her understanding. In fact Elinor's
advocacy of established norms of conduct reflects a faith in communal
standards that her creator appears to share, although aspects of Elinor's
behavior betray her own kind of solipsism. Like Marianne, although
relying on a very different rhetoric, Elinor separates herself from her
community. She does so by refusing to share her pain or to subject the
causer of that pain to external judgment. From one point of view, she
adopts a posture of moral heroism; from another, she displays emo-

tional insufficiency. Her defensive refusal to acknowledge vulnerability even after revealing her secret insists on her difference from those around her. As her mother says in another connection, "You are never like me, dear Elinor" (336). If her divergence from her mother marks Elinor's superiority, it also signals her isolation.

Thus preoccupied with her own concerns, as well as with her perceived obligations toward others, Elinor worries neither about being interesting herself nor about finding others so. She leaves such matters to her sister, who cares about them entirely too much. The novel's narrative presentation, however, reminds us that the category of "interest" presents itself as urgent for virtually everyone at some time or other. Sometimes "interest" clearly means self-interest, as when Mrs. Dashwood acts "against the interest of her own individual comfort" (213), Elinor reflects on how Lucy's "interest and her vanity . . . blind her" (238), Marianne praises Edward for his alleged willingness to act on generous principle "against his interest or pleasure" (244), Lucy perceives the "opportunity of being with Edward and his family" as "the most material to her interest" (254), Willoughby speaks of a relative "whose interest it was to deprive me of [my aunt's] favour" (321), and so on. Sometimes the word draws on its oldest recorded meaning ("the relation of being objectively concerned in something, by having a right or title to, a claim upon, or a share in"). Colonel Brandon's "interest" must facilitate a group's admission to an estate (62); Lucy appeals to Elinor's "interest" to procure a living for Edward (149); Colonel Brandon's "interest" actually provides such a living (284).

More often, though, it appears part of the nature of "interest" to direct attention outward: Lady Middleton's incapacity for interest makes the point negatively. Edward's mother wishes "to interest him in political concerns" (16)—or in just about *anything*, but Edward's resolute depression makes him refuse interest. Even Mrs. Dashwood thinks he "would be a happier man" if he had any profession to "give an interest to [his] plans and actions" (102). The sign of his beginning to cheer up when he visits the Dashwoods is that "his interest in their welfare again became perceptible" (90). To see a mansion that slightly resembles Norland interests the imagination of the Dashwood sisters (40). Mrs. Jennings "takes a very lively interest in all the comings and goings of all [her] acquaintance" (70). Elinor, in distress, "appeared to interest herself almost as much as ever in the general concerns of the family" (104). Elinor and Brandon, preoccupied with other matters, talk to one another "with very little interest on either side" (162) because they feel unable to attend to concerns outside themselves. Elinor reminds Marianne of the painful difficulty with which she has tried "to appear indifferent where I have been most deeply interested" (264). In all these instances, and in many others, involvement with a world beyond the self inheres in the idea of interest. Edward's temporary and Lady Middleton's permanent inability to feel interest in external matters suggest moral inadequacy, as does Marianne's unwillingness to interest herself in anything except her own immediate gratification. Elinor reminds her sister, who complains about the tedium of the Middletons' parties, that "the alteration is not in them, if their parties are grown tedious and dull" (109). The alteration in Marianne that makes her perceive these parties as boring depends on her inability to direct interest toward anyone but Willoughby, a narcissistic extension of herself, whose opinions and emotions duplicate hers in all respects.

Edward's situation suggests the possibility of salvation through interest directed outward. Elinor accepts for herself a discipline of interest. She will go through the motions of finding the world interesting even when her true attention focuses within. Marianne signals her reform by a determination to interest herself in pursuits unrelated to immediate emotional needs. Both postures of interest and failures of interest acknowledge the importance of commitments beyond the self.

Despite the abstract nouns of its title, *Sense and Sensibility* concerns itself more with assessing character than with judging qualities. It raises the issue of how we are to come to terms with the particular minglings of sense and sensibility in each of the Dashwood sisters more loudly than it announces the less compelling question of how we should judge the value of the abstractions themselves. The narrator encourages partial mistakes—encourages us to think Marianne more frivolous, Elinor more rational than they prove to be, guided by what she makes the characters say of themselves.

Of course the narrative action convinces us that these young women have changed in the course of events. When Elinor has her solitary encounter with Willoughby, who has come to justify himself before Marianne dies, she finds him, temporarily, far more "interesting" than she or the reader is likely finally to judge him. Willoughby reveals himself at last as a walking cliché, with his toasts to Mrs. Brandon and his attention to horses and dogs and "sporting of every kind" (379). Like the Middletons' parties, he becomes dull when the protagonists, and the reader, no longer have reason to be interested in him. The point is not that *he* has changed, but that *we* have. I am not sure that Elinor changes either. In narrating the meeting with Willoughby, the storyteller chooses to reveal new aspects of her personality. When she bursts into uncontrollable tears at the news that Edward Ferrars remains free, we see something new about her. But in fact we have been told from the beginning that she has strong feelings, as we are told that Marianne is "sensible" (6). The evidence of Marianne's sense and of Elinor's sensibility is a long time coming, and to the end Marianne remains extravagant in her sense and Elinor restrained in her sensibility. The description of Elinor at the outset remains precisely applicable in the conclusion: "Her disposition was affectionate, and her feelings were strong; but she knew how to govern them" (6). Her rigid self-government long makes her appear monochromatic: she does not arouse curiosity because she does not reveal complexity. Like her mother and sister, though, the reader comes finally to understand more fully the strength of her feelings and their importance to her, her defensiveness and her vulnerability. She forthwith becomes more "interesting."

As for Marianne, she of course undergoes one of those wrenching ordeals of self-realization and self-castigation that abound in Austen's novels. No longer can one say of her that "her sorrows, her joys, could have no moderation" (6), since, punished for emotional extravagance by desperate illness, she has learned as a consequence to moderate at least the expression of her feelings. But she persists in showing herself "eager in every thing" (6), and we are allowed to wonder about the persistence of her moderation. Less engaging than before in her chastened condition, she demonstrates through it at least a temporary capacity to claim moral significance.

That is to say, the narrator manipulates created evidence to make readers perceive both Marianne and Elinor in new ways. The process by which Austen's storyteller sets out to interest her audience is that of changing their assignment of interest to the Dashwood sisters. The change occurs because we have been made to pay attention, in subtle and detailed ways. To *pay* attention: a metaphor of economic exchange that reminds us once more of the process of evaluation going on. Paying attention provides the foundation for the interesting because it enables us to measure value. Marianne's unwillingness to accord genuine attention to Sir John Middleton or to Mrs. Jennings, for instance, prevents her from seeing what virtues they embody, what interest they may provide. Conversely, Elinor's attentiveness to Colonel Brandon first hints the possibility that even he may prove "interesting."

Lucy's actions and her marital and financial success, the narrator observes, "may be held forth as a most encouraging instance of what an earnest, an unceasing attention to self-interest . . . will do in securing every advantage of fortune, with no other sacrifice than that of time and conscience" (376). Attention to the self and its interests in Lucy appears unambiguously reprehensible, partly because of the literal concern for material gain implicit in it. Both Marianne and Willoughby, however, through much of the narrative manifest the same focus of attention, in their narcissism demonstrating a kind of spiritual economics comparable to Lucy's materialistic equivalent. They too concern themselves with gain: with emotional aggrandizement. They too fail to think of the possible effects on others.

But Marianne, at least, finally learns the alternative to self-interest, with its obsessive focus: she commits herself to the attention outward that makes the world more interesting, in the old rather than only the new sense. By paying attention, characters within Austen's narrative come to perceive the importance as well as the appeal of other people. By paying attention, the posture to which novel reading compels us, we the readers learn to find those invented characters interesting: to take seriously the variety of human possibility, to discriminate between the trivial and the important, to allow our emotions to involve themselves with fictional personalities. Austen provides in *Sense and Sensibility* a detailed and provocative pedagogy of the interesting.

This circuitous path leads back to "The Idiot Boy," manifestation of a pedagogical project similar in some respects to Austen's. Unlike Austen, Wordsworth invokes no abstractions, not even that of "interest." Believing that "Our meddling intellect / Misshapes the beauteous forms of things" (Wordsworth and Coleridge 105; "The Tables Turned," lines 26–27), he attempts to educate the reader in the proper locations of the interesting by means not of rational process but of emotional insight. To receive this education, the reader must cultivate "a wise passiveness" (103; "Expostulation and Reply" 24) toward the text as toward the natural world, rather than the linguistic and psychological alertness that Austen demands. Wordsworth invites his reader to trace "the maternal passion through many of its more subtle windings" (241). Such tracing demands its own kind of alertness to understatement ("Betty is not quite at ease" [91; 165), partial articulations ("And how she ran, and how she walked, / And all that to herself she talked, / Would surely be a tedious tale" [92; 214–16]), and fatuous summary ("She's happy here, she's happy there, / She is uneasy every where" [99; 399–400]). It requires that the reader cultivate a large sympathy, sharing the poet's stated assumption that in "low and rustic life . . . the essential passions of the heart find a better soil in which they can attain their maturity, are less under restraint, and speak a plainer and more emphatic language" (239). To an unsympathetic reader, the plainness of the poem's language ("She's happy here, she's happy there") may detract from the emphasis. In such a case, Wordsworth would say, the failure lies in the reader, not in the text. Only a vitiated taste would wish that "the Poet interweave any foreign splendour of his own with that which the passion naturally suggests" (249). The pleasure that the poems aspire to create "must depend entirely on just notions" about the subject of poetic language (249). Lacking such notions, a prospective reader hardly merits the poet's concern.

On the other hand, such poems as "The Idiot Boy" set out to create the taste by which they are to be appreciated. The kind of "taste" required involves more than a sense of immediate aesthetic preference. It must include a quality of moral perception derived from emotional responsiveness. Austen appears to assume that her readers will pay sufficient attention to the text to follow the logic of her moral discriminations. Wordsworth implicitly considers sympathy the necessary concomitant of attentiveness. The sympathetic reader will readily respond to the inarticulate and unarticulated. When Betty Foy pats her son's pony, having found her idiot boy after fearing him lost, she thereby expresses transcendent joy. "She pats the pony, where or when / She knows not, happy Betty Foy!" (99; 402–03): only the exclamation point calls attention to the emotional intensity conveyed by a commonplace act. When the poem's speaker observes, as Betty waits for her son's return, "But yet I guess that now and then / With Betty all was not so well" (90; 147–48), he hints the depth of maternal concentration on the beloved absent child: the mother starts worrying almost as soon as the child leaves. When the narrator confesses his own inability to report Johnny's "adventures," he declares the inadequacy of poetry to render the idiot's experience:

> Oh gentle muses! is this kind?
> Why will ye thus my suit repel?
> Why of your further aid bereave me?
> (97; 352–54)

At the same time, he demands the reader's imaginative participation in the power of the inexpressible. Readers who work at it, the implicit promise has it, can enrich their emotional lives—in a literary version of Marianne's self-aggrandizement—by partaking of the feelings of those who typically go unnoticed. In effect, the reader must reinvent experience too subtle for poetic rendition.

The poem pursues aggressive tactics. Wordsworth's insistence on subject matter not merely "ordinary" but faintly repellent—we conventionally recoil from idiots, whose "otherness" threatens our ordinary assumptions about the human—urges us in directions we may not want to go. The poet is deliberately and self-righteously outrageous in his rejection of the intellectual, his insistence on value located in commonplace, even "subnormal" people. He challenges the reader to feel interested in the emotions of a minimally verbal mother and a nonverbal boy. Despite his refusal of abstractions, he pursues more ostentatiously and consistently than Austen a severe pedagogical agenda that redirects assignment of "interest."

The poetic enterprise of *Lyrical Ballads* absolutely rejects the subjectivity of the interesting. Inasmuch as these poems aspire to educate their readers in the relocation of interest, they insist that all human beings share the same capacity and should feel the same responses. When interest becomes a moral category, as for Wordsworth it does, it loses its aspect of possibly casual preference and proves itself urgent. In Wordsworth's conception there is no ambiguity about the relation between the "touching" and the "important." What is genuinely touching must therefore be important. Or perhaps more accurately, what should be touching should also be acknowledged as important. The cultural significance of Wordsworth's program derives partly from its insistence on community of value, its rejection of the notion that "interest" depends on individual disposition. Communal values alone allow the possibility of transcending the self-interest that taints more subjective definitions of the interesting.

My purpose is not to defend such poems as "The Idiot Boy." As a matter of fact, I dislike that particular poem. It doesn't interest me. I find it boring. An incorrigible left-brain type, I am persuaded by Austen's meticulous discriminations but remain recalcitrant to Wordsworth's pedagogy of sympathy. I can enjoy talking about "The Idiot Boy," arguing about it, even teaching it (the critical act, as I have suggested before, involves our pleasure—our *interest*—in the sound of our own voices). I understand what Wordsworth is getting at and why that matters—it just doesn't grab me.

The possibility of my saying (and feeling, believing) such things calls attention to a problem hinted by Wordsworth's preface to *Lyrical Ballads* and crucial to this book. The doubt that comes to Wordsworth even as he asserts his faith in the beauty and dignity of the human mind reflects his consciousness of inescapable subjectivity, the subjectivity of others. Even his formulation of the mind's capacity for noble excitement betrays doubt, as he acknowledges that others may not "know" what he knows. The craving for base forms of excitement that characterizes his contemporaries cannot be controlled. He may urge his readers toward nobler possibilities, but he cannot make them drink. When, two paragraphs back, I changed "is" to "should" ("What is genuinely touching must therefore be important. Or perhaps more accurately, what should be touching should also be acknowledged as important"), I attempted to replicate Wordsworth's uncertainty. He understands the proper relation between the touching and the important, the relation once contained in the word *interesting*. But he cannot guarantee that others will accept the tie the word conveyed. By the beginning of the nineteenth century, *interesting* had split one meaning from the other. The word that traditionally conveyed precisely the union Wordsworth wishes to enforce now expresses the possibility of unregulated personal response.

When Fielding and Sterne, in their narratorial personae, articulated concern about readers' potential nonacceptance, they worried about those readers' judgment, not about emotional rejection based on some transitory psychic state. You can argue with judgment. You can *judge* it. But there's no arguing with the awful and absolute authority of boredom. If I declare "The Idiot Boy" boring, no one can refute me. It may not bore *you*, but your arguments about its complexity, its importance, its depth of implication can no more change my emotional response than your explanation of how funny a cartoon is can make me laugh.

The uncertainties of modern consciousness (a kind of consciousness apparent in Wordsworth's preface) derive partly from awareness of multiple, multiplying, uncontrollable individual sensibilities. It is the heroic enterprise of poems like "The Idiot Boy" to withstand multiplicity by entering into a kind of detail that demands the reader explore unfamiliar emotional territory and declares that territory's common interest. Bits of uncertainty manifest themselves: moments of coyness and cuteness, like the invocation of the muse, that suggest the author is conscious of strain. Yet his serious effort persists. If *Sense and Sensibility* shows the cost involved in separating appeal from significance, "The Idiot Boy" tries to insist on the gain inherent in discovering at once the importance and the emotional energy of the ordinary. One can admire the undertaking—although the literary history of the next two centuries would reveal its futility, as wide shifts of taste demonstrated the final impossibility of controlling an audience's assignment of interest.

FIVE

"A Dull Book Is Easily Renounced"

How the Interesting Turns Boring

The shift in taste by which the interesting—a work engaging to so many that "interesting," even in the modern sense, appears to constitute an objective description—becomes in a precisely equivalent sense the boring provides a focus for interrogating more fully the meaning of boredom as a cultural construct. At its own historical moment, *Sir Charles Grandison* seemed attractive; now most readers find it dull. That within the past decade or so critical interest in Samuel Richardson's final novel has heightened once more only underlines the truth that our constructions of interest or its opposite depend not just on individual mood or taste but on widely shared systems of assumption and conviction. What is at stake in cultural oscillations of interest? How, exactly, *can* an "interesting" book become "boring"?

My three test cases in this chapter—*Grandison, Coelebs in Search of a Wife, Robert Elsmere*—share a common preoccupation with the didactic. All employ fiction to inculcate moral or theological doctrine; all may therefore provoke premonitory yawns. Many readers have yawned over each of them—although at the time of first publication all these books attracted wide enthusiasm. As J. Paul Hunter observes,

> The difficulty [didactic] focus has caused for modern readers is hard to calculate and almost impossible to exaggerate. The trouble is that readers of our time are not comfortable with such content, such aims, or the tones that support them. . . . All "period" literature —that is, any text that is firmly anchored in some historical present—sooner or later becomes problematic for subsequent readers with different knowledge and different needs, but modern and post-modern contexts of reading present special difficulties for certain traditional modes of writing. (225)

Yet we do not automatically deplore the didactic: only such forms of didacticism as Hunter alludes to, those peculiar to distant historical moments. Instructional books fill best-seller lists of the 1990s, telling us how to lose weight, how to make a million dollars in real estate, how to heal our ailments with home remedies, how to become more assertive, how to find love. Not the fact but the nature of old didacticisms offends us. Offends us? These didacticisms *bore* us: we dismiss them.

What bores us never fully engages our attention. Yet boredom, as psychoanalysts have suggested, often contains hidden overtones of aggression. (Remember Otto Fenichel, puzzling over the difficulty of predicting "when a frustrating external world will mobilize aggressiveness in the subject, . . . and when it will be experienced as 'boring'" [301].) If one takes seriously the charge that a book is boring—meaning that it bores many of its readers—it would seem appropriate to seek what frustrations the book induces, what aggressiveness it may release in its readers.

Such terminology makes no obvious sense in relation to the novels I have mentioned. What in the detailed record of a good man's travails while deciding whom to marry could possibly provoke aggressive feelings or more than trivial frustration? The utter irrelevance to the modern or postmodern situation of *Grandison* and *Coelebs* and *Elsmere* seems the most obvious reason to label them "boring." But Hunter remarks the tendency of early didactic novels "to pursue readers and pry into their private commitments" (225), and such a tendency has manifest potential for generating disturbance. To proclaim works boring evades pursuit—but the irrelevance of those works may be more apparent than real.

In trying to suggest what may have made three outmoded novels "interesting" to their first readers, I hope simultaneously to discover why later audiences should dismiss them as "boring": to locate ways their "prying" may challenge our vital assumptions as well as ways the seriousness of their engagement has become invisible. My argument will involve issues of legibility and of urgency. I shall contend that these novels, offering covert as well as overt didactic messages, raise questions of how they should be read as well as unanswerable ones about how they actually *were* read. In what ways has their legibility altered?

Early in volume 2 of *Sir Charles Grandison* (1753), Harriet Byron reports to her confidante, Lucy, Lady L's retrospective narrative of her own marriage and its preamble. By this point in the text, Richardson's famous technique of "writing to the moment" has oddly changed. Harriet writes not to the moment of her own direct experience, but to that of someone else's narration of long-past experience. Lady L has an "interesting story," so Harriet will pass it on. Not, perhaps, without a qualm. She pauses to justify her long secondhand narrative:

> I thought, my Lucy, that the conversation I have attempted to give, wou'd not, tho' long, appear tedious to you; being upon a *new* subject, the behaviour of a free-liver of a father to his grown-up daughters, when they came to have expectations on him, which he was not disposed to answer; and the rather, as it might serve to strengthen us, who have had in our family none but good men . . . in our resolution to reject the suits of libertine men by a stronger motive even than *for our own sakes.* . . . I am sure, my grandmamma, and my aunt Selby, will be pleased with it; because it will be a good supplement to the lessons they have constantly inculcated upon us, against that narrow-hearted race of men, who live only for the gratification of their own appetites. (2:348–49; letter 18)

The justification of narrative lies in its putative didactic effect, but its presumed interest (it will not, Harriet thinks, appear tedious) depends also on its novelty. Both points apply equally well to the whole long novel, which heavily insists on its own moral purposes and claims novelty in the very conception of the "good man" as hero. Ideally, the fiction of the good man (a fiction about such a man and presumably *by* another) will strengthen its readers by giving them knowledge they cannot gain firsthand, as Lucy and Harriet, with "none but good men" in their family, learn usefully about bad men by hearing other women's stories.

The requirements for "interesting" fiction implied by the lines quoted bear little relation to those a twentieth-century reader might posit. They suggest clearly conceived but alien functions for "character" in the novel. The bad man of Harriet's story, the good man of Richardson's, alike stand in for the "race" of their kind. Their individuality hardly matters. Their "personality" bears lightly on their narrative function. Their moral rather than their psychological natures define their importance. One of the author's female correspondents complains that the men she meets do not resemble Grandison: "Ah! Mr. Richardson, that Sir Charles puts one sadly out of conceit with the ordinary kind of people one meets with; indeed you should not tantalize one with such a pattern, unless you intend to make two or three dozen men by it for the use of your friends, whose tastes you have spoiled" (Richardson, *Correspondence* 4: 131; From Al. Sutton, 26 Oct. 1751). Recognizing Richardson's character as a "pattern," she objects not to that character's lack of realistic specificity but to the failure of actual men to conform to his type. Like Harriet herself, Miss Sutton assumes that effective narrative provides models rather than imitations of life.

Richardson figures in conventional literary histories as a contrast to Fielding, partly because he concerns himself with the inner experience of his characters whereas Fielding dwells more insistently on the external. But that is the Richardson of *Pamela* and especially of *Clarissa*. The Richardson of *Sir Charles Grandison* assigns his characters emphatic internal conflicts: Sir Charles must decide what to do when he loves one woman and is committed to marry another (really, though, he loves them both); Harriet must suffer her apparently unrequited love for Sir Charles. But the novel dwells so little on the intimate dynamics of these conflicts that one hardly believes in them. Instead, it focuses on the moral implications of how each character confronts adversity, on the complexities of their moral, not their psychological, makeup.

These aspects of the novel seem readily to account for why twentieth-century readers, until recently, have found Richardson's final novel boring. On the other hand, the same characteristics made the book enthralling to its earliest readers. Thomas Edwards, for instance, writing to Richardson, speaks of Sir Charles in extravagant terms that clearly locate the book's interest in its protagonist:

> He whom I called in for an ally became my master, and made me spend with him every leisure hour I could command, till I had again gone through the five books; and had they been fifteen, I must have done so. . . . He shall be my master; and it will be my own very great fault, if I am not better for his lessons to the last day of my life. (Richardson, *Correspondence* 3: 71; 28 Jan. 1754).

Edward Young describes the moral effect of the novel in yet more exalted language:

> When the pulpit fails, other expedients are necessary. I look on you as a peculiar instrument of Providence, adjusted to the peculiar exigence of the times; in which all would be *fine gentlemen*, and only are at a loss to know what that means. While they read, perhaps, from pure vanity, they do not read in vain; and are betrayed into benefit, while mere amusement is their pursuit. I speak this not at a venture; I am so happy as already to have had proofs of what I say. (Richardson, *Correspondence* 2: 33; 14 Mar. 1754)

The drama implicit in the playing out of moral identity, the drama Edwards and Young respond to, no longer grips a great many readers. Eighteenth-century audiences thought the Clementina plot thrilling; the graduate students who read *Sir Charles* with me find the Italian scenes tedious. Only if—as in Jane Austen and Henry James—moral drama enacts itself in psychological terms do most readers trained by nineteenth-century fiction experience the drama's force. The breathless attention of an earlier audience testifies to their different response.

But more is at stake here than a modern preference for the psychological over the moral. As I have already hinted, I suspect that "boredom" with a novel like *Grandison* guards against a threat the work covertly offers. More profound than the novel's commitment to its predictable notion of "goodness," more potent—if also rather more concealed—even than its vivid repudiation of libertinism, is its endorsement of an idea of community now both alien and challenging. That endorsement expresses itself in the novel's structure as well as its substance. It explains why it hardly matters whom Sir Charles marries, and why it matters so much. It exposes a crucial difference between mid-eighteenth-century and late twentieth-century readers.

The passage quoted above, in which Harriet explains the moral significance of the story she has just told, inhabits a long scene of narration. Sir Charles's two sisters solidify their developing relationship with Harriet by telling her stories of their experience. Three women sit together; two of them tell stories to a third. The third woman tells those stories again to a fourth, her cousin Lucy. Lucy reads Harriet's letters aloud to the assembled family. In other words, the epistolary structure of the novel, which in *Clarissa* reflected intricacies of intimate relationship, here speaks less of dyadic links than of ever enlarging fellowship. The novel's insistence on community, as immediate pleasure, as standard of conduct, and as glimmering ideal, probably supplied much of its interest to an immediate audience—and much of its ethical force, that force now so difficult to recapture.

In one of his innumerable self-justifications and self-explanations, Richardson wrote a short preface to *Grandison*. In it he explicitly claims the work's interest and links that interest to its length: "Mere Facts and Characters might be comprised in a much smaller Compass: But, would they be equally interesting?" (4). What, he maintains, "will enliven as well as instruct" is "the Variety of Characters and Conversations necessarily introduced into so large a Correspondence" (4). Richardson's vision of *concordia discors* differs from Pope's, for instance, in centering solely on the human. The variety of characters and conversations a novelist can evoke acquires value by constituting a single whole that forms a moral model. The individual human being must learn not only to contain harmoniously all conflicting impulses but also to accept the responsibility to function as part of larger groups whose harmony is perpetually threatened. Grandison and Harriet appear to know these truths instinctually, but even they must learn the complexities of how to put them into practice.

The subject of interest has led me back to didacticism. For Richardson—though perhaps less for his audience—the two remain inseparable: what instructs will also enliven. We in the late twentieth century may assume that a spoonful of sugar makes the medicine go down, that the novelist conceives his message and then invents engaging characters and happenings to make that message palatable. But Harriet's apologia for her long secondhand narrative reveals different assumptions. She expects that her tale will not seem tedious specifically *because of* its generalizable moral implications. Lucy will enjoy it because it warns against libertines, not because it contains any suspense or reveals characterological intricacy. Reading the story (and for Harriet, writing it) will help to affirm the community of the good by restating the assumptions that community lives by.

General truths evoke interest. Thus Grandison's characterization depends on reiteration of moral generalizations about his nature: he remains unfailingly brave, magnanimous, pious, and so on. Richardson's original readers thought it good for them to read about him. They eagerly awaited the book because they anticipated its dramatic presentation of the male counterpart to Clarissa. But that they actually liked it less than they liked *Clarissa* suggests that already, by the mid-eighteenth century, "interest" no longer resided dependably in the moral and the general. Clementina and her story of pathos engaged the audience far more intensely than did Grandison's predictable manifestations of virtue. Clementina too embodies high nobility—but like Clarissa, she also plays out a story of generational conflict with erotic overtones. Yet if one may suspect the widespread interest in Clementina of originating in less high-minded impulses than the desire to improve moral character, it yet remains true that Richardson's representation of her clearly participates in the same program as his depiction of Grandison. Not, of course, that Clementina constitutes an equivalent model of perfection (although we are told repeatedly of her extraordinary piety and virtue). But her story, like Sir Charles's, enforces the value of community and merges didacticism with entertainment.

At several points in the novel, characters announce directly what I take to be Richardson's "program." "We never, I believe," Charlotte observes, "*properly* feel for others, what does not touch ourselves" (2: 334; letter 16). Sir Charles changes the issue from feeling to judgment: "No one can judge of another, that cannot be that very other in imagination, when he takes the judgment-seat" (2: 365; letter 20). Although the brother and sister start from opposite points, Charlotte taking the self as touchstone, Charles privileging the other, both speak for the power and the propriety of emotional identification. The effort to create such identification—to touch readers' selves, thus making them feel for others, to convert the reader to another "in imagination"—permeates *Sir Charles Grandison.*

The Clementina story dramatizes this effort most vividly. At a characteristic moment, the servant Camilla runs to Clementina's mother. "—O madam! it seems she said—*Such* a scene! Hasten, hasten up. They will faint in each other's arms. Virtuous Love! How great is thy glory!" (5: 568; letter 24). *Such* a scene! —the scene of intense sensibility. One may recall Charlotte's wedding day, when everyone weeps over Sir Charles's generosity and Harriet, noting the apparent inappropriateness of such emotion at a wedding, comments, "But how delightfully do such scenes dilate the heart?" (4: 343; letter 16). The scene of sensibility dilates the hearts of spectators within and outside the text. In the Clementina interlude, people hide in closets to watch the spectacle of Clementina's suffering. On occasion, as Camilla's intervention indicates, they troop quite openly to the scene, hoping to see two virtuous lovers faint in one another's arms. To watch suffering (or for that matter, intense emotion of any kind) encourages both kinds of identification. It touches spectators, enabling them to feel for another, and it directly stimulates imaginative participation in someone else's emotion. Watching suffering thus serves moral ends. It creates spectators in the "theater of sympathy" that David Marshall locates through the argument of Adam Smith's *Theory of Moral Sentiments* (1759), published in the same decade as *Grandison.* By Smith's theory, the "spectacle" of suffering "is only a prelude if a precondition for the situation of sympathy which in Smith's view would deny the difference and distance between spectacle and spectator" (D. Marshall 192). To obviate that distance is one of Richardson's purposes.

Clementina's story involves virtually unrelieved suffering. The young Italian woman refuses to marry an appropriate suitor from her own country and class, thereby bringing upon herself relentless persecution by a cousin ostensibly serving the family's interest. In love with Sir Charles, Clementina finally wins her parents' consent to marry him, only to decide that her devout Catholicism precludes her marrying an English Protestant. Emotional strain disorders her intellect, and no one feels confident that she will ever regain mental stability. As many commentators have noted, Richardson had a special gift for recording the confinement and persecution of women. It is not surprising that he wrote with special energy of Clementina.

But the Clementina episodes serve different moral and narrative functions than does the account of Pamela's or Clarissa's beleaguerment. Emphasis on the scene of suffering as one to be watched, literally or vicariously (Sir Charles writes the story of Clementina's distress; it is read aloud to one audience and sent on to another), calls attention to the purpose of such spectatorship. To share the vicarious experience of intense tribulation, identifying imaginatively not only with the victim but with the other witnesses, generates emotional fellowship. Such fellowship, as Sir Charles's comment about the proper position for judgment suggests, can further moral insight, but in *Grandison* it seems essentially an end in itself. People come together in contemplation of other people's manifest sensibility, but their moral and emotional association ensures a kind of stability that *Grandison* apparently assumes almost as an ultimate good. Sir Charles, after all, displays his Godlike goodness (the analogy to the divine occurs repeatedly) principally by drawing people together. He steadily extends his family, claiming both Harriet and Clementina as sisters before he finally makes Harriet his wife, enlarging his figurative family to include all Clementina's relatives, insisting on reconciling alienated members of his own family, moving to include even the mother and stepfather of his ward Emily. One might, from a twentieth-century perspective, comment on the dubious political implications of this ethic of absorption into the aristocratic hierarchy, but Richardson's text neither states nor implies the slightest reservation about the value of community, no matter how generated or for what purposes.

For a novel to support this doctrine, by its manipulation of the epistolary, by its plot, and by its characterization, would have seemed peculiarly emphatic in the mid-eighteenth century. Already a considerable body of moralistic commentary had accrued to the developing genre of the novel, arguing that novels encouraged young girls in particular to value love too highly, that they stimulated admiration rather than opprobrium of dubious behavior (Tom Jones's casual sexual activity, for example), that they failed to offer clear moral models, that they caused people (again, girls especially) to waste their time in fantasy rather than perform their appointed tasks. One could sum up such attacks as directed toward the novel's encouragement of individualism. With their focus on strongly characterized individual men and women, novels implicitly stimulated their readers to think of themselves too as "special." They thus opposed the central assumptions of conservative moral thought—precisely the assumptions that Richardson endorsed in *Sir Charles Grandison*.

In *Grandison*, in other words, the novelist used his genre to subvert itself by an extraordinary endeavor to undermine the value of individualism. For this reason especially it is likely to "bore" modern readers. Clarissa and Pamela, however exemplary, live vividly in the text by virtue of intense personal conflict. We remember about Clarissa not the copybook virtues that Anna Howe attributes to her (How well she uses her time! How generously she helps the poor!) but the anguish of her situation, torn between tyrannical father and tyrannical lover. Sir Charles, theoretically caught in an anguished situation of his own, does not acquire imaginative life through his suffering. One remembers him, rather, for his rather self-conscious and insistent demonstrations of virtue: his discourses on dueling, his determined peacemaking. In his own letters, he tells someone else's story. In other people's letters, he emerges less as center of narrative than as object of admiration. His significant actions—rescuing Harriet, refusing to duel, showering benevolence on the suffering—define his character as Good Man, not his distinctiveness. Never does he act importantly on his own behalf, unless we take his self-interest as located in a desire to be and to be perceived as virtuous.

Implicitly and explicitly, *Sir Charles Grandison* as text and Sir Charles as protagonist oppose the idea and all embodiments of the "modern." A few allusions to the word in the first third of the novel will suggest the prevailing animus. Harriet, just becoming acquainted with the Grandison family, learns that Charlotte has two suitors, both handsome, both attractive to women in general. "This," Harriet comments, "makes me afraid, that they are modern men, and pay their court by the exterior appearance, rather than by interior worth" (1: 180; letter 36). A few pages later, Charlotte observes of some female friends that they never wish to stay home. "Any-where rather than at home: The devil's at home, is a phrase: And our modern ladies live as though they thought so" (1: 191; letter 38). Even bad Sir Thomas Grandison, Sir Charles's father, trying to repel a suitor for his daughter, observes, "Men worth having are so affrighted by the luxury and expensiveness of the modern women, that I doubted not but the characters of my girls would have made their fortunes, with very little of my help" (2: 328; letter 14). (Usually the potential monetary value of the nonmodern remains more decently obscured.)

In each of these instances, and in many more, "modern" means superficial and decadent. It implies, for Richardson as for Swift before him, presumptuous abandonment of the shared values of the past. It connotes the corruption of an age of individuals: superficial, frivolous, and atomistic. As the marriage of Harriet and Sir Charles finally approaches, Beauchamp invokes blessings upon them: "God preserve you both, for an example to a world that wants it" (6: 213; letter 51). He thus restates the novel's project: to offer embodiments of traditional virtue for the edification of a society lost in modern individualism. The past connotes stability; the present, disorder. The single clear textual reference to contemporary affairs alludes to the "troubles . . . in Scotland," caused by a "young invader" (3: 124; letter 20). One more image of modern instability, the political and military effort to unsettle the Protestant succession emphasizes the danger implicit in all challenges to the status quo.

Richardson's attack on the modern implicates twentieth-century readers—also likely to accept individual sensibility as a guide and to admire superficial signs of attractiveness and success. If we no longer fight duels, we have devised other outlets for phallic aggression and competitiveness. Fewer and fewer of us find contentment in staying home. From the point of view of the novel, we are the enemy.

Of course the converse applies equally well: from our point of view, the novel is the enemy. Not merely in its openly didactic sequences but in its fundamental conception—its ways of imagining plot, character, rhetoric, epistolary form—*Sir Charles Grandison* challenges individualistic assumptions. And you can't really argue with a novel. Lengthy passages about the evils of dueling or the joys of benevolence may be easy to dismiss, but the concept of character as exemplary rather than unique retains a capacity to disturb: to arouse feelings of aggression, for instance. To declare *Grandison* (and Grandison) boring obviates the difficulty.

This, like Richardson's other novels, contains flashes of self-subversion that may reassure the modern reader. As Anna Howe in *Clarissa* provides a refreshing note of witty common sense, Charlotte Grandison here offers antisentimental clarity. She even, astonishingly, mocks the emotional excess of Harriet's love. In a wonderfully comic evocation of "a couple of *Loveyers,* taken each with a violent ague-fit, at their first approach to each other," she calls attention to the privileged male narcissism that even exemplary Sir Charles embodies. "I, I, I, I, says the Lover—You, you, you, you, says the girl, if able to speak at all" (6: 66; letter 20). But she draws back almost immediately, and the novel's action relentlessly tames her, humiliating her for an injudicious erotic choice and confining her to domesticity. In the same way, the inter-mittent perception by one English character or another that Clementina's parents are "cruel" in their "persuasion" receives no clear textual ratification. Although Clementina's story does not proceed to full resolution, the novel ends with intimations that she will soon set-tle down and marry the man her parents approve. Here, as in *Clarissa*, men hold all the social power and parents function as autocrats. Richardson objects minimally to such arrangements, yet he allows pos-sible objections to come into view.

But if he provides ironic comment on his own sentimentalities, he also *uses* them. The sentimentalities of *Sir Charles Grandison* attempt to draw readers and characters alike into a community founded on tradi-tional assumptions. As both eighteenth-century and twentieth-century critics have pointed out, sentimentality in its nature supports the status quo: one weeps but doesn't have to *do* anything. In Richardson's final novel, the association of lavish weeping with profound acceptance of things as they are appears not inadvertent but purposeful. The weeping of those sensitive to the emotional force of human unhappiness and also of the generosity that can almost always (in Richardson's world) allay it—that weeping *proves* the rightness of things. In a benevolent patriarchal order, everyone occupies precisely the appropriate position. The richest man is the best man. (It seems no accident that others repeatedly ask Sir Charles to serve as executor of their wills: the Good Man, virtually by definition, knows how to take care of money.) Women may possess great intellectual, moral, and emotional power (the well-known debate in the text about female education concludes by justifying it—within limits), but they occupy a subordinate place. Harriet must pine in silence while Sir Charles waits to see whom he will marry. Not even Charlotte suggests that anything is wrong with the arrangement.

To pay close attention to the moral and social implications of Richardson's novel may entail being irritated by them and by their pow-erful articulation through structure as well as theme. Most of the time, given such a long novel with such paucity of happening, people don't bother. Instead, declaring themselves bored, they keep their distance. The original readers presumably needed no such protection, since the doctrine Richardson preached would have seemed less alien to them. Yet in its reactionary aspects it must already have appeared faintly dubi-ous. The protest articulated by a number of contemporary readers against Sir Charles's willingness to have his prospective daughters reared as Catholics while keeping his sons Protestant (only, of course, if he married Clementina)—this protest perhaps suggests even eighteenth-century discomfort with the novel's insistent, serene hierarchies.

Boredom implies—indeed, *is*, as I have often reiterated—a refusal to pay attention. The self-canceling aspect of the present chapter has become increasingly apparent to me. Books I too considered "boring" when I first read them bore me no longer. (On the other hand, I must confess that I foundered in my attempts to reread Disraeli's novels as possible cases in point: I could not bring myself to attend.) Works that I here declare boring to twentieth-century sensibilities in fact interest me greatly—because I have paid close attention to them. Boredom both causes and is caused by failure or inability to attend. To focus on any work with intense awareness virtually guarantees finding it interesting—not attractive, necessarily, or admirable, but worthy from a historical or sociological or psychological or aesthetic point of view of the consideration one has given it. Yet the question of why we don't and won't pay attention to certain books in certain historical periods remains compelling, even though the object of study may change before our eyes. If Adorno is right in characterizing taste as the seismograph of history,[1] shifts of taste that declare books once greatly admired no longer worth notice at all—not bad, exactly; just not interesting—have importance equivalent to that of our choice of "canonized" texts. They tell us what ideas we can no longer afford to admit to consciousness, as well as what forms of literary embodiment have come to seem meaningless. The point of my investigation has nothing to do with whether *Sir Charles Grandison* "is" boring—only with the fact that many more readers now think it so than would have thus dismissed it in 1753.

In 1808 Hannah More, by this time generally accepted (though not necessarily liked or approved of) as arbiter of morals and spokesperson for Protestantism, published a work of fiction for adults: *Coelebs in Search of a Wife*. An immediate popular success, it passed through twelve editions in its first year (Hopkins 224), with its second edition appearing only three days after the first. In less than a fortnight, it had gone out of print (M. Jones 193). Before More's death in 1833, thirty thousand copies were sold in America (Hopkins 224). The novel had won international success.

Before writing *Coelebs*, More fiercely and frequently attacked novels and their writers and readers. Fiction, in her view, encouraged false and

1. I owe this allusion to David Kaufmann.

dangerous ideas. Its pernicious effects threatened the young particularly, and they threatened females because novels often developed their
plots out of romantic situations all too likely to seem attractive to
women. As speculation developed about the authorship of *Coelebs* (first
published anonymously), the very possibility that More was responsible made the work more exciting. Had the moralist renounced her
obdurate advocacy of uncompromising truth?

In an 1809 letter to William Waller Pepys, More offers her own
explanation for her excursion into fiction:

> I thought there were already good books enough in the world for good peo-
> ple, but that there was a larger class of readers whose wants had not been
> attended to—the subscribers to the circulating library. A little to raise the
> tone of that mart of mischief and to counteract its corruption I thought an
> object worth attempting. (qtd. in M. Jones 193)

The curious implicit antithesis between "good people" and "subscribers
to the circulating library" betrays More's assumption that virtue survives
dependably only in those who eschew fiction. But she expresses her
willingness to serve also the larger population of those susceptible to
the attractions of the printed word, as well as her desire to subvert fiction by writing it. Her transformation of the genre, she hoped, would
refocus the imaginations of the vulnerable.

The reviewers, wary about the question of imagination (although
the *Lady's Magazine* characterizes *Coelebs* firmly as "a work of *religious
imagination*" written by "a writer of ability and genius"),[2] typically
stress doctrine rather than invention in their praise of More's accomplishment. Not infrequently they quarrel with the novel's doctrinal
positions: the *British Critic*, for instance, objects to More's excessive
stress on natural depravity. On the other hand, it observes that *Coelebs*
"may be inferred" to be a "valuable and interesting work" because it has
achieved a fourth edition in three months (481), and the magazine conveys its own endorsement by a reference to "these interesting volumes"
(487).

What the anonymous reviewer appears to find "interesting" is More's

2. The *Lady's Magazine* publishes two extended excerpts from *Coelebs*: "The Visit of
Charity: With Observations on the Paradise Lost" and "The Visit: With Strictures on
Modern Female Education." It appends an evaluative note to the first passage (including
the observations quoted; 100), praising More's novel because it ends not with marriage
"but when Coelebs has attained to the sure and certain hope of a blissful union" (100).
Presumably such a conclusion obviates the chance that readers will find erotic titillation
in the text.

daring. He remarks that the artifice of presenting religious exhortation in the guise of a novel "was extremely judicious; for even the follies of fashionable education are not greater enemies to conjugal happiness than the sentiments which, in early life, are imbibed from novels" (481). Like many eighteenth-century critics of the novel as genre, the reviewer implicitly assigns fiction enormous potential influence over its readers. More has engaged the issue of fiction's power by attempting to redirect it. Even critics who found her novel's emotional force negligible respected her enterprise.

Thus the *Edinburgh Review*, in a long assessment written by Sydney Smith (according to M. Jones 197), adopts a heavily ironic tone toward the exalted reputation of "the celebrated Mrs Hannah More" and declares the reviewer's iconoclastic intention of "treating [*Coelebs*] as a book merely human, —an uninspired production, —the result of mortality left to itself, and depending on its own limited resources" (*Edinburgh Review* 145). The novel's "machinery," the review continues, has "not the slightest claim to merit. Events there are none; and scarcely a character of any interest" (146). Although such assertions sound unequivocally damning, the reviewer does not feel unequivocal. The nature of More's endeavor, if not that of the book itself, wins his qualified approval:

> There are books however of all kinds, and those may not be unwisely planned which set before us very pure models. They are less probable, and therefore less amusing than ordinary stories; but they are more amusing than plain, unfabled precept. Sir Charles Grandison is less agreeable than Tom Jones; but it is more agreeable than Sherlock and Tillotson. (145)

Interest is a relative matter. Since fiction can "amuse" the reader more than theology can, any work of fiction gets higher marks, from one point of view, than does "plain, unfabled precept." By presenting "very pure models," More proves herself to have planned "not . . . unwisely." And her wisdom resides partly in her capacity to make her presentation more "amusing" than plain precept could be.

In its denial of interest to More's characters, its claim that the fiction offers no events, and its judgment that the novel's machinery has no claim to merit, Sydney Smith's review provides a more negative assessment than was offered by any other contemporary critic. But others concurred in locating the novel's interest in its didactic project. The *Gentleman's Magazine* sounds most enthusiastic:

> We earnestly recommend an attentive, impartial perusal of it, both to parents and young people. When pure, sound morality and unaffected benevo-

lence are so pleasingly illustrated, it is sufficient to make us in love with virtue. . . . We are aware that to a certain class of Readers the discussions upon religious topics may appear dry, and uninteresting; for our own part, we can only wish that in these aweful, momentous times, such subjects were more seriously considered. (251)

The critic counters the possible allegation that the book lacks interest by his implicit claim of its significance, relying on the word's older meaning. But he also finds More's book "pleasing" in its illustrations of virtue, and he suggests an intense emotional response to it: "It is sufficient to make us in love with virtue."

The *Critical Review*, complaining about minor infelicities of style but offering abundant quotation and summary with the apparent conviction that readers will find the quoted material compelling, concludes that "the meaning of the author is so good, and the design is so evident to promote the interests of piety and virtue, that we should think ourselves highly culpable if we made any speculative errors or incongruities a subject of severe animadversion" (264). The reviewer will not enter into doctrinal quarrels, nor will he reflect at all on fictional technique or effectiveness, since he considers the inculcation of good "meaning" self-justifying. The *Monthly Review* begins with conventional condemnation of novels in general: "By the usual furniture of circulating libraries, deceptive views of life, a false taste, and pernicious principles, have been disseminated; and it is the commendable object of the writer of the volume before us to counteract the poison of novels by something which assumes the form of a novel" (128). After relating More's plot, the review summarizes, "Such is the story of this novel; which consists more of delineations of character and of discussions than of surprising incidents; and which, though it displays the reading and talents of a male writer, bespeaks in the nature of its plan the ideas and systems of a female" (129). The models of character, the reviewer concludes, may be too flawless to be persuasive, but the moral undertaking of the novel remains praiseworthy. Despite lack of incident, despite implausible character, More's fiction deserves and will reward her readers' attention.

Like *Sir Charles Grandison, Coelebs* has fared badly over time. Twentieth-century readers may peruse it for historical, theological, or sociological reasons, but one can hardly imagine their seeking direct pleasure in it. It supplies virtually nothing readily recognizable as imaginative interest. Like the early reviewers, we will probably find the book's characters unconvincing and its plot almost nonexistent. Moreover, we will doubtless consider its moral doctrine irrelevant—certainly not "pleasing," and perhaps hardly more "amusing" than doctrine unmediated by fiction. What once seemed universally interesting now presents itself as self-evidently boring.

Q. D. Leavis, contemplating the nature and the function of popular fiction, argues that it serves the important purpose of transmitting "cultural news" from one intellectual level to another. "Such work must be done in order that some kind of communication may be kept up, and only the novel can do it, for . . . the general reading public touches nothing more serious than the novel or newspaper" (71). Leavis alludes here to the state of things when she wrote in 1932; her description would apply less precisely to the early nineteenth century. But she goes on to make a transhistorical point about the simplification involved in such cultural transmission: "A pertinent objection is that the process necessitates a simplification of the issues that lets slip the essentials and leaves only some unmeaning and often misleading facts. Hence this kind of novel dies as soon as it has begun to date" (71). By this argument, *Coelebs* would become boring as its doctrine no longer bears on most lives not because of the nature of the doctrine but because of that doctrine's formulation—its simplification to the point of meaninglessness. In contrast, *Paradise Lost* and *The Divine Comedy* retain imaginative life for twentieth-century audiences because they communicate doctrine in complex form.

The argument contradicts the more familiar assumption that Milton, for instance, survives by virtue of nondoctrinal attributes: the power of his language and verse, the vigor of his fable and his characters. Leavis suggests that any doctrine that challenges the intellect by its intricacy and energy can hold the interest even of those who do not believe it. She suggests also a snobbish and ahistorical conviction that what fails to interest a reader like herself thereby declares its inadequacy.

It seems too easy an assumption. Clearly, one can construct more than one explanation for a book's declining interest. The question why *Coelebs* interested so many people in the first place also raises divergent possibilities. More's expressed desire to attract "subscribers to the circulating library" suggests not only the audience she hoped for but the kind of audience she probably won: middle-class women, a specifically gendered subgroup of the "parents and young people" to whom the *Gentleman's Magazine* recommended her work. We need to speculate, then, about what kind of force *Coelebs in Search of a Wife* would have carried for early nineteenth-century women.

The reviewers I have quoted presumably were all male. The lessons and attractions they found in *Coelebs*—lessons and attractions recommended to others; they rarely give evidence of having themselves experienced the novel as directly appealing—constitute prescriptions for rather than reactions by women. About immediate female reactions, I have found no straightforward testimony. M. G. Jones suggests as causes for the book's popularity its presenting of a domesticated form of religion "in an easy and attractive guise" and its providing for middle-class readers "a valued guide to feminine propriety written by a woman of recognized religious and social position" (193). But Jones offers no evidence for these assertions. My own hypothesis will focus on more covert didactic concerns than religion and propriety.

Mitzi Myers economically summarizes Hannah More's didactic accomplishment: "Skillfully modulating the mentorial persona of the female middling classes, she reproved the rich and improved the poor" (266). But one may discern an understrain to the demonstration of female propriety in *Coelebs*, whose perfect candidate for wifehood, Lucilla Stanley, perhaps answers to fantasies besides that of unexceptionable goodness. Although the story nominally issues from the consciousness of a male protagonist, its substance concerns a female rather than a male problem: how to attract a man. The "how" the narrative recommends involves impeccable piety and preoccupation with charitable and domestic activities. But it also allows female learning, as long as its possessor does not obtrude it. In the preface, Coelebs expresses himself as "supposing that females of the higher class may combine more domestic knowledge with more intellectual acquirement, that they may be at the same time more knowing and more useful, than has always been thought necessary or compatible" (More x).

If the notion of usefulness reinforces the orthodoxy of female subordination, that of "knowing" opens wider opportunities. Might "knowing" have supplied a code for female freedom? The admirable Lucilla keeps her learning secret. Not until her lover is on the verge of declaring himself to her (he has long since confessed his love to her father) does she acknowledge that she has read Milton. (Her admiration of Milton's Eve confirms Coelebs's passion, given his own enthusiasm for *Paradise Lost*.) To read Latin or Milton without allowing anyone outside the family to know it constitutes exceedingly innocent knowledge. The principle of secrecy, however, along with the suggestion that young women might "be . . . more knowing," allows for a range of possibilities, not all equally innocent.

Of course one can hardly imagine that a young woman would seek in *Coelebs* justification for a reprehensible predilection for secrecy. Yet the program of decorum *Coelebs* offers amounts to a prescription for disguise. The ideal young woman, as here delineated, spends much of her time in visits of charity. At home, she sews garments to give to the poor and deserving, she helps her mother run the household, and she studies. In social intercourse, she remains largely silent. Rarely and reluctantly (like Clarissa before her) does she presume to offer an opinion. When she does so, her views unfailingly exemplify both wisdom and propriety.

Lucilla, the "she" in question, meets orphaned Coelebs's requirements for the kind of wife his dead parents would have approved. She never says or does anything wrong. By her parents' report, and the servants', and the neighbors', she has always led an exemplary life. The blanks in that life lie concealed by the principle of restraint. When Lucilla explains to Coelebs the special perspective of the gardener, she seems to offer an allegory of her own character. Coelebs has suggested the dullness of winter in the country. The young woman responds that she loves the winter because she imagines what takes place beneath appearances: "When all appears dead and torpid to you idle spectators, all is secretly at work" (273). Just so, Lucilla's silences allow Coelebs to fantasize for her a rich mental existence that marriage will fully expose to him. Nothing, however, guarantees such exposure. The unacknowledged motives and feelings suggested by More's repudiating Wollstonecraft without reading her (see pp. 90–91) perhaps correspond to the hidden possibilities of Lucilla's mind and imagination.

For a modern reader, the question of "character" hardly arises in *Coelebs*. More makes little attempt to differentiate the persons of her narrative except by acquired attributes—religious faith, mainly, but also "accomplishments": one Stanley daughter studies mathematics, another sings, neighboring girls vary their displays of talent according to the eligible men in the vicinity. Nor does More concern herself much with plot in any recognizable sense. Coelebs looks for a wife and finds one. He makes no false starts: no inappropriate woman attracts his attention, although he briefly seeks in the wrong places for a proper wife. He endures no great suspense as to whether his beloved will accept him, although the narrative occasionally suggests, unpersuasively, that he worries about the courtship of a rich young nobleman whom Lucilla has already rejected. As More's preface (written in the voice of Coelebs) accurately puts it, "The texture of the narrative is so slight, that it barely serves for a ground into which to weave the sentiments and observations which it was designed to introduce" (ix). Readers who interest themselves in this text, in other words, must do so on grounds other than those that usually attract us to novels.

To think about the conceivable bases of interest in *Coelebs* calls attention once more to the close link between "interest" and "self-interest." To a culture persuaded that one's fate for eternity depends on choices made in daily life, guidance in those choices becomes a matter of intense self-interest. But the fiction would also have appealed to women on more immediate grounds of self-interest: it has much in common with the "how to find love" books that currently compel large audiences. Written in the voice of a young man (Coelebs narrates his own odyssey), it promises that a young woman who practices the right revelations, the right concealments, may win a rich, independent husband (he will burden her with no in-laws) who adores her, even though she lives in the country, unsupplied with obvious suitors. In other words, it restates a familiar female fantasy, that governing "Cinderella" as well as *Pamela* (although social class does not here become a central issue): a really good girl will get what she wants.

Not only do the "blanks" in Lucilla's life allow the female reader as well as Coelebs—though in rather different ways—to construct hidden possibilities for the good girl's inner experience, they also encourage that reader to identify with the heroine. The novel makes the point explicit when Lucilla's mother observes that her daughter

> is no prodigy dropped down from the clouds. Ten thousand other young women, with natural good sense, and good temper, might, with the same education, the same neglect of what is useless, and the same attention to what is necessary, acquire the same habits and the same principles. . . . If she is not a miracle whom others might despair to emulate, she is a Christian whom every girl of a fair understanding and good temper may equal, and whom, I hope and believe, many girls excel. (225)

Nature, it seems, provides good sense (or "fair understanding") and good temper; nurture supplies the rest of what can make a girl appear a "prodigy" or "miracle." If this summary assigns considerable responsibility to parents, it also allows room for every young woman to fantasize her own position as wondrous image of virtue. Lucilla says rather little in the course of the narrative. She delivers her view of Milton and in particular of his Eve, she expounds her own humility and unworthiness, but rarely does the novelist allow her direct speech. (In contrast, Coelebs and the other male characters, as well as certain grown-up females, talk a great deal: conversation provides most of the novel's substance.) Others talk about her, reporting her virtuous character and actions. The technique further emphasizes her position as a screen on which readers may project their fantasies. She resembles in this respect Lord Orville, the virtuous nobleman of Frances Burney's *Evelina*—the heroine's reward—whose conversation, frequently praised by others, seldom appears in the text. Modern readers typically think him "a stick." His appeal to an eighteenth-century audience must have depended on his very blankness—a blankness inviting the reader to fill it in with whatever constitutes male attractiveness. With Lucilla as with Orville, "attractiveness," nominally not the central issue, is simply displaced from the physical to the moral sphere. If goodness gets a man, it necessarily constitutes attractiveness.

The plot of *Coelebs in Search of a Wife*, as sketchy as the characterization, offers comparable do-it-yourself possibilities. The absence of conflict in Coelebs's progression toward matrimony—and in Lucilla's—promises the reader that virtue smooths every difficulty. Alternatively, it suggests that whatever stresses roughen the path to marital happiness make no significant part of the journey's story: from a Christian perspective, difficulties hardly count, are insignificant by comparison with the end in view: a happy outcome in the afterlife. The young female reader, however, might find herself imagining a more immediately gratifying outcome and seeing her own story as an inevitable progress toward it. Thus plot as well as character invites identification.

If I am right in these guesses, that within three-quarters of a century *Coelebs* no longer seemed readable stems not from the simplifications of doctrine that indeed inform it but from the simplifications of romance that may once have made it attractive. Mothers may have given More's novel to their daughters in the spirit that moved Mrs. Morland (at the end of *Northanger Abbey*) to seek out an appropriate issue of the *Mirror* to deal with a daughter's depression. But daughters perhaps saw in the novel a promise of romantic happiness, a justification for hidden mental lives, a prophecy that they too could prove their profound attractiveness just by *acting like* good girls. As fiction during the nineteenth century increasingly concerned itself with the enactment of inner conflict, as doctrine became contested territory even within fictional genres, scope for identification with More's bland narrative would have diminished. Not because it no longer corresponded to the audience's theology but because it no longer met that audience's dreams, *Coelebs* would have lost its interest for women readers.

My account of the early location of interest in *Coelebs in Search of a Wife* has abounded in *may*s and *might*s. There are no certainties here, since few early nineteenth-century women have left records of their reading to illuminate what More's novel meant to them. Indeed, even if they testified to their utter involvement with the doctrinal problems the novel discusses, one might still suspect that the conventionally good woman of the period would not have allowed herself to say that a work so obviously intended for didactic ends also spoke to romantic fantasies. So we can never know. We can equally well entertain an opposed hypothesis, one firmly grounded in the explicit argument of the novel itself: that "interest," in the early nineteenth century, inhered in matters quite different from those that interest us.

In a passage late in *Coelebs* that contemporary magazines frequently reprinted, the narrator voyeuristically watches, concealed, as his beloved reads the Bible to a poor, dying woman. "It was an interesting sight," he comments, "to see one of the blooming sisters lift the dying woman in her bed, and support her with her arm, while the other fed her, her own weak hand being unequal to the task" (361). The sight's "interest" presumably derives from the contrast between blooming sisters and dying woman, a contrast that stimulates the observer's sensibility. The first time Coelebs sees Lucilla Stanley, he observes, "I have seen women as striking, but I never saw one so interesting." "Her beauty is countenance," he continues; "it is the stamp of mind intelligibly printed on the face. It is not so much the symmetry of features as the joint triumph of intellect and sweet temper" (106). Here too, "interest" depends on paradoxical relations: between intellect and sweetness, mind and body. It implies an interpretive challenge: the viewer must fathom the mingling of qualities, as he must later come to terms with his emotions at the spectacle of beauty and death intertwined. Joking about the lack of difficulty in Coelebs's way as a lover, a friend observes that "a little dejection" would "give interest to your countenance" (159). Interest, in other words, demands and denotes complexity.

Various people suffer boredom in the course of *Coelebs* (the word itself even appears once). They are bad—or at least misguided—people. "The languor, the listlessness, the discontent . . . !" Coelebs exclaims, about urban devotees of pleasure (189). Later he summarizes his London experience: "What was old, however momentous, was rejected as dull, what was new, however insignificant, was thought interesting" (289). Good people leading good lives avert boredom's threat by conscious arrangement. Thus Lucilla, because she loves gardening, prevents herself from spending too much time at it. By limiting her indulgence, her father explains, she guarantees her continued interest: she always stops before she can find her activity tedious. Mr. Stanley, speaking generally, recommends "an orderly division of the day" because it makes time pass faster. "It prevents tediousness by affording, with the successive change, the charm of novelty, and keeping up an interest which would flag, if any one employment were too long pursued" (308). The function of an educated woman is to keep her husband's life from feeling dull. Mr. Stanley contrasts the woman prepared only for display with one educated to fulfill her domestic function. "A woman, whose whole education has been rehearsal, will always be dull, except she lives on the stage." Her virtuous counterpart, on the other hand, "entertains her husband" (190), who otherwise might find amusement only outside the home.

These instances suggest that to avert boredom requires consistent moral effort. If interest inheres in complexity, it may require special kinds of awareness—like Lucilla's about the winter landscape—to perceive the complexity that guarantees pleasure in virtuous experience. *Coelebs in Search of a Wife* deliberately challenges its readers' interest by thematizing the issue of interest. It declares the hidden drama of the commonplace. As Mr. Stanley points out,

> life is not entirely made up of great evils or heavy trials, but . . . the perpetual recurrence of petty evils and small trials is the ordinary and appointed exercise of the Christian graces. . . . To bear with vexations in business, with disappointments in our expectations, with interruptions of our retirement, with folly, intrusion, disturbance, in short, with whatever opposes our will, and contradicts our humor; this habitual acquiescence appears to be more of the essence of self-denial than any little rigors or inflictions of our own imposing. (122)

Coelebs chimes in that he has often thought "that we are apt to mistake our vocation by looking out of the way for occasions to exercise great and rare virtues, and by stepping over those ordinary ones which lie directly in the road before us" (122). Both men thus speak for an invisible moral heroism, for the pervasive though often unapparent value of everyday experience.

By analogy, the ostensible eventlessness of *Coelebs* as a novel conceals its record of moral effort and moral choice that, rightly seen, constitute high drama as well as high virtue. The text trains its readers to redirect interest. Early readers presumably learned its lesson. Later ones, perhaps less attentive because less engaged at the level of romantic fantasy, denied the fascination of the unexceptional.

Both my hypotheses about the possible interest of More's novel to those who originally rushed to purchase it center on the reader's response to plot: to the plot of romantic fulfillment that declares happy marriage the reward of virtue, to the plot of almost invisible happening that identifies significant moral action as inhering in commonplace experience. Without more stress on the intensity of individual psychic response, by the end of the nineteenth century such plots no longer held readers' attention. George Eliot could make one believe in the high importance of a wife's effort to participate imaginatively and intellectually in her husband's futile academic endeavor—but she did so by revealing the precise shape, the exact cost, of such effort. More neither attempts nor believes in such exactitude. For her as for Richardson, the exemplary remains the general rather than the particular.

> Those who have systems or hypotheses to recommend in philosophy, conduct, or religion induct them into the costume of romance. . . . When this was done in *Télémaque*, *Rasselas*, or *Coelebs*, it was not without literary effect. Even the last of these three appears to have been successful with its own generation. It would now be deemed intolerably dull. But a dull book is easily renounced. The more didactic fictions of the present day, so far as I know them, are not dull. We take them up, however, and we find that, when we meant to go to play, we have gone to school. (Gladstone 766)

Eighty years after the publication of *Coelebs*, it figured as the very type of the boring book. The critic of a later generation finds it difficult even to imagine its original success. He feels confident, however, that the didactic novels of his own day (he alludes specifically to Mrs. Humphry Ward's *Robert Elsmere*, subject of his twenty-two-page review) will not prove vulnerable to repudiation. Less than fifty years later, Q. D. Leavis would cite *Robert Elsmere* as representative of books "long forgotten though they caused mighty reverberation in their own day" (71).

The commentator who uses *Coelebs* as an example of dullness and *Elsmere* as an instance of successful didacticism is William Gladstone, prime minister of England. That he commented extensively on Ward's novel in the *Nineteenth Century* suggests the importance assigned to this fiction, the interest aroused by it, at the moment of publication. Within two months the novel had reached its fourth edition. Two months later the seventh full-price edition had appeared (E. Smith 33–34). Half a million copies sold in the United States within a year (E. Jones 82). "The popularity of *Robert Elsmere*," Enid Jones writes, "was as sudden and amazing as a tidal wave" (85).

"The success of this novel," observes a reviewer in the *Quarterly Review*, "is the most interesting, and in some respects the most instructive, literary event of the present year" ("Robert Elsmere and Christianity" 273). The event's "interest," it seems, derives from the religious controversy the novel dramatizes. "Few persons would be at the trou-

ble to read through so long a novel, for the sake of its romantic
episodes, who were not chiefly interested in the religious struggle
which it depicts" (274). Although the reviewer finds many novelistic
virtues in the fiction, he considers its religious interest fundamental.
And he objects intensely to the religious ideas. Early in his long essay,
he claims in patronizing terms that he will not "censure" the author:

> We refrain, in deference partly to Mrs. Ward's services in other departments
> of learning, partly to her earnestness and sincerity, and partly to her sex,
> from expressing the censure which would ordinarily be due to a writer who
> engaged in an attack upon the received Christian faith with so imperfect a
> knowledge of the present conditions of the controversy, and consequently
> with such inevitable misrepresentation. (275)

But the review's subsequent pages consist mainly of detailed quarrels
with the religious positions of individual characters. The reviewer
approves only of Robert's pious wife, Catherine, and suggests that
Elsmere should simply have consulted her: she would have restored his
faith (298). "The victory in this story, to our minds, remains with
Catherine," he concludes, praising her for her "instinctive revulsion,"
her "distrust," and her "loathing" of heterodox positions (302).

The intensity with which the reviewer involves himself in the novel's
religious controversy provides direct evidence of how imaginatively
and emotionally compelling *Robert Elsmere* appeared to its first readers.
Gladstone's sympathetic and perceptive account reveals less immediate
involvement but a comparable assumption that one must take this work
very seriously indeed. "If it be difficult to persist [in reading *Robert
Elsmere*]," he remarks, "it is impossible to stop" (767). He locates the
novel's power in its characterization, finding its doctrinal debates
unpersuasive. The real battle, he maintains, takes place not about religion but about marriage—"fought in a hundred rounds, between
Elsmere and Catherine" (769). (I think he is quite right, and I shall
return to this point.) And he summarizes the nature of Ward's theological enterprise more precisely than does the other reviewer I have
quoted, saying of the book,

> It may, I think, be fairly described as a devout attempt, made in good faith,
> to simplify the difficult mission of religion in the world by discarding the
> supposed lumber of the Christian theology, while retaining and applying, in
> their undiminished breadth of scope, the whole personal, social, and spiri-
> tual morality which has now, as matter of fact, entered into the patrimony
> of Christendom. (777)

Gladstone's *now* is crucial: Ward's novel belongs peculiarly to its historical moment. As Andrew Lang put it in another contemporary review, the novel provides "a vast and crowded picture of our distracted age" (814). The word *modern*, in *Sir Charles Grandison* a term of opprobrium, in *Robert Elsmere* carries more complicated weight. It recurs frequently, especially toward the end, to emphasize that the intellectual conflict central to the novel's plot uniquely characterizes the late nineteenth century. Although Elsmere's decline in orthodox Christian faith and his development of a substitute form of theism plus good works derives from personal experience, from accidents of association and of character, it depends heavily, the narrator often points out, on his period's intellectual and religious history. Catherine, clinging to a faith that in her father was already "old-fashioned," refuses to march with the times. But even she, the narrator observes, has changed her views more than she realizes, by virtue of imperceptible pressures felt by all thinking people. "Modern," in Richardson's novel, meant superficial, self-seeking, and decadent. In the context Ward predicates for it, it connotes responsiveness to intellectual currents from the Continent, faint skepticism about established truth, awareness of recent scientific discovery, uneasiness about such discovery's religious meaning. For Richardson, in short, "modern" has social and moral significance. For Ward, its meanings center on the intellectual.

"The decisive events of the world take place in the intellect." Robert quotes this line, without attribution, adding that "it is the mission of books that they help one to remember it" (Ward 197). Reader, writer, and thinker, Robert believes he has discovered by historical research the illogicality of Christian faith—having learned how cavalierly early writers handled evidence, he can no longer believe in miracles. He must relinquish his role as clergyman, give up the village life he enjoys, and torment his beloved wife. His story recapitulates many a Victorian crisis of faith and accords such crises intellectual dignity. Insisting on its own modernity as well as its intellectual seriousness, it presumably attracted at least some of its original readers by just these means, implicitly promising that they would understand their own immediate experience better for reading it.

Although a man fills the title role, two women—Catherine and her sister Rose—share narrative interest. Rose inhabits a conventional romance plot with a difference: she insists against all obstacles on preparing herself to be a professional musician. (This vocation, however, in the event serves mainly to make her attractive to London society and to draw two men to her.) Catherine, on the other hand, embodies traditional female ways of being. She cares for her invalid mother, she performs charitable works as ardently as does More's Lucilla, she devotes herself, once married, to husband and child. An old-fashioned woman, a New Woman, a saintly man, and (by way of lover for Rose) an attractive, rich, aristocratic man: the novel offers something for everyone.

Its ostensible plot concerns a clergyman's loss of faith and his simultaneous and subsequent moral exaltation. By the time Robert dies, having exhausted himself in the service of the poor and of his moral vision, he has achieved virtual sainthood. Certainly the reviewers showed some justice in attacking Ward's dangerous theological position. She apotheosizes a man who has systematically and logically rejected Christian revelation, offering detailed arguments to support his rejection. The suffering he endures as a consequence of his loss of faith only increases his heterodox heroism. No representative of orthodox Christianity in the novel demonstrates comparable breadth of understanding or energy in good works. The Victorian reader must have felt a thrill of rebellion in the very act of contemplating such a figure as Robert, with such a career.

Yet the novel makes a more complicated claim on our attention than by its exploration of the theologically unorthodox. Its effect, for attentive readers now and presumably for attentive readers always, depends on the coexistence of two other plots. If the action involving Rose clearly constitutes a subplot, the events dependent on Catherine's nature and situation possess importance comparable to that of the Robert plot. Ward's imagining of Catherine, a devout Christian utterly committed to her father's theology, allows her no rebellion. Her commitment to her husband wavers no more than does her devotion to Christ. She conforms to the standards of the good Victorian woman. Yet the reviewer who thought Robert should simply allow Catherine to eliminate his religious doubts missed a great deal in this good woman's characterization. Like Robert himself, Catherine is allotted an inner life of some complexity.

Her initial attraction for Robert derives, like Lucilla's for Coelebs, from the sense she conveys of hidden realities. Robert finds her "interesting."

> She had not yet said a direct word to him, and yet he was curiously convinced that here was one of the most interesting persons, and one of the persons most interesting to *him*, that he had ever met. What mingled delicacy

and strength in the hand that had laid beside her on the dinner table—what potential depths of feeling in the full dark-fringed eye! (35)

"One of the most interesting persons" (as opposed to "interesting to *him*") suggests the old meaning of *interesting* as "significant." Catherine embodies both moral importance and emotional appeal. And Robert's diagnosis of her proves accurate: "delicacy and strength" indeed characterize the young woman. As for the "potential depths of feeling" in her eye, that Victorian code for erotic appeal—Ward comprehends (although Robert does not) not only erotic potential but its capacity for transmutation into other forms of energy. Before and after marriage, Catherine specializes in sublimation.

Despite the fact that Catherine seems the very type of the good Victorian woman, tireless in service to others, dedicated to God and to a life of taking care, Ward avoids or reverses many gender stereotypes: another ground of "interest" in her novel. Robert, official representative of the religious establishment, has entered the ministry on the basis not of intellect (despite his and his creator's high evaluation of the intellectual) but of feeling. Although his intellectual brilliance has brought him academic success, he remains—before and after his marriage—governed largely by feeling, particularly tender feeling. Ward makes the point emphatically and repeatedly, analyzing Robert's attitudes toward the squire (a determined and intelligent atheist and a fine historian, whose beliefs and books finally draw Robert away from the church, but a pathetic man), toward the squire's steward (bitter and destructive, but a man whose pathos Robert also perceives), toward the poor and the sick, in a rural village and in London. Full of religious, erotic, and filial passion, Elsmere remains a man of integrity, but feeling largely controls his destiny. (Lang suggests that even his loss of faith stems from his preexistent "fever of unrest, and of anxiety," product of exhaustion [822].) In this respect he conforms more nearly to a conventionally "feminine" type than to a "masculine" one. Moreover, from childhood on he suffers spells of illness brought on by the sheer intensity of his feelings and his life. His state intermittently verges on invalidism. He ends the novel, and his life, in a tubercular "decline," like many a fictional heroine. Like a heroine too, he finds himself, in all innocence, the object of attempted sexual seduction. His purity protects him; he escapes the designing female's wiles but feels, as a maiden might, . . . soiled.

Catherine, on the other hand, despite her orthodox good womanhood, reveals certain stereotypically "masculine" aspects. Most conspicuously she likes to govern, and in her family of origin she governs well. When we first encounter her, as the angel of her Yorkshire village, she controls her own household (a mother and two sisters), authorized by the dying injunction of her father. Her determination has prevented Rose from leaving the village to study music abroad. Indeed, she has kept the entire family from abandoning the countryside her father loved. She identifies strongly with the dead father (as Robert identifies with his mother). After her marriage, she happily falls into the role of helpmeet, yet her will and her principles remain powerful. In some ways she appears the stronger of the novel's central characters. Although she accepts (perforce) Robert's decision to leave the church and goes with him to London, her silent, steady resistance to him never diminishes. The Angel in the House, in this incarnation, proves not altogether easy to live with.

The marriage of such beings promises—and delivers—drama. Gladstone's perception of that marriage as the novel's center of interest calls attention to tensions at the heart of the Elsmeres' family relations. Robert and Catherine struggle for control: over systems of belief, over how they shall live. Predictably, the struggle ends in the woman's submission: "White and pure and drooping, her force of nature all dissolved, lost in this new heavenly weakness of love" (531). Robert's "sensitive optimist nature" (528), shocked by a would-be seductress's advances, leads him toward new affirmation of connubial love as the greatest of earthly goods. "One task of all tasks had been set him from the beginning—to keep his wife's love!" (529). Domesticity, that traditional preserve of the feminine, triumphs. But if Robert learns that he must value his wife's love above all else, his wife learns that she must respect his way of thinking as highly as her own. Impossible, finally, that she should be right and he wrong: the reviewer who thought that Robert would regain his faith if only he consulted Catherine must ignore the ideological weight of the conclusion.

The affirmation of marriage by no means constitutes a happy ending, from the "masculine" or the "feminine" point of view. It depends too heavily on compromise, on the tempering of conviction and passion on both sides. Infused with awareness of the necessity of relinquishment, with an almost Johnsonian sense of the emotional insufficiency of human experience, this resolution—the Elsmeres live happily together until Robert's death, which follows with considerable speed—issues from a realism startling in its bleakness. If religion does not create happiness or certitude, neither does romance, parenthood, or fam-

ily life. Ward's novel proves iconoclastic not only in challenging orthodox religious pieties but in questioning domestic pieties. Happy fami-
lies are all alike, it suggests, specifically in the compromises they have
made to achieve relative contentment.

The Rose story, superficially a predictable romance, reinforces the
novel's message that experience inevitably proves painful and flawed.
Never imagined as fully as Catherine, Rose seems from the outset
morally inadequate in her self-will and her thirst for glamour as well as
for music. Her flashes of authenticity appear mainly in her more reprehensible moments, as when she reflects, "Robert has been too successful in his life, I think" (263)—calling herself a "wretch" for thinking it.
Her infatuation with Robert's academic friend Langham, quite evidently a misdirected passion, guarantees its own frustration. The rich,
aristocratic, intelligent, kind lover Ward finally conjures up for her has
the air of deus ex machina: his many virtues appear to guarantee his
wife's happiness, but by the time Rose accepts Flaxman, the reader
knows that not even rich, aristocratic, intelligent, kind lovers ensure
contentment. A "loose end" has been built into Rose's character, in her
passion for music. Although she has never quite committed herself to a
professional career, she has clearly established her longing for more
than ordinary social life has to offer. It appears unlikely that Flaxman
will gratify such longing. One kind of storybook marriage or another,
all will entail relinquishing dreams. All demand concessions. All exemplify the radical imperfection of human experience. And remarkably for
a Victorian novel, *Robert Elsmere* holds out little hope that the afterlife
will compensate for the insufficiencies of earthly eventualities
(although it *does* imagine happy reunions in the hereafter, which presumably offset the specific trials of experienced relationship).

For a reviewer to locate a novel's central struggle in the realm of
domestic relations and then pay relatively little attention to that realm
directs attention once more to the problem of "interest." Gladstone
contends that the important conflict in *Robert Elsmere* concerns not religion but marriage, yet the substance of his review focuses on theological rather than domestic problems. The religious could be assumed as
self-evidently important; domestic concerns belonged by custom to the
conventionally trivialized world of women. Does Gladstone find the
struggle between Robert and Catherine "interesting" or consider it a fictional fact with no necessary effect on the reader? And what of the hundreds of thousands of others who composed the original audience? Did
the massed attention of those buyers direct itself to the novel's debates

over the divinity of Christ or to the drama of marital compromise or to both? Or did they claim to care about the theological while actually interesting themselves in the marital?

Such questions are not only unanswerable but in a sense meaningless, since reading remains an individual act performed by readers with individual characters and histories and consequently individual interests. Yet *Robert Elsmere* in 1888, like *Coelebs* in 1808 and *Grandison* in 1753, constituted a cultural event, its popularity a mass reaction. To wonder why a fiction now relatively devoid of life should once have seemed so compelling involves one in speculation about what would have engaged the interests of inhabitants in another culture. And Gladstone's comment about the marital "battle" provides specific focus for such speculation—if no answer to the questions it implies.

The theme of interest and boredom sketched within the text of *Robert Elsmere* makes the specific locations of human interest an urgent matter. At the outset, the attitude toward boredom appears altogether predictable. Rose and Agnes, Catherine's other sister, find the rural valley they inhabit dull; so does the vicar's wife, Mrs. Thornburgh, when her plots for arranging marriages seem not to work out well. Boredom implies disengagement. Catherine, deeply engaged in the human life around her, could not possibly feel bored. But her engagement itself irritates and dispirits her sisters, who believe that nothing interesting will ever happen where they live and blame Catherine that they live there.

Robert, as we have already seen, constructs Catherine as "interesting" virtually from the first moment he sees her. He then goes on to take lively interest in all his surroundings, animate and inanimate, and to create for himself a vivid existence by the vitality of his attention. Catherine, with her intense inner life, also continues to find her experience interesting. But others, lacking the same imaginative and moral capacities, suffer the reiterated fate of boredom. Rose, for instance, considers not only her village but, on occasion, even London tedious. Langham—who fears from Rose the judgment, "You are not interesting—no, not a bit!" (168)—suffers "boredom with the whole proceeding" (177) when he goes to church (although Robert's sermon interests him more than he anticipates), feels conscious that "his friend's social enthusiasms bored him a great deal" (200), and describes his life as one of ever-diminishing interest (218–19). The squire often determines his own course of action out of his fear of boredom. Flaxman, an epicure of feeling, seeks new experience to avert boredom. Madame de Netteville, Robert's would-be seductress, gains social position by her "most remarkable power of protecting herself and her neighbours from boredom" (514). (In this as in other nineteenth-century novels, inhabitants of society's upper reaches prove particularly vulnerable to boredom.)

Implicit moral condemnation hovers around boredom's victims, whose disengagement appears to declare their lack of self-discipline—almost an eighteenth-century view of things. But a life rich in interest does not necessarily merit approval. When Robert faces himself and his failings after Madame de Netteville's attempt on his virtue, he concludes that if his wife "had slipped away from him, to the injury and moral lessening of both, on his cowardice, on his clumsiness, be the blame! Above all, on his fatal power of absorbing himself in a hundred outside interests, controversy, literature, society" (529). To designate as a "fatal power" the capacity for large interest reminds the reader of the high moral stakes implicit in every choice. Perhaps it suggests also what is at issue for that reader in responding to the text.

For choice inheres in the reader's locations of interest, as in the characters'. In *Robert Elsmere*, I have claimed two centers of interest: the public, "masculine" sphere of theology and the private, "feminine" locus of domesticity. When Robert goes through his agony of self-realization, his imagination turns from the scene of seduction to "the image of a new-made mother, her child close within her sheltering arm" (529). As Robert lies dying, his watching wife sees a vision of Christ, but the dying man himself, in an "ecstasy of joy," calls out, "*The child's cry! — thank God!*" Catherine realizes "that he stood again on the stairs at Murewell in that September night which gave them their first-born, and that he thanked God because her pain was over" (604). At these crucial junctures, the domestic, in its specificity and emotional energy, takes precedence over the conventionally religious. Indeed, it defines a new realm of spirituality.

The "public" readers of *Robert Elsmere*, the reviewers, treat theology as the novel's central concern, but it is not hard to imagine people (once more, especially women) reading otherwise. The two fulcrums of interest in effect organize radically different novels. One tells the story of a heroic man who in the course of a self-abnegating career locates for himself a new spiritual center of gravity, whose generosity includes and forgives and accepts the relatively rigid and narrow orientation of the woman he marries. The other focuses on a heroic woman whose considerable gifts realize themselves only in devotion to others. The man she marries, using his intellect to explore uncharted paths, becomes other than she thought him. Emotionally as well as legally unable to leave her husband, dependent on him for her work and for her identity, suffering, as Lang puts it, in "silent misery [which] is not a thing to be read about without pain" (823), she realizes that "her life had been caught and nipped in the great inexorable wheel of things. It would go in some sense maimed to the end" (558). The awkward metaphor, joining the colloquial sharpness of "nipped" with the clichéd vagueness of "the great inexorable wheel," conveys the harshness of Catherine's predicament. But the necessity of religious and of marital devotion remains. She manages to believe that God can accept more than one way of approaching him and to acknowledge the sufficiency of a marriage based on compromise.

Catherine's story is sadder than Robert's, and more persuasive. I think it, in fact, more *interesting.*

More clearly than I have demonstrated why these novels strike modern readers as boring, I appear to have explained why they do not bore *me.* My reaction emphasizes that women might read in different ways than men but also stresses the truth that reading attentively reveals "interesting" things in more than one aspect of a novel. Many early readers presumably found direct didacticism more engaging than twentieth-century audiences consider it, but we need not assume that interest in moralizing necessarily precludes concern with the psychological and social. Widespread modern and postmodern distaste for theology no doubt ensures that many readers now approach *Robert Elsmere* with considerable skepticism—and that stance may protect them from even noticing the energy of the novel's subtext about marriage.

But the putative interest of these novels and the boredom they allegedly generate bear a close relation to one another. Much depends on the expectations a reader brings to the text; much depends on selectivity. All reading is selective, as everyone knows who has had the experience of rereading a familiar novel and discerning in it altogether new meanings: literally seeing different things. Readers often account for such an experience in terms of their immediate life situation, but cultural pressures also help determine what one notices. Current readers are unlikely, for instance, to feel the emotional urgency of Elsmere's quandary over the historicity of miracles—partly because they *anticipate* no genuine urgency in discussion of such matters. Newspapers, talk shows, and magazines reiterate tacit and explicit messages about what interests "us"—that largely fictional collectivity constituted by shared existence in the 1990s. We know in advance that debates over the divinity of Christ or recommendations that women cultivate submissiveness will not excite us. Such knowledge contaminates and controls responses to a text. Similar kinds of assumed knowledge enable readers of our era to recognize and dismiss signals of "sentimentality" or simple "romance"—signals abundantly supplied by all three of the novels at hand. The sources of interest and of boredom in these novels, in short, are not just allied but identical (Robert's problem and its implications, Catherine's dilemma and its meanings, the evangelical version of romantic myths about how to attract a man, the gospel of community . . .): it all depends on how you read.

Hunter's astute observation about the tendency of early didactic novels to pry into their readers' private commitments explains not why such works, when historically distanced, bore us but why once upon a time they bored almost no one. The didactic novelist's pursuit and prying forbid passivity. Soliciting the reader's active response, insisting on how much is at stake for everyone, they allow even repudiation—but not neutrality. Yet Ward's putative prying (and Richardson's, and More's) will no longer trouble most of those few who still pay attention to her: they won't even notice it. By another operation of selectivity, the challenge of these works has become inaudible. The sounds of pursuit fade away, the sense of urgency recedes. Failing to recognize, for instance, Ward's prying into her readers' romantic as well as religious faith, their belief in the possibilities of connubial bliss, we can adopt a serenely historical perspective and believe the novel has nothing to do with *us*. We "know" in advance the irrelevance of the book's central concerns. The state of moral passivity implicit in the reader's refusal to engage expresses itself in the judgment that *Robert Elsmere* is boring.

Or does the twentieth-century reader in fact intuit a kind of prying that seems altogether intolerable? Does cultural guilt attend the general abandonment of the faith of our fathers and mothers, so that Ward's implicit interrogation of the grounds of her readers' belief touches a nerve? In an era of widespread marital instability, do reminders and questions about the costs of stability prove especially troubling? As we celebrate individualism, do we find calls to community unsettling?

I can make up stories about what has happened to make novels like those considered in this chapter vanish from the realm of the self-evidently interesting. Using *Robert Elsmere* as a case in point, I might speculate about what ideas Ward's novel embodies that, as I put it earlier, we—our culture—can no longer afford to admit to consciousness, about how this old-fashioned book may still arouse frustration and aggression that we conceal with a judgment of "boring." My story would go like this. A century ago, a female novelist dramatized the

notion that a man's crisis of faith in the divinity of Christ might generate a woman's crisis of faith in her husband ("He for God only, she for
God in him"). The fictional treatment of theological issues, though
already out of date in the opinion of some reviewers and presumably
some readers, aroused widespread interest attested not only by reviews
but by enormous sales of Ward's book. More covertly, the novel's evocation of marital tension and the compromised resolution of that tension also engaged many. Both subjects, clearly related to one another
and presented with barely concealed didactic purpose, rich in ideological implication, demanded self-questioning about Victorian readers'
intimate commitments and intimate doubts. The interest of *Robert
Elsmere* would have derived partly from the personal challenges it conveyed.

These challenges have not vanished, but they have become textually obscure and often personally offensive in an era when not everyone can assume or accept a connection between faith in Christ and in
a spouse, when a woman's determined fidelity to a self-willed husband
will elicit feminist blame more probably than praise, when theological
disputes seem as outmoded as female submission to many Western
minds, when most people no longer think of theology as part of ideology. *Robert Elsmere* embodies ideas that many, now that a prevailing ethos
glorifies "self-fulfillment," feel actively reluctant to think about: for
instance, the contention that everyone must bear responsibility for his
or her beliefs and failures of belief, and the notion that no conceivable
choice will guarantee satisfaction. Such views—we may wish to dismiss
them as "Victorian views"—call into question dominant assumptions of
our time. To take seriously the implications of *Robert Elsmere* might
indeed provoke aggressive feelings. Far easier to declare the book boring: irrelevant.

Robert Elsmere not only does ideological work acceptable at its cultural
moment, it also raises questions about standard ideologies. It explores
both the theological arguments against the divinity of Christ and the
need for women to embrace less than they dream of, the heroism of
intellectual exploration and that of domestic acceptance. Its legibility
may originally have differed for men and for women; it may differ now.
But its high seriousness still has the capacity to disturb—if people read
it seriously.

That is my story. Ward's novel implies other didacticisms besides
those I have mentioned, and other versions of the explanatory story
might fit other facts about the book. But if one accepts the insistence
of *Robert Elsmere* that something important is at stake in choosing objects

of interest, any such story must entertain the possibility that the repudiation implicit in dismissing a work as boring has more than casual meaning. Often the designation *boring* serves to ward off anxieties and antagonisms entailed in acknowledging the interest of complex works.

A sample of three interesting/boring novels can prove little about the vast category of published material that interests large numbers of people at one time and bores most readers later. To hasty or casual readers, the past may seem immaterial to a complicated present, especially when evoked in unfamiliar vocabulary with moralistic emphasis and complicated sentence structure. Unless they manifestly demand close attention, promising reward, the import of long-neglected books becomes invisible. The books become boring.

Designating books as boring acquires cultural usefulness and energy from its capacity to obviate difficulty. It removes the necessity to confront potential challenge; it justifies inertia. Interest is always constructed: literary critics, in the business of creating and sustaining it, know that. Boredom is constructed too—and a dull book is easily renounced. To try to reconstruct the interest of such a book, however hypothetically, not only teaches us something about ourselves and about our predecessors, it reminds us that "boring books" need not always bore us.

SIX

The Normalization of Boredom

Nineteenth-Century Women
and Their Fictions

English women's lives are unbelievably monotonous, sterile and drab. Time has
no meaning for them—the days, months and years bring no change to this
oppressive uniformity. . . . There are very few things young women can do for
entertainment. The family atmosphere is cold, arid, deadly dull, so they plunge
headlong into the reading of novels.

(Tristan 191, 194)

The indiscriminate reading of novels is one of the most injurious habits to which
a married woman can be subject. Besides the false views of human nature it will
impart, and the waste of time, it indisposes for all serious occupation, it produces an indifference to the performance of domestic duties, and a contempt
for ordinary realities, which will be highly detrimental. . . . [In many] the health
has been destroyed by the excitation produced.

(Freeling 114)

The first of the quotations above comes from the observations of a
Frenchwoman visiting London in the 1830s. The second, published in 1839 but strikingly reminiscent of eighteenth-century commentary, belongs to a work by a man offering good advice to brides.
Together they suggest that the early nineteenth-century Englishwoman
faces a dreary prospect, her direct experience supplying only boredom,
her attempts at escape into the vicarious experience of fiction involving the sinister threat of "excitation."

By the beginning of the Victorian period, the association between
women and boredom—and not coincidentally, between women and
leisure—was well established. As a modern historian puts it, "It might
be said that women of all classes, though in different ways, were confined in a world where they were more the objects than the subjects of
leisure" (Cunningham 132). Their possible arenas for activity limited,

the imperative of leisure powerful in their experience, women would indeed seem likely candidates for boredom. But I do not propose to assess whether the female population of Great Britain actually led boring lives; rather, I shall consider what imaginative use certain Victorian woman novelists made of boredom's alleged immanence in female existence.

The twentieth century—in which the conventional association of female domesticity with boredom has by no means disappeared—provides a useful starting point. In October 1987 the *New Yorker* published a profile of Miriam Rothschild, ecologist and member of the famous Rothschild family who now, in her eighties, lives in a vast English mansion. Her schizophrenic sister, Liberty, inhabits one wing of the mansion under the care of a resident nun. Miriam Rothschild tells of her sister's eccentric behavior, concluding with this anecdote: "Once, we were all at dinner and she was bored with the conversation. She didn't know that's what it was, but she was *bored*. So she got an orchid out of the middle of the table and ate it. Munched her way through it. *Very* slowly. Ha! That stopped us in our tracks!" (Fraser 73).

For me this story provokes a number of questions. What, if anything, is the relation between Liberty's boredom and her psychosis? Would her behavior have differed had she *known* she was bored? How did eating an orchid help her? Why do people laugh at this anecdote? Would it have equal comic edge if someone ate an orchid because she was insane, not because she was bored? What, if anything, does this bizarre anecdote have to do with the ordinary female situation? Does it bear at all on the realm of textuality?

From a literary (as opposed to a psychiatric) point of view, psychosis and boredom are tropes for one another. The defining aspect of boredom—"a complex stalemate between fantasy, impulse, and threat" (M. Waugh 548)—is the incapacity to engage fully: with people, with action (one may act, but without complete emotional participation), with one's own ideas. Psychosis, for different reasons, generates the same incapacity. Boredom's characteristic condition of inhibition and dissatisfaction frustrates action, thought, even emotion beyond the unsatisfying emotion of boredom itself. Like the psychotic, less tragically only because less permanently, the victim of boredom finds all outlets mysteriously blocked.

To understand oneself as bored implies understanding the possibility of remedy: hence the importance of Liberty's alleged failure to *know* she was bored. However much most of us suffer through dull dinner parties, we generally comprehend our suffering as a temporary condition, not a permanent state of the soul. A woman aware of the nature of her malaise would not have to eat an orchid. She might shift the conversation in more interesting directions, retreat into her own consciousness, or hold out until dessert.

How does eating an orchid solve Liberty's problem? Miriam Rothschild's final comment provides a clue: "That stopped us in our tracks!" To eat the orchid, slowly, directs everyone's attention toward the eater. Her condition of desperate isolation—psychosis, to be sure, but also boredom—finds apparent remedy as eyes focus on her. She manages an illusion of engagement.

Boredom provides a provocative literary subject partly because the internal experience of paralyzing monotony often impels its victims to dramatic action in an attempt to evade what they feel. "Strange that boredom, in itself so staid and solid, should have such power to set in motion," Kierkegaard remarks. Calling boredom's influence "magical," he points out "that it is not the influence of attraction, but of repulsion" (*Either/Or* 281). Boredom, in this view, becomes the opposite of desire, but like desire a principle of action. Liberty eats an orchid, Jane Austen's Emma Woodhouse plots other people's lives, a character in a Maria Edgeworth novel amuses herself by "daily jealousies, conflicts, and comparisons" (*Helen* 146), less because they want what they get than because they do not want what they have. Boredom provides a negative stimulus for action, thus an impetus for narrative.

Would Liberty's flower eating engage us in the same way without the presumption of boredom? The hypothesis of boredom as causality acquires entertainment value because the flower-eating episode has been made into a story, governed by a reassuring view of boredom's triviality. Consider, in contrast to the Liberty story, a cinematic instance in which a bored woman eats an orchid. The scene occurs in the film *The Last Emperor:* the emperor's wife, deprived of all meaningful function, alone at a huge, magnificent party, quietly begins munching orchids from a splendid flower arrangement. The spectator, compelled at least fleetingly to imagine the internal experience of a woman driven to flower eating, feels the disturbance of fundamental disorder.

The story of Liberty does not encourage disturbance, because Miriam Rothschild and Kennedy Fraser generate a saving distance between the reader's consciousness and that of the orchid eater. Liberty's sister formulates the episode as a joke. She dwells on the reaction of the guests, she invites the amusement of her listener. Hinting that boredom as an experience need not be taken seriously, ignoring Liberty's aggression, deprecating her misery, she shapes the story for reassurance.

Yet in life and literature alike, boredom may entail profound human consequences. Pre-twentieth-century fictional explorations of those consequences rely less on the clearly aberrant than on the commonplace, but women novelists' investigations of the female situation often interrogate, as do the two anecdotes I have cited, the predicament of the woman forced inward. What interests me in their narratives is what Freeling terms "excitation": we might call it desire. In their grotesque actions the emperor's wife and the ironically named Liberty display the intensity of distorted desire, the intensity that boredom itself disguises. Female figures in nineteenth-century fiction by women, imagined as doing nothing at all extreme, suggest the same story of literally inexpressible desire. Boredom by its nature denies desire. It may also reveal desire's presence.

Like Liberty Rothschild, Jane Austen's Emma Woodhouse does not understand herself as bored. More precisely, she knows her condition from time to time, in specific situations (in the company of Miss Bates, on the eve of Miss Taylor's wedding), but suppresses her awareness that boredom inheres in her circumstances. Although much of what she does attempts to alleviate tedium, she rarely acknowledges the problem. As a consequence, her remedial activity, like Liberty's, displays a certain randomness.

What does Emma want? What she does *not* want emerges more distinctly. Notoriously, she does not want to marry, to the bewilderment of her seventeen-year-old protegée Harriet. Although the narrator allows us to glimpse some posturing in Emma's proclamations of self-sufficiency and power and her certainty that her sister's children will fill her emotional needs, it seems true that she consciously experiences no erotic desire. In one of Austen's brilliant jokes, Emma actually confuses boredom with erotic feeling. "This sensation of listlessness, weariness, stupidity, this disinclination to sit down and employ myself, this feeling of every thing's being dull and insipid about the house! —I must be in love" (262). Through most of the narrative, Emma neither loves nor recognizes in herself any desire to love. She toys with the notion of Frank Churchill's infatuation with her, but the point of the exercise is that it involves no emotional vulnerability. Erotic energies do not govern her consciousness.

Imaginative energies *do*, as she tirelessly constructs plots around other people. Thus she responds to her limited opportunities for action, making others her surrogates for excitement. "Absolutely fixed" in her village, she cannot even change locale. Emma can and does care for her father; she visits the poor; she participates in her limited society and takes long walks with Harriet. Mr. Knightley tells her that she has a spirit of seriousness and a spirit of vanity. When the former controls her, she combats boredom by involving herself fully in concern for her father; under the pressure of the latter, she invents narrative plots.

The narrator permits us to see some of the effort involved in Emma's maintaining her own conviction that her life supplies adequate pleasure and occupation. For one well-known instance:

> Emma went to the door for amusement. —Much could not be hoped from the traffic of even the busiest part of Highbury; —Mr Petty walking hastily by, Mr William Cox letting himself in at the office door, Mr Cole's carriage horses returning from exercise, or a stray letter-boy on an obstinate mule, were the liveliest objects she could presume to expect; and when her eyes fell only on the butcher with his tray, a tidy old woman travelling homewards from shop with her full basket, two curs quarreling over a dirty bone, and a string of dawdling children round the baker's little bow-window eyeing the gingerbread, she knew she had no reason to complain, and was amused enough; quite enough still to stand at the door. A mind lively and at ease, can do with seeing nothing; and can see nothing that does not answer. (233)

The reader does not necessarily concur with Emma's "knowledge" that she has no reason to complain. On the contrary, the impoverished scene may generate a moment of pity for its witness. She names actual people—Mr. Petty, Mr. Cox, Mr. Cole—but this male cast of characters exists here only as a figment of her imagination, a nucleus for a nonexistent plot, representing the most she can hope for, a vision of action and of possibility that does not materialize. Only the anonymous butcher, old woman, children, and curs, limited sources of amusement, limited centers of action, inhabit the Highbury landscape.

The crucial last sentence of this account, the one about "a mind lively and at ease," generated by Austen's technique of free indirect discourse, records Emma's characteristic compensatory self-congratulation. She invents lives for other people, she fabricates interest in two dogs and a bone, and she reassures herself that her capacity to do so implies her superiority. Thus she both combats and denies boredom, insisting that "seeing nothing" sufficiently occupies her lively mind. She claims superactive engagement with the world outside herself—the opposite of boredom.

Yet one might argue that for Emma, often though not always, the world outside hardly exists. Bored people have trouble making reality real. Emma does not truly interest herself in butchers or in quarreling dogs, only in the operations of her own consciousness. She never attends to Harriet Smith—the real Harriet—enough to understand the girl's limitations and their bearing on her conceivable destiny, as she never attends to Mr. Elton's emotional actuality, or to Jane Fairfax's. Boredom, entailing incapacity for engagement, implies alienation. Emma, despite her social leadership in Highbury, has little real connection to most of her fellows. To return to what Emma wants, her principal desire, although she does not formulate it in negative terms, derives from the movement of repulsion Kierkegaard describes. She wants not to be bored. She uses others as instruments to fulfill this negative desire.

First-time readers of *Emma* often dislike the central character and eagerly anticipate her comeuppance. Experiencing the desire for completion operative in the reading of all narrative, they may have difficulty conceiving appropriate terms for resolution. Only after Emma realizes her love for Mr. Knightley can the new reader subside into conventional wishes and expectations. Hardened novel addicts will understand that Emma must find both reward and discipline in marriage, but like Emma herself they may remain at a loss about whom she might marry. The novel entertains with its wit and its verbal energy but long leaves its readers in emotional limbo: a moral equivalent for boredom. Yet Emma's boredom palpably belongs to a fiction. The fiction maker can be trusted to dissolve it in good time and to satisfy her readers.

In fact that fiction maker resists boredom even in the act of representing it. We may contemplate by way of example a bit of conversation involving Emma, her sister Isabella, and their father:

> "You seem to me to have forgotten Mrs and Miss Bates," said Emma. "I have not heard one inquiry after them."
>
> "Oh! the good Bateses—I am quite ashamed of myself—but you mention them in most of your letters. I hope they are quite well. Good old Mrs Bates—I will call upon her to-morrow, and take my children. —They are always so pleased to see my children. —And that excellent Miss Bates! — such thorough worthy people! how are they, sir?"
>
> "Why, pretty well, my dear, upon the whole. But poor Mrs Bates had a bad cold about a month ago."

"How sorry I am! But colds were never so prevalent as they have been this autumn. Mr Wingfield told me that he had never known them more general or heavy—except when it has been quite an influenza."

"That has been a good deal the case, my dear; but not to the degree you mention. Perry says that colds have been very general, but not so heavy as he has very often known them in November. Perry does not call it altogether a sickly season."

"No, I do not know that Mr Wingfield considers it *very* sickly except—" (102)

Isabella breaks off there, but the conversation continues for more than four pages.

This is not the sort of talk one would wish to hear in one's own living room, but to read Austen's version of vacuity reveals how effectively the distance of representation converts banality into comedy. Avoiding the potential terror of boredom—the terror of its potential persistence—we can acknowledge how ludicrous are the preoccupations that generate it, as we enjoy the related yet opposed obsessions of father and daughter. Fiction, framing triviality and fatuousness—the monotony, sterility, and drabness that Flora Tristan declared characteristic of British women's lives—transforms them into aesthetic phenomena. Inviting us to laugh at the tedious, it reassures us that triviality and fatuousness have no immediate connection with our own lives.

The prosing of Isabella and Mr. Woodhouse and loquacious Miss Bates provides pleasure through the precision with which Austen renders the workings of limited minds. In the passage of conversation just quoted, the narrator's voice never intervenes, yet the rendition's exactitude reveals its control by the shaping intelligence that has long since claimed the reader's confidence. Trusting that we will not be forever abandoned in a morass of observations about sickness and its remedies, that some purpose dictates the representation of tedium, we can—miraculously—enjoy the vignette.

As Emma tries to steer the conversation away from what might disturb her father, she demonstrates her self-control and responsiveness at a level approaching ethical heroism. The narrator clearly approves. The reader, acknowledging Emma's good manners—she even finds herself "very happy to assist in praising" Jane Fairfax, for the sake of keeping off dangerous conversational ground (104)—yet may notice that Emma on her good behavior, fulfilling the injunctions of conduct books, is readily absorbed into a consummately boring social texture. Her social life, unless she takes steps to enliven it, consists almost entirely of enactments of tedium. During one especially entertaining evening party, for instance, there are "a few clever things said, a few downright silly, but by far the larger proportion neither the one nor the other— nothing worse than every day remarks, dull repetitions, old news, and heavy jokes" (219). Such is the young woman's habitat: the verbal equivalent of the Highbury square.

The Emma one enjoys and remembers does not spend her time steering her father away from dangerous subjects. She occupies herself in making excitement, not in preserving boredom. Exerting inner control over external circumstance, she compensates for dull repetitions and old news by inventing new news. In a social environment from which desire has largely vanished, to be deflected by pretense (Frank Churchill and Jane Fairfax) or redirected into concern about gruel (Isabella and Mr. Woodhouse), Emma dramatizes a yearning for excitement that declares her desire for desire. Although she accepts boredom as filial duty, she defies it when she can. Given the limitations of female prospects, her "excitation" must derive from the operation of her imagination. Hence she must be chastened by the action of the novel.

The best-known of Sarah Ellis's books of advice for Victorian young women provides a useful retrospective gloss on *Emma*. Published in 1842, *The Daughters of England* offers authoritative and reiterative counsel. Its central issue emerges early in the text:

> It is this waiting to be interested, or amused, by anything that may chance to happen, which constitutes the great bane of a young woman's life, and while dreaming on in the most unprofitable state, without any definite object of pursuit, their minds become the prey of a host of enemies, whose attacks might have been warded off by a little wholesome and determined occupation. (48)

The dangerous enemies, it soon emerges, are feeling and imagination. Ellis warns repeatedly that girls must find things to do, must maintain constant activity, "wholesome and determined occupation," in order to avoid the sinister potential of "dreaming": Emma's form of self-indulgence. Lacking sufficient "wholesome and determined occupation," Emma must have a husband. Otherwise her unconscious desire for desire will endanger her.

Bored people may eat the centerpiece, create imaginary romances, whatever. As Haskell Bernstein puts it, "For the chronically bored, something must happen. Boredom may lead them to anything" (515). Bernstein evokes the same situation—the state of waiting for something exciting to happen—that Sarah Ellis declared characteristic of women. It is a situation that encourages moralizing in others besides Ellis, even in the twentieth century, because of the sense of danger readily associated with it. Emma Woodhouse creates moral dilemmas for the reader as well as for herself: readers quite conscious of the difference between real people and textual representations have been known to say that they *disapprove* of Austen's central figure. Yet when she stops behaving like a spoiled child, many of the same readers feel a troubling sense of repression.

Through the normative voices of Knightley and of the narrator, Austen's novel solicits a steady stream of intimate judgment about everything Emma does. Consistently we are invited to approve her "proper lady" (i.e., "good girl") behavior and to disapprove her efforts to create for others stories more dramatic than their actual experience and to make herself significant as mistress of others' destinies. In other circumstances, in real life, we might admire the imaginative force of a woman so determined to make her existence interesting, and the narrative invites us to admire it here too—but only when Emma keeps it under control. The text leaves little doubt about the judgment it invites. It values proper female devotion to the interests of others, of which the established sign is marriage, more than extravagance of imagination.

Emma, then, accepting boredom as a condition of women's experience, distinguishes between acceptable and unacceptable responses to it. The reader, previously repelled by Emma's arrogance, finding it difficult to know what to want for the character, can relax into familiar wishes for the socially defined happy ending roughly a hundred pages before the novel's conclusion, when the protagonist first recognizes her erotic wishes. Boredom then disappears as an issue. Emma at last has plenty of legitimate business to occupy her, not only in the dangerous inner world (dangerous because not subject to external control—dangerous in the way Sarah Ellis would recognize) but in the realm Highbury designates as actuality. The text encourages its readers' easing into familiar fictional patterns in order to reinforce the ethical judgment that Emma's salvation must consist in her compliance with norms of respectable femininity. The proper response to boredom is not rage, not imagination, but a kind of acceptance, through the conformity that implies boredom as a dimly recognized inevitability. Austen, finally endorsing orthodox female conduct, provides her character with legitimated desire and satisfies in her readers the most conventional forms of narrative yearning.

Here as elsewhere the subject of boredom implicates that of fiction. For novelists and for Emma Woodhouse, constructing fictions counteracts life's tedium. Reading fiction (and Emma of course reads fictions in the lives around her) has rescued millions from ennui, though not necessarily without danger, as Sarah Ellis and Arthur Freeling suggest. Yet a fearful fantasy for authors hovers round the image of the bored woman, figuring a reader traditionally assumed, like women, to inhabit a position of receptivity but capable, like women, of the passive aggression inherent in boredom. To reject as uninteresting what conventional life has to offer, as Emma Woodhouse for a time surreptitiously does, constitutes a psychic act of profound hostility. Correspondingly, for a reader to declare tedious what a novelist offers devastates the authorial enterprise.

Perhaps this covert analogy between bored woman and recalcitrant reader helps explain the pedagogical resolution of *Emma*, with its marriage designed to instruct the protagonist in proper behavior. The imagining of the Knightley-Emma union evinces a need to control, even to eliminate, the disruption of desire that boredom implies. As the negative of desire, boredom threatens conventional structures not only of experience but of fiction. Its unpredictability as a principle of action menaces orthodox notions of plot and of female conduct. Austen creates a bored heroine, only to eliminate her boredom: it cannot be allowed to utterly subvert the text.

On the other hand, it provides a useful means for Austen to pursue her usual course of qualified subversion. For two-thirds of *Emma*, boredom in effect supplies a disturbing metaphor for the ordinary condition of women. If the novel ends by declaring the emotional state impermissible, it also explores its consequences. Emma must be chastened, but first she is allowed to demonstrate the severe difficulties of being handsome, clever, and rich with little acceptable outlet for one's talents. The intensity with which the narrative quells the impulse to combat boredom by messing with other people's lives declares the power of that impulse and hints the threat implicit in the "oppressive uniformity" of female experience.

"The most self-sustaining achievement of genderism," two recent commentators write, referring to the twentieth century, "is the normalization of *boredom* for women." They go on to quote someone they call "a Beautiful Person from the 1960s," one Princess Pignatelli, who says, "I was so bored I used to remove the hairs from my legs, one by one, with tweezers" (MacCannell and MacCannell 210). But as Austen's novel shows, the normalization of boredom for women long precedes the twentieth century. Men write sentences; women inhabit the parentheses. Knightley has his estate to take care of, Mr. Elton preaches. Emma, by comparison, has little occupation and little choice of occupation. These commonplace distinctions become crucial in relation to boredom and its "normalization." The opposite of boredom is engagement; one must have something to engage with.

As a matter of historical fact, the daughters of the gentry in nineteenth-century England typically found little obvious pretext for engagement in their daily lives. The most passionate statement of the difficulty I have found considerably postdates Austen, coming from a book published in 1866. The situation that book describes, however, duplicates the one Austen evokes for Emma. Emily Davies formulates the problem of the unmarried Victorian young woman in relation to the expectations of men. She points out that in the past, women served a kind of apprenticeship in household management, participating actively in "household labours [which] would supply a very considerable variety of useful occupation. . . . Probably a great many fathers, profoundly ignorant as they are of the lives of women, cherish a vague imagination that the same kind of thing is going on still" (Davies 38). By no means, Davies explains. No longer needed for household tasks, young women have no clear responsibilities and no meaningful occupation. It is unreasonable to expect them to invent things to do: "Women are not stronger-minded than men, and a commonplace young woman can no more work steadily without motive or discipline than a commonplace young man" (42).

The search for "something" to occupy the virtuous young woman— for legitimate objects of female interest—constitutes a subtext in nineteenth-century novels less obviously concerned than *Emma* with the problem of female boredom. Maria Edgeworth's *Helen* (1834) offers a case in point. The study of a naïvely honest girl whose efforts at straightforwardness run into difficulty because of a friend's deviousness, it nominally focuses on moral dilemmas rather than social perplexities. Yet because Helen must discover not only how to live virtuously but how to live in the world, she faces also the pressures of finding occupation for her imagination and intellect in a social environment that stresses the trivial—that, in short, normalizes boredom.

Her creator faces comparable challenges in devising a narrative about a virtuous and conventional young woman inhabiting a conventional environment. Like her eighteenth-century predecessors, Edgeworth can invent complicated miseries for her protagonist. Indeed, Helen suffers greatly as a result of false perceptions of her by many, including her lover. But the novel claims as its ground of interest the central character's psychological struggle rather than her suffering. It implicitly argues for the appeal of the inner life—as literary subject and as object of personal attention. The novelist and the character alike try to discover what interests them, and they reach the same conclusions.

Interest first appears as a subject in the text when triply orphaned Helen (her parents have both died in her early childhood; at the beginning of the novel, her guardian uncle dies) encounters her old mentor, Lady Davenant, mother of her friend Cecilia. Nineteen years old, Helen can now, the narrator suggests, see with adult eyes. She finds Lady Davenant's character compelling. "Even her defects—those inequalities of temper of which she had already had some example, were interesting as evidences of the power and warmth of her affections" (18). Needing to attend to matters of business, Lady Davenant suggests that Helen occupy herself by looking over a portfolio of letters on the table, letters saved, apparently, because of their literary value. The girl glances through many of the letters, until she is "struck by a passage" in one. "She read the whole, it was striking and interesting" (19). Going on to read other letters by the same writer, she comments to herself on their lack of affectation, their ease and naturalness, and the evidence they provide of "something romantic and uncommon in the character of the writer" (19). Such qualities, presumably, constitute the "striking and interesting."

These instances suggest that Helen seeks (and finds "interesting") the emotionally authentic and the genuinely individual. Conventional though she is, she values the "uncommon." She looks beneath surfaces to discover complexities that compensate for the blandness of decorous existence. Beneath her own surface lie comparable complexities. As her companions register this fact, their "interest" in her increases. General Clarendon, for instance, the husband of her old friend Cecilia, becomes "more and more interested about Miss Stanley" (34). So do the young men who encounter her socially. Finally, just before her catastrophic loss of reputation, her lover, Granville Beauclerc (author of the interesting letters), hears others at a large party say that "though there were some as handsome women in the room, there were none so interesting" (326): the ultimate accolade, in this novel's vocabulary.

The word's serious weight comes partly from overtones of its old meaning: something "interesting" implies something worth being interested in. But the novel also attends to the term's subjectivity by contemplating not only what merits interest but what allows people to feel it. A discussion about embroidery raises the question indirectly, as a group containing two women sewing and three or four idlers considers the value of the needle. Lady Davenant declares her categorical respect "for work and workers." Her husband, agreeing with her, wishes that men too could sew: "How many valuable lives might have been saved, how many rich *ennuyés* would not have hung themselves, even in November!" (146) This persiflage calls attention not only to the issue of occupation but to the closely related matter of interest. Lord Davenant's remark suggests that the value of embroidery as activity consists specifically in its capacity to focus attention and involvement—thus to prevent ennui. (John Gregory, a century earlier, had said the same thing, but without acknowledging that men as well as women might suffer from idleness.) Lady Cecilia, on the other hand, finds even the sight of sewing distasteful, because those who interest themselves in their needles withdraw interest from the larger world. She, like everyone else, makes choices about where she will assign interest. Her range is relatively small. Needlework bores her, she shows little inclination for serious discussion or reading, but she enjoys contemplating the natures of men and women—a sufficiently large subject.

Helen, who shares Cecilia's interest in the human, also likes to embroider, to read, and to talk seriously. Not ordinarily a speechmaker, on one occasion she makes a little speech about the sources of interest:

> As we advance in life, it becomes more and more difficult to find in any book the sort of enchanting, entrancing interest which we enjoyed when life, and books, and we ourselves, were new. It were vain to try to settle whether the fault is most in modern books, or in our ancient selves; probably not in either: the fact is, that not only does the imagination cool and weaken as we grow older, but we become, as we live on in this world, too much engrossed by the real business and cares of life, to have feeling or time for factitious, imaginary interests. But why do I say factitious? while they last, the imaginative interests are as real as any others. (150)

As the utterance of a nineteen-year-old girl, this sounds a bit implausible. One hears the voice of the novelist, wishing to provide in her book "enchanting, entrancing interest," troubled to realize that interest derives not only from the nature of the book but also from the emotional makeup of those engaged with it. The move from *imaginary*, in the next to last sentence, to *imaginative* in the final sentence marks an important perception. Imaginary interests may be by definition unreal; imaginative interests, as Helen says, "are as real as any others." The imaginative faculties must engage themselves in order to generate interest in anything at all. By her large capacity for taking interest, Helen demonstrates the quality of her mind and heart.

The "large capacity" involves discrimination as well as acceptance.

For instance, Helen finds Horace Churchill, the mannered fop who finally decides to woo her, altogether uninteresting. Beauclerc, watching her, feels pleased to note that although Churchill amuses Helen, "she would never be interested by such a man" (145). Lady Davenant, eager to know "what degree of interest" Beauclerc and Churchill excite in Helen's mind (139), leads her to confess Churchill amusing while declaring "Mr. Beauclerc's conversation much more interesting" (140). By such distinctions she reiterates the importance of the interesting and of her ability to locate it. Not everyone can. Announcements of boredom recur among the aristocrats who largely populate the novel. One man feels bored with falconry, although another finds it peculiarly absorbing because his commitment to the sport attracts women. A frivolous woman declares intellectual females all "blue bores"—the worst kind, she says. Even Helen, although she does not use the word, endures boredom in the company of the fatuous aide-de-camp who fills the air with empty speech. As in eighteenth-century women's novels, boredom figures here as entrapment: people forced to stay in temporarily or permanently uncongenial social environments suffer it. Helen never feels bored when alone or when able to choose her own occupation: only when forced into unchosen company.

Two early comments, one to, the other by Lady Davenant, help to justify the importance assigned to interest and the interesting in this novel. During a carriage ride with Helen, Lady Davenant says she has a mind to tell her young companion some episodes from her own life. It soon emerges that these events will prove painful to recall and to relate, but Lady Davenant remains determined to pass them on because

> general maxims, drawn from experience are, to the young at least, but as remarks—moral sentences—mere dead letter, and take no hold of the mind. "I have felt" must come before "I think," especially in speaking to a young friend; and, though I am accused of being so fond of generalising that I never come to particulars, I can and will: therefore, my dear, I will tell you some particulars of my life, in which, take notice, there are no adventures.

She then claims for herself a life of feeling rather than incident: "nothing, my dear, to excite or to gratify curiosity." Helen's response reiterates the high importance of feeling, once more in relation to the matter of interest. Quite apart from curiosity, she says, "there is such an interest in knowing what has been really felt and thought in their former lives by those we know and love" (57).

The story Lady Davenant then tells involves her youthful, not altogether conscious, deviation from the path of integrity and the emotional consequences of her moral straying. In an effort to gratify her own vanity, she risked her husband's love. Reporting the critical confrontation, she says, "I cannot tell you exactly how it was—it was so dreadfully interesting to me that I am unable to recall the exact words" (74).

Both Helen's response and Lady Davenant's remark reflect the close relation between interest and other sorts of emotion. On the one hand, human attachment, as Helen notes, creates interest; on the other, interest can be itself the sign of feeling so potent as to destroy memory. Both kinds of connection link interest and meaning. Lady Davenant, assuming Helen's interest in what has happened to her, can take it for granted that the lesson she wishes to teach will communicate itself most forcefully through an anecdote eliciting this personal interest. When Lady Davenant forgets her husband's words, she does so partly because of their intense meaningfulness. Indeed, their meaning essentially inheres in their interest. So "dreadfully interesting" is the husband's apparent repudiation of her that it sears her consciousness, transcending language even while employing it.

The cataclysmic effect of the "dreadfully interesting" event suggests that interest can resemble passion more than inclination. For women in conventional early nineteenth-century society, men provide the most plausible focus of interest, although other ostensible directions of concern may conceal this central one. Flora Tristan's view of Englishwomen does not obviously describe Helen and her friends, who find abundant entertainment for themselves and never appear to perceive their own existence as cold, arid, or deadly dull. Yet the external occupations that present themselves—embroidering, visiting, contemplating architectural improvements, taking drives, painting landscapes—involve no urgency and serve little useful purpose beyond filling time. The not always acknowledged urgency in women's lives as rendered in this novel concerns the problem of finding love: finding something to love as well as discovering how to be loved.

By "love" I mean not only, or not necessarily, sexual love—although obviously marriage constitutes the most widely accepted goal of female aspiration—but love conceived in a wider sense, as devotion to an object of any kind. Given such a definition, the relation of "interest" to "love" becomes readily apparent. Helen's most intense interest, as I have already suggested, focuses on human objects. She can learn from Lady Davenant because she loves her; she interests herself in Beauclerc's letters because she imagines the person who has written them. Edgeworth celebrates such location of interest. In the character of Helen (as well

THE NORMALIZATION OF BOREDOM / 179

as in the normative adult female, Lady Davenant), the novel offers a powerful counterclaim to the hypothesis of female boredom by demonstrating that traditional female qualities—the talent for relationship, the gift of sympathy—can heighten experience, vitalizing an apparently uneventful course of life. It is in some ways a deeply conservative argument, inasmuch as it implies no need for enlargement of women's opportunities or intellectual resources. Given the implicit essentialist view of the female nature, women can solve any potential problem of boredom simply by being women. *Helen*, in other words, considers the "normalization of boredom" for women a mistake of the observer. Tristan and Davies are wrong: Englishwomen may appear to lead boring lives, but their emotional resources protect them from boredom.

The thematizing of interest in this novel, however, does not have altogether conservative implications. If boredom functions once again as the negative of desire, interest serves as desire's surrogate; if love, and interest, *need* not be sexual, both *can* be. Her husband's words are "dreadfully interesting" to Lady Davenant because of the erotic connection between them. When he addresses her as "Lady Davenant" rather than using her first name, she instantly changes course: the threat of lost intimacy chastens her. Helen's claim of interest legitimates her desire. Because Beauclerc's letters, emanations of mind and heart, first attract her, because she feels interest long before she acknowledges love, she proves herself not primarily a sexual being. But she also gives herself room for sexuality. Emma denies desire by inventing happenings outside herself. Helen ignores it by interesting herself in actuality, especially human actuality. But Emma's inventiveness not only chastens her, it also reveals the imaginative vitality that attracts others; and Helen's interest in other human beings readily lends itself to erotic redirection.

Near the beginning of his monumental study of ennui in Western literature, Reinhard Kuhn specifies forms of boredom that do not concern him in his present undertaking. One, he says,

> is illustrated by the typical portrait of the suburbanite. She is tired of the magazine that she is reading or the television show that she is watching and mixes another cocktail for herself. Or perhaps she telephones an equally bored friend and they talk for hours about nothing, or perhaps she drifts into an affair that means as little to her as the television show or the magazine article. (7)

A comparable tone of contempt for the "typical" bored woman emerges from many utterances of the nineteenth and twentieth centuries.

Women do not wish to identify with this unattractive figure; men find her hardly worth noticing.

Kuhn returns to his imagined suburbanite, two pages after the passage quoted above, in a comparison with Emma Bovary. "It is a generally accepted interpretation," he writes,

> that Flaubert's Emma Bovary presents symptoms similar to those felt by the bored suburbanite. And yet to reduce her ennui to this level is to misunderstand the very complex condition of which she is a victim. The former suffers from a metaphysical malady, and the latter only feels a superficial and vague disquiet. It is this difference in dimension that makes of the one a great literary figure and of the other an undistinguished and uninteresting representative of a group. (9)

A "metaphysical malady," worth careful consideration, may characterize a "great literary figure." The "undistinguished and uninteresting representative of a group," on the other hand, in Kuhn's view can hardly inhabit a significant text. The "group" she represents, however, has existed for a long time and has included many members. Edgeworth and Austen—and I am about to add Susan Ferrier to their company—take seriously the problem of boredom, even boredom defined as "superficial and vague disquiet." Not that they condone succumbing to it: quite the contrary. But they recognize it as an enemy that demands considerable resources to combat. Women may be, often are, forced into "undistinguished and uninteresting" lives, doomed to trivial pursuits. How do they nonetheless declare the meaning of their lives? Nineteenth-century answers do not altogether duplicate their eighteenth-century counterparts.

I have argued that assignment of boredom and interest carries cultural as well as personal meaning. Helen's eagerness to engage with Lady Davenant and with Beauclerc helps to define her exemplary status. In general, her concern with relationship declares her good-womanhood; in particular, her interest in a morally upright woman and an intelligent, responsive, responsible man shows her capacity for right thinking and feeling. If her interest focused instead on superficial and selfish Horace Churchill, she would no longer embody her culture's standards. Indeed, Edgeworth could hardly have imagined a heroine with such an interest: Helen would no longer *be* a heroine if she valued a fop. Nor could she fill the heroine's role if her interest directed itself primarily to matters intellectual or abstract. A woman with such interests, in the early nineteenth century, would serve more plausibly as object of satire rather than admiration. Helen's interests make her culturally, socially acceptable. They give her the potential to become a heroine.

In the nineteenth century as in the eighteenth, boredom signals psychic inadequacy. The nature of that perceived inadequacy, however, has changed. When a late eighteenth-century essayist excoriates a wealthy self-made man for having no interests to occupy him once he has retired from commerce, the point is that the object of satire lacks intellectual resources. Given proper education, he would not find himself in such a plight. The bored figures in *Helen*, on the other hand, lack *emotional* resources. They fail not in thought but in feeling. Feeling attests character. The good woman's primary interest in other people demonstrates appropriate emotional orientation. That Beauclerc's financial mistakes derive from his loyalty to a friend, even though that friend proves unworthy, reveals Beauclerc as worthy of admiration. Incapacity for interest in others, conversely, signaling emotional incapacity, marks the morally inadequate.

This point becomes vivid in Susan Ferrier's *Marriage*, published in 1818, in which boredom associates itself with elevated social class or the aspiration to rank, and opprobrium attaches to leisure as the sign of self-indulgence. As a Scotswoman Ferrier, like Edgeworth (who was Irish), did not belong to the dominant English culture. Although Edgeworth elsewhere wrote of Ireland, in *Helen* she makes no reference to anyplace outside England. Ferrier, on the other hand, uses her knowledge of Scotland to comic effect in *Marriage*. The Scottish life she displays is culturally deprived, crude, and difficult. By the way outsiders respond to it, they reveal their true natures.

Almost two hundred of the novel's five hundred-odd pages concern the experience of the heroine's mother, Lady Juliana. After eloping with an officer of Scottish origin, Juliana manifests no adaptive capacity and no ability to empathize even with her own husband. Her concerns focus entirely on herself. She wants a life of pleasure, superficially defined, and reacts with horror to what she finds at her husband's home in Scotland. That horror most often expresses itself as boredom. Juliana exists in a state of "languid dejection, or fretful repinings," by which she passes the "tedious hours" of her time in Scotland (65). The "demon of *ennui*" repeatedly possesses her "vacant mind" (103). Her relatives by marriage struggle in vain to entertain her, but her days grow "more and more tedious" (104). "The inability to experience one's own feelings directly and intensely is the root of chronic boredom," Haskell Bernstein writes (518). Juliana exemplifies this description, translating her every emotion into the catchall category of boredom. When she sees another woman making stockings for the poor, she yawns repeatedly and remarks, "It must be a shocking bore! and such a trouble!" (57). The knitter replies, "Not half such a bore to me as to sit idle," but Lady Juliana fails to get the point. When she gives birth to twin girls, they do not "interest" her (125). A nurse manages to attract her narcissistic involvement to the infant who grows fat and beautiful, but she feels so little concern for the other twin, weak and complaining, that she actually gives the child away. (This daughter, Mary, will become the novel's heroine.)

The word *bore* and its cognates, central to Juliana's vocabulary, figure largely in the novel's early sections. Used to designate anything that does not immediately engage the spoiled young woman, the word itself in its vagueness and inclusiveness suggests her mental and emotional impoverishment. It belongs to the jargon of fashion, which Juliana eagerly embraces. Indeed, she cannot even hear the linguistic discriminations that characterize the speech of Mrs. Douglas, the intelligent, virtuous woman to whom she gives Mary.

The privileged mother who gives away her infant daughter exemplifies the horror of boredom. Her incapacity for genuine interest in anything outside her self registers most sharply in her emotional incapacity for motherhood. The action of the novel turns on degrees of emotional capacity: Mary's largeness of feeling in contrast with her mother's severe limitation, Mrs. Douglas's generosity of spirit in contrast with the narrowness of the other Scotswomen, and so on. Boredom is a trope for emotional limitation of all kinds. Inadequacy of feeling matters far more than intellectual inadequacy—although in fact the two seem to go together here. The capacity to feel properly measures virtue. Thus both Mary's scrupulosity about not involving herself with a man who might court her only because his mother wants him to and her insistence on marrying for love rather than for social advantage testify to her emotional and consequently moral force—the reverse of her mother's languid moral insufficiency.

Juliana as an imagined figure resembles the "typical . . . suburbanite" Kuhn describes, tired of ordinary pursuits, ready to drift into almost any form of plausible entertainment. Her "disquiet," like that of Kuhn's paradigmatic woman, might be characterized as "superficial and vague," and she as a person could be called "undistinguished and uninteresting." Yet her importance in the novel she inhabits far exceeds her stature as a personality. The significance of her malaise, even though it lacks the metaphysical implications Kuhn seeks, permeates Ferrier's fiction. Even trivial forms of boredom carry meaning.

In both *Helen* and *Marriage*, boredom figures as a sign heavily weighted with moral import, a pointer to crucial thematic concerns. The critical plot complication in *Helen* concerns the heroine's inadvertent involvement in Cecilia's double dealings. Before her marriage, Cecilia entangled herself romantically with a man of dubious morals and wrote compromising letters to him. From the beginning of their relationship her husband expresses his determination never to marry a woman who has loved someone before him; consequently Cecilia denies any previous involvement. She implicates Helen in her lie by suggesting that Helen, rather than she herself, was once the object of D'Aubigny's attentions. When D'Aubigny's partly fictionalized correspondence becomes public, Helen is compromised. She declares her inability to marry Beauclerc, since she will not clear her name by exposing her friend, and retreats into exile. Eventually, of course, the truth emerges, and Helen can marry, her integrity reaffirmed.

Cecilia's moral insufficiency derives from emotional flaccidity. She does not exert herself enough to feel richly for her friend, to enter imaginatively into Helen's experience, to realize the implications of her own behavior. Preferring emotional ease to effort, she fails to speak or to act when she should. Her passivity contrasts with Helen's energetic effort to meet Lady Davenant's standards and her own. It corresponds to her limited range of interests, in opposition to Helen's active involvement. Helen's defense of the imaginative power of reading exemplifies her capacity for self-extension: the capacity that enables her insistent interest in other people and in various forms of action. The novel's moral concerns and its plot developments, in other words, constitute extensions from the polarities of boredom and interest as in effect postures of the soul.

"Postures of the soul" become a profoundly complicated issue in Charlotte Brontë's *Villette*, published in 1853 (the year of *Bleak House*) and reworking Brontë's Brussels experience of 1844. Lucy Snowe, the novel's narrator and protagonist, suffers various sorts of anguish, some described, some implicitly indescribable. Impoverished, a worker by necessity, she can never experience the luxury of boredom. Nor does she see a great deal of it in others. Nonetheless, boredom exists as a largely unspoken and specifically female alternative to Lucy's ceaseless industry. The tacit polarities of this novel are not boredom and interest but (as for Dr. Johnson) boredom and action. Both carry moral weight.

> All those strong energies which belong to the body, such as loving and hat-
> ing, fighting, subduing, coveting, grasping, getting, having, and enjoying,
> —these are all growing and gaining strength along with the body, and have
> actually to be overtaken, borne down and compelled to submission by the
> higher powers. (Ellis, *Education* 22)

These words appeared in 1856. Loving, having, and enjoying, in Sarah
Ellis's formulation, must be subdued as savagely as hating, fighting, and
grasping. All constitute dangerous female energies—energies, shock-
ingly, of the body. As Charles Bathurst puts it, "Passion is passion" (5).
He is arguing against female cultivation of feeling:

> We often see girls . . . affect that behaviour which shows liveliness and quick-
> ness, even of temper, as well as of affectionate feeling, rather than sense and
> quietness: cultivate (in plain English) *passion*, feelings, and emotions, and
> what is called animation; not always meant to be confined to the kindly and
> affectionate feelings, but to nurse up, heighten, and exaggerate both likings
> and dislikings of any sort; as opposed to a cool, calm, peaceful state of mind,
> suited to reason, consideration, patience, and self-control. (3–4)

Charlotte Brontë and Lucy Snowe inhabit the culture that produced
Ellis's words and Bathurst's, a culture fearful of female emotional force,
willing to jettison love and enjoyment, liveliness, emotion, and anima-
tion for women in favor of "reason, consideration, patience, and self-
control." *Passion* was a dirty word. This was a world of which a woman
could write that her fellow females are generally "satisfied with employment that is little better than digging holes and filling them up again"
(Taylor 62), that they engage in needlework for the sake of "the sooth-
ing effect of sedentary monotonous occupation, the advantage of having a subject of common interest that the silliest can understand, and,
above all, the filling up of time" (71).

Lucy Snowe claims for herself just that "cool, calm, peaceful state of
mind" that Bathurst recommends. The narrative that contains her dramatically demonstrates that coolness and self-control belong only to
the surface, that a woman can spend her time docilely digging holes
and filling them up again while yet seething with various forms of just
that passion she has obediently compelled to submission.

In 1826 an anonymous work titled *Diary of an Ennuyée* appeared in
London. Its editor explains that the diary was found after the author's
death. "As a real picture of natural and feminine feeling, the Editor
hopes that it may interest others as much as it has interested him"
(Jameson 1). The diarist describes herself as a victim of grief for an
unspecified calamity, who travels in the hope that "continual motion,

continual novelty, the absolute necessity for self-command may do something for me" (5). Although Paris, for instance, excites her, she soon reverts to melancholy. "Why was I proud of my victory over passion?" she inquires. "Alas! what avails it that I have shaken the viper from my hand, if I have no miraculous antidote against the venom which has mingled with my life blood, and clogged the pulses of my heart!" (44). Her mood does not appreciably improve, but she concludes, "I can allow that one half at least, of the beauty and interest we see, lies in our own souls" (207). This writer's incapacity to take an interest in the world stems not from boredom but from depression.

A cultural gap divides 1826 from 1853. Lucy Snowe too suffers from depression. The trope of the viper of passion shaken off yet leaving its venom behind might apply to her, and the perception that much of "the beauty and interest we see, lies in our own souls" is fully exemplified in *Villette*. Yet an author could no longer assume in quite the same way that "a real picture of natural and feminine feeling" would "interest" readers in general—or that a picture of self-pity, rage, and self-dramatization could be perceived as either "natural" or "feminine." The anger that invigorates all of Brontë's fiction expresses itself in *Villette* largely through the figure of disguise. Lucy Snowe is a woman in hiding, compliant with social expectations for a female in her state of life, yet bursting with unacceptable passion. Her self-respect depends on successfully concealing most of her feelings. Feeling, outside a very limited range, is no longer respectable.

Yet of course feeling is Charlotte Brontë's subject. I have described *Emma, Helen,* and *Marriage* as all concerned with the nature of an acceptable inner life for women. *Emma* argues for the necessity of imposing limits on imagination, for the subterranean identity of desire and imagination, and for the possibility of controlled gratification of desire. *Helen* and *Marriage* both maintain the necessity of "interest" as a female attribute, a sign of the woman's concern for others, of her capacity for benign and outwardly directed feeling. "Interest" also serves as surrogate for desire, and even as justification. Brontë, though, at a historical moment when women were urged to subdue loving and hating and getting and having and enjoying, would find it harder to speak even indirectly of desire, harder to celebrate the life of feeling, however benign. After all, as Bathurst had pointed out, one kind of feeling leads all too easily to another: passion is passion. So Brontë constructs her "have it both ways" narrative: the story of a woman who behaves impeccably except when seriously ill, who consciously and explicitly avoids unduly disturbing readers' sensibilities but also avoids any displays of "womanly" feeling, whose turbulent inner life rarely erupts but nonetheless compels attention.

Lucy Snowe occasionally feels bored. When she finds herself in this state, she takes prompt steps to alleviate it. Ginevra Fanshawe, a student in the establishment where Lucy teaches, demands that Lucy do her sewing. "A compliance of some weeks threatening to result in the establishment of an intolerable bore, I at last distinctly told her she must make up her mind to mend her own garments" (79). Much earlier, less emphatically, Lucy inhabits a household along with the child Polly. At times Polly sits dutifully on a stool, sewing or drawing or "learning her task," never showing a spark of peculiarity. "I ceased to watch her under such circumstances," Lucy observes; "she was not interesting" (19). These two instances exemplify Lucy's emphatic insistence on controlling her own situation when to do so lies within her power. In this respect as in others, she contrasts vividly with Ginevra, who often complains of being bored by some person or some necessity of life, and indeed with the female students she teaches, who find their lessons boring and rail about boring tasks. Once, to be sure, Lucy finds herself helpless against—not boredom, really: a vicious form of ennui. Left alone during a school vacation, feeling the days long, silent, and lifeless, the premises "vast and void," the garden "gloomy," she hardly knows how she will live to the end of the eight weeks. "When I had full leisure to look on life as life must be looked on by such as me, I found it but a hopeless desert; tawny sands, with no green fields, no palmtree, no well in view" (150). She diagnoses the problem clearly as due to the withdrawal of "the prop of employment," her customary recourse against boredom and depression alike. Never does she willingly suffer boredom: she does not accept it as the female condition.

Or at any rate as *her* female condition. Lucy's relation to other women composes a compelling subtext of *Villette*. For some women she feels a good deal of affection: for Polly, first in her knowledge a tiny child, later a charming woman; for Polly's mother, who cares for Lucy in her illness; even for Madame Beck, secretive, conniving, but as a worker worthy of respect; and for Ginevra, whose meretriciousness Lucy knows clearly. Ginevra and Madame Beck emerge as more or less contemptible, Polly and her mother as admirable. As far as Lucy is concerned, though, *all* other women appear objects of contempt, to greater or less degree. They have not experienced such suffering as she has endured; they live, by comparison, sheltered lives. Untested, they do not belong to her kind. Companionable, helpful, even dependent though she may temporarily be, Lucy does not, cannot, consider them equals.

On occasion she seems to imagine the common lot of women—of *other* women, that is—as boredom. At any rate, her imagery for that lot emphasizes uneventfulness. The best-known instance:

> I will permit the reader to picture me, for the next eight years, as a bark slumbering through halcyon weather, in a harbour clear as glass—the steersman stretched on the little deck, his face up to heaven, his eyes closed: buried, if you will, in a long prayer. A great many women and girls are supposed to pass their lives something in that fashion; why not I with the rest? (30)

A sense of superiority to the ignorant and emotionally timid reader merges with the condescension toward ignorant and emotionally timid women who exist as women are supposed to. Such women, in Lucy's understanding of them, live emotionally as well as physically uneventful lives. Never forced to struggle for emotional or physical survival, they belong to a world different from hers. In her explicit formulations, Lucy makes the difference a sign of her worth.

Yet it stands also as a mark of her inferiority. Ginevra has not a fraction of Lucy's intelligence, spirit, or imagination, yet she consistently patronizes the slightly older woman, flaunting her superior sexual attractiveness. Lucy believes herself unattractive. She reminds the reader repeatedly of her lack of physical beauty, insisting that even elegant clothes cannot beautify her. Conscious of erotic feeling toward a young doctor, she suppresses it with a rigidity and insistence worthy of Sarah Ellis herself—suppresses it not on moral grounds but because she understands the impossibility of its gratification. Although she believes herself more intelligent, more emotionally experienced, more fully tested by suffering than any other woman she knows, she also sees that other women attract men and that they manage lives of ease and grace. The involuted tone and diction of *Villette* convey Lucy's utterly opposed attitudes: her convictions both of superiority and of worthlessness.

The eventlessness and boredom she implicitly and explicitly posits in other women's lives correspondingly mark both their inferiority and their superiority. Lucy takes pride in her capacity to do things well. Although she claims to have no ambition, once challenged by Madame Beck to assume the role of teacher, she determines to succeed at this new work, as she determines to triumph as an actress when Monsieur Paul persuades her to assume a last-minute part. Her self-esteem depends on her self-sufficiency, which she repeatedly demonstrates. (Hence the special horror of her collapse into dependency under the strain of illness.) From the point of view of a self-sufficient woman, the passivity and dependence of most women, their acceptance of unpro-

188 / CHAPTER SIX

ductive existences, declare the relative inadequacy of other members of her sex. From the point of view of the woman forced to labor for sustenance, however, the life of passivity and dependence—and imagined boredom—also signifies comfort and relief. Lucy is both these women: the self-sufficient worker, the forced laborer. And she conveys both points of view.

A man does find Lucy attractive, it turns out. Monsieur Paul wishes to marry her (and she to marry him), but not to doom her to dependency. As a sign of her specialness and his, he dramatizes his love by making it possible for her to establish her own school. Waiting for him to return from the West Indies, where he has gone on a mission of duty, she does not loll on a sofa, like the image of Cleopatra for which she feels disgust and contempt. Instead she continues to work, passing the three happiest years of her life because she considers herself her lover's steward, because she works for him. "The spring which moved my energies lay far away beyond seas, in an Indian isle" (478). No longer does Lucy declare the old form of self-sufficiency. Instead, she glories in her sense of connection as well as in the work it sustains. But her happiness promises no happy ending for the novel: she returns to her tone of ambiguous contempt in alluding to those of "sunny imaginations" who believe in happy endings, able to picture for her "union and a happy succeeding life" (481).

Because Lucy's tone here closely resembles that with which she refers to the eventless lives of girls and women, I feel tempted to suggest that she connects sunny imaginations with emotionally ignorant females. Sunny imaginations belong to those who do not know what life is really like, those whose lives Flora Tristan characterized as marked by "deadly uniformity," those whose experience Lucy considers boring—even while she envies it. Happiness, Swift's Hack claimed, is the perpetual possession of being well deceived. Lucy seems inclined to believe the same thing. Her energies perforce direct themselves toward survival, which depends partly, at the novel's end as at its beginning, on the suppression of desire. Suppression, but not total denial. No more able to afford the luxury of self-deception than that of boredom, Lucy demonstrates the operation of an imagination not fueled by the reading of novels, not directed toward creating interest for herself by rewriting other people's lives, but focused primarily on establishing a self-image that can help her in the task of survival. That self-image includes full awareness of what she has lost.

Brontë's enterprise in writing *Villette* differs from Austen's in *Emma* as dramatically as the novels' protagonists differ. Both works appear to uphold the necessity of keeping feeling and fancy under control. Lucy, who specializes in understatement, rarely allows herself imaginative liberty; Emma learns to curb her own freedom of fancy. But Brontë, unlike Austen, emphasizes the pains of curbing, giving tragic dignity to Lucy's rigorous self-discipline and presenting it as an aspect of her unrelenting anguish—as well as a defense against that anguish. Instead of the manifest decorum of civil existence that Emma's refraining constitutes, Lucy's necessary reticence reveals itself as part of the high cost paid for existence in society. Austen hints the loss involved in social maturity by making the reader enjoy Emma's imaginative vitality. Brontë goes beyond hints, duplicating her character's ambivalence as she simultaneously endorses and undermines Victorian proprieties for women.

Emma never mentions boredom, but she constantly withstands it. Lucy directly speaks of it only rarely and trivially. By implication, though, she judges as boring female forms of existence different from her own, and she at least partly envies the monotony of such lives. For Emma, for Lucy, and for Edgeworth's Helen, boredom is the largely unmentionable alternative to self-constructed modes of possibility. Even in the nineteenth century, many texts suggest the normalization of boredom for women and the felt need for women to resist that normalization. To experience their own desire, women had to evade the deadening power of severe restriction. Fiction suggests they found ingenious ways to do so.

To consider this group of novels together under the rubric of boredom, even though boredom by no means supplies their central subject, calls attention once more to the by now much reiterated fact that an experienced, though often suppressed, sense of tedium belongs to the daily life of many modern women as rendered in fiction. Such consideration reminds us again of the amount of cultural condensation implicit in the idea of boredom. But it also helps clarify the curious sense of urgency many readers feel in Austen's, Edgeworth's, and Brontë's novels. Only *Villette,* of the three works centrally considered in this chapter, evinces a (fairly) clear aspect of social protest. Yet all three novels throb with an energy of resistance that provides power. What they resist is the social prohibition for women of many forms of meaningful action. The struggle against boredom is one consequence of such prohibition. Emma, Helen, and Lucy refuse to accept boredom as their fate. Misguided or conventional in form, their resistance helps constitute their characters and the plots that contain them.

If I have succeeded in demonstrating the cultural importance of boredom, the demonstration implies literary consequences. A notion that distills such a rich array of moral and psychological meanings must carry those meanings into the texts it inhabits. In nineteenth-century England, and even more insistently in the twentieth century, most works of fiction (and many of drama, poetry, and autobiography) contain at least the vocabulary, and often the rendered condition, of boredom, an ever more central aspect of cultural experience. Even when they make no point of the fact or the language of boredom, the emotion's presence contributes to textual impact, often in complicated fashion. Such presence does not make a literary work itself boring: often quite the contrary.

SEVEN

Society and Its Discontents

Cultural Contexts of Nineteenth-Century Boredom

Nineteenth-century women, as imagined by nineteenth-century women, understood boredom as a malady threatening their sex but resistible by individual effort and imagination. Twentieth-century readers contemplating female representations in fiction published more than a hundred years earlier may perceive the malady as an inevitable result of social impositions on women, but the texts of novels by such writers as Austen and Brontë provide only indirect and ambiguous evidence that the novelists understood the situation in comparable ways. Victorian male novelists, on the other hand, typically stress the direct connection between a decadent and corrupt society and the boredom of its participants.

Publishing *Don Juan* between 1819 and 1824, Byron could comment that his own "Society is smooth'd to that excess, / That manners hardly differ more than dress" (Byron 789; *Don Juan* 13: 751–52). He goes on to connect this smoothing out of difference to the problem of boredom:

> there is nought to cull
> Of folly's fruit: for, though your fools abound,
>   They're barren and not worth the pains to pull.
> Society is now one polish'd horde,
>   Form'd of two mighty tribes, the *Bores* and *Bored*.
>   (789; 13: 756–60)

Describing a country house party, he suggests the participants' primary interest in "Ambrosial Cash" (790; 13: 799), then reports their daily activity. Young and middle-aged men go out hunting:

> The middle-aged, to make the day more short;
> For *ennui* is a growth of English root,
>   Though nameless in our language: —we retort
> The fact for words, and let the French translate
> That awful yawn which sleep can not abate.
>   (790; 13: 804–08)

Those who remain behind have yet more trouble finding entertaining occupation. Boredom threatens everyone.

Byron, an aristocrat writing of aristocrats, established the tone for many of his century's imaginative renditions, particularly of life among the idle rich. The sense of society as a "polish'd horde," barbarity slicked over by social decorum; the insistence on "Ambrosial Cash" as a primary interest of people at every social level; the description of men and women desperately seeking occupation—all reappeared in many a novel. More important than any specific detail was the prevalent imagining of boredom as a social rather than an individual malady. Inflicted on those with little significant function in life, therefore associated especially with the rich, boredom signaled social discontent that did not recognize itself as such. The novelists who render it, however, rely on it as a means of criticizing existing social arrangements and assumptions. Even when a character in these fictions understands herself (usually) as responsible for her own discontent, the novelistic pattern suggests social causes for individual maladies. The aristocratic subject, in the imagining of middle-class writers, figures the sickness of the age. Yet boredom also continued to serve highly specific and individual novelistic functions.

Bleak House virtually begins with yawns, the response to the tedium of Jarndyce and Jarndyce in its slow progress through the courts. Boredom in the eventless courtroom seems explicable. Lady Dedlock's emotional deadness is another matter.

> My Lady Dedlock (who is childless), looking out in the early twilight from her boudoir at a keeper's lodge, and seeing the light of a fire upon the latticed panes, and smoke rising from the chimney, and a child, chased by a woman, running out into the rain to meet the shining figure of a wrapped-up man coming through the gate, has been put quite out of temper. My Lady Dedlock says she has been "bored to death." (Dickens, *Bleak House* 9)

The narrator's sentimental vignette purports to explain the lady's asserted boredom. Although the account announces no direct reason for either boredom or being "put quite out of temper," the shining man and the running child function as sufficient causes. The episode establishes a simple psychological situation: childless woman, saddened by the sight of happy domesticity, feels cross and bored.

But a heavy weight of irony impinges, implicit in the contrast between the lyrical rhythms of the domestic vision and the flatness of the final sentence; in the references to "*My* Lady Dedlock," the pronoun recalling the deference accorded to a member of the nobility; and in the generalized attitude established by the preceding paragraphs on "the world of fashion." "It is a deadened world, and its growth is sometimes unhealthy for want of air" (8). When Lady Dedlock asserts that she is "bored to death," her claim, in this context, has almost literal force. (The novel's action will fully literalize her inexorable movement toward death.) The text invites a response to her situation involving something more than, opposed to, sentimental sympathy. Her boredom, conventional though it is, demands a gloss—partly because, *Bleak House* repeatedly suggests, all conventionality needs glossing. The novel's subsequent chapters, interpreting Lady Dedlock's boredom, will make it more perplexing even as it becomes more comprehensible.

Sir Leicester Dedlock, the lady's husband, accepts her boredom as an aristocratic appurtenance. He himself "is generally in a complacent state, and rarely bored. When he has nothing else to do, he can always contemplate his own greatness" (154). His narcissism averts tedium. We can draw no general conclusions from this fact, though, for Lady Dedlock's narcissism fully implicates itself in her stance of boredom.

This emphasized boredom helps to focus several of the novel's paradoxes. Lady Dedlock's position contrasts with that of her daughter, Esther, who strives from childhood "to be industrious, contented, and kind-hearted, and to do some good to some one, and win some love to [her]self if [she] could" (18). None of the adjectival virtues Esther invokes obviously characterize her mother, who is never industrious, never content, and though not devoid of kindly impulse, conceals her kindness. But the text raises questions about the value of conventional virtues. Mrs. Jellyby as parodic figure makes one wonder about the morality of industry ("I love hard work; I enjoy hard work" [103]), that mode of self-defense epitomized by Lucy Snowe, and even about the desirability of wanting to do good, like Edgeworth's Helen. Mrs. Jellyby's cheerful spirit (parodically duplicating Esther's customary resolute good cheer) marks her insensitivity. By comparison, boredom signals moral awareness. For Lady Dedlock, "the desolation of Boredom" associates itself with "the clutch of Giant Despair" (154). If her reaction to that clutch (always to "fly") does not command respect, her "weariness of soul"—alternatively termed boredom and despair—acknowledges her consciousness of and responsibility for past sin. Her daughter, also threatened by despair, makes up her mind "to be so dreadfully industrious that [she] would leave [her]self not a moment's leisure to be low-spirited" (235). The adverb gives one pause. Why "dreadfully"? The shadow of Mrs. Jellyby looms again.

Esther neither elucidates nor recurs to the momentary perception hinted by her adverb. The reader, however, may speculate that the refusal to allow herself "a moment's leisure," defending not against boredom but against the closely connected malady of depression (Lucy Snowe's malady, withstood in comparable ways), records Esther's reluctance to fully confront her own feelings. The possible dreadfulness of her industry indeed reflects, at immense distance, the dreadfulness of Mrs. Jellyby's, a defense against emotional actuality. Industry as the alternative to boredom possesses its own ambiguities, calling attention by contrast to the honesty implicit in Lady Dedlock's boredom.

That may seem a peculiar judgment, since most readers perceive such boredom as a pose. Boredom as a public stance emphasizes Lady Dedlock's acquired aristocracy. It marks the difficulty of pleasing her, the luxury of her aloofness. If the text conveys that boredom constitutes suffering, it also suggests how boredom conceals other suffering by disguising its nature.

Yet boredom as spiritual and emotional inertia declares the truth of Lady Dedlock's condition as aristocrat by marriage and as suffering human being. Esther's determined industry obscures from herself as from others the intensity of her pain. Lady Dedlock's boredom works in comparable ways for most observers (not for Mr. Tulkinghorn, not for Esther), but it conceals nothing from herself. Moreover, it dramatizes what has happened to her. To live the life she has chosen, she must destroy the passion and the maternal devotion for which she no longer has occasion. Both manifest themselves in isolated moments, but most of the time they effectively do not exist. Their absence amounts to deadness, with boredom its sign.

The novel's third-person narrator exploits the tension between boredom as pose and as spiritual malaise in portraying Lady Dedlock and in extending her boredom to other members of the Dedlock tribe, stereotypical participants in aristocratic society. Thus Cousin Volumnia, a cause of boredom in others, "being one of those sprightly girls who cannot long continue silent without imminent peril of seizure by the dragon Boredom" (790), lapses readily into yawns. Her male equivalent, "the debilitated cousin" (570), too languid and uninvolved to utter a comprehensible sentence, likewise embodies aristocratic moral decay. The posturing of these minor characters, like Lady Dedlock's behavior, reveals emotional entropy.

In the mythology of *Bleak House*, boredom's true opposite is not Esther's compulsive industry but her embracing capacity for interest. She marks her recovery from illness as a process by which "I became useful to myself, and interested, and attached to life again" (490). Attachment to life, of course, depends on interest. The scope of Esther's interests, focused primarily on other people but also on her own and others' activities, guarantees her survival, as the severe limitation of Lady Dedlock's interest ensures her death. The lady concerns herself with a village girl named Rosa. When she sends Rosa away, she herself next appears "as indifferent as if all passion, feeling, and interest, had been worn out in the earlier ages of the world, and had perished from its surface with its other departed monsters" (652). To figure passion, feeling, and interest as monsters suggests the sinister transformative power that even the pose of boredom may possess. And the sentence uncovers what boredom destroys: emotional capacities, gifts of involvement beyond the self. Having left passion, feeling, and interest in the antediluvian past, Lady Dedlock can only die.

Failure of interest is implicit in Lady Dedlock's boredom, in that of the Dedlock cousins, and in Richard's feeling "languid about the profession" of medicine, which he thinks, according to Mrs. Badger, "a tiresome pursuit": "He has not that positive interest in it which makes it his vocation" (229). (Richard, of course, has been corrupted not by the possession but by the fantasy of riches.) In each case, the failure emphasizes the inability to extend attention outward that boredom fosters. Lady Dedlock reveals narcissism as tragedy. Her concentration on self and the boredom that accompanies it alike derive from the sin (in Dickens's moral universe) of bearing a child out of wedlock. Motherhood, the emblem of commitment to another, for Lady Dedlock entails isolation. When her husband reads aloud to her an essay he admires, by a man with "a well-balanced mind," she cannot concentrate: "The man's mind is not so well balanced but that he bores my Lady, who, after a languid effort to listen, or rather a languid resignation of herself to a show of listening, becomes distraught" (402). Languid resignation to a show of listening belongs to boredom as pose. Distraught misery inheres in boredom as (fictional) actuality.

Less concerned to document Lady Dedlock's suffering than to suggest its meanings, the third-person narrator implies compassion,

reminding the reader of the association between the character's boredom and her despair. Inasmuch as he also calls attention to the connection between her boredom and her sin, he adumbrates a moral judgment on her state. The reader presumably shares Mr. Tulkinghorn's
admiration for the lady's self-discipline. She displays courage as well as
control, and loyalty to the man she has married. But the insistent link-
age of boredom with sin and misery makes us understand Lady Dedlock most profoundly as victim—not of a tedious world (despite the
undeniable tedium of her social environment) but of her own actions.
On the other hand, those actions—both the premarital impropriety
and the aristocratic marriage—reveal the consequences of an oppressive social system. In it individual virtues—the discipline, courage, and
loyalty that characterize Lady Dedlock—have no redemptive power.
Esther can rescue herself from despair by energy and interest focused
outward. Lady Dedlock, doomed to boredom, therefore lacks the
capacity for such focus. The lack defines her misery and her consequent
moral inadequacy.

As a subject for the novel's moral commentary, boredom accumulates
an impressive weight of meaning. But Dickens's moral focus differs not
only from that of the medieval theologians who understood states of
nonengagement as antithetical to faith but also from that of eighteenth-
century thinkers who concerned themselves with the proper use of
human faculties. Lady Dedlock's boredom is by its nature incurable.
The medieval monk and the eighteenth-century citizen have it within
their power to remedy their states, and they know their responsibility
to do so. Not so the lady whose sexual sin entails her psychic suffering.
She can undo neither the sin nor its consequences.

If Dickens's narrator resembles his predecessors in understanding
boredom as imbued with moral weight, he differs from them, then, in
considering it essentially an unchangeable condition. Inasmuch as it
conveys spiritual emptiness and alienation, it declares itself unalterable.
As despair by its nature denies the possibility of change, so Lady Dedlock's boredom, closely allied to despair, rejects modification.

The moral positions of the bored often inhere in position of another
sort: in roles of wealth and power, acquired or hereditary, and in association with such roles. The cousins thus take on their boredom by con-
tiguity with Sir Leicester and his wife; Richard's boredom derives from
his obsessed fantasies of approaching wealth; and Lady Dedlock's
depends partly on the opportunities provided by her social position.

Connecting boredom as psychic condition with the burdens and
privileges of aristocracy, inherited or acquired, is a nineteenth-century

move. To link boredom with wealth has always seemed tempting. A lady, by *being* a lady, has leisure for boredom. But social realism plays a relatively small part in Dickens's characterization of Lady Dedlock, which depends more vitally on middle-class fantasies and projections about the upper classes: not their wealth, but their style. Flora Tristan's view, that of a foreign visitor to England, echoes with more emphasis the fantasy of native middle-class observers. Tristan comments that rich "English women not only do nothing at home, but they imagine that touching a needle would reduce them to the status of working women. Time weighs heavily on them" (196). Men of the same social class, in their clubs, "all appeared to be supremely bored" (246). The attitude of those who must work toward those who need not inevitably betrays at least ambivalence, often resentment.

Those who work feel contempt for those who do not. They both express that contempt and reassure themselves by imagining the boredom of people without meaningful occupation: hence the tendency of middle-class writers to represent upper-class characters as bored. But Dickens's narrator, contemptuous of the enervated cousin, conveys more complicated class-inflected attitudes toward Lady Dedlock. If aristocratic boredom marks a class's alleged moral inferiority (as non-workers), it also epitomizes that class's claim to superiority. Tristan's nonsewing women use their boredom as a sign of rank. So, for different reasons, does the imagined figure of Lady Dedlock. Refusal to find or to make the world "interesting" marks the languor of a group that feels entitled to its difference. Both envy and resentment infuse the middle-class response.

Lady Dedlock justifies in action the implicit claim of superiority made by her personal style. By her constantly dramatized boredom she asserts her position as Sir Leicester Dedlock's wife. Her boredom implies the world's incapacity to provide adequate stimulus for her, and it heroically conceals her anguish. Boredom as concealment marks her moral achievement. If the plot punishes her with death for a sexual lapse, it also allows her to reveal her pain openly in her final self-destructive wandering. Previous to that last fatal expedition, Lady Dedlock has demonstrated her heroism by preserving the aristocratic pose that irritates the middle classes.

The character thus embodies the scope of boredom both as pose and as psychic deadness. Such "deadness" provides Lady Dedlock's necessary defense against feeling. When penetrated, it allows little but pain. Moreover, it *constitutes* pain: the vacuity of the lady's days, the alienation that leads to her death. In this Victorian novel as in the work of medieval theologians, inability to find the world interesting constitutes loss of faith: despair. By calling this inability "boredom" rather than "ennui," Dickens, employing a term in his time still associated with upper-class slang, links the trivial and the profound, external irritation and internal misery. The stance that in the enervated cousin seems reprehensible as well as foolish, in Lady Dedlock appears bitter necessity. Dickens transmutes a Victorian social cliché by examining it closely in a single imagined case.

The matter of boredom does not organize the full multiplicity of Dickens's novel, but it condenses important other concerns of *Bleak House*. Most significantly, perhaps, it demonstrates the complex impositions of social pressure on individuals often barely conscious of it. The dynamic of self and other, embodied and examined in Esther's selflessness, in Mr. Jarndyce's magnanimity, in Caddy Jellyby's moral education, in her mother's moral blindness, in Richard's selfishness and Harold Skimpole's, in Ada's devotion, in the courts' operation, in the ramifications of friendship—this dynamic plays itself out also in the manifestations of boredom, with its incapacity for involvement. In a single passionate sentence, the narrator suggests the moral obligation to be *interested*: "Stand forth, Jo, in uncompromising colours! From the sole of thy foot to the crown of thy head, there is nothing interesting about thee" (641). The novel makes us, its readers, interested in Jo. Its allegation that the waif is uninteresting calls attention to the others' refusal of interest in Jo's world, and to the subjectivity of "interest" as concept. In its emphatic formulation, the "nothing interesting" sentence paradoxically demands interest for Jo and, by extension, for all unfortunates.

Boredom in its refusal of interest constitutes a moral flaw on a continuum of other flaws. Lady Dedlock's ambiguous ennui provides a central image of death-in-life for a work preoccupied with various forms of death-in-life generated by the operations of law. It defines one pole of the opposition between stasis and energy played out through many manifestations and exemplifies the possible discrepancy between outer forms and inner life. The notion of boredom epitomizes the allegorical implications of Lady Dedlock's name. Her spiritual deadlock, product of past choices, limits her capacity for energy and desire: precisely the operation of boredom. *Bleak House* embodies the intricacy of implication inherent in the word *boredom* through a character organized by boredom's meanings. And though the psychic state is never emphasized as a crucial motif, it calls attention by analogy and by contrast to other vital issues in *Bleak House*.

Many of the attitudes toward boredom that reveal themselves in *Bleak House* will sound familiar by now. The celebration of interest, the attachment of moral weight to boredom, the claim of boredom's enmity to energy and desire, the use of industry as defense: we have encountered these before. But the presence of boredom as sign of superiority and the likelihood of boredom as pose, as well as the association between boredom and the upper classes, suggest new complexities. Lucy Snowe's ambiguous attitude toward the posited boring lives of women implies ways that, from the point of view of the underprivileged, boredom might constitute a mark of privilege; but Lady Dedlock indicates further possibilities. Boredom, always already rejecting what it has not yet experienced, makes intimacy inconceivable. As a posture of rejection, it repudiates attempts to establish a mode of equality and thus inevitably constitutes a mark of superiority: therefore, presumably, a desirable pose.

The prospect of boredom as pose, the conception of it as bearing on considerations of class, the association of boredom with superiority—all shift emphasis from inner experience to life in the world. In chapter 1 I suggested that a developing "sociological view" of boredom characterized the nineteenth century. Although Dickens's representation of Lady Dedlock evinces subtle psychological and moral awareness, it also shows his not altogether comfortable consciousness of boredom as social construct. Lucy Snowe's vivid recognition of the discrepancy between her self-presentation and her inner experience suggests one cause for discomfort: the notion that displayed emotion might constitute a pose has unnerving implications. Yet more troubling is the conceivable corollary—by now all too familiar—that social intercourse depends on the manipulation of false selves.

A year after *Bleak House*, Dickens published *Hard Times*, with its more sinister though less central exemplar of boredom as pose. In the character of James Harthouse, near seducer of Louisa Gradgrind, the novelist proposes the pose of boredom as a mark of moral insufficiency. When Louisa asks Harthouse if he has no opinions of his own, he sums up his moral position:

> I have not so much as the slightest predilection left. I assure you I attach not the least importance to any opinions. The result of the varieties of boredom I have undergone is a conviction (unless conviction is too industrious a word for the lazy sentiment I entertain on the subject) that any set of ideas will do just as much good as any other set, and just as much harm as any other set. (162)

This pronouncement embodies its speaker's slippery mingling of appearance and substance. His insistence that he cares about nothing, with the attached explanation that his lack of caring derives from the "varieties of boredom" he has "undergone," sounds like a fashionable affectation. On the other hand, one would hardly conclude from Harthouse's statement that he *does* care about much of anything. His bored attitudinizing has infected him. Pretending he doesn't care has made him, finally, not care.

To term Harthouse's bored stance a *fashionable* affectation calls attention to its origins, explained parenthetically shortly before he disappears from the novel. Harthouse ends as he began, "still true to his conviction that indifference was the genuine high-breeding (the only conviction he had)" (251). Genuine high breeding demands the "conviction" he alleged earlier, that any set of ideas or experiences is as good as any other. He

> had tried life as a Cornet of Dragoons, and found it a bore; and had afterwards tried it in the train of an English minister abroad, and found it a bore; and had then strolled to Jerusalem, and got bored there; and had then gone yachting about the world, and got bored everywhere. (158)

Stance or genuine emotional response? James Harthouse hardly knows the difference. Dickens, however, invents for him a situation that engages unequivocally real feeling, although the narrator never specifies that feeling's nature. Lust? Pleasure in the chase or in the activity of his mind in planning it? At any rate, projecting Louisa's seduction, "He was not at all bored for the time, and could give his mind to it" (206). Louisa's ultimate evasion distresses Harthouse:

> He was positively agitated. He several times spoke with an emphasis, similar to the vulgar manner. He went in and went out in an unaccountable way, like a man without an object. He rode like a highwayman. In a word, he was so horribly bored by existing circumstances that he forgot to go in for boredom in the manner prescribed by the authorities. (249)

By specifying Harthouse's agitation as a state of being "horribly bored," the narrator defines boredom as pain, suggesting that the unemphatic "manner prescribed by the authorities" constitutes only a mask of boredom having little to do with the actuality. Harthouse has previously concerned himself with manner rather than substance. Now he feels something so authentic that he fails to worry about how he looks. By his own standards, though, he has deviated from aristocratic behavior in allowing himself "emphasis." He will soon revert to ways of acting that protect him from revealing, and perhaps even from feeling, feeling.

Such a description of Harthouse's deportment may make him sound ridiculous, but he is more sinister than that. The novel hints that his moral danger to others stems from the fact that something in most human beings responds to the temptation of not caring. When Louisa confesses to her father, "My dismal resource has been to think that life would soon go by, and that nothing in it could be worth the pain and struggle of a contest" (241), she transposes Harthouse's indifference into a more plangent key. Boredom can seem preferable to more active forms of pain. Louisa's steady misery draws her to Harthouse. Similarly, Harthouse's influence over Tom stems from the alternative he offers to direct and difficult experience. His own moral insufficiency also derives from the illusion of ease that boredom offers. "The not being troubled with earnestness was a grand point in his favour, enabling him to take to the hard Fact fellows with as good a grace as if he had been born one of the tribe, and to throw all other tribes overboard, as conscious hypocrites" (194–95). Boredom as pose or as actuality—either obviates making discriminations.

Finally, Harthouse like Lady Dedlock reveals that the distinction between boredom as manner and as substance has little meaning. In Dickens's apparent view, the refusals alike implicit in boredom as stance and as emotion imply abrogation of responsibility. To associate boredom as a posture with "genuine high-breeding" condenses a biting criticism of the upper classes, who, by implication, reject involvement with others, claim superiority to passion or principle, and condescend to those so ill bred as to care about anything. Harthouse is an imitation aristocrat: occasionally he lapses into feeling. To real aristocrats belongs the repudiation of feeling—passion and compassion—that constitutes boredom.

William Makepeace Thackeray's brilliant exploration of the British social scene, *Vanity Fair*, appeared in 1847–48, before the two Dickens novels we have been considering. Although the representation of Becky Sharp lives in most memories as the book's crucial component, *Vanity Fair* concerns itself more essentially with society than with individuals. In the society it depicts, boredom fulfills complicated cultural functions.

Becky Sharp enrages, entices, fascinates, appalls. She never bores.

One cannot say the same thing about her foil, virtuous Amelia Sedley. Although Thackeray's narrator lavishes sentimental praise on Amelia, he reveals occasional uncomfortable semiawareness that the more impeccable the behavior of the good girl, the more boring.

Attributions of who or what is boring, I must say once more, depend on the attributer. Devoted Dobbin presumably does not perceive Amelia as boring (although he turns out to like his daughter better). Indeed, nobody ever quite labels this admirable woman as dull. On the other hand, the notion seldom seems far away, and the narrator protests rather too much about her moral (as opposed to entertainment) value. Amelia's cultural place differs dramatically from that of Edgeworth's comparably virtuous Helen, who invariably *interests* others.

The narrator formulates the problem explicitly as one of incident. "Miss Sedley was not of the sunflower sort," he explains, going on to specify that

> the life of a good young girl who is in the paternal nest as yet, can't have many of those thrilling incidents to which the heroine of romance commonly lays claim. . . . While Becky Sharp was on her own wing in the country, hopping on all sorts of twigs, and amid a multiplicity of traps, and pecking up her food quite harmless and successful, Amelia lay snug in her home at Russell Square. (150)

The ironic, colloquial, metaphoric specificity lavished on Becky ("pecking up her food quite harmless and successful") contrasts with the vague negatives ("not of the sunflower sort," "can't have many . . . incidents") and the equally vague positive formulation ("lay snug in her home") applied to Amelia: the texture of the prose itself tells us that Becky is more fun. But the narrator evades or denies the point. He claims that women find Amelia dull but that men appreciate her sweetness, gentleness, passivity. He acknowledges that in many circumstances she does not have much to say, but he explains her verbal inadequacies as the consequence of limited experience. When he admits how "insufferably tedious" (664) an account of her "solitary imprisonment" with her father would be, he hastily adds a characteristic invocation to remind us of Amelia's undeniable and admirable virtue: "May we have in our last days a kind soft shoulder on which to lean, and a gentle hand to soothe our gouty old pillows" (664).

A week after their marriage Amelia's husband, in her apparently accurate perception, is "already suffering *ennui*, and eager for others' society!" (291). His eagerness stems largely from Becky's wiles: "She brought his cigar and lighted it for him; she knew the effect of that manoeuvre, having practised it in former days upon Rawdon Crawley. He thought her gay, brisk, arch, *distinguée,* delightful" (291). By contrast, Amelia appears "mute and timid": uninteresting. She talks more when Becky is not around, but not to much purpose. She specializes in smoothing pillows and bringing soup—that sort of thing.

The narrator insists, through demonstration as well as assertion, on the essential frivolity of such categories as "interesting" and "boring," which derive from relatively superficial immediate response to stimuli. However "interesting," Becky remains also monstrous: a sinister mermaid with repellent, scaly underparts (intense sexual fear and loathing mark the description), cannibalistic. To call her interesting (or brisk, *distinguée,* delightful) obscures more important truths about her.

Quite so. Yet the truth of her "interest" remains also palpable and powerful. Becky promises to all who associate with her freedom from boredom. For many, that promise proves irresistible.

England's sense of itself in the mid-nineteenth century included belief in the dullness of its social existence. One can draw on other sources than *Vanity Fair* to support the point. Leonore Davidoff, writing about society etiquette, sums up Victorian social life:

> The unique feature of Victorian society is that . . . essentially middle-class patterns of behaviour were grafted on to the honorific code of the aristocracy or gentry to produce the widened concept of "gentility," which was, without doubt, one of the most effective instruments for social control ever devised. (36)

She does not add that the increasing elaboration of social codes resulted in an intolerable sense of restriction, but much contemporary commentary conveys the oppression and tedium of, for instance, dinner parties at which the order of seating, the menu, and the conversation, all predictable, proceeded by dreary rule.

In 1842, for instance, Mrs. Humphry Ward published an account of "A County Dinner-Party," a detailed narrative of entirely ritualistic social procedures, during which no one feels the slightest real interest in what is happening. After the guests leave, the hostess talks to her husband:

> Only eleven o'clock, is it? Gracious me! I thought it was at least one—that Lady Broadlands is such a stupid, proud fool, and he *such* a bore. . . . I am quite worn out. What a set of tiresome people. Thank goodness, I have done with them for this year: when they give a return dinner I shall contrive to be engaged. Why, Mr. Myddleton, I protest you're asleep—! (251)

204 / CHAPTER SEVEN

The hostess finds her guests boring, the host considers the hostess boring, an aura of boredom suffuses the entire enterprise. It is, other commentators intimate, the atmosphere of England.

Thus Charles Bathurst, in 1850, generalizes that "the present generation is so incessantly haunted with the not unfounded fear of being heavy and dull, that perhaps we run into the disagreeable merely to avoid the insipid" (131). Edward Bulwer-Lytton, more inclusively and more emphatically, comments, "It is reserved for us to counteract the gloomiest climate by the dullest customs!" (1: 36). He elaborates:

> From the tone of Society which I have attempted to describe, arises one of the most profound of our national feelings; that listless and vague melancholy which partakes both of the Philosophical and the Poetic; that sad and deep sentiment which is found only in the English and the German character, and is produced in each nation by the same causes; it is the result in both of an eager mind placed in a dull and insipid circle. (1: 173)

An anonymous "woman of fashion," visiting in Paris, contrasts the French gentleman's willingness to converse with women to the rudeness of his English counterpart.

> Is not this more amiable than John Bull's selfish system of sitting till past midnight over the bottle? —his poor wife and daughter the drowsy guests of the weary and exhausted lady of the mansion, all dying with *ennui*, while the carriage waits, and the horses and servants are perishing; the latter, perhaps, imitating their master in potent libations to pass away the time. (*Private Correspondence* 1: 207)

Whether specific or general, these accounts convey the same impression of "dull and insipid"—and painfully rigidified—social circumstance, the kind of circumstance George Osborne alludes to in *Vanity Fair* when he exclaims, "Curse the whole pack of money-grubbing vulgarians! I fall asleep at their great heavy dinners. I feel ashamed in my father's great stupid parties" (246). Eager minds, Bulwer-Lytton maintains, become melancholy as a result of the dulling environment. More immediately, the eager and the inert both yield to boredom, melancholy's close relation. No way out presents itself—not for the weary and exhausted women, not for the drinking men.

Becky Sharp, who does not belong by birth to the society she inhabits, promises rescue from tedium. Given her presence, social gatherings turn lively, conversation becomes entertaining. Because of her outsider status, she does not feel bound by the social conventions of the middle class, although she can at will use them to her advantage. She alleviates the problems of many forms of social exchange: settings besides the dinner party, in the world of Vanity Fair, generate boredom. Thus life at Queen's Crawley, where Becky first goes as a governess (she calls it Humdrum Hall), follows a dreary and tedious routine. Here is Becky's account of it:

> Lady Crawley is always knitting worsted. Sir Pitt is always tipsy, every night; and, I believe, sits with Horrocks, the butler. Mr Crawley always reads sermons in the evening, and in the morning is locked up in his study, or else rides to Mudbury, on county business, or to Squashmore, where he preaches, on Wednesdays and Fridays, to the tenants there. (115)

The Bute Crawleys, and particularly Mrs. Bute, produce nothing but tedium. As Mrs. Bute reflects, trying to think how to get Miss Crawley into her clutches, "She always used to go to sleep when Martha and Louisa played their duets. Jim's stiff college manners, and poor dear Bute's talk about his dogs and horses, always annoyed her" (228). But Mrs. Bute herself annoys Miss Crawley. As the narrator sums up, she "had committed the most fatal of all errors with regard to her sister-in-law. She had not merely oppressed her and her household—she had bored Miss Crawley" (389). When young men get together, they find it hard to pass the time. "Tell us that story about the tiger-hunt," George Osborne begs Jos Sedley. "Here George Osborne gave a yawn. 'It's rather slow work,' said he, 'down here; what *shall* we do?'" (262). They decide to go watch the stagecoach arrive to alleviate their boredom. A final instance: when Becky returns, as Rawdon's wife, to Queen's Crawley, now under a new regime, she finds a life of "calm pursuits and amusements" (495): a boring life.

In each of the situations I have mentioned—and the novel specifies many more—Becky intervenes to create interest, excitement, stimulation. She offers malicious imitations, flirtatious invitations, witty stories, attentive listening of a sort that convinces the speaker of his or her own interest. She laughs at herself, making a funny story of her encounter with Lady Southdown's medicines. She laughs at other people, creating instant conspiratorial alliances with those who hear her mockery. She flatters, connives, insinuates. Wherever she goes, she generates fun, although she herself sometimes experiences boredom in the very act of alleviating it.

How should we feel about this talent for creating pleasure? In a heavy-handed and authoritative way, the narrator intervenes to tell us. He has just quoted a letter from Becky to Amelia that makes comedy of the dreary life at Queen's Crawley. Then he explains his own moral instincts: he loves his good and kindly characters, laughs at the silly, abuses the wicked and heartless. "Otherwise," he worries,

> you might fancy it was I who was sneering at the practice of devotion, which Miss Sharp finds so ridiculous; that it was I who laughed good-humouredly at the reeling old Silenus of a baronet—whereas the laughter comes from one who has no reverence except for prosperity, and no eye for anything beyond success. Such people there are living and flourishing in the world—Faithless, Hopeless, Charityless; let us have at them, dear friends, with might and main. Some there are, and very successful too, mere quacks and fools: and it was to combat and expose such as those, no doubt, that Laughter was made. (117)

No doubt. The very phrase introduces doubt into the discourse, which does not lack perplexities. First the narrator dissociates himself from Becky's laughter. Then he defines her as the target of his satire: she is the person with no reverence except for prosperity. Moving from her to her kind ("such people"), the writer insists not only that one should attack them, but that laughter—no doubt—exists for the purpose of exposing this human species.

But Becky herself, with her eye for revealing detail, her sense of metaphor, her alertness to visual and verbal nuance, has already engaged our interest, and our laughter. Here is most of a sample paragraph from her letter, describing Lady Crawley:

> She was an ironmonger's daughter, and her marriage was thought a great match. She looks as if she had been handsome once, and her eyes are always weeping for the loss of her beauty. She is pale and meagre and high-shouldered; and has not a word to say for herself, evidently. Her step-son, Mr Crawley, was likewise in the room. He was in full dress, as pompous as an undertaker. He is pale, thin, ugly, silent; he has thin legs, no chest, hay-coloured whiskers and straw-coloured hair. He is the very picture of his sainted mother over the mantlepiece—Griselda of the noble house of Binkie. (113)

When Becky laughs, the narrator tells us, we should not share her sense of the comic, since it emerges from pernicious values. Why, then, does he make her so brilliant a comedian? Her capacity to convert tedious experience into verbal humor engages the reader as it engages Miss Crawley and George Osborne and Rawdon Crawley and the rest. By comparison, the narrator's unexceptionable abstractions seem pallid and a bit automatic.

No doubt, indeed, laughter was made to combat quacks and fools. In the world, though—in our Vanity Fair as well as Thackeray's—it serves other functions as well, including that of alleviating boredom. If one takes the narrator's intervention about laughter seriously, it suggests that we should perceive boredom as morally superior to iconoclasm. When Mr. Crawley leads the family in prayer, we must respect the enterprise. We must not laugh at Mr. Crawley, or at Lady Crawley, one of an array of life's female victims. We should laugh, if at all, at Becky, who has the nerve to invite us to mock the sacred. The manifestation of social discontent that we label boredom, caused, according to Thackeray's novel, largely by the emptiness of existing forms of social intercourse (including marriage)—this manifestation, inherent in our social systems, we must accept as necessary.

On the one hand, *Vanity Fair* is the first text we have encountered that pays serious attention, through the character of Becky Sharp, to the possibility of alleviating boredom. On the other hand, it displays considerable anxiety about whether boredom in fact should be alleviated—but not about whether it *can* be. Lady Dedlock's boredom, if that is what her complexities of pose and feeling should be called, is not subject to external modification. Although one can attribute responsibility for her state to existing social arrangements, her internalizations defend definitively against outside intervention. James Harthouse, who takes his boredom as a mark of distinction, reveals a state equally invulnerable to modification from without. But the bored characters in *Vanity Fair*—and they abound, including on occasion even Becky herself—yearn for and respond to entertainment.

Like readers of a novel?

Becky's capacity to avert boredom depends on three conspicuous aspects of her character: abundant energy, will to succeed, and desire to provide pleasure. Although, as the narrator directly states, her interest focuses solely on herself, she recognizes that only through others can she achieve what she wants. If she pleases others, perhaps they will provide the wealth and social status she craves. The energy of her self-interest extends outward. Clever and inventive, she revitalizes a world that has become monotonous to many who live in it. But because she is, the narrator says, a quack and fool, a scaly monster, an appropriate object of mockery and contempt, the qualities she possesses—energy, desire to please, cleverness, inventiveness—are compromised, associated with wickedness.

Interesting is not an important word in this novel, and not a term of value. Becky's hypocritical letter to Miss Briggs, announcing her elopement, is "affecting and interesting" (200): the interesting accompanies the meretricious. Helen in Edgeworth's novel, when declared interesting, receives the ultimate social accolade. Amelia and Dobbin in

Thackeray's novel, each monomaniacally focused on a hopeless love, each flawlessly good, hardly merit the same label. Becky is interesting, they are good. Being good is preferable to being interesting.

Well, yes. But where does all this leave the novelistic enterprise? Another of the narrator's uncomfortable recognitions, acknowledged more than once, involves his awareness that readers want interest and excitement. Early in the story, he hypothesizes other sorts of narrative options than those he actually pursues. One involves a burglar who abducts Amelia. The narrator characterizes the novel that would have resulted as "a tale of thrilling interest, through the fiery chapters of which the reader should hurry, panting." The present narrator, how-ever, offers "only a homely story" (88). Later, though, he makes more grandiose claims: "I am going to tell a story of harrowing villainy and complicated—but, as I trust, intensely interesting—crime. My rascals are no milk-and-water rascals, I promise you. When we come to the proper places we won't spare fine language—No, no!" (117). In both sequences, the idea of interest arouses uneasy irony. It worries the fic-tion maker that readers desire fictions of interest, because he wants to provide fictions of morality or because he fears he cannot sustain inter-est or because he does not know for sure where interest lies, from the point of view of his audience. He places himself morally, as he must, with Amelia and Dobbin. The problem remains of how to place him-self imaginatively. He can hardly avoid metaphoric association with beguiling, inventive, fanciful Becky, like other fiction makers the enemy of boredom—but also like other fiction makers untrustworthy.

Boredom derives, in *Vanity Fair*, from social custom, social repres-sion, social forms. The efforts of an outsider, a determined individual-ist, can combat it. But boredom, the ally of repression, is morally prefer-able to its alternatives: so the novel suggests. Although the novelist in his enterprise necessarily plays a role more like that of Becky Sharp than that of Amelia, he textually allies himself with Amelia. She isn't *really* boring, he says, when you get to know her. And anyhow, she's so *good*. But such a defense hardly suffices for the novelist himself. *Vanity Fair* never resolves the dilemma. It plays a noteworthy part in the liter-ary history of boredom, though, because it explicitly places itself on the side of social repression, announcing that boredom should not be too readily rejected: what opposes it may be worse.

Roughly a quarter century after the appearance of *Vanity Fair*, Anthony Trollope published his own fictional exposé of British society in *The Way We Live Now*. The idea of goodness no longer caused the novelist the kind of difficulty that plagues Thackeray's work. "I suppose we ought to love the best people best; but I don't, Paul," announces Hetta Carbury, the novel's nearest approach to a heroine. When her lover responds that *he* loves the best of all possible persons, she will have none of it. "You must love me best," she pronounces, "but I won't be called good" (150). Imagine Amelia Osborne saying such a thing! The character in Trollope's novel who unquestionably epitomizes the good, Roger Carbury, ends by not achieving what he desperately wants and must relinquish his deeply held convictions about family and inheritance.

As for boredom, it figures more importantly as verbal convenience than as experiential category. Young gentlemen confronted with a distressing event or situation often term it "a frightful bore," thus justifying their failure even to attempt to remedy what they dislike. In an environment largely devoid of pleasure, like the world of this novel, the idea of boredom can have little real meaning. Everyone (almost everyone) seeks money rather than happiness—seeks it with single-mindedness comparable to Becky Sharp's. Assuming comparable single-mindedness in their companions and acquaintances, the inhabitants of Trollope's fictional universe judge any means justifiable for the sake of the necessary end. They will not take action against cheating at cards any more than they will reject the acquaintance of the triumphant cheating financier, so long as he remains triumphant. They may consider a given social environment "dull"—a country house, say, with no significant visitors; a club with no card game in progress—but they do not think enough about their own feelings to regard themselves often as either bored or interested. Their boredom or interest in any sense really connected with pleasure has no bearing on their fundamental pursuit: the pursuit of their self-interest—their financial interest.

In the mildest form of the malady that afflicts most of the novel's characters, the seekers for wealth and position assume rather than examine the connection between their goals and pleasure. Thus Mr. Melnotte, the great financier, plots to marry his daughter to the eldest son of the marquis of Auld Reekie, attaching high value to the notion of the British aristocracy. "How glorious would it be," he reflects, "to have a British Marquis for his son-in-law!" The narrator comments, "Like many others he had failed altogether to inquire when the pleasure to himself would come, or what would be its nature" (2: 215). In a more sinister version of the same configuration, plotters know the irrelevance of pleasure to their situation and the impossibility of finding it.

Lady Carbury shows not the slightest sympathy with her daughter's heartbreak when Hetta believes herself betrayed by the man she loves. "Who," she asks herself, "were the happy people that were driven neither by ambition, nor poverty, nor greed, nor the cross purposes of unhappy love, to stifle and trample upon their feeling? She had known no one so blessed." She understands the hard bargain that must be made by women in the world:

> A woman, she thought, if she were unfortunate enough to be a lady without wealth of her own, must give up everything, her body, her heart, —her very soul if she were that way troubled, —to the procuring of a fitting maintenance for herself. Why should Hetta hope to be more fortunate than others? (2: 383)

Mr. Melnotte and Lady Carbury fulfill paradigmatic functions in Trollope's novel. In some respects more sympathetic than other characters similarly driven by ambition (or by what they understand as necessity), both demonstrate the capacity to engage their wills fully in the effort that preoccupies them. Trampling on their feelings or denying feeling's relevance, they illustrate why boredom and interest are concepts with limited bearing on *The Way We Live Now*.

Although the novel reveals few successful alternatives to the moral positions of Melnotte and Lady Carbury, it does not fail to register the high cost of those positions. Marie Melnotte, the financier's daughter, puts the case most succinctly. "I suppose I shall marry that young man," she observes, referring to the man her father wants for her, "though it will be very bad. I shall just be as if I hadn't any self of my own at all" (2: 111). Sacrifice of the self is the cost that must be paid. The novel dwells on the practiced hypocrisies of Melnotte, determined right up to the point of his suicide to present the world with a powerful version of himself, and of Lady Carbury, who with dizzying shifts of self-presentation prepares a face to meet the faces that she meets. In many instances, the fiction represents characters virtually devoid of sense of self at the point when we encounter them—the young men who keep citing boredom are conspicuous examples. Nidderdale, constrained by his father and hers to woo Marie Melnotte, when the object of his approaches tells him she loves someone else observes, "It's an awful bore. That's all" (1: 334). Dolly Longstaffe, asked whether he would go on playing with someone demonstrated to cheat at cards, responds, "Yes I should. It'd be such a bore breaking up" (1: 267). Sir Felix, also wooing Marie, doesn't bother to tell her he loves her. "He had no objection to tell her so, but, without thinking much about it, felt it to be a bore" (1: 165). Such specimen responses to experience represent the situation of people devoid of the capacity to discriminate, lacking any sense of self to propel them toward choice or action.

On the other hand, external observers of the life led by these young men and by the young women they court and their parents might well term that life boring. Thirty years before the publication of Trollope's novel, it had been possible to imagine a world energized—*revolutionized*—by the new railroad and its implications.

> There is a revolution going on in men's minds now; the new fact, of matter acting strongly upon spirit; wheel power directing men's thoughts and calculations. Locomotion seems to set in order the energy of men's actions— makes the daudle [sic] active, and the loiterer quick and busy. With the improved value of time so manifest to their eyes—seeing what can be done by the best application of man's ability, they also begin to calculate upon minutes, and advantages in odd hours, and really so improve themselves. A railway, a passing carriage upon a railway, is a new teacher in the world. (*Letters of a Citizen Haberdasher* 130)

But the new sense of time that the Citizen Haberdasher perceived and imagined has vanished from the society that Trollope represents. Far from calculating upon minutes and finding advantage in odd hours, the inhabitants of this society have trouble filling minutes and hours. Sir Felix provides an extreme example:

> But he was chiefly tormented in these days by the want of amusement. He had so spent his life hitherto that he did not know how to get through a day in which no excitement was provided for him. He never read. Thinking was altogether beyond him. And he had never done a day's work in his life. He could lie in bed. He could eat and drink. He could smoke and sit idle. He could play cards; and could amuse himself with women, —the lower the culture of the women, the better the amusement. Beyond these things the world had nothing for him. (2: 156)

To call Sir Felix "bored," though, would imply the existence, or the conception, of a true alternative to his state. In a world so nearly devoid of pleasure, boredom has little meaning. Becky Sharp takes a certain delight in the exercise of her talents as she seeks wealth and position. Melnotte, who suffers a compulsion (as, in different terms, do Lady Carbury and the other parents of listless young men), does not enjoy himself in the process of enacting it. Although plotting to achieve the desired goal fills time fairly energetically, in comparison with the card playing that occupies the young men, Melnotte and Lady Carbury receive little gratification even as in various degrees they get what they believe they need. They remain largely governed by anxiety over all that remains to be done—and to be needed.

The self-reflexiveness of most characters in Trollope's novel differs sharply from what I have called "the narcissism of boredom." In *The Way We Live Now*, concentration on the self typically does not imply preoccupation with feelings. (On the contrary, the relatively few characters who *do* show genuine feeling—I'll come to them later—are the least rather than the most self-absorbed.) In this represented world of burgeoning capitalism, an ethos of self-indulgence reigns; yet those governed by it worry more about what they have (or lack) than about how they feel. Indeed, emotion and its assessment seem unacceptable luxuries. "Affluence provides the freedom from necessity and its attendant intense activity that allows the pressing ache of boredom to emerge into awareness," writes a twentieth-century social scientist (Bernstein 521). Perhaps so in the late twentieth century, but not in the Victorian context that Trollope establishes. Yet his imagined men and women feel aches of their own, although they suppress them as unworthy of consideration.

Trollope's big book ranges beyond the domestic, to the House of Commons, the meetings of boards of directors, the planning of financial coups. It remains, however, strangely airless. The House of Commons, as represented, really has nothing to do. The board of directors merely occupies time, to create an illusion of activity. Melnotte's financial plots come to nothing and seem insubstantial from the outset. In *Vanity Fair*, Thackeray conveys the sense of a teeming, if unattractive, world, in which the conflicts that kill people on battlefields parallel the struggles that drive some to bankruptcy and others to social supremacy in the houses of London. *The Way We Live Now* is also heavily populated. If it lacks battlefields, it offers huge parties, events with casts of thousands—architects and workmen who help to produce the occasions as well as aristocrats and social aspirants who attend them. But one does not acquire from the representation of such happenings much sense of social texture, of cultural intertwining. Instead, the novel reiterates with disturbing intensity its renditions of isolated individuals, all suffering their own anxieties, each alone amid multitudes. The relations of the idle young men to one another epitomize the social situation. Linked by membership in a club that they have founded, they nonetheless feel no loyalty. If, out of moral cowardice, Sir Felix appeals to one of his fellows to support his condemnation of cheating at cards, it comes as no surprise that the other man will provide no backing. These men do not help one another, they hardly think of one another. Their association remains formal rather than substantial, a matter of convenience, not feeling; and they duplicate in this respect the social arrangements of others in their world.

Of course the atomization effected by the dominion of money constitutes one of Trollope's principal targets in his indictment of how the British live. Lack of community betrays the same loss of tradition as the universal toleration of corruption or the rejection of social distinctions. A population that has abandoned connection to its past will inevitably, in the logic of this fictional argument, also reject the connections between one human being and another. One point of this depiction of "English society" is that no society in fact exists.

But the novel has a happy ending—a comic resolution of marriages that apparently counteract the theme of fragmentation and isolation. Hetta and Paul, the man she loves, marry. So do Lady Carbury and the editor she has earlier rejected. Even Marie Melnotte, who in the course of the novel gradually discovers her selfhood, matches herself with a financially ambitious American. If only one of these marital arrangements conforms to conventional novelistic renditions of romance, all suggest the possibility of relationship—or perhaps the impossibility of appealing to a popular audience with an altogether bleak delineation of contemporary existence.

Even the cheerful resolution, though, has bleak undertones. For one thing, we must consider Roger Carbury, Hetta's rejected wooer, who only with poignant difficulty retains his place in the general winding up of affairs. By far the most passionate figure in the novel—arguably the *only* passionate figure—Roger feels intensely not only about Hetta but about the various traditions he insistently partakes in. He upholds the value of property, of family, of squirearchy. He takes his inherited responsibilities with the utmost seriousness. He believes in and fulfills obligations to others, helping Lady Carbury although he despises her son, behaving with rigorous justice to Paul Montague, who has, in Roger's view, stolen the woman he loves. When he realizes Hetta wants to marry Paul, Roger constitutes himself a "father" to the woman he loves, grandfather to her putative children. She suggests for him the role of brother, but he will have none of it: he already feels old; he believes himself, indeed *wills* himself, to be aging rapidly. He hopes Hetta and Paul will spend much of their time at his family home; he wants their children to inherit it.

Thus the man who has valued family continuity above all plans to violate it; the man who has loved more intensely than any other character in the novel denies the erotic in himself. If this denouement emphasizes once more Roger's largeness of spirit, it also stresses his failure. The arrangement of things that Trollope depicts leaves no room for such as Roger, except as an appendage to the lives of others. Throughout the novel, Roger has stood for older ways of behaving, older forms of value. His association with age long predates his final willed aging: Hetta's first mention of him insists that he is far too old for her to marry. His is the voice of true value, from the point of view of the narrator, but his voice sounds only faintly for those around him. The sense of despair that mingles with the rage of the novel expresses itself most clearly through the representation of Roger.

Hetta and Paul, less extreme in their views, the nearest exemplars of romance, might promise hope, but Trollope's version of young lovers leaves little room for optimism. Hetta displays no reprehensible attributes, but she lacks energy. Although like generations of novelistic heroines before her she successfully resists the marriage a parent wishes for her (only narrowly: repeatedly she tells herself that she should marry Roger because he is so good), her general stance seems singularly passive. She does what her mother wants even at the risk of moral taint. Obediently she attends the party given by Melnotte; without protest she subordinates herself to her worthless brother, to whom her mother is devoted. The narrator asserts her love for Paul, and she asserts it herself, but the text never makes that love real in the way it renders Roger's hopeless passion. One cannot feel that Hetta offers much prospect for a better future. She will not be governed by a compulsion to seek wealth or position, but she does not stand for anything in particular.

Or Paul either. Like Hetta, he fills passive roles through most of the novel. Helpless, he finds himself entangled in the affairs of a corrupt entrepreneurial company. Helpless, he does the bidding of the forceful American woman he once agreed to marry but no longer wants any connection with. She asks him to escort her to the seaside for her health: What can he do? Only because she finally decides to let him go can he free himself. Only with the constant coaching of a wiser friend can he untangle his business affairs. He too lacks the energy that might foretell better things ahead. He doesn't *want* to be corrupt, but perhaps he won't be able to resist. . . .

As for Lady Carbury, we are asked to consider her love for her hopelessly decadent son a redeeming element in her character. This obsessive love motivates her first rejection of her suitor, as it motivates her wish for Hetta to marry Roger and also her entire writing career, an effort to make money for Felix's sake. Mother love thus constitutes an important element of plot. Quite outside the realm of choice, it drives

Lady Carbury as her will for money does and is coextensive with that will. Its redemptive force does not appear powerful. The marriage Lady Carbury finally acquiesces to will be comfortable both financially and socially. Uniting two worldly though agreeable people, it conveniently links two centers of self-interest: a cheerful outcome in a fragmented world. Marie's marriage, also a product of convergent self-interest, establishes a place for a young woman who has previously had no place of her own. Only in this limited sense does it contribute to the "happy ending."

The Way We Live Now paints a dark picture—but to its shades, I repeat, boredom contributes little. Getting and spending, men and women in the novel's world lay waste their powers, but only rarely do they suffer the malaise that the late twentieth century often associates with capitalism. The young men who proclaim all inconvenience or emotional disruption a bore do not on the whole appear to endure any condition so self-aware as boredom, although Sir Felix has his moments of ennui. A young woman seeking marriage but cut off from the social environment in which she might find it may experience a sense of frustration and tedium roughly equivalent to the dullness of boredom, but her affliction is unusual. Those fully engaged in social or financial routines find them absorbing, generating desire. Trollope's narrator, or the reader guided by him, may judge Lady Carbury or Mr. Melnotte to be leading futile lives, dominated by unworthy desire, but these characters themselves do not experience futility.

One story implicit in the foregoing sequence of novels—*Bleak House* to *The Way We Live Now*—concerns the relation between boredom and discrimination as well as that between boredom and social class. Lady Dedlock's boredom, all-inclusive though it seems, judges her experience, registering the impossibility of her full engagement with a social world from which she has definitively separated herself. Harthouse, in *Hard Times*, only appears to judge experience: he imitates an aristocratic psychological stance. *Vanity Fair*, continuing the association between boredom and aristocracy, depicts a social universe in which upper-class men and women require unusual stimulus (that of Becky Sharp) to avoid boredom and in which "goodness" connects itself with tedium. In each of these fictions, boredom provides both a luxury and a burden for those who need not struggle for advancement, much less survival. But it also, in its authentic aristocratic manifestations, assesses moral and psychological environment. Lord Steyne's reliance on Becky to entertain him calls attention to the genuine lack of entertainment in his ordinary routine. Compared with Dickens's conception of Lady Dedlock, Thackeray's imagining of Lord Steyne reveals no moral or psychological depth. One hardly feels troubled by the lord's need for excitement. Nonetheless, his state of boredom says something real about his experience.

In *The Way We Live Now*, those who offer real judgments of their experience—the American divorcée, for instance, and Marie Melnotte—declare the misery rather than the tedium of what they endure. Such suffering as these female pawns undergo requires little judgment or discrimination: it presents itself as an ineluctable fact. The disappearance of boredom as a meaningful category of evaluation suggests that the society Trollope evokes no longer concerns itself with psychological adjudications. Dickens imagines Lady Dedlock's boredom as a register of her inner state, willfully presented as a judgment of the world around her. Even Harthouse's professions of boredom betray a psychic condition, if not precisely the one he wants to represent. Lord Steyne's boredom, on the other hand, tells us more about his surroundings than about himself. Describing him as bored, the narrator suggests that actuality justifies him.

No one in Trollope's novel has enough sense of alternatives to make a genuine assessment of boredom. Negative evidence, of course, is all too richly interpretable. That boredom has almost vanished from the represented world, except as a kind of verbal tic, allows a range of meanings, including inadvertence: Trollope may have cared not at all about the presence or absence of boredom. Yet the textual recurrence of the young men for whom "It's a bore" constitutes the appropriate comment on all experience calls attention to the issue. The young men emphasize the virtual disappearance of discrimination from the world depicted. Their reiterated pronouncement obviates all distinctions, avoiding the need for judgment. Declaring a temporary shortage of money or entertainment and a friend's cheating at cards to belong to the same category, they achieve a condition of life in which they can believe nothing whatever is required of them. Their linguistic laziness and moral laziness reflect one another.

These idle youths reveal a perverse relation to time, which exists for them as a psychic space to be filled with pleasure. Comparable perversity governs the many characters in the novel for whom boredom is not even an alternative. The men and women who seek wealth or literary fame or social status keep themselves busy psychically and physically; for them time exerts a painful urgency. The absence of boredom from their perception denotes dullness of consciousness, inability to know psychic reality or to distinguish one psychological state from another.

Imagining, back in chapter 1, the nature of experience before the invention of boredom, I posited a harmonious state in which leisure did not exist as a separable condition, in which focus on community and on spiritual obligation obviated the need for extended introspection, in which people did not worry about the precise degree of happiness and fulfillment in their lives. Trollope provides a bitter parody of this idyllic situation. His characters cannot afford to worry about what they feel. The young men who declare their boredom, like the young woman cut off by financial exigencies from the conditions under which she might realize her marital ambition, use the idea of the boring as an escape from unconfrontable emotions such as rage, despair, and envy. The older men and women absorbed in their fight for "success" do not define their feelings because feelings might take time and energy away from the crucial struggle. Unlike inhabitants of the imaginary preboredom world, they operate on the basis of motive rather than purpose, their ceaseless endeavor an extension of the kind of meaningless enterprise characterizing Dickens's Mrs. Jellyby: industry more "dreadful" than any Esther Summerson might imagine. The relative absence of boredom from their existence marks their loss of feeling, judgment, and discrimination. Despite the rather pallid comparatively "good" characters who provide Trollope's "happy ending," *The Way We Live Now* represents a community marked by lack of difference among its members.

Lady Dedlock's boredom signals her despair. Mr. Melnotte's complete lack of boredom declares Trollope's despair—with a society where, in his apparent view, people no longer use their feelings as a guide to moral perception or allow moral perception to affect their feelings. For Dickens, Thackeray, and Trollope, boredom, constituting a taken for granted condition of possibility, supplies an index of moral as well as psychic actuality. Charting a relation between internal and external reality, it helps to measure a developing sense of social emptiness as the nineteenth century continues.

EIGHT

The Ethics of Boredom
Modernism and Questions of Value

As the twentieth century opened, the statistician Francis Galton, narrating his own life, reminisced about his confrontation with boredom as an objective condition:

> Many mental processes admit of being roughly measured. For instance, the degree to which people are bored, by counting the number of their fidgets. I not infrequently tried this method at the meetings of the Royal Geographical Society, for even there dull memoirs are occasionally read. . . . The use of a watch attracts attention, so I reckon time by the number of my breathings, of which there are 15 in a minute. They are not counted mentally, but are punctuated by pressing with 15 fingers successively. The counting is reserved for the fidgets. These observations should be confined to persons of middle age. Children are rarely still, while elderly philosophers will sometimes remain rigid for minutes altogether. (278)

Galton's conviction that observation will elicit fact, as well as his a priori assumption that fidgets necessarily betray boredom, reveals a confident sensibility far removed from the modern. On the other hand, his imagining of boredom not as psychic state but as mental process prepares the way for new kinds of perception. The restlessness of a child and the rigidity of an elderly philosopher, like the measurable fidgets of the middle-aged, externalize internal action. The modernist reassignment of ethical weight to boredom, this chapter's subject, depends on understanding it as action: active repudiation that can constitute either moral superiority (as in D. H. Lawrence's Birkin) or moral inadequacy (Grandcourt in *Daniel Deronda*, Gilbert Osmond in *The Portrait of a Lady*), since a modernist ethic would deny the unambiguous systems that earlier moralists such as Johnson could draw on.

Fictional (and poetic) evocations of boredom multiply exponentially in the twentieth century, partly for reasons implicit in the common understanding of modernism, which posits an isolated subject existing in a secularized, fragmented world marked by lost or precarious traditions: a paradigmatic situation for boredom. Boredom provides a convenient point of reference for the cultural and psychic condition of those deprived alike of meaningful work and of pleasure in idleness. At once trivialized and magnified, boredom in its early twentieth-century representations alludes to the emptiness implicit in a life lacking powerful community or effective tradition. Since "everybody" feels it, it hardly distinguishes its sufferers. It can constitute a way of life, a fashion of speech, or both. Casual and focused allusions to its pervasiveness establish the atmosphere of much modernist fiction and often control that fiction's characterizations.

All of which is just what we might expect. Perhaps less predictably, modernists often embark on more or less covert ethical interrogation of boredom as a category. What does it mean to make assertion of boredom a register of discrimination, as I claimed Victorian novelists do? Can boredom be a sign of virtue? Does it reveal its victims' mode of perception? In a society where everything is up for grabs, the nature of emotional response becomes an urgent matter. Modernist writing reflects that urgency.

I propose to consider, in chronological order, a sequence of important novels published between the late nineteenth century and the mid-twentieth century. Disparate in emphasis, they yet share boredom as a common signifier of ethical crisis. No longer do the acts of refusal inherent in boredom necessarily mark moral inadequacy: D. H. Lawrence makes such refusal a property of heroism. No longer does a clear line divide tedious from "interesting" experience: Gertrude Stein insists on the value of the repetitious and trivial. Even novels that make the conventional association of boredom with aristocratic, willed inertia investigate the concept in searching terms. Modernism's questioning of established assumption extends to the realm of the boring, although boredom is not the central subject of any novel considered in this chapter.

A year after Trollope issued *The Way We Live Now*, marked by nostalgia for the old and anger at the new, George Eliot published *Daniel Deronda*. To claim for Eliot a position among the modernists challenges orthodox historical categories, but the novelist's fictional investigation of "the Jewish question" in fact charts at least patches of new ground. The tensions of *Daniel Deronda* register anxiety about the impingement of the modern without resolving that anxiety in Trollope's insistently conservative fashion. Eliot preserves her commitment to "the nineteenth-century English mode of successivity" that Gertrude Stein deplored (DeKoven 24). Her novel, despite its double structure, has a clear beginning, middle, and end, its conceptual order evident. It values "tradition" and "morality." On the other hand, by making Judaism the locus of significant tradition, by exploring the value of different kinds of relation to the past, and by figuring the Jew, that customary English outsider, as center of consciousness, *Daniel Deronda* raises questions about standard nineteenth-century assumptions. And its "resolution" leaves large issues in the air.

The enterprises of this dense, difficult novel include interrogating the category of boredom in ethical terms. For eighteenth-century thinkers, the moral issue of boredom had concerned the obligation to interest oneself in the life beyond this world. Dr. Johnson's distaste for lethargy marked his conviction of individuals' responsibility to commit themselves to spiritual effort. To acknowledge even the possibility of boredom implies willingness to forgo such effort. Nineteenth-century writers, by contrast, conscious of the ways society forms and threatens the individual, located the moral problem of boredom firmly in the realm of daily experience, suggesting kinds of self-discipline necessary to withstand it and opposing to the flaccid state of disengagement the arduous cultivation of interest or endeavor focused not on the hereafter but on what comes to hand. Dickens demonstrates moral import in the aristocratic pose of boredom, Thackeray connects the malaise with social deterioration, Trollope depicts an environment in which even boredom has lost its meaning. It remained for Eliot to diagnose boredom as ethical sickness, its personal significance extending inevitably to the social but not only socially defined.

Daniel Deronda deviates from the typical Victorian novel in incorporating Judaism as a dramatic issue, but its system of rewards and punishments, like its characterization of Mirah, seems all too predictable. Yet the fiction's acute inquiry into the culture of alienation—specifically of *boredom* as alienation—calls attention to the difficulties and the importance of that sense of estrangement and fragmentation often taken to mark the modern. The polarity of interest and boredom central to *Daniel Deronda* defines spiritual potential in a context where people feel far less oriented toward their postmortem destinies than did Dr.

Johnson. It also elucidates the inadequacy of a social environment that no longer nourishes its participants.

For Eliot as for other nineteenth-century woman writers we have considered—Austen, Edgeworth, Ferrier, Brontë—human beings provide the fundamental locus of interest, not because women traditionally concern themselves with relationship but because the obligation of attention to one another signifies the ethical. The double plot of *Daniel Deronda* opposes a man and a woman linked in shared boredom to a man and a woman united in passionate interest. Bored Gwendolen Harleth appeals to passionate Daniel to help her discover interest. Her education in that possible discovery, and in its alternative, focuses the novel's didactic concerns. Daniel's finding his proper interest in life determines his fate. More insistently than any other work we have looked at, Eliot's novel demands that its readers take seriously the moral and psychological dynamics of boredom.

The first chapter of *Daniel Deronda* opens with Daniel's construction of moral and aesthetic interest in the spectacle of Gwendolen gambling and closes with her expression of a desire to meet Daniel—allegedly because, according to her hostess, he looks bored and Gwendolen claims she herself is "always bored." The hostess expresses some skepticism about this self-description, pointing out Gwendolen's perpetual eagerness in activity. Gwendolen explains it: "That is just because I am bored to death" (9). In the next chapter the narrator effectively confirms the characterization by revealing that the young woman "had gone to the roulette-table not because of passion, but in search of it" (13).

Like Sir Leicester Dedlock, Gwendolen appears to consider boredom an aristocratic appurtenance (an attitude confirmed when she subsequently encounters Grandcourt), and she attests her fitness for socially higher things by her inability (the inability Evelyn Waugh would later scrutinize) to invest full or consistent attention in the stimuli her life offers. Like Lady Dedlock, she cultivates boredom as social style. It serves her, however, more as aggression than as defense. The perception that aggression inheres in being bored as well as in being boring initiates Eliot's subtle investigation of what seems in Gwendolen almost a form of automatism. She and Grandcourt have both learned that the stance of boredom can be used to manipulate others—which only intensifies its danger to the self. Because of their other attributes, they can use boredom as power. Gwendolen's beauty and grace give observers an initial impression of her superiority, which she supports by her assertions of boredom. Grandcourt's wealth functions in comparable ways. Without beauty and wealth as marks of specialness, Gwendolen and Grandcourt could not enforce lack of engagement as the sign of excellence.

In other words, the meaning of boredom as a consistent attitude in Eliot's important bored characters depends in the first instance on their attitudes toward themselves. Both demonstrate a set of characteristics that our post-Freudian era readily describes as *narcissism*. The novelist's examination of boredom's link to narcissism helps account for the interest in boredom displayed in *Daniel Deronda*.

Narcissism, of course, had long been Eliot's subject: Rosamond, in *Middlemarch*, provides a detailed case history. The narrator's warning in that novel that the world does not offer an udder for our supreme selves reminds us how insistently she sees focus on self as the primary moral danger—in this respect following moralists of previous centuries. To connect such a focus with boredom, however, is a new move, presumably responsive to new social actualities. Gwendolen's boredom—incapacity, refusal, sign of power—derives from the narcissism that impedes her vision of the world. Her increasing recognition that she needs objects of interest outside herself signals her effort to escape that narcissism and the desperation it implies—an effort obviously imperfect, since the desire for interest may only extend the reach of narcissistic entitlement, but nonetheless morally promising.

As the connection to narcissism suggests, Gwendolen's boredom, although it constitutes an aggressive stance, a means to power, feels to her painfully real. She connects it with the perverseness of other people (consisting in their failure always to conform to her desires) and understands it as a gender issue. In an early conversation with her cousin Rex (which occurs, like the scene of her initial interest in Deronda, within the context of book 1, "The Spoiled Child": a rubric designed to inform all judgments of Gwendolen), she complains that she cannot experience only what is gratifying because the world is not sufficiently pleasant. "Girls' lives are so stupid," she concludes; "they never do what they like." Rex declares his belief that men exist in a worse condition: "They are forced to do hard things, and are often dreadfully bored, and knocked to pieces too" (62). Female boredom derives from prohibitions inhibiting female action, male boredom from imperatives demanding action of socially mandated sorts. Despite the immaturity of the conversationalists, they enunciate genuine perceptions. But if such is the nature of things—if girls cannot act and men must—the fact establishes the outlines of their moral problem. To defy the social order is self-evident folly: Gwendolen's folly. Speaking to Grandcourt during what passes for their courtship, she complains once more about the situation of women: "We are brought up like the flowers, to look as pretty as we can, and be dull without complaining. That is my notion about the plants: they are often bored, and that is the reason some of them have got poisonous" (120). She does not, however, sufficiently consider the implications of her own analogy. She too has become "poisonous" as a result of indulged boredom.

The poisonous aspect of Gwendolen's boredom consists partly in its destruction of the capacity to discriminate: a familiar perception employed in a new context. Understanding her boredom as caused by others' failure to submit to her desires, Gwendolen sees in Grandcourt's boredom the promise of noninterference. Boredom announces that one does not care about anything. If Grandcourt doesn't care, surely he would not obstruct her course of self-indulgence, which his abundant money would only facilitate. The woman who has used her own boredom to exert power over others succumbs to the power of a man's boredom—the response of a man "whose grace of bearing has long been moulded on an experience of boredom" (320), a man for whom boredom indeed constitutes power. She fills the languid pauses of his conversation with internal speculation about what impression she is making and what life with him might be like. Surely his coolness promises distance. An alliance with him would not imply the impediments of intimacy. He would not meddle, he would only provide for Gwendolen a more glamorous aura. His boredom creates a blank to fill with a woman's fantasies.

But Grandcourt's boredom, far more consciously and consistently than Gwendolen's, helps him control and manipulate others. If Gwendolen's brief resistance to his advances piques his interest, it also intensifies his determination to dominate her. His ostentatious boredom does not diminish after their marriage, but Gwendolen painfully comes to understand the sadism it masks. As he ever more completely subjugates her, her own boredom expresses itself as passivity concealing murderous wishes. The state of feeling that had earlier seemed to her an attractive instrument of social and erotic power becomes a sign of helplessness. Well before Grandcourt's death, the text, in pursuit of its ethical program, has converted boredom into ugliness and misery.

The opposed possibilities of boredom as sadism and as passivity may direct attention to the state's utility as a sign of divided sensibility. Anthony Cascardi, alluding to "the mobile psyche of modernist desire," goes on to suggest that "the modern subject is defined by its insertion into a series of separate value-spheres, each one of which tends to exclude or attempts to assert its priority over the rest. Subjective experience is itself the conflictive `totality' described by all of these" (3). The description oddly evokes the conventional situation of women, "inserted" into various spheres by the necessity, to put it in eighteenth-century terms, of "belonging to" a series of males, and thus often constrained to inhabit a "conflictive `totality.'" Modernism has been linked in various ways with the "feminine." To consider Gwendolen a modernist representation helps to delineate a complex connection. Accustomed to present at least a facade of compliance, Gwendolen almost automatically adjusts herself to Grandcourt and to Daniel as she has previously adjusted to her uncle. The conflicting ethical demands implicit in different male characters forcibly impinge on her. Afraid to confront the nature of her own desire, she aligns herself alternately with Grandcourt's values and with Daniel's. The "conflictive" experience characteristic of modern consciousness thus seems in her to derive from her entanglement, as a woman, in a highly traditional social system.

But Eliot analyzes Gwendolen's consciousness more subtly than this summary suggests. The reader first encounters the character as a determined young woman, skillful in promoting her own interests. Even in this premarital state, however, before her wavering allegiance has divided itself between two men, Gwendolen seems alienated from herself as well as from others. Unable to judge or to comprehend her self, divided in ways signaled by her hesitation in accepting Grandcourt as well as by outbursts of violence or terror (she strangles her sister's canary, for instance, and faints at the unexpected sight of a painting of death), outbursts belying her controlled self-presentation, ignorant of the scope of human nature, she blindly pursues what she half knows she does not want. Both her ignorance and her self-control reflect her social compliance. Her self-division betrays the costs of that compliance and signals Gwendolen's participation in the modern condition.

Boredom's importance as an ethical issue in *Daniel Deronda* hinges on the significance assigned to personal involvement. From the beginning, Daniel demonstrates wide capacity for interest. He interests himself, for instance, in the fate of women, partly, we are told, because of his uncertainty about his mother's destiny. Originating in aesthetic consideration of an ambiguously attractive object, his initial contemplation of Gwendolen rapidly develops into moral awareness, marked by his redeeming the necklace Gwendolen pawns to pay her gambling debts. His first sight of Mirah, whom he will marry, also registers an aesthetic spectacle. Daniel wants to watch her because of "the delicate beauty, the picturesque lines and colour of the image," imagines a "probable romance" connected with her, and smiles at himself for his "prejudice that interesting faces must have interesting adventures" (172). Her look of misery contributes to the aesthetic effect, but when action (dipping her cloak in the water so its weight will help her drown) signals misery's immediacy, Daniel's "interest" once more generates moral energy. His gradual involvement in Jewish nationalism, originating in his contact with Mirah, comes to symbolize the scope of his moral imagination—in fact, of his interest. In this connection, the narrator comments directly on the moral importance of interest, the enlarging of self it involves, and on its relation to boredom (or ennui: she uses the terms interchangeably). "This wakening of a new interest—this passing from the supposition that we hold the right opinions on a subject we are careless about, to a sudden care for it, and a sense that our opinions were ignorance—is an effectual remedy for *ennui*" (335).

The vast distance between Gwendolen and Daniel along the spectrum from boredom to interest paradoxically links them. Daniel pities Gwendolen's moral insufficiency, demonstrated by her boredom; Gwendolen envies and finally longs for his capacity to invest interest outside himself and to guide himself by it. This potentially redemptive desire for outwardly focused interest intensifies as she endures a boredom marking doom (moral vacuum and despair) rather than entitlement. By the time Grandcourt bears her off on a miserable yacht trip, Gwendolen knows that she has married an alien being whom she can never escape. Grandcourt, entirely aware that she does not love him, anticipating the pleasure of forcing her into subordination, feels vaguely threatened by the recurrent contacts between Gwendolen and Deronda. He would scorn to acknowledge jealousy, but he wishes to take his wife away, into a situation where, alone with him, she must profoundly experience his domination. In premarital conversation Grandcourt has repeatedly pronounced most activities, most situations, and most people "a bore." Now, cruising the Mediterranean with his beautiful wife, he recapitulates such pronouncements. Now, for the first time, she really understands them.

The intercourse between husband and wife on the yacht consists mainly in "well-bred silence." Occasionally Grandcourt remarks on, for instance, the sugarcane that he sees through his telescope and asks Gwendolen if she wishes to see it. Remembering Daniel's injunction that she interest herself in "something outside her personal affairs," she dutifully looks (625). But the confinement of her life with a man toward whom she now feels moral repulsion becomes increasingly nightmarish, the nightmare consisting in endless repetition of the meaningless. She asks how long they will continue yachting. He sees no reason to stop: "There's less to bore one in this way. . . . I'm sick of foreign places" (628). Gwendolen finds "wearisome" the prospect of continued close contact with her husband. Only Grandcourt's death rescues her, but into another kind of nightmare, that of imagined responsibility for a crime committed only mentally but mysteriously resulting (so her fancy has it) in her husband's drowning.

The yachting sequence dramatizes boredom's threat to narrative. As a girl, not bored, Gwendolen, fascinated with her own potential, could imagine for herself glamorous stories of marriage and self-indulgence. As a woman doomed to share her husband's languor, in her induced boredom she—unlike Daniel, whose intense interest projects a vivid life narrative—can neither invent nor envision any satisfactory story for herself. The idea of motherhood, for example, fills her with dread. The narrative of guilt generated by her husband's death at least opens prospects. As for Grandcourt, despite his privileged position as wealthy male he too proves unable to construct a sufficient extended story— beyond that of persecuting his wife—and death emphatically concludes his inadequate narrative.

Gwendolen's habit of boredom, Daniel's habit of interest epitomize their different relations to others. For Gwendolen—capable of kissing her image in the mirror—the world of other people constitutes a vast audience. She willingly makes herself an object for contemplation because she understands such objectification as a source of power. Given her beauty, she believes that all she wants to have should come to her, all she wants to do should be possible. Herr Klesmer, a true artist, reveals her incapacity for a career on the stage, shocking as well as mortifying her because he declares strict limits on the possible. Her family's new poverty exposes further limits, once she understands that she cannot rescue them from it by her talent and beauty. Her uncle suggests that she will find the life of a governess "interesting" because it will open new experience. She cannot comprehend the idea. Though prepared to do her duty, to serve as governess if nothing else offers, she is not prepared to discover interest in such service, which would place her in a relation to others virtually inconceivable to her: one of social inferiority. If she considers others not as contemplators of her beauty but as separate beings, they become in her consciousness objects of manipulation, to be controlled by her wishes, subordinated to her power. Even after her enlightenment by suffering and by Daniel, she cannot imagine a relationship between equals. Her marriage makes her more "interesting," the narrator observes, "more fully a human being," because "less confident that all things are according to her opinion" (631). But neither the marriage nor its aftermath allows her to understand herself simply as one among many consciousnesses, all limited, all within their limits entitled.

Daniel, on the other hand, acutely aware of other people's feelings and situations, treats everyone as an equal. Eliot goes to considerable pains to emphasize the fact. His benevolence to Mirah and to Mordecai, for instance, avoids the faintest suggestion that his relative good fortune corresponds to any significant superiority. Unlike eighteenth-century fictional bestowers of charity, he does not understand suffering as spectacle or as stimulus for his own emotions. He accepts helpfulness as a natural obligation, grasping his inherent connection to others—*all* others. If his unfailing virtue in this respect risks irritating the reader, it emphasizes a crucial point: interest in others, commitment to a human world outside the self, enlarges the self (as well as the scope for narrative). Nothing else will serve.

These perceptions ground Eliot's moral condemnation of boredom as the antithesis of such interest. A second basis for condemnation, more distinctly allied with modernist assumptions, depends on boredom's inherent connection to time. *Daniel Deronda* contemplates the contrast between time sacred and secular, public and personal. In reclaiming his Jewish heritage its protagonist—for whom time, like space, measures an objective external realm—discovers the sacred, which depends on no notion of the afterlife. Rather, the tradition Daniel recovers locates the sacramental in history, future as well as past, sanctifying his sense of responsibility by placing it in the context of Jewish destiny.

Gwendolen, on the other hand, vividly experiences time's relativity. Matei Calinescu claims as one of the marks of "modernity" a set of values based on "the personal, subjective, imaginative *durée*, the private time created by the unfolding of the `self'" (5). Only this kind of time generates boredom. Gwendolen's experience on the yacht, one endless day succeeding another, exemplifies the problem of "personal" time. Altogether relativistic, its progress marked by the self's investigation of itself, time becomes for Gwendolen an element in which to drown (Grandcourt literalizes the metaphor) or at best to tread water—not, like Daniel's version of time, one to swim in. Boredom, given this perception of time, consists in the paradoxical incompatibility of the self and the concept of time it generates. Such boredom typifies not only narcissism but narcissism's inadequacy to create satisfaction. A sign of moral insufficiency in Grandcourt and in Gwendolen, boredom declares both their self-confinement and their uncomfortable relation to time.

Eliot's ostentatious moralism appears to ally her firmly with her Victorian contemporaries, but the morality she associates with the problem of boredom, like her suggestion that British tradition no longer has moral power, points forward. Her consideration of the dynamic of interest and boredom securely links the two plots of *Daniel Deronda*, which many have seen as essentially disconnected. It also suggests that, in her awareness of "private time" and the difficulties it creates and in her sensitivity to the temptations and the dangers of narcissism, she looks to a future in which both problems would become increasingly acute.

Henry James, more orthodoxly "modern," in *The Portrait of a Lady* (1881) rewrote the Gwendolen plot of *Daniel Deronda* with intensified stress on the psychological force and moral inadequacy of the bored man. The relationship between Gilbert Osmond, perpetually bored, and Isabel Archer, never bored, more intimate and inescapable than that between Gwendolen and Daniel, allows full ethical analysis of boredom as aggression, as narcissism, as self-chosen style, as sign of a painful relation to time. Less moralistic than Eliot, James yet understands as she does the moral issues implicit in boredom as modern experience. Isabel marries Gilbert Osmond and stays with him even after she realizes the devastating moral implications of his stance—stays with him because of her own understanding of moral issues. James's imagining of this attraction of opposites reveals his grasp of an intricate ethical dilemma.

Osmond, like Grandcourt, presents himself as a social aristocrat, elegant by tradition and by taste. As Isabel early concludes about him, "He had consulted his taste in everything—his taste alone perhaps, as a sick man consciously incurable consults at last only his lawyer: that was what made him so different from every one else" (220). Isabel's consciousness, conceiving this metaphor, fails to interpret it. Her image oddly assimilates Osmond to her cousin Ralph Touchett, literally incurable and, though uninterested in lawyers, conspicuously concerned with legacies. She does not analyze the all too accurate implications of imagining the lover of art as a "sick man" who has rejected forms of consultation that might take him outside himself. She finds him endlessly "interesting." He in turn interests himself in her—partly because he imagines her as one who might "publish . . . to the world" his remarkable "style"—"without his having any of the trouble" (255).

Gilbert Osmond's desire to have no trouble belongs to his self-presentation as bored, which Ralph considers part of his pervasive, carefully articulated *pose* (325). But if Osmond's boredom is partly pose, an aspect of his determination to present himself as superior and untouched, it also has deeper meanings. The mask has grown to the face. Osmond's enactment of boredom, like Lady Dedlock's, only disguises boredom's experiential reality.

Osmond's distaste, even before his marriage, for Isabel's ardent impetuosity calls attention to boredom's protective function. Pose or reality, boredom guards Osmond from the unexpected. His refusal to interest himself in anything but the rare beautiful object (Isabel being one such object), his reliance on the aristocratic life as "a thing of forms, a conscious, calculated attitude" (354), his perception of "the infinite vulgarity of things" (353)—all these varieties of nonengagement amount to moral equivalents of boredom, the declaration that nothing possesses sufficient interest to be worthy of attention. "He was easily bored, too easily," as Madame Merle observes (207).

Long before Osmond appears in James's pages, the novel recurs frequently to the verb *bore* and its cognates. Lord Warburton in particular, the honorable and attractive young Englishman who woos Isabel, uses the vocabulary of boredom as an aristocratic tic. Ralph says of him that he "pretends to be bored" (21). "You wouldn't be bored if you had something to do," Mr. Touchett admonishes him (22), failing to recognize the degree to which his boredom consists merely in a social style. Inasmuch as Warburton's allusions to boredom reflect artifice more than experience (as when he worries that he might bore first Isabel, then Pansy), he invites comparison with Osmond. The vast gap between them helps to focus and solidify a negative evaluation of Isabel's husband. Osmond's boredom rejects experience; Warburton's language of boredom disguises commitment. In fact the young lord has much to do. He pretends disengagement as a courtesy, as he pretends to believe himself potentially boring to the women he courts. In contrast with Osmond, whose "traditions" have no discoverable source and whose "honor" consists in appearances, Warburton lives with and from a profound sense of family honor. His claim of boredom and his willingness to see himself as boring provide pretexts for refusing to demand much from others; Osmond's boredom fulfills the opposite function. (And if

Osmond imagined himself as boring—an unlikely eventuality, given his narcissism—he would presumably delight in the aggression thus concealed.)

The word *interesting*, opposite of *boring*, with its cognates also figures importantly in this fiction. "I'm not in the least bored," Ralph Touchett announces, setting up the opposition: "I find life only too interesting" (21). (Caspar Goodwood much later echoes him, likewise denying the imputation of boredom [416].) Isabel shares this apparently enviable situation. "She had a fixed determination to regard the world as a place of brightness, of free expansion, of irresistible action" (53). As Mrs. Touchett explains to her son, "She has no idea of being bored." The mother adds that she doesn't think Isabel finds her a bore: "Some girls might, I know; but Isabel's too clever for that" (46). Boredom is in the mind of the beholder.

If people are not inherently boring but only judged so by those not clever enough to perceive their interest, it may follow by extension that not the external world but the internal alone provides cause for boredom. Robert Nisbet suggests "it is probable that only a nervous system as highly developed as man's is even capable of boredom," which stands fairly high on the scale of afflictions (22). For James too, boredom appears to depend on the "nervous system," even though external causes may be assigned for it, external happenings said to alleviate it. Thus Ralph, despite his proclamation of interest in the world, acknowledges a bit later that he "had never been more blue, more bored, than for a week before [Isabel] came" (63); her arrival resolves his difficulty. But not because she is inherently "interesting," although many people find her so. Her husband, for instance, learns to feel her presence quite the reverse of interesting. Ralph's capacity to take interest, rather than particular external stimuli, makes his boredom temporary. Osmond's refusal of interest keeps his chronic.

"Refusal" implies choice. Indeed, Osmond's boredom, whether pose or actuality, is *chosen* in exactly the same sense as Isabel's endless interest in what lies outside herself—the product, as we have seen, of "fixed determination." James's fiction characteristically concentrates on how people create themselves. In *The Portrait of a Lady*, this most central of human activities dramatizes itself through the dialectic of "boring" and "interesting."

Isabel's sense of life's infinite interest connects itself with her commitment to action. "When Isabel was unhappy she always looked about her—partly from impulse and partly by theory—for some form of positive exertion. She could never rid herself of the sense that unhappiness was a state of disease—of suffering as opposed to doing" (341). Boredom, a form of unhappiness from which Isabel never suffers, lends itself particularly well to the remedy of "positive exertion." Nisbet declares that "work, more or less properly attuned to the worker's aptitudes, is undoubtedly the best defense against boredom" (23). Isabel neither finds nor seeks gainful employment, but she has what one might call a fatal attraction—certainly it determines her fate—for other kinds of work. "The desire for unlimited expansion had been succeeded in her soul by the sense that life was vacant without some private duty that might gather one's energies to a point" (291). If her dedication to duty, like that of Eliot's Maggie Tulliver, generates ambiguous results, it yet proves morally superior to Osmond's inertia, manifestation and emblem of his boredom.

Isabel's concern for duty opposes itself to Osmond's rejection of moral categories to provide a specific form of the polarity that preoccupies me. The man dedicated to boredom as a way of life extends the resultant state of alienation to separate himself from the realm of conventional moral judgments, despite the love of convention he proclaims and in other respects displays. Like Madame Merle, he concerns himself with morality only at the level of social appearance. His mistress must not present herself as his mistress, the illegitimacy of his daughter must not emerge, his wife must not appear to leave him. But his boredom itself has the effect of moral judgment. It isolates him in his rejections (even Madame Merle comes to bore him). It allows him to insist tacitly on his superiority to those around him. Declaring his human environment uninteresting, he re-creates the world in the image of his boredom, condemning the behavior, the taste, the very existence of others.

The ardent woman inevitably violates the standards of the bored man. Isabel struggles to please her husband. She masters many of the social forms he values, but her being remains, as she perceives, an offense to him. James demonstrates in persuasive detail how boredom and interest, personified in Mr. and Mrs. Osmond, criticize one another. Like Browning's "last duchess," Isabel does, thinks, feels everything too intensely. Her husband hates her as a result: so she believes, and the reader can believe it too. But his stance of boredom mutes hatred's expression. Almost never does he allow himself open passion.

The struggle between boredom and engagement covertly centers on issues of control. The bored person almost necessarily wins in the short term, because boredom, unlike engagement, implies no respect for the identity of the other. A monstrous egotism in its persistent denial of value, boredom wields the power of its singleness. Osmond enforces the negative. Under his influence Isabel learns to curb expressions of her interest in others, in the world. She largely complies with the forms he demands. And though she appears temporarily to escape by virtue of her emotional intensity, she returns to Osmond in the end.

James knew the disturbing force of this resolution and the ambiguities associated with it. I have used increasingly emphatic judgmental language ("no respect for the identity of the other," "monstrous") in characterizing Osmond and the boredom he represents; the novel solicits such judgment. But not only of Osmond, or of boredom. Isabel's ardency also invites assessment, while making it difficult.

The intense interest in the world that Isabel brings with her from the United States converts itself, given more experience, into her equally intense desire for a duty to provide the arena for committed action. Osmond (and later Pansy as well) supplies her with such a duty. She marries him to help him. She returns to him, after experiencing Caspar's passion and devotion, with the feeling that she is now "free" and that "there was a very straight path" (482). Now, for the first time, she really knows what she is giving up. The knowledge generates the freedom of conscious choice. Her departure, James wrote in a notebook entry, "is the climax and termination of the story" (487).

The capacity for interest and engagement that Isabel so richly displays duplicates Keats's "negative capability," implying a gift for feeling into the life of others. Whereas boredom implies rejection of others' claims, even of their full reality, Isabel's engagement involves, on occasion, richer recognition of others' needs and desires than they might themselves possess. Thus her return to the misery of her marriage tacitly acknowledges claims of Osmond's more profound than he would ever make himself, responsibilities to Pansy that Pansy could not presume to imagine. She has accepted the consequences of her gift for interest: specifically the consequences of the interest that she self-deludedly felt in Osmond, whom she created in the image of her need. She has made an ethical decision, rejecting love for duty, putting her obligations to others before her own needs and desires. James's imagining of her thus has disturbed generations of readers.

And with reason. Isabel's self-sacrifice seems all too familiar, the kind of suppression long celebrated in women, a manifestation of the moral superiority the Victorians readily granted, partly as a social convenience, to "good" females. The doctrine of women's moral guardianship of the family kept them home, encouraging them to sublimate any yearning for public achievement. Isabel's rejection of erotic desire for domestic duty denies the importance of self-fulfillment. James makes her wonderfully, compellingly attractive, traces the trajectory of her increasing awareness, her knowledge of self and others, then . . . throws it all away.

Yet the ending of *The Portrait of a Lady* does not read like a verbal gesture of conformity.

The ethical problem of Osmond and his boredom helps to clarify the ethical problem of Isabel. Alasdair MacIntyre writes, in the context of an examination of modern moral relativism, that in *The Portrait of a Lady* "James is concerned with rich aesthetes whose interest is to fend off the kind of boredom that is so characteristic of modern leisure by contriving behaviour in others that will be responsive to their wishes, that will feed their sated appetites" (23). MacIntyre understands the novel as belonging to a long tradition of moral commentary.

> The unifying preoccupation of that tradition is the condition of those who see in the social world nothing but a meeting place for individual wills, each with its own set of attitudes and preferences and who understand that world solely as an arena for the achievement of their own satisfaction, who interpret reality as a series of opportunities for their enjoyment and for whom the last enemy is boredom. (24)

These sentences in part characterize Osmond's moral malady. Isabel's husband indeed typifies the aesthete (rich, of course, only by virtue of his marriage) who manipulates others to gratify his wishes, who sees his own satisfaction as of paramount importance, and who elevates the significance of his own will. But it is by no means true that he tries to "fend off" boredom or considers it "the last enemy." On the contrary, his boredom constitutes the sign of his manipulative power. By virtue of his incapacity for engagement, he can "contrive" the behavior of others. By virtue of it he himself remains relatively invulnerable.

Kierkegaard, most epigrammatic and most profound of Western experts on boredom, writes, "Boredom, extinction, is precisely a continuity in nothingness" (*Concept* 133). The sense of nothingness, of *absence*, of the extinction of human capacity, becomes ever stronger in relation to Osmond. In contrast, Isabel grows into a richer presence. In her final imagined choice, she rejects the cliché of self-gratification and the pursuit of happiness, thus eliminating the danger of boredom (nothingness) such pursuit implies. Her choice affirms the vitality of her continued capacity for "interest."

Alternative endings, in which she might choose life with Caspar, or at least choose to explain herself to Caspar and to us, or even rest in indeterminacy, might better satisfy the reader's desire for assurances of human possibility. We would probably feel better even if the narrator made it clear that he considered Isabel's return a tragic denouement, registering Clarissa-like arrogance or female delusion. But he does nothing of the sort. Caspar, Henrietta suggests, will be all right in the long run. And Isabel? The question mark lingers.

Osmond in his boredom, Osmond's sister in hers, damage other people less by destructive will than by refusal of interest: determined, if unconscious, unawareness. The pursuit of happiness often reveals itself, in modern times, through the search for the interesting. Wayne Booth, playfully sketching a history of boredom, points out that

> As the causes of tedium moved outward, so did the causes of its opposite, and people more and more asked the world to *interest* them by being novel, surprising, or relevant. . . . It is scarcely surprising that people enjoying a newly discovered individualism, demanding of the world that it be *interesting*, discover[ed] that in fact the world bored them. (283)

The futile demand that the world be interesting perpetuates the dulling form of dissatisfaction perhaps most characteristic of modern middle-class and upper-class culture. Osmond and his sister, their environment ever unsatisfactory to them, endure the consequences of their leisure. Isabel affirms the option of work, through which, finally, she creates interest. If we as readers reject her definition of her work, we ally ourselves dangerously with the nonethical participants in James's fictional universe.

James's study of ethical triumph and failure seems more up-to-date than George Eliot's partly because it stresses its psychological concerns more obviously than its moral ones. Yet even more emphatically than its predecessor, *The Portrait of a Lady* insists on the moral danger of indulging in an antagonistic relation to time and to society, focusing on imagined needs of the self, allowing boredom to become a habitual stance. Osmond faces little struggle, Isabel struggles constantly. Through struggle she increases and defines her moral stature. Yet she also demonstrates that the morality of "interest"—recommended earlier by Maria Edgeworth—may entail debilitating demands on the individual who embraces it.

James's nineteenth century by inevitable progression becomes T. S. Eliot's twentieth century. Gilbert Osmond's inability to interest himself in the world signals in familiar ways his claim of aristocracy. By the time Eliot writes the fragments of "Sweeney Agonistes," working-class rather than aristocratic men and women can be imagined as experiencing—though also as fearing—boredom. If, as other contemporary texts indicate, boredom could still serve as a sign of superiority, it could also signal pervasive social danger. Neither Grandcourt nor Osmond is introspective. T. S. Eliot's viciously imagined Doris (in "Sweeney"), however, reveals a degree of moral inertness not imaginable fifty years before. At least Grandcourt and Osmond demonstrate highly developed consciousness. Grandcourt knows exactly what he is doing to Gwendolen, Osmond knows the precise aesthetic value of the objects he contemplates. Doris knows nothing, except that she needs distraction.

In an interlude of pseudoerotic playfulness titled "Fragment of an Agon," Sweeney fantasizes carrying Doris off to a cannibal isle. He'll be the cannibal, she'll be the missionary, he'll eat her in a lovingly imagined stew. The island, as Sweeney evokes it, lacks the appurtenances of civilization. It has no telephones, gramophones, automobiles; it offers only palm trees and the sea as objects of contemplation, only fruit to eat, only the surf to hear. Three things make up the island's activities. What things? Doris inquires:

> SWEENEY: Birth, and copulation, and death.
>   That's all, that's all, that's all, that's all,
>   Birth, and copulation, and death.
> DORIS: I'd be bored.
> SWEENEY: You'd be bored.
>   Birth, and copulation, and death.
> DORIS: I'd be bored.
> SWEENEY: You'd be bored.
>   Birth, and copulation, and death.
>   That's all the facts when you come to brass tacks:
>   Birth, and copulation, and death.
>   (147)

Later, after others have elaborated the ease of island existence, Doris reiterates her prospective boredom more emphatically: "That's not life, that's no life / Why I'd just as soon be dead," and Sweeney explains to her that "Life is death" (150).

Despite Eliot's distasteful snobbery, he has found a compelling image for modern frivolity and the alienation it entails in the figure of a woman who rejects fundamental experience on the ground that it would fail to entertain her. Doris's idiom ("I'd just as soon be dead") has no thought behind it, but Sweeney's embracing generalization in

236 / CHAPTER EIGHT

response indicts modern life. Separated from basic natural process, avid for titillation, the persons Eliot evokes lack the superficial dignity that characterizes Grandcourt and Osmond. They stand not even for their style. Sweeney, with his dim perception of "all the facts," uses that perception only to harass a woman possibly dimmer than he. The result Eliot imagines for consistent refusal to engage seriously with others involves the utter destruction of human substance. Life is death.

The ethical implications of such a presentation inhere mainly in its disgusted tone (which also, paradoxically, reflects its ethical insensitivity). One can imagine no realm of moral choice for Sweeney and Doris, evoked as almost subhuman. But Eliot's representation of "Apeneck Sweeney," as he is designated in "Sweeney among the Nightingales" (65), and his companions implicitly exhorts the poet's contemporaries to choices that will allow them not to resemble these grotesques, or condemns them for choices that make them moral equivalents of Sweeney. To indulge or to refuse boredom, with its self-absorption and its rejections, illustrated as well in Doris as in Osmond, becomes a choice definitive of moral nature.

Other modernists reiterated Eliot's vision even when they returned to the upper classes. Evelyn Waugh's upper-class young have plenty of style but little more substance than Doris. For the characters in *A Handful of Dust* the term *boredom* has become an empty social counter—yet it also accurately defines the essence of their experience. More fully than his predecessors, Waugh examines the implications of employing boredom as a category of interpretation.

Husbands and wives in Waugh's novel easily get bored with one another; both feel bored with the houseguests they compulsively invite to stay with them and accordingly apologize for the likelihood that the guests too will find the visit boring; people readily dismiss one another as bores. Out of boredom, Brenda Last embarks on a love affair with unattractive, unpopular John Beaver, challenged by her initial belief that he feels "terribly puzzled, and rather bored in bits" with her (65), only to find herself victimized by her own unanticipated passion. The affair provides a spectacle to alleviate boredom for Brenda's social set. Her husband, Tony, bemused by her assertions that she must spend more time in London to study economics, decides she must have been bored at home. Then, drunk, he confides that Brenda's new friends think him "a bore" (87). Correspondingly, Brenda herself, plagued by at least vestigial guilt, decides Tony must find it "pretty boring" on his estate without her (110) and produces a young woman to entertain him.

The reiterated, virtually automatic complaint of boredom betrays the limited imaginations of complainers who understand the social universe as operating by monotonous principles of causality. To label "boring" the self or others or experience in general registers incongruities between fantasy (the narcissistic fantasy that life can be always interesting) and actuality (it isn't). The paucity of analytic terms available to Waugh's characters, as they dichotomize experience into "boring" and "amusing," reveals their conceptual constriction, their incapacity to understand what happens to them: the incapacity that condemns them to the tedium they hate and fear. Neither work nor leisure provides them with meaningful relation to time. They live desperately, unaware of their desperation, encased in social confidence that protects them from realities larger than those of their privileged world.

The theme of boredom in *A Handful of Dust* reiterates the pattern controlling the novel as a whole, whereby trivia reveal profundity. Men and women who know not what they fear declare their own and others' boredom and work to forestall it. They thus assert, among other things, their discomfort in relationship. Although the Lasts posit one another's boredom as a function of lack of companionship, more typically the novel's characters understand boredom as resulting from the company of bores. Everyone at every minute risks relegation to that dread category.

To find the cause of boredom consistently in other people implies alienation that does not know itself as such. A friend once remarked to me that she considered it a sin to call someone a bore. Such dismissal denies the uniqueness—which implies the necessary interest—of every human being. Emily Post, in the 1945 version of her patronizing recommendations about manners and morals, makes the same point immediately after offering some harsh words about bores. "On the other hand," she concludes,

> to be bored is a bad habit, and one only too easy to fall into. As a matter of fact, it is impossible, almost, to meet anyone who has not *something* of interest to tell you if you are but clever enough yourself to find out what it is. Also you might remember that in every conversation with a "dull" person, half of the dulness is your own. (46)

Waugh's characters remember nothing of the sort. Assessing one another by entertainment value, they keep finding their companions inadequate. The novel's narrator does not take sides. If he suggests Brenda's moral inadequacy in her flight into adultery, he also uncovers in Tony a comparable failure of discrimination and nerve.

We last see Brenda burying her face in a pillow, "in an agony of resentment and self-pity" (279), deprived alike of money and of what passes for love. Events have judged her. Tony, also devoid of money and love, also suffering understandable resentment and self-pity, ends more luridly, condemned to spend the rest of his life reading Dickens aloud to an old man he has encountered in the jungles of Brazil. Dickens, most immediately compelling of novelists, thus becomes the center of a parable of social boredom. Tony must endure, without intimacy, the endless intimate company of a man who does not interest—much less entertain—him. Doomed to Dickens (if he refuses to read, he doesn't eat), he discovers the tedium of repetition. His ordeal is boring in the most precise dictionary sense—"that annoys, wearies, or causes ennui"—not only in the loose usage of his London friends. His sadistically narcissistic companion, Mr. Todd, experiences no boredom in the situation. For him Dickens remains endlessly interesting. Moreover, he has the power to control every aspect of his society. The natives, like Tony, do his will. The contrast between his condition and Tony's enables one to understand boredom as partly a function of powerlessness: a "modern" recognition.

In the light of that understanding, the novel's earlier allusions take on new meaning. Characters' reiterated complaints about the tedium of their companions or their condition may reflect their painful experience of impotence, regardless of how much money or "love"—most powerful of social counters—they possess. Boredom, then, is not a trivial complaint, however inexactly defined, however much its sufferers deserve it. On the contrary, it epitomizes the impossibility of effective action or knowledge in a world dedicated to the dulling of consciousness by meaningless activity, meaningless talk. The social environment inhabited and partially created by Gwendolen and Grandcourt has expanded. At London parties, on their country estates, in bed, Waugh's personages find it impossible to change even briefly. They have no control over their real situations. Brenda may leap into implausible adultery, but only superficially does she alter her condition. Tony's jungle doom reiterates his earlier social fate. The complaint of boredom reflects the experience of futility at the center of a secular, frivolous society.

Waugh's narrator makes no direct claims of significance for the story he tells, certainly none for boredom as literary subject or as personal emotion, and none for the characters of *A Handful of Dust,* who inhabit a glittering social world and live mainly to entertain themselves. They are not serious people. (Tony Last feels a serious interest in his anachronistic estate, but circumstances—and his wife—soon deprive him of the opportunity to indulge it.) Yet the satiric energy of Waugh's narrative suggests that the apparent lack of seriousness in plot, subject, and characters may be exactly the point, given the moral evasiveness implicit in refusal to take things seriously. Enjoying the frivolity of the world Waugh depicts, one must also judge it—partly for its inability to move beyond boredom as ground of interpretation.

Boredom appears everywhere in the early twentieth century, often, as in Waugh, assumed rather than discussed. I shall focus briefly on D. H. Lawrence and Gertrude Stein for final examples from the period of how the language of boredom condenses ethical issues. In *Women in Love,* Lawrence allows admirable and seriously flawed characters alike to experience boredom. Their capacity for the experience proves nothing. What matters is to what ends they use their boredom. For Stein, in *Ida,* boredom, nonexistent as a rendered state, lurks as a hypothetical experience for the reader: a fact creating considerable moral perplexity.

Women in Love (1920) offers an arrangement of characters as schematic as that of *Daniel Deronda:* a pair of "good" lovers, Ursula Brangwen and Rupert Birkin, coexist with a pair of "bad" ones, Gudrun Brangwen and Gerald Crich. All prove capable of boredom. Rupert, sometimes bored with people in general, sometimes with specific individuals, considers his boredom a sign of righteousness. He clearly thinks himself superior to Ursula, for instance, when she feels interested and he bored. Unlike the narrator of *The Portrait of a Lady,* Lawrence's narrator appears to align himself solidly with the bored man, whose boredom, like that of Osmond and Grandcourt, derives from his lack of interest in other people. Ursula talks "with lively interest, analysing people and their motives"; Rupert responds that "he was not very much interested any more in personalities and in people" (296). He sees Ursula's interest as "destructive," her analysis as "a real tearing to pieces" (297). On this occasion as on others, he declares himself on the side of "impersonality." Ursula has earlier summarized his position (with which, at the moment of summary, she believes she agrees) as a conviction that "human beings are boring, painting the universe with their own image" (257). He wants something larger than the human, beyond the personal. Sometimes he imagines love as that "something." "Let love be enough then," he says in his first explicit declaration to Ursula; "I'm bored by the rest" (146).

Each of Birkin's many announcements of his boredom expresses categorical rejection: of personalities and individual people, of all except love, of suffering, of reaction, of another man's ideas or discursive style or stance toward life. Unlike Waugh's characters, Birkin uses the language of boredom with exact and literal meaning. All that he rejects wearies him; he finds it tedious, he prefers not to engage. His intellectual and metaphysical snobbery corresponds to Gilbert Osmond's aesthetic snobbery.

To link Birkin with Osmond may seem wildly implausible because Birkin lives in the mind as a man of energy, in sharp contrast with Osmond's determined languidness. One remembers Osmond as a corrupt figure, Birkin as an upright one. Yet the sign of Osmond's corruption oddly resembles that of Birkin's virtue. Osmond's denials of experience, condemned by their contrast with Isabel's eager engagement, correspond to Birkin's refusals to connect, even in antagonism, with Mr. Brangwen—his rejection of the merely personal.

One must account, though, for his undeniable energy, not usually a concomitant of boredom. Investigating other bored characters in Lawrence's novel helps distinguish Birkin's special qualities. Gerald, for instance, also endures boredom, or its threat, with a meaning as precise as Birkin's. Yet his state of being differs utterly from the other man's. Before his father's death, Gerald "had never known what boredom was" (258). That is to say, he had never consciously experienced boredom, although the patterns of his life conformed to what others might define as boring. Afterward, no desire lasts long enough or has sufficient intensity to carry him into action. He has lost interest in women, who once could stimulate him; now he believes that his mind needs stimulation before his body can find it. He experiences his own emptiness. Drink or hashish might help, he thinks, or a woman (despite his earlier realization of lost interest), or Birkin. He can do nothing for himself.

Given the recent loss of his father, one might characterize him as suffering from depression or grief. Birkin, however, suggests boredom as the explanation for his state (259). Gerald tacitly accepts the diagnosis, declaring work or love the cure but unable to make use of either. The famous nude wrestling scene follows; Gerald says he feels better as a result. But his inability to commit himself remains. Although he takes Gudrun to Switzerland with him, their alliance holds them only tenuously. Subsequently enraged with his partner, he almost strangles her, then realizes he does not care enough about her to kill her. His death in the snow derives from the failure in him of all desire except longing to come "to the end" (464).

Gerald feels human connection (with Birkin, with a woman) as salvation but achieves it precariously, temporarily. On occasion he desires to desire, but at other times he longs for mechanical routine to free him from desire. Boredom, neither sign of superiority nor willed refusal, marks his human insufficiency. Ultimately it entails his death.

The schematic narrative opposition between Birkin and Gerald, in other words, extends to their boredom, which means differently depending on who feels it. Gerald hates the boredom he endures, Birkin takes apparent satisfaction in his. Boredom overtakes Gerald—who in this respect resembles most human beings—as an affliction for which he seeks a remedy. It comes to Birkin as a consequence of his conscious rejections. Boredom diminishes Gerald, aggrandizes Birkin. Boredom belongs to Birkin's program for himself, as it belongs to Gilbert Osmond's. In Osmond, though, it constitutes a sign of impoverishment. Not so for Birkin: at any rate, Lawrence's novel suggests nothing of the sort. Boredom, paradoxically, epitomizes the force of concentration with which Birkin organizes his perceptions of the world. Whereas Osmond systematically limits his universe, his boredom the image of his refusals, Birkin tries insistently to expand, rejecting other people and their suffering for the sake of the transcendent consciousness he seeks. The novel gives him the last word. Ursula tells him he can't have everything—specifically, that he cannot have both the deep love of a woman and that of another man. "It's an obstinacy, a theory, a perversity," she says; "it's false, impossible." "I don't believe that," Birkin replies (473). So *Women in Love* ends, with the rejection of Ursula's good common sense. But then Birkin always rejects common sense, in the service of what he considers higher values. Lawrence's apparent transvaluation of the boredom that, like Osmond's, repudiates other people and other ways of being provides a means to articulate his character's distaste for the conventional in all its forms. Birkin's boredom disavows not only common sense but common—meaning ordinary—people. It declares his participation in a moral rather than a social aristocracy.

Gudrun allows herself to get rid of Gerald by indulging in a small frenzy of boredom, stimulated by the distasteful German Loerke. Loerke announces that love is "a bore." "Women and love, there is no greater tedium." Gudrun assents: "Men and love—there was no greater tedium" (450), and her concurrence seduces her. Alone in her room, she reiterates how greatly Gerald bores her: "His maleness bores me. Nothing is so boring, so inherently stupid and stupidly conceited." The nature of maleness changes as she contemplates it. At first it consists primarily of sexual confidence and seductiveness. Men's erotic constitution makes them boring. Yet they bore her not only as lovers, but as workers too. "These men, with their eternal jobs—and their eternal mills of God that keep on grinding at nothing! It is too boring, just boring" (455). This categorical dismissal of men as boring specifically includes Birkin and as specifically excludes Loerke, because he is "a free individual," an "artist," not a repeater of useless motions. Gerald, however, remains her primary target. After almost four pages of reflection about the boredom he induces, she concludes, "Poor Gerald, such a lot of little wheels to his make-up! He was more intricate than a chronometer-watch. But oh heavens, what weariness! What weariness, God above! A chronometer-watch—a beetle—her soul fainted with utter ennui, from the thought" (458). She has convinced herself.

In the *willed* quality of her boredom Gudrun resembles Birkin. Both seem to *choose* their boredom because it reminds them of what they wish to stand for. But Lawrence's novel insistently distinguishes among its characters, and the differences between Gudrun's and Birkin's boredom matter more than the similarities. Gudrun, although she makes her boredom into an argument and situates it in a discourse about large social arrangements, in fact chooses it in the service of her immediate desire. To construct Gerald, indeed all men except Loerke, as boring merely aids her erotic choice. The novel invites its readers to understand her limitations as a result of that choice and of the willful boredom that enables it.

Gerald too, we are to understand, lives a severely limited life, makes limited choices, and dies because of his own failures of comprehension. He retreats into various versions of the mechanical, his embracing boredom a sign of that retreat. Birkin, in contrast, makes his boredom into deliberate protection from forces that might threaten his efforts at mental enlargement. Although Ursula does not consistently accept it, she feels a kind of awe at Birkin's endless capacity for theorizing, which declares his intellectual power and his refusal of conformity. Boredom separates him from what he does not wish to consider fully. He consciously employs it as a resource.

For him too, boredom aids the fulfillment of desire—not only for Ursula but for his sense of himself as remarkable and superior. To return to the term used earlier in this chapter, Birkin's boredom supports his narcissism, justifying a self-absorption that its possessor insists on explaining as something larger. Birkin, the novel would have us believe, wishes desperately to get beyond self. To find suffering and limitation and humanity boring amounts to a moral discipline by which he evades traps of feeling that might interfere with his effort to evolve a balanced, suprapersonal love, a perfect love, two stars balanced in their orbits.

The ethical system supported by *Women in Love* does not condemn him: quite the contrary. Gilbert Osmond appears reprehensible not only in his egotism but in the system he constructs to bolster it, a system that employs boredom as a critical weapon. Birkin, an egotist who ignores the fact of his own self-absorption, also constructs a large system of belief that justifies his behavior and his rejections. Boredom functions within that system too as a critical implement. If Ursula on occasion finds her lover's theorizing false or foolish, the novel as a whole never supports her position. It adumbrates a new ethic of boredom (as well as a new ethic in other respects) that accepts it as a principle of moral action, or inaction: a legitimate principle of rejection. Some of the attributes that make Gilbert Osmond distasteful are alleged to make Birkin morally attractive. The capacity for full engagement with whatever presents itself no longer seems a self-evident good.

My comments on *Women in Love* have not significantly modified traditional readings of the novel. Lawrence's moral schematic has long seemed quite apparent. By focusing on the place of boredom in that schematic, however, I hope to suggest yet another aspect of the intricate meanings boredom acquired for literary purposes as the twentieth century moved on. In the secularized world, with the importance of the individual becoming ever more fully assumed even as the stability of the individual subject wavered, the mandate of responsibility for one's neighbor no longer dominated even theoretically. Boredom, often seen as an upper-class affectation concealing self-absorption and moral insufficiency, might also, Lawrence suggests, signal the operations of a human spirit engrossed in the high enterprise of perfecting itself.

Gertrude Stein opens yet another set of possibilities. In *The Autobiography of Alice B. Toklas* (1933) she employs boredom as a rhetorical and psychological principle of meaning within a plot of self-invention that defies conventional expectations both in the story it tells and in its mode of telling it. Boredom provides the initiating pretext in the narrative of a literary career. It emerges as an explicit theme roughly a third of the way through *The Autobiography*, to inaugurate Stein's existence as someone whose life holds intense interest—for herself and presumably for any reader. The autobiographer explains that her first two years of medical school were all right because "she always liked knowing a lot of people and being mixed up in a lot of stories and she was not awfully interested but she was not too bored with what she was doing," but "the last two years at the medical school she was bored, frankly openly bored" (100). (She puts the point differently in *The Making of Americans:* "I went to the medical school where I was bored and where once more myself and my experiences were more actively interesting me than the life inside others" [Stein, *Selected Writings* 212–13].) Boredom becomes a figure for the impossibility of narrative. Only lots of people and lots of stories—the two sources of delight closely related to one another, as Eudora Welty for one has frequently pointed out— can avert it; as commitment to medicine begins to interfere with Stein's interest in both, it becomes intolerable.

Or so, at any rate, she says. "Gertrude Gertrude remember the cause of women," a friend pleads, and Stein reports herself as replying, "You don't know what it is to be bored" (101). She gives up her proposed career and goes to Europe. She also, *The Autobiography* suggests, reinterprets her past. Retrospectively, she understands the pleasures of medical school as those of story. She thereupon dedicates her life to such pleasure.

Boredom, then, provides a form of a posteriori interpretation as well as a mode of self-justification. For Stein it means the absence of available story. Women have been thought to suffer boredom at home and to alleviate it by seeking careers. Stein, according to her friend, will harm the cause of women by abandoning a profession not readily accessible to females. She decides, however, to help the cause of women in quite another way: by committing herself to her chosen form of pleasure, by sharing that pleasure with others, by justifying in a new kind of narrative the responsiveness and attentiveness long associated with women.

The Autobiography of Alice B. Toklas makes no attempt to render the imaginative dimensions of boredom as experience. It simply asserts boredom as fact, taking for granted the sense of distaste aroused in the reader by even an allusion. Everyone understands the need to escape. By choosing writing as her career, Stein demonstrates her capacity to find acceptable modes of evasion.

Boredom fulfills benign purposes in *The Autobiography* because of its immediate literary consequences in the story the writer makes of her life. The claimed experience promptly converts itself into productive compensatory activity. Looking back, a woman who believes she has suffered boredom declares her suffering the instrument of change. She functions more distinctly as analyst than as victim of the condition. Indeed, she trivializes the state in evoking it: something that must be, and easily can be, escaped. In the long project of her post-medical school writing, Stein implicitly argues, and demonstrates, that nothing is inherently boring. Constructing narrative out of commonplace experiential repetition, she demands for it the reader's interest.

In "Composition as Explanation" Stein describes her early writing: "There was a groping for using everything and there was a groping for a continuous present and for using everything by beginning again and again" (*Selected Writings* 457). The description applies also to a late work of fiction, *Ida* (1941), which by its refusal to acknowledge boredom as a possibility suggests a new direction for the ethics of boredom. The back cover of the Vintage paperback edition accurately characterizes the novel: "This is the story of Ida, whose life consists mainly of resting, because she is always tired; of talking to herself; and of getting married, time after time." The successive marriages, which would provide plausible centers of interest in most books about women, here recede in importance. On the whole, resting comes to seem a more significant activity than getting married.

Although Stein's book calls itself a novel and provides narrative of a sort, it does not emphasize event—nor does its protagonist:

> One day did not come after another day to Ida. Ida never took on yesterday or tomorrow, she did not take on months either nor did she take on years. Why should she when she had always been the same, what ever happened there she was, no doors [Ida dislikes doors] and resting and everything happening. Sometimes something did happen, she knew to whom she had been married but that was not anything happening, she knew about clothes and resting but that was not anything happening. Really there was never really anything happening although everybody knew everything was happening. (135)

Everything happening, not anything happening, time become meaningless because a person remains the same: the narrator describes Ida's experience in long rhythms of repetition and variation that deny the importance of isolated individual events, suggesting that large, unanalyzed patterns of experience hold paradoxical meanings ("there was never really anything happening although everybody knew everything was happening") that create the textures of human life. That Ida "never took on" measures of time suggests both that she never assumes time as part of her being and that she never accepts time as antagonist. She simply exists within it, confident of her identity (although she changes names, occupations, friends, spouses), confident of her capacity to accept happening and nonhappening alike. Boredom, given her special relation to time, cannot plague her. Time is as nearly as possible irrelevant, a fact so fundamental as not to be worth considering. Whether it passes slowly or quickly, whether occupations feel enjoyable or tedious—such discriminations do not belong to Ida's mental activity.

On the other hand, she frequently invokes the category of "interest." She assesses people, dogs, events as interesting or not. Sometimes nothing at all seems interesting to her, except herself.

> Ida thought she would go somewhere else but then she knew that she would look at everybody and everything and she knew it would not be interesting.
> She was interesting.
> She remembered everything and she remembered everybody but she never talked to any of them, she was always talking to herself. (44)

But the arbitrariness with which Ida assigns interest suggests its final irrelevance as a form of classification. She has an extended connection with someone named Andrew, who becomes less and less Andrew as she becomes more Ida, whose name "changed to Ida and eight changed to four and sixteen changed to twenty-five and they all sat down" (94), but who later "came to be Andrew again and it was Ida" (95). Given his metamorphoses, Andrew can be designated indifferently by masculine or feminine pronouns. "He" and "she" at once, s/he takes a walk every day and tells Ida about it. These activities—the walking and the talking—the text designates twice as "very pleasant." They epitomize the ordinariness of daily life and the substance of this "novel": a work about the permanence and impermanence of identity ("For which it made gradually that it was not so important that Ida was Ida" [95]) and about the deep pleasure of the commonplace.

Or perhaps one should say, the deep pleasure of the commonplace rendered in language. The arbitrary assignments of interest correspond to the apparent arbitrariness of happening on the page—eight changing to four and sixteen to twenty-five, new characters appearing out of nowhere, Ida getting married or getting a job or changing location for no obvious reason. Taking a walk and talking about it constitute unremarkable activities. Taking a walk and talking about it as Andrew becomes Ida and Ida becomes less important and eight becomes four— this is quite another matter. Such a concatenation depends on a specific sort of representation. When Stein reports, in *The Autobiography*, the pleasure of being mixed up with lots of people and lots of stories, one may realize retrospectively that she *makes* the stories she enjoys, as she makes out of next to nothing the story of Ida. Such making is the work of language. Its importance to *Ida* emerges with particular clarity in a playful extended sequence concerning superstition. Andrew, it turns out, likes to hear about good luck and bad luck because they seem unreal to him: walking and talking fully define his reality. Someone tells him he must worry about spiders, cuckoos, goldfish, and dwarfs. Then a representative of each class of beings speaks for itself in long, rhythmic, engaging soliloquy. A bit from the spider's soliloquy, in its entirety a single sentence occupying a full page, will suggest the flavor of the whole:

> I am I, I am a spider and in the morning any morning I bring sadness and mourning and at night if they see me at night I bring them delight, do not mistake me for the sky, not I, do not mistake me for a dog who howls at night and brings no delight, a dog says the bright moonlight makes him go mad with desire to bring sorrow to anyone sorrow and sadness, the dog says the night the bright moonlight brings madness and grief, but says the spider I, I am a spider, a big spider or a little spider, it is all alike, a spider green or gray, there is nothing else to say, I am a spider and I know and I always tell everybody so. (123)

This fragment has no obvious connection with real-life spiders: its speaker belongs to a fairy tale. Its fanciful rhymes and repetitions and allusions create their own delight. Inasmuch as such a passage bears on boredom, it suggests a new opposition, an ethical opposition, one hinted in Stein's account of her medical school career: language—writing—opposes boredom. Given the capacity to transform experience into its verbal rendition, boredom becomes impossible. I have suggested before that to pay full attention to anything rescues it from the category of the boring. Transmuting something into language constitutes paying attention. Stein's project, in *Ida* and in her other writing, involves the conversion of the ordinary—everyday components of life—into the extraordinary: highly individual forms of language. She thus denies boredom and implicitly reproaches those who find eventless lives (in particular, the eventless lives of women) devoid of interest. The covert ethical point is more emphatic than its equivalent in Eliot or James. Refusal of interest means laziness.

The book you are now reading began with the assertion that all writing and all reading by their nature resist boredom. The kind of ethical consideration initiated by the works considered in this chapter may return our attention to the hidden dynamic of interest and boredom that infuses fiction in particular. The dialectic of boredom and interest so crucial to *The Portrait of a Lady* operates in all writing. Isabel's "interest" creates her "work," the vocation of responsibility she embraces; Osmond's refusal of interest, his commitment to the posture of boredom; constitutes his ethical failure. Inasmuch as ethics involves individuals' relations and obligations to their fellows, it implies the fundamental imperative of interest, the ground of action in relation to or on behalf of another. To understand boredom, and even the passivity that boredom creates and reflects, as other forms of action (a move implicit in the kind of ethical analysis examined here) intensifies the threat that boredom constitutes for the novelist both as entertainer and as would-be guide.

James's preface to *The Portrait of a Lady* resounds with the words *interest* and *interesting*. Summarizing his hopes for the novel, he writes, "The interest was to be raised to its pitch and yet the elements kept in their key; so that, should the whole thing duly impress, I might show what an `exciting' inward life may do for the person leading it even while it remains perfectly normal" (14). To raise interest to a compelling pitch must be the desire—indeed, the urgent necessity—of every writer. As the narrator of *Tom Jones* pointed out, if the novelist keeps an inn for the entertainment of all passersby, those travelers always have the option of rejecting the offered entertainment. Only by interesting the reader (the point is almost too obvious) can the writer set in operation the fundamental transaction of his or her art.

But consciousness of a reader, in a modern or postmodern era, implies awareness of indeterminacy. No matter how "interesting" the novel, the putative reader may decline to be interested. Such refusal can imply serious criticism, suggesting the text's moral inadequacy (cf. Birkin) or the insufficient attention it pays to experience or its inadequacies of language (cf. Stein). On the other hand, the refusal may only reflect the reader's moral and aesthetic laziness. In either case, it effectively nullifies the writer's achievement.

NINE

Cultural Miasma

Postmodern Enlargements of Boredom

About nine o'clock most nights, when I am reading, my cat leaps to the top of a small chest of drawers and begins with deliberation to knock objects—perfume bottles, framed photographs—one by one to the floor. "He's bored," I say. "He wants attention."

"Fly the Concorde around the World," an advertisement urges. "The future way to fly—NOW. Everything else is boring."

Such attributions of boredom, to an animal probably incapable of this form of psychic distress, implicitly to billions deprived of Concorde luxury, call attention to the concept's late twentieth-century value as an all-purpose index of dissatisfaction. Advertisers could hardly do without it. A sexy woman lolls on a Directoire chaise. "I gave up chocolates," the copy reads. "I gave up espresso. I gave up the Count (that naughty man). And his little house in Cap Ferrat. The Waterman, however, is not negotiable. I must have something thrilling with which to record my boredom." Transgression and boredom: the only alternatives. The sphere of transgression enlarges: not just adultery and cocaine, but coffee and chocolate as well. So does that of boredom. We gaze at television to forestall boredom, and television generates more of it. Postmodern architecture works on the viewer in roughly the same way. The church socials and bingo games that contented previous generations strike contemporary intellectuals as quaint, perhaps, but ludicrously dull. Watching football bores some people, baseball unaccountably bores others. The Reagan administration was declared boring, and so was George Bush, but no political party has a monopoly: Michael Dukakis was widely felt to be terminally tedious. Cities, regions (Switzerland, the Middle West), occupations (toll collector, file

249

clerk): vast categories fall by assertion into limbo. On the other hand, I keep meeting people who insist that they themselves are never bored.

Never bored, finding a great deal boring, attributing boredom to others: What are we, collectively, up to?

Sociologists and psychologists tell us that the prevalence of boredom has greatly increased in recent years, and they eagerly tell us why. Sean Desmond Healy, for instance, whom I quoted in the first chapter as defining the problem (in 1984) in these terms: boredom is caused by "the growing metaphysical void at the center of Western civilization, not such more obvious conditions as wealth, leisure, personal pathology, or human nature" (87). Haskell Bernstein (1975) finds the cause in "the early and vigorous expectation of behavioral compliance when that can be accomplished only by the imposition of massive repression of feelings" (528–29). Many commentators associate the problem with the loss of a proper relation to leisure: given a pervasive lack of serious purpose in life, leisure "declines to mere amusement, time-filling, and becomes, like work and perhaps even more so, something to be got through" (Allen 26). In its ideal state, according to Josef Pieper, leisure implies "an attitude of non-activity, of inward calm, of silence; it means not being 'busy,' but letting things happen" (27). In other words, while constituting a state utterly opposed to boredom, it involves a kind of deliberate "emptiness" that postmodern observers often automatically associate with boredom. False leisure, the "time-filling" kind, only imitates its true counterpart, generating discontent.

Affluence creates boredom's conditions, according to some; yet assembly-line workers as well as rich people allegedly suffer the malady. A myth persisting from the eighteenth century has it that middle-class women in particular endure boredom. Consider Walter Kerr on the subject, from 1962:

> The buzz of her husband's power saw seems to drive her as well, though neither to fatigue her nor to satisfy her in quite the same degree. When she has completed the social tasks assigned to her by her husband, and has momentarily finished with the tasks she has assigned to herself, she is often to be found writing to one or another counselor in the women's magazines. We have all become accustomed to the lament that is here given voice: "I do not have enough to do, I do not respect the place I occupy in the world." (36)

Although much has changed since 1962, the familiarity and the symbolic resonance of this figure persist. Loss of political power generates boredom, Anton Zijderveld explains (81–83). The observation applies to Kerr's imagined woman, and to many a male as well.

For the first time, in the second half of the twentieth century, some of those attempting to account for boredom as a social pattern offer political exegesis. The group of Paris intellectuals who labeled themselves "the Situationist International," active in the French revolt of May 1968, presented a conspiracy theory:

> Leisure time was expanding—and in order to maintain their power, those who ruled, whether capitalist directors in the West or communist bureaucrats in the East, had to ensure that leisure was as boring as the new forms of work. More boring, if leisure was to replace work as the locus of everyday life, a thousand times more. What could be more productive of an atomized, hopeless fatalism than the feeling that one is deadened precisely where one ought to be having fun? (Greil 50)

Again, locating the conspiracy slightly differently:

> In modern society, leisure (What do I want to do today?) was replaced by entertainment (What is there to see today?). The potential fact of all possible freedoms was replaced by a fiction of false freedom: I have enough time and money to see whatever there is to see, whatever there is to see others do. Because this freedom was false, it was unsatisfying, it was boring. . . . It was leisure culture that produced boredom—produced it, marketed it, took the profits, reinvested them. (Greil 51)

Like the vaguer sociological and philosophic analysis I have cited, such political explanation assumes boredom to be a product of social forces rather than a matter of individual responsibility. The specific exegesis proved erroneous: leisure, in fact, has not increased. But the importance of political interpretation as a mode of confronting boredom remains.

Boredom has become an embracing rubric of discontent. Although those who explain its omnipresence typically attribute it to large cultural causes, advertising thrives on the suggestion that specific remedies will alleviate it. "I dreamed I found a 365-day-a-year cure for boredom," announces a newspaper ad for a Bethesda condominium, over a photograph of a beringed and manicured hand holding a pool cue. "Live your fantasy with The Christopher's Grand Opening Limited Offer," the ad continues, promising that life will always hold interest if only one lives in the right place. "ROMANCE GREED DECEPTION LUST." These words, in boldface capitals, preside over an advertisement in *Lingua Franca* and, reiterated around the edges, provide a frame for the copy. Immediately under the nouns as headline, another set of capital letters explains them: "THE CLASSICS DON'T HAVE TO BE BORING!" What will rescue the classics from the imputation of boredom and reveal (for

the first time?) their connection with ROMANCE GREED DECEPTION LUST
is their translation into video versions, all available "for the new low
price of just $29.98 each!"

If boredom functions for advertisers and village explainers as a generalized sign of dissatisfaction, challenging elucidation and remediation, it serves approximately the same purpose for postmodern writers
of fiction. No longer does it provide a locus for ethical interrogation,
no longer does it mark individual corruption. The pursuit of happiness
implies boredom's threat. Ever taking our emotional temperatures, we
rediscover that life more often than not provides neither misery nor
ecstasy. The reaches between include the hypothetical poise of calm
contentment, but also a condition more familiar to twentieth-century
humanity, one in which the world presents itself as uniformly gray.
Many consider such grayness implicit in the postmodern situation.
"Life, friends, is boring. We must not say so" (Berryman 16). Cultivated
and sophisticated observers have been known to dismiss as "boring"
people they encounter, meetings they attend, sentiments they hear or
read. To do so attests the fineness of their sensibilities. Boredom
declares itself an aesthetic or intellectual or emotional category, not an
ethical one.

Among other things, it provides an all-purpose index of alienation.
The privileged man or woman, separated by good fortune from the
mass of humanity, transforms the sense of separation into psychic
inability to find experience—the kind of experience others have—gratifying.

> Life, friends, is boring. We must not say so.
> After all, the sky flashes, the great sea yearns,
> we ourselves flash and yearn,
> and moreover my mother told me as a boy
> (repeatingly) "Ever to confess you're bored
> means you have no
>
> Inner Resources." I conclude now I have no
> inner resources, because I am heavy bored.
> Peoples bore me,
> literature bores me, especially great literature,
> Henry bores me, with his plights & gripes
> as bad as achilles,
>
> who loves people and valiant art, which bores me.
> (Berryman 16)

We flash and yearn, the world outside us, of nature and of art, vibrates with possibility, we possess the rich resources of mind and imagination—yet, whether we say so or not, we may at any moment find ourselves "heavy bored."

But whom, exactly, does that "we" designate? The strategy of Berryman's lines depends on the speaker's initial association with humankind, unspecified "friends" potentially involved in his plight. Yet the poem increasingly emphasizes the isolation of his boredom. He participates in an aristocracy not of social class but of intellect, ironically superior to his mother's platitudes, knowledgeable about "great literature," aware of high art and of epic. Even his own creativity bores him, as he rejects "Henry," protagonist of many of the *Dream Songs*. The effort to connect himself with others dwindles as "me" becomes the pronoun of choice. "We," in other words, serves as a temporary hopeful fiction within the poem's embracing fiction. On the other hand, many or most readers will surely respond imaginatively to the speaker's plight, recognizing it as an endemic state, potential in all experience. So "we" may, at any given time, include many—though, importantly, never *everyone*. Always it implies its exclusions.

Berryman's verses do not call for the reader's moral judgment, nor do they make such judgment easy. Because they express consciousness of the world's abundant stimuli, the reasons no one need ever be bored, even while asserting the bored man's inescapable dilemma, they forestall easy moralizing. We all know the intermittent inaccessibility of "inner resources," the pain of the situation in which the world's beauty holds for us no immediate power. On the other hand, the poem opens with a direct assertion that the boring quality of "life" constitutes a universal unspeakable secret. "Inner resources," like the beauties of art and nature, then, become irrelevant. Boredom is the human doom. Yet since the poem's strongly marked tone insists on its speaker's individuality, one can attribute this categorical assertion to his presumably temporary state of mind. The voice of boredom itself speaks to declare all life its domain. The assessment's universality attests its falseness.

If the poem does not solicit ethical judgment, it demonstrates what makes such judgment difficult in the contemporary world. Although it evokes sympathy for its speaker, it also shows that speaker with increasing emphasis declaring his isolation from his kind. Implicitly he claims his state as itself the result of unblinking judgments that reveal the inadequacy of what he is offered. The reader's relation to the rendered situation depends on willingness to identify with an imagined person who implicitly rejects identification (other "peoples" bore him). The evocation of boredom may provoke moral and psychological repugnance, or sympathy, or simply recognition. By the complexity of his rendition, Berryman makes it hard to know what kind of judgment would be an appropriate response. The speaker's mother adheres to standards by which he might be condemned—but one hardly wants to participate in that mother's moral simplicities.

Berryman's lines exemplify in miniature both the aristocracy of boredom and the way the condition can seem to forestall judgment by drawing everything to itself. Fiction writers obviously have fuller scope for investigating how boredom can present itself as a form of response that judges the world while making judgment difficult for the reader. In postmodern times they have on occasion fairly reveled in boredom. Donald Barthelme makes entertainment out of psychological malaise. For instance:

> I remember once we went out on the ups and downs of the West (out past Vulture's Roost) to shoot. First we shot up a lot of old beer cans, then we shot up a lot of old whiskey bottles, better because they shattered. . . . But no animals came to our party (it was noisy, I admit it). A long list of animals failed to arrive, no deer, quail, rabbits, seals, sea lions, condylarths. It was pretty boring shooting up mesquite bushes, so we hunkered down behind some rocks, Father and I, he hunkered down behind his rocks and I hunkered down behind my rocks, and we commenced to shooting at each other. That was interesting. ("Views of My Father Weeping" 12–13)

This parodic rendition of intergenerational tedium achieves its comedy by deadpan tone and wild inventiveness. Its introduction of one animal we (at any rate, I) have to look up ("Condylarthra: An order . . . of Eocene Ungulata . . . more or less plantigrade ["walking on the sole with the heel touching the ground"], with five-toed limbs" [*Webster's New International Dictionary*, 2nd ed.]) into a commonplace array calls attention to the resolute simplicity, even the willful reliance on cliché, predominant in diction and sentence structure. The bizarre sequence insists on its own ordinariness. Yet it also vividly displays its writer's capacity to make interest out of nothing: literally out of the nonpresence of animals that achieve their brief vitality from language alone.

Typically in Barthelme's work, interest resides, as here, in rhythmic exactitude and in a daring inventiveness that aggressively asserts its power to absorb the reader in banality. One more case in point, necessarily extended:

> Q: I have a number of error messages I'd like to introduce here and I'd like you to study them carefully . . . they're numbered. I'll go over them with you: undefined variable . . . improper sequence of operators . . . improper

use of hierarchy . . . missing operator . . . mixed mode, that one's particularly
grave . . . argument of a function is fixed-point . . . improper character in
constant . . . improper fixed-point constant . . . improper floating-point con-
stant . . . invalid character transmitted in sub-program statement, that's a
bitch . . . no END statement.
   A: I like them very much.
   Q: There are hundreds of others, hundreds and hundreds.
   A: You seem emotionless.
   Q: That's not true.
   A: To what do your emotions . . . adhere, if I can put it that way?

   Q: Do you see what she is doing?
   A: Removing her blouse.
   Q: How does she look?
   A: . . . Self-absorbed.
   Q: Are you bored with the question-and-answer form?
   A: I am bored with it but I realize that it permits many valuable omis-
sions: what kind of day it is, what I'm wearing, what I'm thinking. That's a
very considerable advantage, I would say.
   Q: I believe in it. ("The Explanation" 73–74 [all ellipses in text])

Computer jargon, isolated for attention, comments on the arbitrariness of meaning. Barthelme invites us to take pleasure in this language
on the page—in its odd relations to ordinary structures of meaning—
although we would hardly enjoy it on our computer screens. When the
speaker identified as Q (not always the questioner) emphatically
announces that "there are hundreds of others," one can fancy his delight
in the abundance the technological world supplies. It comes as something of a surprise that A chooses this moment to comment on his inter-
locutor's apparent lack of emotion, since Q's previous statement seems
to betray feeling. But A's observation calls into question the attribution
of emotional import to a simple statement about quantity. More important, it challenges the responses of that "one" I blandly posited ("one
can fancy"). True, one can fancy. But one can also *not* fancy, or fancy
something quite different.
   In their refusals to create resolution (even to answer questions: To
what *do* Q's emotions adhere?) or to assign clear meanings, Barthelme's
stories may appear to assume no coherent community of readers, no
"one" or "we" whose responses can be controlled or anticipated. The
narrator gives no direct evidence of caring about response. He supplies
reiterated narrative frustrations that actively taunt his readers, toward
whom his aggression emerges in such sequences as the one about the
woman removing her blouse. That woman reappears in another story,
"Kierkegaard Unfair to Schlegel":

Q: What is she doing now?
A: She appears to be—
Q: How does she look?
A: Self-absorbed.
Q: That's not enough. You can't just say, "Self-absorbed." You have to give
more . . . You've made a sort of promise which . . .
  A:
Q: Are her eyes closed?
A: Her eyes are open. She's staring.
Q: What is she staring at?
A: Nothing that I can see.
Q: And?
A: She's caressing her breasts.
Q: Still wearing the blouse?
A: Yes.
Q: A yellow blouse?
A: Blue. (91)

Here the text makes explicit the aggressive relation of narrator to
reader: "You have to give more . . . You've made a sort of promise
which. . . ." And A, temporarily a figure for the narrator, says nothing
in response, although he intensifies the tease by adding, after further
questions, sparse erotic detail.

The passage quoted earlier likewise comments on itself, in the
exchange about the question-and-answer form that declares it boring,
values its exclusions, and announces Q's belief in it. In both instances
the text calls attention to its own refusal of narrative satisfaction. In
Barthelme's stories, boredom undergoes significant displacement, less
important as a condition within the narrative than as an aspect of discourse inherent in most processes of reading and writing. Unlike James,
Barthelme lacks apparent faith in the possibility of making fiction
"interesting" to a postmodern audience. In fact, I know readers who
declare they are bored by him, by the lack of substance in the stories'
raw material and the preciosity of Barthelme's manipulations. Such
readers do not include me. What interests me is less the stories' content than their daring in using and shaping that content to reveal once
more the mind's fundamental enmity to boredom.

To be sure, boredom may also have demonstrable effects within a
Barthelme story: a father and son shoot at one another to allay their
malaise. This parodic episode only underlines the narrative problem.
Boredom, democratized, permeates experience. How, then, can a storyteller find material for compelling story? Doesn't any claim of interest falsify the texture of late twentieth-century life? Aggression, the

shooting incident suggests, supplies the only feasible alternative to boredom. The storyteller dramatizes the possibilities he narrates, beginning potentially absorbing narrative (a woman caressing her breasts) only to frustrate, in a transparent act of aggression, the reader's developing desire to know more; or providing the empty words of computer error messages to remind us of meager and tedious actuality. The notion of "compelling story," no longer relevant, vanishes.

Yet Barthelme's fictions exercise their own kind of power, for reasons not unrelated to the dominion Gilbert Osmond possesses over Isabel. If evocation of character and event stresses the democratized presence of boredom (though in fact few important characters in Barthelme's fiction appear to do any work: they too are a privileged class), the narrator himself more clearly exemplifies boredom's aristocracy. Like Osmond, he adopts a stance of not caring much about anything. His insouciant bricolage glories in arbitrariness. Rarely does he commit himself even to completion: his "stories" compose themselves from fragments. Like Osmond's aesthetizing of experience, this narrator's rejection of the consecutive, of climax, of plot, functions as judgment, not only declaring his entitlement (he has the capacity and the pre-empted right to judge) but substantiating his self-protective disengagement. Unwilling to validate any "story line," the narrator tacitly asserts the lack of coherence and of *point* in experience.

The characters of Barthelme's fictions interest themselves briefly in something and then get lost. They recite computer messages for one another, they like them very much, but their attention wavers, they cannot focus long on a single matter. They talk to one another in ways they themselves find boring. They experience the erotic only at a remove. They shoot at cans or bottles or one another, seeking in vain to make their lives interesting to themselves. They are victims of a culture of boredom.

Paraphrasing James, J. Hillis Miller remarks that "writing is not only a field for doing, but a field in which responsibility for the effects of doing may be conspicuously and stringently kept in view" (101). The "doing" involved in writing a work of fiction includes most fundamentally the familiar obligation to *pay attention*. By virtue of paying attention, fiction tells its truth.

I open Barthelme's *City Life* at random:

> Twenty thousand policemen of all grades attended the annual fete. The scene was Camelot, with gay colors and burgees. The interior of the Armory had been roofed with lavish tenting. Police colonels and generals looked down on the dark uniforms, white gloves, silvery ball gowns.

"Tonight?"
"Horace, not now. This scene is so brilliant. I want to remember it."
Horace thought: It? Not me?
The Pendragon spoke. "I ask you to be reasonable with the citizens. They
pay our salaries after all. . . . I know that for instance when you see a big car,
a '70 Biscayne hardtop, cutting around a corner at a pretty fair clip, with
three in the front and three in the back, and they are all mixed up, ages and
sexes and colors, your natural impulse is to—I know your first thought is, All
those people! Together! And your second thought is, Force!" ("The Police-
men's Ball" 54–55)

Such satiric brilliance derives from careful cognizance of the nature of
contemporary "fetes," the clichés of sex, the vagaries of narcissism, the
impulse to violence and its transmutations, the images of television
police shows. Nothing rendered in this scene is inherently "interesting."
On the contrary, for the kind of people likely to read Barthelme police
balls represent the epitome of tedium. The young man who asks,
"Tonight?" the young woman who answers in platitudes, the police
chief (by a charming joke transformed into an ancient British chief of
chiefs) with his double message—all themselves constitute clichés. But
Barthelme's version irradiates the familiar and enlightens by its conjunctions. The narrator's inconsequence, his refusal of narrative development, amount to courtesies toward a reader posited as a product of
that culture on which the storyteller has intensely concentrated, a
reader of limited attention span, limited capacity for sustained interest.
The teller of the story demands attention but acknowledges the chance
of resistance. He reminds us once more that the presence of the interesting depends always on the observer.

Although the subject of boredom often holds great interest for makers of fiction, although the superficial stance of boredom may provide
a resource for narrators, the actuality of boredom remains intolerable—
morally as well as creatively intolerable—for writers. Even Barthelme,
whose characters appear to suffer boredom as doom rather than choice,
by the activity of his narrator suggests alternatives. Whatever may be
true in other spheres of life, as a writer one has no right to be bored,
even in the most dismal circumstances. Indeed, the writer in his action
denies boredom's conceivable hegemony. However emphatically a
writer asserts alienation, he or she simultaneously contradicts the assertion, inasmuch as writing almost necessarily entails engagement. Every
successful book temporarily rescues its readers from boredom as an
imaginable fate, abandoning them finally to a world less populated, less
satisfying ("the real world") than they have recently enjoyed on the

page. The world we inhabit contains police chiefs but not pendragons. Writers like Barthelme, making the commonplace entertaining, provide satiric emphasis for readers' putative tendency not really to look at either the poverty or the richness of their own experience.

In its nature, as we have seen before, boredom opposes desire. More precisely than repulsion, the negative form of desire, it constitutes desire's antithesis, assuring its victim of the utter impossibility of wishing for anything at all. The sufferer from boredom finds it impossible to invest fully in any action, to believe any action worth the effort of involvement. "The thing that hath been, it is that which shall be; and that which is done is that which shall be done: and there is no new thing under the sun" (Eccles. 1.9). Why bother? The hope of something new may dimly remain: one can always go round the world in the Concorde. But a sense of futility precedes and forestalls endeavor. As the protagonist of Maria Edgeworth's 1809 novel *Ennui* observes, "Had I known how to enjoy the goods of life, I might have been happy" (7). No bored person possesses that vital knowledge.

Boredom may signal (though it also conceals) the simultaneous presence of depression and its antecedent, rage. If boredom disguises depression, depression's symptoms may also obscure the presence of boredom. The psychoanalyst Robert Seidenberg has suggested that women in particular often suffer misdiagnosis by professionals who fail to take seriously the psychological effects of social limitation. Reporting a case history of a housewife bored by her life's triviality, he observes that she endures real, external psychic dangers that "may not be apparent except to the observer who has thought about them" (357). The distinction between depression and boredom, in other words, hinges on causality. At least in the twentieth century, we typically attribute the causes of boredom to conditions outside ourselves: the tedious meetings we must attend, the dreary classrooms we inhabit.

Thus high-school students, convinced of their oppression by an uncomprehending world of adults, respond with unyielding, often highly dramatized, boredom. I would guess that every newspaper in the United States has published at least one feature story about adolescent boredom, explaining academic failure and recourse to drugs and violence as its consequences. One example of the genre, from the *Washington Post* (8 Dec. 1991), carries the headline, "FOR VA. TEENS, EMPTINESS AMID PLENTY." The subhead elaborates: "Battling Boredom, Some in Suburbs Turn to Drinking, Crime." "Regardless of the money their parents have," the article explains, "the clothes, the houses, the cars, the opportunities at school and the proximity to a major city, they say they are bored out of their minds." A West Springfield high-school senior is quoted: "This is the most boring place I ever lived. There is nothing for a teenager to do."

Six months later (15 June 1992), the *Post* did it again, under the sub-head, "Everyone Experiences Boredom, But It May Be Worst for Teens."

> Teenage boredom doesn't always have a name, it can be the heavy sighing, the rolling of the eyes, the tapping of the foot, the constant eating, napping, talking on the phone, watching television for hours into the night, the inability to study, concentrate, and the need to be with friends *every single minute*. The words "I'm bored," may mean the short-lived ennui when relatives come for dinner, when a class is dull, or the game has been rained out. Or it can be the deadly excuse defiantly given for binge drinking, stealing cars, or random shooting. (C-5)

Boredom, in other words, can explain most manifestations of the adolescent psyche.

The testimony of newspaper articles and pop psychologists frequently suggests that teenage students believe in an adult conspiracy dooming them to tedium. "My life has been one big bore from the beginning!" complains Calvin in Bill Watterson's comic strip "Calvin and Hobbes" (26 Jan. 1989). He has been asked to do a "dumb assignment," to write about an adventure he has had. His perception of his own experience as boring quickly leads to a paranoid conviction of deprivation: "I never get to have adventures!" Grown-ups, presumably, are responsible.

The diagnoses (self-diagnoses and evaluations by others) of middle-class adolescents and housewives as sufferers from boredom exemplify the imaginative functions boredom serves in our culture. As pretext and justification for behavior ranging from the irritating (rolling the eyes, tapping the foot) to the antisocial (drugs and violence), the claim of boredom now locates the causes of conduct firmly outside the self. The victim's insistence, or the diagnostician's, on external causes, typically unremovable causes, guarantees continued suffering—and the continuing opportunity to exploit the state of victimization. Boredom as universal explanation and complaint reveals the scope of twentieth-century entitlement: Calvin's sense of a right to adventures, the teenager's right to "be with friends *every single minute*," the housewife's right to mental stimulation. As its declared dominion spreads, boredom becomes a metaphor for the postmodern condition.

Surprisingly, it provides a metaphor for desirable as well as undesirable situations. An unknown woman approached me at a cocktail party. She wanted to know what I was writing these days. When I told her, she exclaimed, "Oh, I *love* to be bored!" Pressed to elaborate, she maintained that she always sought out boring movies, she looked for the most boring person at every party ("Thanks a lot," I said), she treasured boring books. Boredom, she insisted, was the best escape from anxiety. It filled the mind; it kept worse things away.

Walter Benjamin: "If sleep is the apogee of physical relaxation, boredom is the apogee of mental relaxation. Boredom is the dream bird that hatches the egg of experience. A rustling in the leaves drives him away" (91).

Enthusiasts of boredom find the state desirable for the lack of desire and—at least in fantasy—of tension that it embodies. As Joanie says in Garry Trudeau's "Doonesbury" (7 Aug. 1992), "Boredom? I would *welcome* boredom! I would *love* my life to be less interesting!" Such imagined boredom may imply a kind of suspended attention comparable to that of a listening psychoanalyst. It "hatches the egg of experience" by allowing the semiconscious brooding that integrates and interprets past happenings. Avoiding distraction, it makes space for creativity. In Benjamin's view, it constitutes creativity's necessary precondition. It sounds like Pieper's form of leisure.

It does not have much to do with the resentment-loaded endurance most people bring to the two-hour meeting about nothing, or to the companion with a compulsion to report minutiae of his gallbladder surgery. Such meetings, such companions, feel like cultural clichés. We assume the inevitability of suffering them, but also maintain our right to be aggrieved by them. The tedium of required activity, of compulsory contact, of repetitive demand: these generate the tension we associate with boredom in the negative construction of the condition, leaving no room for creativity. This variety of boredom figures important ways in which human beings impinge on one another in crowded, anxiety-ridden societies.

The views of boredom as fructifying force and as almost universal misery have something in common. Both give remarkable authority to the state. In the accounts of journalists and of Walter Benjamin, in the remarks of the woman at the cocktail party and the adolescent in West Springfield, one glimpses the power widely assigned to boredom as myth and as state of mind. How much it accounts for, how much it is assumed to affect almost everyone! How could we get along without it?

It is far from surprising, then, that twentieth-century novelists assume boredom as a point of reference, often taking it (as sociologists and journalists also tend to do) as the paradigmatic ailment of our time. The ennui that afflicted characters in nineteenth-century Continental fiction—Werther, Raskolnikov—or defined the pose of such poets as Baudelaire typically declared the sufferer's awareness of society's intractable corruption and of alienation as its consequence for the sensitive spirit. *Only* for the sensitive spirit: if society bears some responsibility for the individual's boredom, the special person's special responsiveness bears more. Now, though, boredom has new forms of utility for fiction writers. Although the bored character still may make at least formal gestures of superiority, he or she most often conveys the belief that "society" consists in a set of internalized forces. The bored man or woman in fiction embodies conflicts of necessary involvement in a society so organized that its members grate on one another's nerves. Even characters unafflicted by the condition may take incidental opportunities to discuss it. Thus a bit of dialogue in a mildly amorous scene in A. S. Byatt's *Still Life:*

> "What do you want?" . . .
> "I want something *not boring* most of all. Sexy, of course, and warm and kind, but lots of women are that. Only most women are *so boring.*"
> "Maybe they find you boring."
> "Possibly. That's not the point. I doubt if *you'*d even understand what I'm talking about. You aren't bored and you don't bore—you'd make your own amusement anywhere, I suppose." (314–15)

The male assumption that not only life in general but women in particular almost inevitably prove boring (an assumption only faintly and implicitly contested by the individual woman on the scene) delineates not only the speaker's discouragement but the dimensions of his entitlement. Although he does not necessarily expect to get what he feels he should have, he clearly believes it appropriate that some woman should constantly stimulate and entertain him—in addition to being "of course" sexy, warm, and kind. His description of the woman he speaks to as neither bored nor boring stamps her as remarkable, and she readily accepts the flattery that differentiates her from others of her gender.

Byatt can safely assume that most of her readers will participate in the general late twentieth-century conviction that boredom, always impending, constitutes a devastating malady. The aversion and despair with which many confront the possibility or likelihood of boredom help to make it a subject of discussion not only familiar but provocative. Thus Julian Barnes introduces almost gratuitously into *Staring at the*

Sun a set of paradoxical reflections about boredom. Jean, the protagonist, is watching a German movie.

> Jean disliked it strongly, but also found it completely interesting. This sort
> of response was something she increasingly noticed. Previously—a word
> which covered all her life—she had been interested in what she liked, and
> not interested in what she disliked; more or less, anyway. She had assumed
> everyone was like this. But a new layer of responsiveness seemed to have
> grown; now she was sometimes bored by what she approved of and could
> sympathize with what she disapproved of. (117)

A little later, she exposes to her companion another paradox of boredom: "I was unhappy, and bored too, I expect, but all the time I seemed
to be understanding more about things. About the world. The more
unhappy I became, the more intelligent I felt" (118). Boredom brings
intelligence; it bears no relation to approval; interest can inhere in what
one dislikes. Such specific observations matter less, for my purposes,
than the simple fact of boredom as a point of reference. Jean's increasingly subtle perceptions about boredom convey her psychological
growth. They serve this purpose because, although boredom can be
assumed to constitute an acknowledged common experience of readers—like, say, fear and love—its precise workings have not yet been
fully explored.

Novelists like to say profound things about boredom. The champion
at such pronouncements must be Saul Bellow, who in *Humboldt's Gift*
invents a first-person narrator planning to write a book about boredom,
about "the chronic war between sleep and consciousness that goes on
in human nature" (108). This device allows Bellow to explicitly assert
the high importance of boredom as subject and as contemporary condition. Before long, however, Charlie Citrine's announced subject has
transmuted itself into "great bores of the world": a significant change.

The world of *Humboldt's Gift* appears both sordid (it contains crooked
lawyers and incompetent ones, gangsters, women eager to sell themselves) and serious, with high stakes involved in most of its transac-
tions. Charlie is in some sense an intellectual, not just a frivolous exemplar of self-indulgence. Yet he, like Waugh's Brenda Last, suffers
resentment and self-pity; he too finally locates the causes of boredom
in other people. He generalizes, politicizes, distances his concern.

> Suppose . . . that you began with the proposition that boredom was a kind
> of pain caused by unused powers, the pain of wasted possibilities or talents,
> and was accompanied by expectations of the optimum utilization of capac-
> ities. . . . Nothing actual ever suits pure expectation and such purity of expec-

tation is a great source of tedium. People rich in abilities, in sexual feeling, rich in mind and in invention—all the highly gifted see themselves shunted for decades onto dull sidings, banished exiled nailed up in chicken coops. (199)

[Postrevolutionary Russia is] the most boring society in history. Dowdiness shabbiness dullness dull goods boring buildings boring discomfort boring supervision a dull press dull education boring bureaucracy forced labor perpetual police presence penal presence, boring party congresses, et cetera. What was permanent was the defeat of interest. (200)

Humboldt had become boring in the vesture of a superior person, in the style of high culture, with all of his conforming abstractions. Many hundreds of thousands of people were now wearing this costume of the higher misery. A terrible breed, the educated nits, mental bores of the heaviest caliber. (443)

Such dicta alleviate Charlie's plight by providing the illusion of saving intellectual activity and by implying his superiority to the state he describes. He locates boredom elsewhere, condemning others as bores. Yet he suffers from the disease he purports to analyze. (It is even possible that he is himself a bore.) He worries a lot about "the boredom of the grave" (373); he experiences, inexorably, the boredom of the study, the courtroom, the couch, the car, the restaurant, the nightclub: the educated urban man's environment.

Like Waugh's characters, Charlie Citrine flees to sexual indulgence as an escape. (In his world as in Brenda Last's, money and "love" constitute power.) He keeps a young, glamorous, sexy mistress whose presence at his side testifies to his vitality. She exploits him and he knows it. He even knows that his need for such a mistress betrays his fear of the boring grave, of declining force, of his own intellectual and moral inadequacy. But knowledge brings no salvation. Like the Lasts, Charlie and his kind are doomed—to boredom and to what boredom means.

What it means, here too, is the failure of intimacy, the impossibility of power (in a society grown too complex and too dangerous to allow persons within it the sustained experience of power), the incapacity of individuals to take responsibility for themselves. Charlie is an at least moderately appealing character, partly because the reader can know him and his inner workings rather fully, partly because his environment bears a close relation to ours, partly because he tries constantly to understand and articulate his plight. Yet the effort at understanding and articulation only complicates that plight. Waugh's characters rely on a superficial and limited vocabulary to convey and reflect their straitened experience; Charlie appears to possess endless verbal resources. But he too employs language as a defense against the intolerable; he too finds change impossible. Tony Last reading Dickens novels aloud over and over, chapter after chapter; Charlie Citrine speculating repetitively about Humboldt—both supply figures of inescapable tedium.

If the story of Tony in his jungle captivity constitutes a parable of boredom, so does the novel that contains it. And so does *Humboldt's Gift*. In both works the idea of boredom—through Charlie's exegeses and his experience, through the Lasts' life in and out of "society"—focuses an indictment of twentieth-century failure. It calls attention to pervasive lassitude, to a malaise of futility. It summarizes something fundamentally wrong in the response of contemporary men and women to their circumstances.

The most characteristic postmodern imaginative use of boredom is not as fictional subject but as fictional atmosphere. Anita Brookner, for instance, has written many novels concerned with the lives of more or less isolated women for whom boredom is the assumed ground of experience. Sometimes they consciously combat it, sometimes they simply accept its necessity. It creates a light fog in their bedrooms, their sitting rooms, and their consciousness. Its pervasiveness and apparent inevitability give it a kind of defining force, even when—perhaps *because*—the text does not dwell on it.

In *A Closed Eye* (1991), the narrator observes, "Lizzie [who has just seen a performance of *Swan Lake*] could not have been said to have been reassured by her contact with art, since art casts so critical a light on life itself" (174). Brookner's art casts a critical light indeed. It unsparingly delineates a world in which good people receive no reward, meretricious characters frequently get exactly what they want, and possibilities for pleasure appear highly limited. In *Look at Me* (1981), boredom assumes an emphatic place. The narrator-protagonist, Frances, works in the reference library of a medical institute. Organizing and caring for pictorial renditions of doctors and patients through the ages, she contemplates representations of melancholy, an ailment particularly associated, in its less dramatic forms, with women. When a friend becomes "depressed," Frances feels in a position, given her study of images, to reclassify the condition "as plain boredom" (67). But boredom, it turns out, can produce effects at least as sinister as those of depression.

It all depends on who's bored. Frances herself suffers from boredom but cannot afford to dwell on the fact. Rigidly controlled, she knows the dullness of her isolated and carefully regimented life. Sometimes, she says, "I wish I were beautiful and lazy and spoiled and not to be trusted. I wish, in short, that I had it easier" (19). But she must live the life ordained for her, accepting boredom as its condition, trying not to think about it.

Frances knows someone as beautiful and lazy and spoiled and not to be trusted as she could possibly imagine. Alix, wife of Nick Fraser, a doctor working at the institute, has a much easier life than Frances's. Having it easier implies making life harder for others. Dutiful, careful, controlled Frances collides emotionally with the self-indulgent Frasers, who attract and betray her. The novel's chilling effect derives from its utter predictability and from the painful way its tone elaborates and dramatizes its substance—a point I shall return to.

Telling in retrospect a story whose ending she already knows, Frances conveys the almost willful blindness with which she allows herself to become captivated and entrapped by Alix and Nick. At the time she understands her experience as liberation. Rescued from boredom, she worries that she might bore the Frasers. Boredom both stems from and entails isolation—not merely the failure of intimacy I spoke of in *Humboldt's Gift*, but the lack even of companionship. The Frasers save Frances for a time but also create new anxieties in her. Alix, Frances knows, considers her dull: "simply because I was loyal and well-behaved and uncritical" (57). The narrator's virtues, in other words, become in the perception of amoral others the signs of tedium. She works to modify or conceal them. Educated, as she says, by the Frasers, she becomes "sharper, funnier, more entertaining" (67), making her experience at the library into a continuing comic narrative to help alleviate Alix's boredom.

The dynamic between the boredom the Frasers enable Frances to escape and the boredom that constitutes Alix's unending entitlement and demand drives the narrative. Alix's boredom (a less immediately recognizable form of isolation—spiritual isolation—than Frances's) is an insatiable appetite. "I am interested in absolutely everything," she announces (41), yet her life does not offer her adequate "continuous satisfaction." Consequently she seizes on gossip or any other evidence of intrigue and interrogates strangers about "the central drama of their lives." Some lives, she believes, are inherently more interesting than others. Relating to others as spectator, she yearns for "a drama that would last until something else claimed her attention, one that would fill an empty afternoon, or a week, or, at the very longest, a month" (68). Frances argues that dramas in life take a long time to develop, that all lives hold interest that need only be perceived; Alix denies the argument. Ultimately she denies Frances herself, whose drama has diminished in interest. Wantonly, she shatters Frances's evolving romance, in which she has claimed a proprietary interest, and begins to contemplate a new drama, which she has helped to create.

The sinister effects of Alix's boredom, which seems almost *willed*, a condition to be announced and placated, a maw ingesting endless "stories"—the sinister effects of this dangerous boredom are readily apparent. One could not call Alix's boredom an atmosphere: it resembles a focused intent. It subordinates everything and everyone, presenting itself as a raging need. And because its alleviation demands emphatic short-term stimulation—no drama lasting longer than a month—it destroys sustained relationship. Yet it functions as a sign of privilege. Alix's enormous sense of entitlement expresses itself most fully through her reiterated claims of boredom, always entailing demands on others.

The Prodigal Son, Frances reflects, was "so much more amusing than his tedious brother" (163–64). The others must have felt dull without him, "so extremely bored with only the spectacle of virtue and hard work to beguile them" (164). She herself, providing only such a spectacle, feels unsurprised when the Frasers no longer find her interesting. Those who demand endless interest in their lives, those like Alix, ratify the value of others by declaring them beguiling. When the Frasers' interest in Frances lapses, she can no longer feel her own worth. Bitterly, she perceives her life as a series of makeshifts. And once more she must confront its boredom.

The kind of boredom Brookner knows most about (by the evidence of her other novels) is Frances's kind, the atmospheric variety that envelops its sufferers in a soft but impenetrable haze. Alix's drama-seeking boredom exists in constant tension with Frances's intuitions of tedium, which are just this side of despair. Alix uses her proclaimed boredom to challenge response; Frances's boredom expresses her awareness that the world will offer her no response. Alix's boredom has sinister effects on others, Frances's threatens herself.

It threatens her with desperation. One can perhaps posit desperation underlying Alix's constant demand for stimulation, but it remains hidden from its victim, who believes herself nourished by the excitement she demands and manufactures. For Frances, on the other hand, awareness of boredom implies the need to acknowledge her life's inadequacies. Indeed—and this seems a view unique to the late twentieth century—in Brookner's presentation Frances's boredom in itself constitutes a form of perception. My imagery of fog, haze, miasma suggests boredom as obscurantism, but although Frances's boredom dims her capacity to respond to her experience, it also constitutes a recognition and a judgment of that experience. Her boredom tells her what is wrong with her life.

> I have been aware of a boredom, a restlessness, that no ordinary friendship can satisfy; only an extraordinary one. I have grown tired of my lot, I suppose, and have wanted strenuously to change it. So I write, and I take a lot of long walks, and I ferment my ideas, and if I am lucky they come out as vivid as I should like real life to be. (70)

This summary of her condition details her defenses against it: irony ("if I am lucky"), fantasy ("only an extraordinary one"), tentativeness ("I suppose"), and of course the writing, walking, and fermenting. Defense is necessary, for the full acknowledgment of boredom would imply acceptance of despair.

Eighteenth-century thinkers associate boredom unambiguously with moral failure. Its remedy involves mental, moral, or spiritual discipline. Nineteenth-century commentators connect it with class arrogance, with inadequate responsiveness to others, sometimes with capitalistic false value. They too frequently imply that it can be remedied by self-discipline. Brookner, on the other hand, conveys no glimmer of hope. Frances disciplines herself stringently without solving her problem—because her problem inheres in the conditions of her life. Young, attractive, intelligent, prosperous, virtuous, eager to work at human relationships and at whatever arena of effort presents itself, she cannot control her circumstances. Boredom constitutes, in the novel's argument, an appropriate response to those circumstances. The fiction represents other sufferers of boredom as painful atmosphere. A man and a woman who haunt the reading room, seeking company, change of scene, stimulation to counteract the tedium of their condition remind us that society has room for millions of isolated victims. More troubling still is Miss Morpeth, the retired librarian who understands that the Frasers don't visit her because she is "simply not interesting enough for them to bother about, . . . a boring old woman" (139), and who sees Frances—not with affection, but with distaste—as like herself. The bored (Frances understands this too) are perceived as boring (unless, like Alix, they convert boredom into a sign of power). And they lack the capacity to alter their condition.

To understand boredom as the sign that one accurately perceives a life situation is a bleak view. Brookner does not even offer the vague comfort of believing that the creation of dismal and tedious situations is part of a capitalist plot. It seems, rather, part of the nature of things: a form of fate. And there's not much one can do about it. To say that the novel holds out no hope of remediation is not quite accurate, since in fact Frances vigorously combats her situation. Combat creates something to do, but its defeat of boredom proves little more than a mirror trick.

At the novel's end, when her hope of love has vanished, Frances embarks with determination on a program of fiction writing that involves, she says, transforming dreary experience into the stuff of comedy. It sounds theoretically like the best possible solution. In practice, it doesn't make much difference.

I commented earlier on the way Brookner's tone elaborates her substance in *Look at Me*, and the point bears on any assessment of Frances's "solution." The self-punishing timbre of the voice that tells the story speaks eloquently of pain, and particularly of the painfully acquired lack of confidence that impedes Frances. When her almost lover rejects her, she quickly interprets his action as the consequence of her failures. Perceiving herself as containing only "emptiness," she wonders how to conceal it. Only association with the successful, those filled with vitality and expectation, she decides, can help her. She will live henceforward as an observer, claiming no right to engage in serious experience.

Her determination to involve herself seriously in writing, then, declares defeat rather than victory. Writing, she has said in the middle of the novel,

> is your penance for not being lucky. It is an attempt to reach others and to make them love you. It is your instinctive protest, when you find you have no voice at the world's tribunals, and that no one will speak for you. I would give my entire output of words, past, present, and to come, in exchange for easier access to the world, for permission to state "I hurt" or "I hate" or "I want." Or, indeed, "Look at me." (84)

Writing, for Frances, constitutes an attempt "to do everything I could not do in real life" (132). Those who can, do; those who can't, write.

To the list of things Frances wants permission to state, one might add, "I am bored." Her conviction that all her emotions are impermissible includes the emotion that, unarticulated, she believes makes her boring to others. As her experience of Alix tells her, boredom expressed proclaims itself as a demand for activity by others directed toward satisfying the bored person's need. But Frances cannot express her feelings. Moreover, she believes it incumbent on her to satisfy her own needs, not to expect others to do so. Hence the project of writing witty, entertaining fiction: it will give her something to fill her time.

"As a writer one has no right to be bored," I announced earlier.

Frances believes the same thing. But *Look at Me* establishes a large gap between "writer" and "woman." Given the connection between being bored and being perceived as boring, a solitary woman cannot afford to *appear* bored. Her chosen role as novelist provides prima facie evidence of her interest in the human world around her. It serves as a mask behind which she continues to participate in the sad fellowship of the lonely and bored, those who must manufacture occupation and preserve appearances.

Boredom marks the powerless in Brookner's imagined world. Not a universal condition but a sign of society's insufficiency, it speaks of social rather than political vulnerability. Frances appears to consider her state an index of personal failure, and perhaps it is: the text, written in its protagonist's voice, provides no unambiguous evidence. In any case, boredom constitutes an apparently incurable as well as agonizing ailment. If it provides a mark of privilege for those like Alix, in more sinister and authentic form it signals the plight of the solitary woman for whom society provides no comfortable place.

The same contrast between boredom as entitlement and as pain occurs repeatedly in Brookner's fiction. Sometimes it is a gender contrast: in *Brief Lives* (1990) Fay, who considers herself utterly commonplace and whom some find boring, marries Owen, in whom she notes from the beginning "a restless fatigued expression, which I later came to identify as boredom" (31). That boredom creates constant uncertainty in their marriage, since "Owen's boredom meant that he had a limited attention span: he always needed new people to break what he experienced as the monotony of the old" (32). Similarly, Fay's dazzling friend Julia, who makes no secret of considering her boring, demands constant stimulation and constant attention. When Fay herself, widowed and alone, falls into boredom, she never names it. Nonetheless, it constitutes the element in which she moves:

> As the light faded, and it took longer to do so in the lengthening spring days, I would scan the street for signs of life, watch the hairdresser over the way locking up for the night, hear the home-going traffic in the distance, and reflect with sadness that the children would all be gathered safely in, watching television, and that none would pass my window, waving, as they sometimes did. (178)

Or the contrast may be generational, as in *A Closed Eye*, where virtually everyone suffers from boredom but members of different generations appear to confront it differently. Harriet, the protagonist, a dutiful wife following an empty routine, suffers because her daughter,

Imogen, finds her parents "boring and unsatisfactory" (178). Another glamorous and demanding creature like Julia, Imogen—beautiful, sexy, knowing—dies in an automobile accident at age eighteen, leaving her mother without psychic occupation. Because of her beauty and imperiousness, Imogen, in Harriet's view, has the right to be bored. She herself does not. She nonetheless endures boredom's pain.

The privileged practitioners of boredom interest Brookner far less than the sufferers who war against their own misery, often without naming it. Thus Blanche, in *The Misalliance* (1986),

> maintained an excellent appearance, not so much because she valued such excellence as because she could thus use up much superfluous time. She calculated that she could spend up to an unwanted hour every morning by simply putting herself to rights, and producing a pleasing effect to lavish on the empty day. (7)

The narrator calls her effort "heroic" and describes it as warding off "despair" or "panic," but the evocation of Blanche's daily life makes it clear that the departure of her rather disagreeable husband has doomed her to persistent boredom.

Sometimes the victims deny their state. Rachel, protagonist and narrator of *A Friend from England* (1987), announces with pride, "I had cut my losses early—no more sleepless nights for me, no more boredom either" (105). Like Frances in *Look at Me*, Rachel has in her past painful experience of which she never speaks. Frances's past apparently includes a devastating love affair; Rachel's includes the death of her parents and an unspecified trauma that has left her afraid of water. She resembles Brookner's other wounded central figures in her consistent effort to suppress and deny feeling, but her denial of boredom does not prevent her suffering it.

For Rachel and for others in Brookner's novels, as my quotations will already have suggested, boredom often inheres in others. (Perhaps this fact partly explains the prevailing loneliness of these figures.) Like Charlie Citrine, Brookner's characters ardently believe in the existence of bores, aggressively uninteresting people who make life miserable for their companions. Such people provide useful targets of blame, useful ways to account for the experience of vague and generalized discontent, a valuable means of projecting such discontent outward. The perception that bores abound in the world—increasingly common in recent "realistic" fiction: Margaret Drabble's late novels provide a striking case in point—registers the degree to which widespread complaints of boredom accompany the sense that society provides not psychic support but only causes for irritation. Boredom, in Brookner's novels and in many others, declares the world (meaning, specifically, the world of other people) out of joint.

Brookner's characteristic contrast between the privileged, who loudly announce their boredom, and the unprivileged, who merely suffer it, apparently opposes a kind of *constructed* boredom—what the entitled manufacture to justify their large claims—to an unavoidable experience of dreariness. Such an opposition suggests how completely the idea of boredom has been naturalized in the late twentieth century. The exegeses offered by sociologists and psychologists make it sound inevitable, a "natural" consequence of late capitalist society or of woman's fate. Often, as in the newspaper articles and advertisements I have cited, boredom is felt to need no explanation. It simply exists, itself sufficient explanation for multitudinous other phenomena. The woman writing out her boredom with her Waterman pen resembles Brookner's Frances in her acceptance of "recording" as a response to but not an alleviation of an inevitable state of being.

The appropriate question to ask about such social conditions is not, Why is everyone bored nowadays? (or depending on your everyone, Why does everyone so vigorously deny boredom?) but How has boredom come to be so deeply *assumed* in our culture? In these pages I have sketched some arcs of its development over the past two centuries— enough to show both that boredom is not an ineluctable category of interpretation and that it is for many purposes a remarkably useful one.

The history of boredom in its cultural constructions matters partly because boredom itself now appears to matter so much. If boredom can provide plausible justification for acts of violence or self-destruction, if the desire to forestall it sells fountain pens and trips around the world, if fiction writers assume it as the substratum of experience and journalists draw on it as a readily comprehensible realm of reference—if all of the above are true, it would seem that boredom has assumed broad explanatory power in a society widely felt to be baffling. The narcissism many writers of the past associated with boredom as psychic malady now appears to be a collective condition; so too does boredom. It has haunted Western society ever since its eighteenth-century invention. Its twentieth-century magnification absorbs ever more experience into the maw of the meaningless and provides ever more material for the imaginative writer, in a paradoxical relation that has intensified since the English fabricated the notion. To pay attention to the state, now as always, helps to clarify the anxieties of writers and of readers as well as the cultural assumptions that are often obscurely implicated in such anxieties.

WORKS CITED

Allen, R. T. "Leisure: The Purpose of Life and the Nature of Philosophy." *The Philosophy of Leisure.* Ed. Tom Winnifrith and Cyril Barrett. London: Macmillan, 1989. 20–33.

Anson, Elizabeth, and Florence Anson, eds. *Mary Hamilton, Afterwards Mrs. John Dickenson, at Court and at Home.* London: John Murray, 1925.

Arendt, Hannah. *The Human Condition.* Chicago: U of Chicago P, 1958.

Austen, Jane. *Emma.* 1816. Vol. 4 of *The Novels of Jane Austen.* Ed. R. W. Chapman. 3rd ed. 5 vols. Oxford: Oxford UP, 1933.

————. *Northanger Abbey* and *Persuasion.* 1818. Vol. 5 of *The Novels of Jane Austen.* Ed. R. W. Chapman. 3rd ed. 5 vols. Oxford: Oxford UP, 1933.

————. *Pride and Prejudice.* 1813. Vol. 2 of *The Novels of Jane Austen.* Ed. R. W. Chapman. 3rd ed. 5 vols. Oxford: Oxford UP, 1933.

————. *Sense and Sensibility.* 1811. Vol. 1 of *The Novels of Jane Austen.* Ed. R. W. Chapman. 3rd ed. 5 vols. Oxford: Oxford UP, 1933.

Bailey, Anthony. "A Young Man on Horseback." *New Yorker* 5 Mar. 1990: 45–77.

Bailey, J. C. *Studies in Some Famous Letters.* London, 1899.

Bailey, Peter. *Leisure and Class in Victorian England: Rational Recreation and the Contest for Control, 1830–1885.* London: Routledge, 1978.

Barnes, Julian. *Staring at the Sun.* 1986. New York: Harper and Row, 1988.

Barrett, William. "Leibnitz's Garden: Some Philosophical Observations on Boredom." *Social Research* 42 (1975): 551–55.

Barthelme, Donald. *City Life.* New York: Farrar, 1970.

Barthes, Roland. *The Pleasure of the Text.* Trans. Richard Miller. New York: Hill and Wang, 1975.

Bathurst, Charles. *Letters to a Niece.* London, 1850.

Baudelaire, Charles. *The Flowers of Evil.* Sel. and ed. Marthiel and Jackson Mathews. 1963. New York: New Directions, 1989.

Bellow, Saul. *Humboldt's Gift.* New York: Viking, 1975.

Benjamin, Walter. "The Storyteller: Reflections on the Works of Nikolai Leskov." *Illuminations.* Ed. Hannah Arendt. Trans. Harry Zohn. New York: Schocken, 1969. 83–110.

Bernstein, Haskell. "Boredom and the Ready-Made Life." *Social Research* 42 (1975): 512–37.

Berryman, John. *Seventy-seven Dream Songs*. New York: Farrar, 1964.

Booth, Wayne C. "The Meaning of Dedication." *The Vocation of a Teacher: Rhetorical Occasions, 1967–1988*. Chicago: U of Chicago P, 1988. 281–87.

Boswell, James. *Boswell's Life of Johnson*. 1791. Ed. George Birkbeck Hill. Rev. L. F. Powell. 6 vols. Oxford: Clarendon, 1934.

———. *The English Experiment, 1785–1789*. Ed. Irma S. Lustig and Frederick A. Pottle. New York: McGraw-Hill, 1986.

———. *The Hypochondriack*. Ed. Margery Bailey. 2 vols. Stanford: Stanford UP, 1928.

———. *London Journal, 1762–1763*. Ed. Frederick A. Pottle. New York: McGraw-Hill, 1950.

———. *The Ominous Years, 1774–1776*. Ed. Charles Ryskamp and Frederick A. Pottle. London: Heinemann, 1963.

British Critic 33 (1809): 481–94.

Brontë, Charlotte. *Villette*. 1853. Introd. Q. D. Leavis. New York: Harper and Row, 1972.

Brooke, Frances. *The History of Lady Julia Mandeville*. 1763. Vol. 27 of *The British Novelists*. London, 1810.

Brookner, Anita. *Brief Lives*. 1990. New York: Random House, 1992.

———. *A Closed Eye*. New York: Random House, 1991.

———. *A Friend from England*. London: Jonathan Cape, 1987.

———. *Look at Me*. 1981. London: Triad Grafton, 1982.

———. *The Misalliance*. 1986. New York: Harper and Row, 1988.

Brown, Thomas. *A Legacy for the Ladies: Or, Characters of Women of the Age*. 1704. London, 1720.

Brubach, Holly. "In Fashion: Retroactivity." *New Yorker* 31 Dec. 1990: 74–81.

Bulwer-Lytton, Edward. *England and the English*. 2 vols. London, 1833.

Burnett, John, ed. *Destiny Obscure: Autobiographies of Childhood, Education and Family from the 1820s to the 1920s*. London: Allen Lane, 1982.

———. *Useful Toil: Autobiographies of Working People from the 1820s to the 1920s*. London: Allen Lane, 1974.

Burney, Frances. *Cecilia: Or, Memoirs of an Heiress*. 1782. New York: Penguin-Virago, 1986.

———. *The Early Diary of Frances Burney*. Ed. Annie Raine Ellis. 2 vols. London: George Bell, 1907.

———. *Evelina: Or, The History of a Young Lady's Entrance into the World*. 1778. New York: Norton, 1965.

———. *The Wanderer: Or, Female Difficulties*. 1814. Ed. Margaret Anne Doody, Robert L. Mack, and Peter Sabor. Oxford: Oxford UP, 1991.

Burton, Elizabeth. *The Georgians at Home, 1714–1830*. London: Longmans, 1967.

Byatt, A. S. *Still Life*. 1985. New York: Macmillan, 1991.

Byron, George Gordon, Lord. *Byron*. Ed. Jerome McGann. *The Oxford Authors*. Oxford: Oxford UP, 1986.

Calinescu, Matei. *Five Faces of Modernity*. Durham, NC: Duke UP, 1987.

Cascardi, Anthony J. *The Subject of Modernity*. Cambridge: Cambridge UP, 1992.

Cassian, John. *The Institutes of John Cassian*. Vol. 11 of *A Select Library of Nicene and Post-Nicene Fathers of the Christian Church*. Ed. William B. Philip and Henry Wace Schaff. Grand Rapids, MI: Eerdmans, 1986.

Chapone, Hester. *Letters on the Improvement of the Mind*. 1773. London, 1822.

Clark, S. H. "'Pendet Homo Incertus': Gray's Response to Locke." *Eighteenth-Century Studies* 24 (1991): 273–91.

Critical Review: Or, Annals of Literature 3 (1809): 252–64.

Cunningham, Hugh. *Leisure in the Industrial Revolution, c. 1780–c. 1880*. New York: Saint Martin's, 1980.

Davidoff, Leonore. *The Best Circles: Society Etiquette and the Season*. 1973. London: Cresset, 1986.

Davies, Emily. *The Higher Education of Women*. 1866. Ed. Janet Howarth. London: Hambledon, 1988.

de Grazia, Sebastian. *Of Time, Work and Leisure*. New York: Twentieth Century Fund, 1962.

DeKoven, Marianne. "'Why James Joyce Was Accepted and I Was Not': Modernist Fiction and Gertrude Stein's Narrative." *Studies in the Literary Imagination* 25.2 (1992): 23–30.

Delany, Mary Granville. *The Autobiography and Correspondence of Mary Granville Delany*. Ed. Lady Llanover. First Series. 1861. 3 vols. New York: AMS, 1974.

———. *The Autobiography and Correspondence of Mary Granville Delany*. Ed. Lady Llanover. Second Series. 3 vols. London, 1862.

Dickens, Charles. *Bleak House*. 1853. London: Oxford UP, 1948.

———. *Hard Times*. 1854. Ed. David Craig. Harmondsworth, Eng.: Penguin, 1969.

———. *Sunday under Three Heads*. London, 1836.

Donne, John. *The Poems of John Donne*. Ed. Herbert J. C. Grierson. 2 vols. Oxford: Oxford UP, 1912.

Drew, Elizabeth. *The Literature of Gossip: Nine English Letter-Writers*. New York: Norton, 1964.

Edgeworth, Maria. *Ennui; Or, Memoirs of the Earl of Glenthorn*. 1809. New York: Garland, 1978.

———. *Helen*. 1834. Introd. Maggie Gee. London: Pandora, 1987.

Edgeworth, Maria, and Richard Lovell Edgeworth. *Practical Education*. 1798. 2 vols. New York: Garland, 1974.

Edinburgh Review: Or, Critical Journal 14 (1809): 145–51.

Eliot, George. *Daniel Deronda*. 1876. Ed. Graham Handley. *The Novels of George Eliot*. Oxford: Clarendon, 1984.

Eliot, T. S. *Collected Poems, 1909–1935*. New York: Harcourt Brace, 1936.

Ellis, Sarah. *The Daughters of England, Their Position in Society, Character, and Responsibilities*. London, 1842.

———. *The Education of Character: With Hints on Moral Training*. London, 1856.

Escott, T. H. S. *England: Its People, Polity, and Pursuits*. 2 vols. London, 1879.

Espriella, Manuel Alvarez [Robert Southey]. *Letters from England*. 3 vols. London, 1807.

Febvre, Lucien. "History and Psychology." 1938. *A New Kind of History from the Writings of Febvre*. Ed. Peter Burke. London: Routledge and Kegan Paul, 1973.

———. "Sensibility and History: How to Reconstitute the Emotional Life of the

Past." 1941. *A New Kind of History from the Writings of Febvre.* Ed. Peter Burke. London: Routledge & Kegan Paul, 1973.

Fenichel, Otto. "The Psychology of Boredom." *The Collected Papers of Otto Fenichel.* First Series. New York: Norton, 1953. 292–302.

Fenwick, Eliza. *Secresy: Or, The Ruin on the Rock.* 1795. London: Pandora, 1989.

Ferrier, Susan. *Marriage.* 1818. Introd. Rosemary Ashton. New York: Penguin-Virago, 1986.

Fordyce, David. *Dialogues concerning Education.* 2 vols. London, 1745.

Fordyce, James. *Sermons to Young Women.* 1765. 3rd ed. 2 vols. London, 1766.

Fraser, Kennedy. "Fritillaries and Hairy Violets." *New Yorker* 19 Oct. 1987: 58–74.

Freeling, Arthur. *The Young Bride's Book: Being Hints for Regulating the Conduct of Married Women.* London, 1839.

Galton, Francis. *Memories of My Life.* London: Methuen, 1909.

Gentleman's Magazine 79 (1809): 151.

Gisborne, Thomas. *An Enquiry into the Duties of the Female Sex.* 1797. New York: Garland, 1974.

Gladstone, W. E. "'Robert Elsmere' and the Battle of Belief." *Nineteenth Century* 23 (1888): 766–88.

Golby, J. M., and A. W. Purdue. *The Civilisation of the Crowd: Popular Culture in England, 1750–1900.* New York: Schocken, 1985.

Gray, Thomas. *The Correspondence of Thomas Gray.* Ed. Paget Toynbee and Leonard Whibley. Rev. H. W. Starr. 3 vols. Oxford: Oxford UP, 1971.

Greer, Germaine. *The Obstacle Race: The Fortunes of Women Painters and Their Work.* New York: Farrar Straus Giroux, 1979.

Gregory, John. *A Father's Legacy to His Daughters.* 1774. London, 1816.

Greil, Marcus. *Lipstick Traces: A Secret History of the Twentieth Century.* Cambridge: Harvard UP, 1989.

Griffith, Elizabeth. *The Story of Lady Juliana Harley.* 2 vols. London, 1776.

Harris, James. *Three Treatises.* London, 1744.

Hawkins, Laetitia Matilda. *Letters on the Female Mind, Its Powers and Pursuits.* 2 vols. London, 1793.

Haywood, Eliza. *The History of Miss Betsy Thoughtless.* 1751. 4 vols. New York: Garland, 1979.

Hazen, Allen T. *Samuel Johnson's Prefaces and Dedications.* New Haven: Yale UP, 1937.

Healy, Sean Desmond. *Boredom, Self, and Culture.* Rutherford, NJ: Fairleigh Dickinson UP, 1984.

Hervey, Mary Lepel, Lady. *Letters of Lady Mary Lepel Hervey.* London, 1821.

Hill, Bridget. *Women, Work, and Sexual Politics in Eighteenth-Century England.* Oxford: Blackwell, 1989.

Hopkins, Mary Alden. *Hannah More and Her Circle.* New York: Longmans, 1947.

Horace. *The Satires and Epistles of Horace.* Ed. Smith Palmer Bovie. Chicago: U of Chicago P, 1959.

———. *Satires, Epistles and Ars Poetica.* Trans. H. Rushton Fairclough. Loeb Classical Library. London: Heinemann, 1926.

———. *Satires, Epistles, and Art of Poetry.* Trans. S. Dunster. 5th ed. London, 1739.

Hunter, J. Paul. *Before Novels: The Cultural Contexts of Eighteenth-Century English Fiction.* New York: Norton, 1990.

Iso-Ahola, Seppo E., and Ellen Weissinger. "Leisure and Boredom." *Journal of Social and Clinical Psychology* 5 (1987): 356–64.

James, Henry. *The Portrait of a Lady*. 1881. Ed. Leon Edel. Boston: Houghton Mifflin, 1963.

Jameson, Anna. *Diary of an Ennuyée*. London, 1826.

The Jerningham Letters (1780–1843). Ed. Egerton Castle. 2 vols. London, 1896.

Johnson, Samuel. *The History of Rasselas Prince of Abissinia*. Ed. Robert W. Chapman. Oxford: Clarendon, [1927].

———. *The Idler* and *The Adventurer*. Ed. John M. Bullitt, W. J. Bate, and L. F. Powell. Vol. 2 of *The Yale Edition of the Works of Samuel Johnson*. New Haven: Yale UP, 1963.

———. *The Lounger*. Ed. Alexander Chalmers. Vols. 30–31 of *The British Essayists*. Boston, 1856.

———. *The Rambler*. Ed. W. J. Bate and Albrecht B. Strauss. Vols. 3–5 of *The Yale Edition of the Works of Samuel Johnson*. New Haven: Yale UP, 1969.

Jones, Enid Huws. *Mrs Humphry Ward*. London: Heinemann, 1973.

Jones, M. G. *Hannah More*. Cambridge: Cambridge UP, 1952.

Kerr, Walter. *The Decline of Pleasure*. New York: Simon and Schuster, 1962.

Kierkegaard, Søren. *The Concept of Anxiety: A Simple Psychologically Orienting Deliberation on the Dogmatic Issue of Hereditary Sin*. 1844. Ed. and trans. Reidar Thomte in collaboration with Albert B. Anderson. Princeton: Princeton UP, 1980.

———. *Either/Or*. Trans. David F. Swenson and Lillian Marvin Swenson. Rev. Howard A. Johnson. Vol. 1. Princeton: Princeton UP, 1971.

Klapp, Orrin E. *Overload and Boredom: Essays on the Quality of Life in the Information Society*. New York: Greenwood, 1986.

Kuhn, Reinhard. *The Demon of Noontide: Ennui in Western Literature*. Princeton: Princeton UP, 1976.

Lang, Andrew. "Theological Romances." *Contemporary Review* 53 (1888): 814–24.

Lawrence, D. H. *Women in Love*. 1920. Introd. Richard Aldington. New York: Viking, 1960.

Leavis, Q. D. *Fiction and the Reading Public*. 1932. London: Chatto and Windus, 1968.

LeFanu, Elizabeth Sheridan. *Betsy Sheridan's Journal: Letters from Sheridan's Sister, 1784–1786 and 1788–1790*. Ed. William LeFanu. New Brunswick, NJ: Rutgers UP, 1960.

Lennox, Lady Sarah. *Life and Letters of Lady Sarah Lennox*. Ed. Countess of Ilchester and Lord Stavordale. 2 vols. London: John Murray, 1901.

Letters from a Peeress of England to Her Eldest Son. London, 1784.

Letters from Mrs. Elizabeth Carter to Mrs. Montagu, between the Years 1755 and 1800. Ed. Montagu Pennington. 1817. 4 vols. New York: AMS, 1973.

Letters of a Citizen Haberdasher to a Young Friend. London, 1847.

Lowell, Robert. *Imitations*. New York: Farrar, Straus and Cudahy, 1961.

Lynch, William F., S.J. *Images of Faith: An Exploration of the Ironic Imagination*. Notre Dame, IN: U of Notre Dame P, 1973.

Macaulay, Catharine. *Letters on Education, with Observations on Religious and Metaphysical Subjects*. 1790. New York: Garland, 1974.

MacCannell, Dean, and Juliet Flower MacCannell. "The Beauty System." *The Ideology of Conduct: Essays on Literature and the History of Sexuality*. Ed. Nancy Armstrong and Leonard Tennenhouse. New York: Methuen, 1987. 206–38.

MacIntyre, Alasdair. *After Virtue: A Study in Moral Theory*. Notre Dame, IN: Notre Dame UP, 1981.

McKendrick, Neil. "The Commercialization of Fashion." *The Birth of a Consumer Society: The Commercialization of Eighteenth-Century England*. Ed. Neil McKendrick, John Brewer, and J. H. Plumb. London: Europa, 1982. 34–99.

McKeon, Michael. *The Origins of the English Novel, 1600–1740*. Baltimore: Johns Hopkins UP, 1987.

Marlborough, Sarah, Duchess of. *Private Correspondence of Sarah, Duchess of Marlborough*. 2 vols. London, 1838.

Marshall, David. *The Figure of Theater: Shaftesbury, Defoe, Adam Smith, George Eliot*. New York: Columbia UP, 1986.

Marshall, Jane. *The History of Alicia Montague*. 2 vols. London, 1767.

Mason, John. *Self-Knowledge: A Treatise, Shewing the Nature and Benefit of That Important Science, and the Way to Attain It*. London, 1745.

Miller, J. Hillis. *The Ethics of Reading: Kant, de Man, Eliot, Trollope, James, and Benjamin*. New York: Columbia UP, 1987.

The Mirror. Edinburgh, 1780.

Montagu, Elizabeth. *The Letters of Elizabeth Montagu*. Ed. Matthew Montagu. 1809. 4 vols. New York: AMS, 1974.

————. *Mrs. Montagu, "Queen of the Blues": Her Letters and Friendships from 1762 to 1800*. Ed. Reginald Blunt. 2 vols. Boston: Houghton Mifflin, n.d.

Montagu, Lady Mary Wortley. *The Complete Letters of Lady Mary Wortley Montagu*. Ed. Robert Halsband. 3 vols. Oxford: Clarendon, 1965–67.

Monthly Review: Or, Literary Journal 58 (1809): 128–36.

More, Hannah. *Coelebs in Search of a Wife*. 1808. Philadelphia, 1884.

Myers, Mitzi. "Hannah More's Tracts for the Times: Social Fiction and Female Ideology." *Fetter'd or Free? British Women Novelists, 1670–1850*. Ed. Mary Anne Schofield and Cecilia Macheski. Athens: Ohio UP, 1986. 264–84.

Nietzsche, Friedrich. *The Gay Science*. Trans. Walter Kaufmann. New York: Vintage, 1974.

Nisbet, Robert. *Prejudices: A Philosophical Dictionary*. Cambridge: Harvard UP, 1982.

Oakley, Ann. *Woman's Work: The Housewife, Past and Present*. 1974. New York: Vintage, 1976.

The Observer. Ed. Alexander Chalmers. Vols. 32–34 of *The British Essayists*. Boston, 1856.

Osborn, Sarah Byng. *Letters of Sarah Byng Osborn, 1721–1773*. Ed. John McClelland. Stanford: Stanford UP, 1930.

Parker, Stanley. *The Sociology of Leisure*. London: Allen and Unwin, 1976.

Peters, Edward. "Notes toward an Archaeology of Boredom." *Social Research* 42 (1975): 493–511.

Phillips, Adam. *On Kissing, Tickling, and Being Bored: Psychoanalytic Essays on the Unexamined Life*. Cambridge: Harvard UP, 1993.

Pieper, Josef. *Leisure: The Basis of Culture*. 1952. Trans. Alexander Dru. New York: Pantheon, 1964.

Plumb, J. H. "The Acceptance of Modernity." *The Birth of a Consumer Society: The Commercialization of Eighteenth-Century England*. Ed. John Brewer, Neil McKendrick, and J. H. Plumb. London: Europa, 1982. 316–34.

———. "The Commercialization of Leisure in Eighteenth-Century England." *The Birth of a Consumer Society: The Commercialization of Eighteenth-Century England*. Ed. John Brewer, Neil McKendrick, and J. H. Plumb. London: Europa, 1982. 265–85.

———. "The New World of Children in Eighteenth-Century England." *The Birth of a Consumer Society: The Commercialization of Eighteenth-Century England*. Ed. John Brewer, Neil McKendrick, and J. H. Plumb. London: Europa, 1982. 286–315.

Pope, Alexander. *Imitations of Horace*. Ed. John Butt. *The Twickenham Edition of the Poems of Alexander Pope*. London: Methuen, 1961.

Post, Emily. *Etiquette: "The Blue Book of Social Usage."* New York: Funk and Wagnalls, 1945.

The Private Correspondence of a Woman of Fashion. 2 vols. London, 1832.

Redford, Bruce. *The Converse of the Pen: Acts of Intimacy in the Eighteenth-Century Familiar Letter*. Chicago: U of Chicago P, 1986.

Richardson, Samuel. *Clarissa: Or, The History of a Young Lady*. 1747–48. 4 vols. London: Dent, 1932.

———. *The Correspondence of Samuel Richardson*. Ed. Anna Laetitia Barbauld. 1804. 6 vols. New York: AMS, 1966.

———. *Familiar Letters on Important Occasions*. Intro. Brian Downs. New York: Dodd, Mead, 1928.

———. *The History of Sir Charles Grandison*. 1753. Ed. Jocelyn Harris. Oxford: Oxford UP, 1986.

"Robert Elsmere and Christianity." *Quarterly Review* 167 (1888): 273–302.

Roberts, William. *Memoirs of the Life and Correspondence of Mrs. Hannah More*. 4 vols. London, 1834.

Rudd, Niall. *The Satires of Horace*. Cambridge: Cambridge UP, 1966.

Russell, Bertrand. *The Conquest of Happiness*. New York: Liveright, 1930.

Said, Edward. *Beginnings: Intention and Method*. New York: Basic, 1975.

Saintsbury, George. *A Letter Book, Selected with an Introduction on the History and Art of Letter-Writing*. London: G. Bell, 1922.

Seidenberg, Robert. "The Trauma of Eventlessness." *Psychoanalysis and Women*. Ed. Jean Baker Miller. Harmondsworth, Eng.: Penguin, 1973. 350–64.

Seward, Anna. *Letters of Anna Seward: Written between the Years 1784 and 1807*. 1811. 6 vols. New York: AMS, 1975.

Shakespeare, William. *A Midsummer Night's Dream*. *The Complete Works of Shakespeare*. Ed. George Lyman Kittredge. Boston: Ginn, 1936. 229–56.

Sheridan, Frances. *Memoirs of Miss Sidney Bidulph*. 1761. London: Pandora, 1987.

Shimmin, H. *Town Life*. London, 1858.

Sisk, John P. "The End of Boredom." *Georgia Review* 39.1 (1985): 25–34.

Smith, Esther Marian Greenwell. *Mrs. Humphry Ward*. Boston: Twayne, 1980.

Smith, Logan Pearsall. *The English Language*. New York: Holt, 1912.

Stein, Gertrude. *The Autobiography of Alice B. Toklas*. New York: Literary Guild, 1933.

———. *Ida: A Novel*. 1941. New York: Vintage, 1972.

———. *Selected Writings of Gertrude Stein*. Ed. Carl Van Vechten. New York: Random House, 1946.

Sutherland, John. *Mrs Humphry Ward: Eminent Victorian, Pre-eminent Edwardian*. Oxford: Clarendon, 1990.

Taylor, Mary. *The First Duty of Woman*. London, 1870.

Thackeray, William Makepeace. *Vanity Fair*. 1848. Ed. J. I. M. Stewart. London: Penguin, 1968.

Thomas, Elizabeth Marshall. *The Hidden Life of Dogs*. Boston: Houghton Mifflin, 1993.

Thrale, Hester Lynch. *Thraliana*. Ed. Katharine C. Balderston. 2nd ed. 2 vols. Oxford: Clarendon, 1951.

Tristan, Flora. *London Journal: A Survey of London Life in the 1830s*. Trans. Dennis Palmer and Giselle Pincetl. London: George Prior, 1980.

Trollope, Anthony. *The Way We Live Now*. 1875. Ed. John Sutherland. Oxford: Oxford University Press, 1982.

"The Visit of Charity: With Observations on the Paradise Lost." *Lady's Magazine: Or, Entertaining Companion for the Fair Sex* 11 (1809): 100–104.

Ward, Mrs. Humphry. "A County Dinner-Party." *Ainsworth's Magazine* 1 (May 1842): 249–51.

———. *Robert Elsmere*. 1888. Ed. Clyde de L. Ryals. Lincoln: U of Nebraska P, 1967.

"Watch Sermon Descriptions, Rabbi Pleads to Congregations." *Knoxville News-Sentinel* 25 Jan. 1992: B2.

Waugh, Evelyn. *A Handful of Dust*. 1934. New York: New Directions, 1945.

Waugh, Martin. "Boredom in Psychoanalytic Perspective." *Social Research* 42 (1975): 538–50.

Wenzel, Siegfried. *The Sin of Sloth: Acedia in Medieval Thought and Literature*. Chapel Hill: U of North Carolina P, 1967.

Wilbur, Richard. "Lying." *New and Collected Poems*. San Diego: Harcourt, Brace, Jovanovich, 1988. 9–11.

Williams, Raymond. *Keywords: A Vocabulary of Culture and Society*. New York: Oxford UP, 1976.

Wollstonecraft, Mary. *A Vindication of the Rights of Women*. 1792. Ed. Charles W. Hagelman, Jr. New York: Norton, 1967.

Wordsworth, William, and Samuel Taylor Coleridge. *Lyrical Ballads*. Ed. R. L. Brett and A. R. Jones. London: Methuen, 1963.

Zijderveld, Anton C. *On Clichés: The Supersedure of Meaning by Function in Modernity*. London: Routledge, 1979.

INDEX

Schmitt